Professor Kane's Contribution
to
Dharmaśāstra Literature

Professor Kane's Contribution to Dharmaśāstra Literature

compiled and edited by

S.G. Moghe

PRINTWORLD

Publishers of Indian Traditions

Cataloging in Publication Data – DK
[Courtesy: D.K. Agencies (P) Ltd. <docinfo@dkagencies.com>]

Kāṇe, Pāṇḍuraṅga Vāmana, 1880-1972, **author.**
[Works. Selections]
Professor Kane's contribution to Dharmaśāstra literature / compiled and edited by S.G. Moghe.
pages cm
English and Sanskrit.
Reprint. Originally published: 1997.
Includes bibliographical references and indexes.
ISBN 9788124600757

1. Dharma. 2. Hindu law. I. Moghe, S. G., editor. II. Title.

LCC BL1213.52.K36 2022 | DDC 294.548 23

ISBN: 978-81-246-0075-7
First published in 1997
Second impression published in 2017
Third impression published in 2022

Published and printed by:
D.K. Printworld (P) Ltd.
Regd. Office : "Vedaśrī", F-395, Sudarshan Park
(Metro Station: ESI Hospital)
New Delhi - 110015
Phones : (011) 25453975; 25466019
e-mail : indology@dkprintworld.com
Web : www.dkprintworld.com

Dedicated to

The Asiatic Society of Bombay, Bombay

which has witnessed the sustained and laudable efforts of Professor Kane

and

The Bhandarkar Oriental Research Institute, Pune

which may take the largest credit for his worldwide reputation

Preface

I have great pleasure in presenting the book *Professor Kane's Contribution to Dharmaśāstra Literature* to the world of Indology. *Dharmaśāstra* is my favourite subject and hence Dr. Kane's writings on *Dharmaśāstra* have proved to be a perennial source of inspiration for me.

In this book, I am presenting nineteen papers of Dr. P.V. Kane dealing with different aspects of Indology such as authenticity of the text, the chronological position of some works and authors, estimates of the style and views of some commentators, restoration of the lost text, the views of some authors whose works are not available to us now, evaluation of the rare manuscript on the *Dharmaśāstra*, challenging the meaning of the word *Dharmaśāstra* as interpreted by other scholars, the resemblance and differences between Vedic and Purāṇic traditions, filling up the gaps in the works of scholars and in Dr. Kane's own work as well, influence of one work over the other, offering illuminating explanations of some important words and removing some doubts relating to court matters in the works, cultural study of some practices (the *tilaka* mark, etc.) and examining the utility of other sciences in studying *Dharmaśāstra*.

In the 'Introduction' to this book, I have discussed most of these points for the interest of the readers of Indology.

I have added a chapter titled 'Dr. Kane's Method and

Interpretation — A review', in which I have also surveyed some articles, books and Ph.D. theses written on *Dharmaśāstra* over the last thirty years or so.

It must be mentioned here that I have included some material in the 'References' to the papers either in the light of the matter in the *History of Dharmaśāstra*, or in the light of the further progress made in the subject so as to make the discussion complete, as much as my ability would allow.

I take this opportunity to express my heart-felt thanks to Kane Memorial Trust, Bombay, for providing me with a substantial grant for the publication of this book. In fact, I do not have the words to express my feelings of indebtedness to the Kane Memorial Trust which has always encouraged me in my research activities.

For bringing out this valuable collection of papers of Dr. Kane, full credit must be given to D.K. Printworld (P) Ltd., New Delhi.

23-8-1996 **S.G. Moghe**
Bombay

Contents

Abbreviations

AitBrā	*Aitareya Brāhmaṇa.*
ĀpDhs	*Āpastaṁba-Dharmasūtra.*
BaudDhs	*Baudhāyana Dharmasūtra* (in the Ānandāśrama Collection of *Smṛtis*).
BB	*Bhujabala.*
BP	*Bhīmaprakaraṇa.*
BṛUp	*Bṛhadāraṇyaka Upaniṣad.*
BrahmaP	*Brahma Purāṇa.*
ChāUp	*Chāndogya Upaniṣad.*
EI	*Epigraphica Indica.*
Gautama	*Gautamadharmasūtra.*
GṛR	*Gṛhastharatnākara.*
JBORI	*Journal of the Bhandarkar Oriental Research Institute.*
KaṭhaUp	*Kaṭha Upaniṣad.*
KauśītakiUp	*Kauśītaki Upaniṣad.*
KṛR	*Kṛtyaratnākara.*
Manu	*Manu-smṛti.*
MPā	*Madana-Pārijāta.*
MBhā	*Mahābhāṣya* (ed. by Kielhorn).

Mbh	*Mahābhārata* (Bombay oblong edition with Nīlakaṇṭha's Commentary).
PraśnaUp	*Praśna Upaniṣad.*
PūMīSūtra	*Pūrva Mīmāṁsā Sūtra.*
RM	*Rājamārtaṇḍa.*
ṚV	*Ṛgveda.*
SBE	*Sacred Books of the East* (ed. by Max-Müller).
ŚatBrā	*Śatapatha Brāhmaṇa.*
TāndyaBrā	*Tāṇḍya Brāhmaṇa.*
TaitĀ	*Taittirīya Āraṇyaka.*
TaitBrā	*Taittirīya Brāhmana.*
TaiS	*Taittirīya Saṁhitā.*
V/vv	*Verse/Verses.*
VājS	*Vājasaneyi Saṁhitā.*
VR	*Vivādaratnākara.*
VS	*Vyavahārasamuccaya.*
VaDhs	*Vasiṣṭha Dharmasūtra.*
Yāj	*Yajñavalkya-smrti.*

1

Introduction

Dr. P.V. Kane, one may say, does not require any kind of formal introduction as his name is well-known to many and, in particular, to all those interested in the field of Indology. His contribution to this discipline is vast and of great depth, so that it is next to impossible to attempt to study it in a single book. What we have undertaken to do in this book, *Professor Kane's Contribution to Dharmaśāstra Literature*, is to present some of Dr. P.V. Kane's highly interesting papers on *Dharmaśāstra* literature.

Bharat Ratna Dr. P.V. Kane's achievement is remarkable and, indeed, unique. A scholar whose literary output exceeds nearly 15,000 printed pages in three languages, Dr. P.V. Kane's *magnum opus* is the *History of Dharmaśāstra* which has been universally acclaimed as an authoritative work on the Hindu religious and civil law of ancient and medieval India.

Dr. Pandurang Vaman Kane (1880-1972) was born in a middle class family of Koṅkan. He completed his schooling and college studies against heavy odds but with flying colours, securing many prizes and scholarships in the offing. His essays, "Aryan Manners and Morals as Depicted in the Epics" and "History of Alaṁkāra Literature", won prizes of the Bombay University. Dr. Kane distinguished himself as an advocate with a penchant for higher Sanskrit studies. He was made Wilson Philological Lecturer and Springer Research Scholar by the Bombay University and he served as the Professor of Law for six years.

Profesor P.V. Kane's vast literary output is contained in his books and articles, and his reviews. His *History of Sanskrit Poetics* is regarded as a work of fundamental significance. His monographs on the *Pūrvamīmāṁsā* system and the ancient geography of Maharashtra, and his critical edition of Nīlakantha's *Vyavahāramayūkha* are valuable works. His most remarkable achievement, however, is his *History of Dharmaśāstra* on which he worked steadfastly for nearly 35 years. The first volume of the *History of Dharmaśāstra* appeared in 1930 (later revised). The successful completion of this monumental project was formally announced in 1962 by the then President of India, Dr. Radhakrishnan. This 6,500 page, five-volume work said to have been accomplished single-handedly is known for its authoritative and thorough treatment of ancient and medieval India's Hindu religious and civil law.

In the paper, 'Dharmasūtra of Śaṅkha-Likhita', Dr. Kane restores the text of Śaṅkha-Likhita, which is now lost to us but which was available to the scholars of *Dharmaśāstra* up to the beginning of the fourteenth century AD. Dr. Kane, in his introduction to this restored text, points out the position of this *Dharmasūtra* in the vast range of *Dharmaśāstra* literature. He notes that it was studied by the students of the white *Yajurveda*. The ordinances of this *Sūtra* were to be followed, according to Parāśara, only in the *dvāpara* age. Besides, this *sūtra* work is in prose and verse. Dr. Kane confidently remarks that the *smṛti* or the *Dharmasūtra* of Śaṅkha-Likhita as published in the Jīvānanda collection or in the Ānandāśrama collection (Poona) are later works. With his vast knowledge of *Dharmaśāstra*, he points out that Śaṅkha-Likhita is quoted as an authority by Vijñāneśvara in his *Mitākṣarā* on the *Yājñavalkya-smṛti*, Medhātithi, and Lakṣmīdhara in his *Kṛtyakalpataru*. In this respect, he also points out that comparatively early writers sometimes ascribe verses or passages to Śaṅkha only or Likhita alone.

Dr. Kane places this work which resembles the style of Kauṭilya's *Arthaśāstra* more than that of the *Dharmasūtras* by Āpastamba and Gautama between 300 BC and AD 100 He says that the *Dharmasūtra* of Śaṅkha-Likhita was fortunate in getting an early commentator though his name cannot be identified. But since the commentator of this *sūtra* is referred to by Kalpataru and Caṇḍeśvara in his *Vivādaratnākara*, it is evident that the commentary was written before AD 1100.

While discussing the importance of the *Dharmasūtra* of Śaṅkha-Likhita, Dr. Kane points out that it enumerates several kinds of ordeals on which other *Dharmasūtra* works are silent. On some topics like separation, inheritance and succession, this *Dharmasūtra* gives us more detailed information as compared to the information available in other *sūtra* works. In passing, he adds that the limits of Āryāvarta as described in this work are more extensive than those indicated by the information available in the *Dharmasūtra* works of Vasiṣṭha and Baudhāyana. But he also significantly points out that there are discrepancies in the prose and poetry portions ascribed to Śaṅkha-Likhita. The prose Śaṅkha (passage No. 64), for instance, allows a brāhmaṇa to have a śūdra wife, though the verse Śaṅkha does not allow it (No. 65).

This contribution on the part of Dr. Kane can be held as a model by others in the field of Indology in their efforts towards restoring any lost text in any branch.

In the paper, 'Asahāya, the Commentator of the Gautama-Dharmasūtra and the Nāradasmṛti', Dr. Kane utilises the knowledge of *Dharmaśāstra* literature for throwing light on the work of Asahāya. He discusses the peculiar views of Asahāya and tries to fix the probable date of this commentator (traces it to earlier than AD 850).

Dr. Kane points out with the help of *Hāralatā* of Aniruddha that Asahāya is the author of a commentary on the *Gautama-dharmasūtra*. On the basis of Pratāparudradeva's *Sarasvatīvilāsa*, Dr. Kane states that Asahāya also seems to have written a commentary on the *Manusmṛti*. In this regard, he refers to the *Vivādaratnākara* which quotes the words of Asahāya on the *Manusmṛti*. Asahāya's commentaries on the *Nāradasmṛti*, *Gautama-dharmasūtra* and the *Manusmrti* are lost to us.

Dr. Kane enlightens the readers on the position of Asahāya in the later *Dharmaśāstra* literature. He shows that Asahāya's views were supported by Vijñāneśvara on the rights of sisters when their brothers are separated. Caṇḍeśvara in his *Vivādaratnākara* quotes the work *Prakāśa* as referring to the views of Asahāya. Dr. Kane also informs us that the *Sarasvatīvilāsa*, which of all works on *vyavahāra* quotes Asahāya the most, tells us that the views of Asahāya, Medhātithi and Vijñāneśvara coincide to some extent.

In his paper titled 'The Tantravārtika and the Dharmaśastra Literature', Dr. Kane takes up important passages from the *Tantravārtika* of the *mīmāṁsaka* Kumārilabhatta (eighth century AD) which have a bearing on *Dharmaśāstra* literature, for study. He notes that these passages help us in understanding the development and chronology of *Dharmaśāstra* literature.

On Kumārila's references, Dr. Kane notes that the author refers to the work of Gautama more frequently than other authors of the *Dharmasūtra*s (there being at least a dozen quotations). In a few cases, the *Dharmasūtra* of Āpastamba is referred to; a little of Baudhāyana's *Dharmasūtra* and that of Śaṅkha-Likhita also find a place. According to Dr. Kane, quotations from other *Dharmasūtra*s cannot be identified — that is, if they exist at all in the *Tantravārtika*. Dr. Kane points out that the *Tantravārtika* stands in a special relation to the *Manusmṛti*. More than twenty verses from the extant *Manusmrti*, wholly or partly, find a place in the *Tantravārtika* It is remarkable, Dr. Kane notes, that a verse treated as interpolated in the *Manusmṛti* editions because it has not been commented upon by commentators like Medhātithi and Kullūka, is quoted in the *Tantravārtika*. Dr. Kane asserts that the extant *Manusmṛti* must be many centuries older than AD 750, and Śabara would have belonged to a period certainly before AD 500 and may be earlier by a few centuries.

Dr. Kane observes that Kumārila, in his interesting discussion on *sadācāra*, sets out in detail how the high personages of old transgressed the Law but also tries to explain away most of the transgressions. It may be relevant to note that Dr. Kane, in his *History of Dharmaśāstra* (Vol. III), refers to such an attempt on the part of Kumārila under the 'Mīmāṁsā Apologetics'.

Dr. Kane states that as Kumārila looks upon the *Purāṇas* as authoritative works, some of the extant *Purāṇa*s would have been composed many centuries before AD 750.

In 'Passages from the Rājamārtaṇḍa on Tithis, Vratas and Utsavas', Dr. Kane presents portions of the *Rājamārtaṇḍa* (a work of King Bhoja concerned with astrological matters in relation to the *Dharmaśāstra*) dealing with *tithis*, *vrata*s and *utsava*s which are compiled from three manuscripts. He informs us that a total of 1462 verses are contained in the *Rājamārtaṇḍa* (of which he presents 286 in this paper).

Dr. Kane includes references to some medieval digests from where some of the verses occurring in the *Rājamārtaṇḍa* are quoted. He has consulted digest works such as *Kālaviveka* of Jīmūtavāhana, *Kṛtyatattva* of Raghunandana, *Kṛtyaratnākara* of Caṇḍeśvara, *Tithi-tattva* of Raghunandana, *Śuddhi-kaumudī* and *Varsakriyākaumudī* of Govindānanda, and *Purāṇa*s where some of the stanzas are found. Dr. Kane reminds us in this context that not only does the *Rājamārtanda* borrow many verses from other works without acknowledging but also, some digests quote these borrowed verses as those of the *Rājamārtanda*.

'The Meaning of Ācāryāḥ' is an attempt by Dr. Kane to show that the use of the word *ācārya* by Kauṭilya should not be taken as a reference to the author's teacher but to previous great writers. Dr. Kane examines the correctness of this meaning by consulting the tradition in respect of usage of this expression. He examines the *Āpastamba-dharmasūtra*, *Gautama-dharmasūtra*, *Manusmṛti* and *Vasistha-dharmasūtra* to conclude that the first meaning of the word is 'teacher of the *Veda*'. Another meaning that developed was 'founder or any great teacher of a *śāstra*'. Dr. Kane gives other meanings from usage by various writers and works: 'great men endowed with the qualities of an *ācāryāḥ*' (Sāyanācārya); 'predecessors' (Yāska); 'inspired seers of the *Upanisads*' (*Hārīta-dharmasūtra*); 'all teachers'; 'great teachers of *dharma, artha* and *mokṣa*' (Vātsyāyana's *Kāmasūtra*). Finally, Dr. Kane cites passages from Kauṭilya's own writings to conclude that the word was used by him in the sense of 'some teachers' and thus referred to great writers of earlier times.

In the paper titled 'The Mahābhārata Verses and very Ancient *Dharmasūtras* and other Works', several verses are set out which occur in the *Mahābhārata* as well as in the *Mahābhāṣya* of Patañjali, *Āpastamba-dharmasūtra, Baudhāyana-dharmasūtra, Vasistha-dharmasūtra* and some other works (*Yājñavalkya-smṛti, Venīsaṁhāra, Nārada-smṛti*), and the different readings available are noted. Such occurrence is interpreted by Dr. Kane as a result of the same family devoting itself to the growth of the *Itihāsa-Purāna* and *Dharmaśāstra* literature.

Dr. Kane begins by stating that the *Mahābhārata* (the original work) out of which the present text of the epic grew must have been composed before 500 BC. In an attempt to explain the *itihāsa* and *purāna*, Dr. Kane conjectures that the *itihāsa* of the *Upaniṣad* period was gradually incorporated into what became the *Mahābhārata* and the *Purāṇa* of that period was expanded into the many *Purāṇas* that emerged later. Dr. Kane concludes that the *Manusmṛti* might have originally contained verses in the *tristubh* metre but later, the *anuṣṭubh* metre was uniformly employed.

In the paper on the *Dvaitanirṇaya*, a work authored by Śaṅkarabhaṭṭa, Dr. Kane points out that the purpose of that work is to dispel doubts on ceremonial usages and rites, and on matters of impurity in births and deaths by giving decisive opinions.

The *Dvaitanirṇaya*, he informs, has various specific issues for discussion including the *navarātra*, a question whether the maternal grandfather is to be included in the *prausthapadī śrāddha* along with paternal ancestors and the *siddhānta* view regarding the giving of gifts. In discussing Śaṅkarabhatta's response to the views of others, Dr. Kane points out that Śaṅkarabhaṭṭa agreed with as well as refuted both Hemādri and Mādhava (Parāśara-Mādhava). He looked upon Vijñāneśvara with great respect but also found fault with him.

Dr. Kane, through his study, attempts to shed further light on a major controversy — whether Haradatta, the author of commentaries on the *Dharmasūtras* of Āpastamba and Gautama, is the very same Haradatta who authored *Padamañjarī*, the celebrated work on grammer. Śaṅkarabhaṭṭa, he shows, made no distinction between the two authors. Dr. Kane quotes a passage on adoption attributed to Śaunaka which is of much interest to modern students of Hindu law and gives Śaṅkarabhaṭṭa's view on it.

Dr. Kane mentions the *sutras* and *adhikaraṇas* of Jaimini referred to by Śaṅkarabhaṭṭa and the other works quoted by him in the *Dvaitanirnaya*. Śaṅkarabhaṭṭa is also identified as the author of a commentary on the *Śāstradīpikā* of Pārthasārathi.

Dr. Kane warns us against dismissing the *Dvaitanirnaya* as an uninteresting work dealing with trivialities. The value of the work should be ascertained bearing in mind that Śaṅkarabhaṭṭa was writing for his time.

In his paper 'Vedic Mantras and Legends in the Purāṇas.' Dr. Kane maintains that though it is generally held that the Paurāṇic tradition is different from the Vedic tradition, yet it should not be forgotten by a careful student that the Purānic tradition has not ignored the Vedic tradition. In fact, it tries to build on the foundations of the Vedic tradition. This is proved by Dr. Kane by taking examples from the *Brahma Purāṇa*.

He points out that in the *Brahma Purāṇa*, several Vedic verses and texts are reproduced without accents. Besides, the *Purāna* authors make the best use of Vedic legends such as

Saramā-Paṇi, Hariścandra Upākhyāna, Indra killing Vṛtra, Namuci, etc. for glorifying the importance of holy places, such as Soma Tīrtha, Mṛgavyādha Tīrtha and Pūtra Tīrtha. Some passages of the *Brahma Purāṇa*, though not quoting words from the *Veda*, give a close paraphrase of the Vedic texts.

In a lengthy but studious article, Dr. Kane studies the views held by the predecessors of Vijñāneśvara, the author of *Mitāksarā*, and estimates Vijñāneśvara's debt to them. Six writers named by the *Mitākṣarā* who wrote commentaries or *nibandhas* on the *Dharmaśāstra* are taken up for study.

Dr. Kane points out that Vijñāneśvara and the commentator, Asahāya agree on certain matters, such as the definition of *dāya* and the explanation of the word 'fourth share' in the verse of Yājñavalkya stating that unmarried sisters are entitled to have their marriages celebrated by their brothers who must give a fourth share to them.

Dr. Kane discusses the different views of Viśvarūpa and the *Mitāksarā* of Vijñāneśvara. Their interpretation of the *Yājñavalkya-smṛti,* in this context, is well illustrated. Viśvarūpa's commentary, *Bālakrīdā* on the *Yājñavalkya-smṛti*, Dr. Kane points out, is saturated with the lore of the *Pūrvamīmāṁsā*. The views of Viśvarūpa quoted by other writers are examined. Some general conclusions are also made — that the printed text of Viśvarūpa is largely authoritative and some later commentators have wrongly ascribed certain views to Viśvarūpa.

Some interesting observations are made concerning Bhāruci, a propounder of the *Viśiṣṭādvaita*, such as the period when he flourished and that he could be identified with Bhāruci, the writer on *Dharmaśāstra*. Disagreements in the views of Vijñāneśvara and Bhāruci are discussed with some interesting examples. The views of Bhāruci are collected mainly from the *Sarasvatīvilāsa*.

Dr. Kane maintains that the commentary of Śrīkara is in the nature of a comprehensive digest and explains some of Śrīkara's views in thirteen examples obtained from the works of

Jīmūtavāhana, the *Smṛticandrikā*, the *Sarasvatīvilāsa* and the *Vīramitrodaya*. A view of Śrīkara's relating to succession of widows as heirs which is disapproved by the *Mitākṣarā* is noted by Dr. Kane.

Dr. Kane observes that the *Mitākṣarā* refers to the views of Medhātithi who wrote a *bhāṣya* on the *Manusmṛti* and Bühler in his introduction to the *Manusmṛti* does give a good deal of information about Medhātithi. Dr. Kane then makes a concise statement of the results of Bühler's study and adds details which, he says, were not noticed by Bühler. An attempt is made to trace the probable date of Medhātithi.

According to Dr. Kane, there are many considerations favouring identification of Dhāreśvara with Bhojadeva of Dhāra. Dr. Kane fixes the period of reign of Bhoja of Dhāra. The *Mitākṣarā* and the views of Dhāreśvara are compared and discussed.

Dr. Kane begins the paper on *kalivarjya* by discussing the meaning of the terms *yuga*, and *kṛta, tretā, dvāpara* and *kali* (the four ages) and he reaches some conclusions, such as, it is doubtful whether the theory of the four ages was known to ancient Vedic literature. He asserts that the theory became a formidable weapon to writers on *dharma* when they had to explain away inconvenient texts. Practices allowed by Parāśara are condemned by later writers as forbidden in the *kali* age. In many digests including the *Smṛticandrikā*, long extracts are given from *Purāṇa*s and Śaunaka which condemn certain practices as forbidden in the *kali* age (*kalivarjya*s). Dr. Kane then lists the several *kalivarjya*s mentioned in the *Āditya Purāna* and verses on *kalivarjya* collected from the *Smṛticandrikā*.

The interesting paper, 'Tilaka Mark' sheds light on some aspects of the practice of applying *tilaka*. Dr. Kane takes up literary references — the *Nāṭyaśāstra* of Bharata, the *Rāmāyaṇa*, the *Kādambarī* of Bāṇa, etc. — to show that from at least the beginning of the Christian era women applied a mark or *tilaka* on their forehead. He also states that there is no indication that it was a necessity then. It is likely that the necessity emerged later with the practice of applying a *pundra* mark on the forehead by men.

In 'The Pārijātā and the Madana-Pārijāta', Dr. Kane's efforts are to convince scholars that the *Pārijāta*, often quoted by the *Kalpataru* and the *Ratnākaras* of Caṇḍeśvara, is different from the *Madana-Pārijāta*. He takes up the task by considering passages where (i) certain remarks are attributed to the *Pārijāta* which are not found in the *Madana-Pārijāta*; (ii) the explanation of the *Pārijāta* differs from that of the *Madana-Pārijāta*; and (iii) certain texts or views are stated as not mentioned in the *Pārijāta* even while they are found in the *Madana-Pārijāta*. Dr. Kane also points out that the dates of the two works clarify the issue.

Dr. Kane begins 'Purāṇa-Dharma' by arguing that centuries before the Christian era, there was a single work called *Itihāsa-Purāṇa* or there were two works, *Itihāsa* and *Purāṇa*. That work or works are now lost and the extant *Purānas* may be only recasts. Dr. Kane then proceeds to discuss some features of the *Purānas* that, in a sense, are distinct from the Vedic features. The *Purāṇas* speak highly of the *Vedas*, utilise Vedic legends and prescribe Vedic *mantras* for religious rites and ceremonies but also introduce changes in rites and usages of the people. The key-note is how great results could be secured with little effort. Thus, Dr. Kane notes, they emphasise *dānas*, pilgrimages to and baths in sacred places, *vratas*, *bhakti* and *nāmasmarana*, and the performance of *śrāddha*.

The paper titled 'The Arthaśāstra of Kautilya' studies the author and his work with specific reference to the controversies regarding the work's authorship and authenticity.

Dr. Kane notes that there is no weighty evidence why Kauṭilya cannot be regarded as the author of *Arthaśāstra*. In the sphere of administration of justice, Kauṭilya is much in advance of the *dharmasūtras* of Gautama, Āpastamba and Baudhāyana and so is much later than these. Yājñavalkya is much later than Kauṭilya for a similar reason. *Kauṭilīya*, says Dr. Kane, is much older than the extant *Manusmṛti*. Regarding the date of the *Kautilīya*, it is stated that no evidence has been brought forward to suggest a date later than 300 BC.

The lengthy discussion titled 'King Bhoja and his Works on Dharmaśāstra and Astrology' is on works ascribed to Bhojadeva that are concerned with astrological matters in relation to *Dharmaśāstra*. Dr. Kane takes up the *Bhīmaparākrama*, the earliest work of this type, the *Bhujabalanibandha*, the *Rājamārtaṇḍa*, the *Vyavahārasamuccaya* (which, he says, could be a work of Bhoja) among others.

Professor Kane details significant aspects of Bhoja's work including the unfavourable *lagnas*, *yogas* like *amṛtasiddhi, dagdha yoga* and rules about the *tithis*. He also observes that a number of verses are repeated by two or more texts. Exactly opposite views appear at some places in the *Bhujabala* and the *Rājamārtaṇḍa*. There are also contradictions between quotations from *Rājamārtaṇḍa* in digests and the manuscript of *Rājamārtaṇḍa*. Dr. Kane is of the view that the *Rājamārtaṇḍa* and the *Bṛhad-rājamārtaṇḍa* are distinct works, with the former being more popular than the latter.

In his brief 'Mahābhārata Citations in the Śābara-Bhāṣya', Dr. Kane states that a verse from Śabara's remarks on Jaimini is taken from the *Ādiparva* of the *Mahābhārata* which is in the *Anukramaṇīparva* and differs from Śabara's quotation only as to the first *pada*. This point will have an important bearing on the antiquity and authenticity of the *Anukarmaniparva*. Some interesting observations are also made on the *sūtras* of Jaimini.

In 'Utpala and the Arthaśāstra of Kauṭilya', Dr. Kane uses a work on astrology — Utpala's *Vivṛtti* on the *Yogayātrā* of Varāhamihira — to reveal some new aspects related to the *Arthaśāstra*.

An interesting paper lists some passages of the *Matsya Purāṇa* and Kauṭilya's *Arthaśāstra* where the words used are strikingly similar. Dr. Kane concludes that the *Matsya Purāṇa* is based on the *Arthaśāstra* and on no other work, and it cannot be assigned to a period later than the sixth century AD.

The paper on issues relating to naming of a child or a person adds to the matter presented by Dr. Kane in his *History of Dharmaśāstra*. Dr. Kane observes that elaborate rules are given in the *Grhyasūtra*s and proposes to compare these rules with the practices deducible from the Vedic literature to discuss this practice since the ancient times in India.

Dr. Kane points out that in the *Ṛgveda*, the same person had four names though usually a person is referred to in Vedic literature by two names. The *Gṛhyasūtra*s refer to odd and even syllables in names and names with a *visarga* at the end for sons. Dr. Kane notes that it appears that the *nakṣatra* name was a secret name in ancient times though gradually such names ceased to be so. There are also examples of Buddhist names derived from *nakṣatra*s. Dr. Kane also takes up various other aspects for study, such as giving names of deities and the matronymic style.

Dr. S.G. Moghe

2

Dharmasūtra of Śaṅkha-Likhita

THE *Dharmaśāstra* of Śaṅkha-Likhita is a very ancient one. Kumārila in his *Tantravārtika* (p. 179) tells us that the *Dharmasūtra* of Saṅkha-Likhita was specially studied by the Vājasaneyins (i.e., by students of the white *Yajurveda*). The *Tantravārtika* also quotes a few words from the work of Śaṅkha-Likhita, which constitute an *Anuṣṭubhpāda*. The story of the two brothers Śaṅkha and Likhita occurs in the *Mahābhārata*, *Śāntiparavan* ch. 23. The *Yājñavalkyasmṛti* (I.5) enumerates Śaṅkha-Likhita along with Gautama and Hārīta among the writers of *Dharmaśāstra*. The *Parāśarasmṛti* (I.24) says that in the four ages, *Kṛta*, *Tretā*, *Dvāpara* and *Kali*, the ordinances of Manu, Gautama, Śaṅkha-Likhita and Parāśara are to be respectively followed. Commentators and authors of digests from the times of Viśvarūpa down to the latest quote very largely from Śaṅkha-Likhita. Viśvarūpa says that Śaṅkha and Likhita pondered over the *dharma* promulgated by Manu and composed their work, after drawing upon the *Veda*.* A considerable portion of these quotations is in prose. Hence it appears that the *Dharmasūtra* of Śaṅkha-Likhita was once available, though it has not yet been discovered. Therefore it is highly desirable to collect together from the numerous books on *Dharmaśāstra* the quotations

---

* समीक्ष्य निपुणं धर्मभुषिभ्यो मनुभाषितम्।
आम्नायात्सम्यगुद्धृत्य शङ्खश्च लिखिस्तथा।।

on या० III, 248

attributed to Śaṅkha-Likhita. In the following pages an attempt has been made to collect from a few well-known works the fragments of Śaṅkha-Likhita and to reconstruct the *Dharmasūtra*. Though the following reconstruction is far from professing to be exhaustive, it will, I hope, serve as a basis for future research and is sufficient to convey an idea of the character and contents of the *Dharmasūtra* of Śaṅkha-Likhita. Jīvānanda (collection of *Dharmaśāstras*, part II, pp. 344-74) printed in 18 chapters and about 330 verses a *smṛti* of Śaṅkha and a *smṛti* of Likhita in 92 verses (part II, pp. 375-82). The same text of the *Śaṅkha-smṛti* has been published in the collection of *Dharmaśāstras* by M.N. Dutt (1988, vol. I) and in the Ānandāśrama edition (1905). The last edition also contains a *laghu Śaṅkha-smṛti* in 71 verses and a Śaṅkha-Likhita-*smṛti* in 32 verses. It is obvious that these are later works. The *Śaṅkha-smṛti* in 18 chapters seems to be comparatively an early work. The relation of the *Śaṅkha-smṛti* in verse to the *Dharmasūtra* seems to be this. The versified *smṛti* is a paraphrase of the already existing work in prose (*vide* Nos. 56 and 61, 69-70, 93-94, 199-200). It is not unlikely that the original *Dharmasūtra* also contained a few verses as Āpastamba's *sūtra* does now (e.g., No. 105). The prose Śaṅkha allowed a brāhmana to have a śūdra wife (64), but the verse Śaṅkha does not do so (No. 65). Even so early a writer as Viśvarūpa regarded the prose and verse portions as the compositions of the same author (*vide* No. 379). About fifty verses from it are quoted in the *Mitākṣarā*. A few prose passages occur in the eleventh and twelfth chapters of the work, one of which is quoted even by so early a writer as Medhātithi. But the numerous prose quotations ascribed to Śaṅkha-Likhita do not occur in the printed *smṛtis* ascribed to Śaṅkha and Likhita. There is another point which is worth noting. Comparatively early writers sometimes ascribe the same text to Śaṅkha-Likhita or simply to Śaṅkha (*vide* Nos. 270-71, 293, 302). Sometimes the passages quoted by the writers are similar, but not quite identical. The well-known *sūtra* about the inheritance to a sonless man is ascribed to Śaṅkha-Likhita and Paiṭhīnasi by Aparārka and to Śaṅkha by Viśvarūpa and the Mitāksarā. Therefore in the following all quotations whether cited as from Śaṅkha or Śaṅkha-Likhita have been brought together. Quotations from Likhita alone are very few and far between. Even ancient commentators make no distinction between the verses attributed to Śaṅkha (most of which are found in the printed Śaṅkha) and the *sūtras* of Śaṅkha-Likhita (*vide* Aparārka pp. 1149, 1154, 1161, 1165 &c). A few quotations are cited as from Bṛhat or Vṛddha Śaṅkha. It is likely that instead of citing the double name, authors briefly cited a quotation as from Śaṅkha. In some of the Mss of Śaṅkha and Likhita *smṛtis* deposited in the Deccan College, the same work is sometimes attributed to Śaṅkha and sometimes to Likhita.

The *Dharmasūtra* of Śaṅkha-Likhita appears to have found a *bhāṣyakāra* very early. Lakṣmīdhara in his *Kalpataru* (Ghose's *Hindu Law* Vol. II. p. 504) draws attention to the fact that the *bhāṣyakāra* read a well-known *sūtra* as *sa yadyekaḥ syāt* instead of as *sa yadyekaputraḥ syāt* (omitting the word *putra*). Lakṣmīdhara, flourished between AD 1100 and 1160 as he was a minister of Govindacandra of Kanauj. The *Vivādaratnākara* of Caṇḍeśvara (AD 1314) twice cites (pp. 234 and 466) the *bhāṣyakāra* of Śaṅkha-Likhita. Hence it follows that a *bhāṣya* on the *Dharmasūtra* was composed before AD 1100 and was available in the beginning of the fourteenth century.

The *Dharmasūtra* of Śaṅkha-Likhita would appear, from the text here presented, to have resembled the other extant *sūtras* on *Dharma*. It embraced almost all the topics treated of in such works as the Gautama or Āpastamba *dharmasūtra*. It agrees very closely with the *Dharmasūtras* of Gautama and Āpastamba and sometimes has the same *sūtras* as in those works. A few such coincidences have been pointed out in the notes (*vide* Nos. 35, 36, 39, 62, 133, 135 for Gautama and Nos. 95, 105, 116, 276 for Baudhāyana). A quotation from Śaṅkha makes Śaṅkha-Likhita as an authority on *Dharma* (No. 3). The *Dharmasūtra* seems to have approved of *Niyoga*, speaks of the secondary sons, was not favourable (just like Gautama and Āpastamba) to the claims of females to succeed to males. On certain points the *Dharmasūtra* of Śāṅkha-Likhita shows a more advanced state of opinion than is the case with Gautama, Āpastamba and Baudhāyana. For example, Śaṅkha enumerates several kinds of ordeals, while the above-named *sūtrakāras* are silent on that point. Śaṅkha enumerates no less than twenty authorities on *Dharma* (including himself). As regards partition, inheritance and succession Śaṅkha-Likhita gives more detailed and definite information than Āpastamba or Baudhāyana. It is further to be noted that in Śaṅkha-Likhita the limits of Āryāvarta (No. 7) are more extensive towards the east and west than is the case with Baudhāyana (I.1.25) or Vasiṣṭha. (I.8-9). The style of the work of Śaṅkha-Likhita resembles that of Kauṭilya more than that of Gautama and Āpastamba (*vide* Nos. 243-245). The quotations hardly exhibit any ungrammatical forms. One quotation includes Yājñavalkya among the writers on *Dharmaśāstra*. If it is the extant *Yājñavalkya-smṛti* that is meant, the *Dharmasūtra* will have to be assigned to a late date. But this does not seem to be likely. From the fact that the *Yājñavalkya-smṛti* itself cites Śaṅkha-Likhita among ancient authorities, from the general style of the work and from its doctrines about the rights of women and other matters, it appears almost certain that the *Dharmasūtra* of Śaṅkha-Likhita is much earlier than the extant *Yājñavalkyasmrti* though it is certainly later than Gautama and Āpastamba. There is close correspondence between Śaṅkha-Likhita and *Yājñavalkyasmṛti* in several cases (*vide* Nos. 14, 27, 69). It would not be far from the truth if the *Dharmasūtra* of Śaṅkha-Likhita be placed somewhere between, 300 BC to AD 100. The prose quotations from Śaṅkha-Likhita refer to the *Vedāṅgas*, *Sāṅkhya, Yoga, Dharmaśāstra* (No. 199). Śaṅkha-Likhita recognised eight forms of marriage (Nos. 66-68). The views of Śaṅkha-Likhita about the status of the offspring of mixed marriages differ from those of Baudhāyana and Manu and are intermediate between the latter two (No. 75). The *Tarpana* (No. 116) which resembles that in *Baudhāyana-dharmasūtra*, refers to the six *Vedāṅgas*, to Bhārata (but not *Mahābhārata*), to twenty writers on *Dharmaśāstra*, and contains numerous details about geography, mythology and cosmogony which are generally found in the *Purāṇas*. The *Dharmasūtra* refers to the opinions of others in the words *eke*

(Nos. 358, 363). It mentions by name the views of Yama (182, 223, both in verse), Kātyāyana (No. 207), Prajāpati (No. 278), Āṅgirasa and Uśanas (No. 289), Pracetasa (290), Vrddhagautama (No. 377), Śaṅkha himself (432). It is better, however, to leave out of account the verse quotations in drawing chronological conclusions. The same verses are ascribed to Manu and Śaṅkha (Nos. 33, 38, 148) and some of the *sūtra*s closely resemble *Manusmṛti* (*vide* No. 72). Six verses occur both in the *Vāsistha-dharmasūtra* and also in the versified Śaṅkha (No. 105). Probably both works borrow them from another source. Same passages are ascribed to several other writers along with Śaṅkha (e.g., No. 293). The idea seems to be that all those exhibited the verse or passage or held identical views.

In the footnotes an attempt has been made to point out the earliest sources from which the *sūtra*s are collected. In only a few cases have parallel passages from other works been cited, as it was thought undesirable to encumber the notes. In my forthcoming work on the history of *Dharmaśāstra*, I hope to utilise the materials collected here for further research.

अपरार्क — commentary of अपरार्क on याज्ञवल्क्य (Ānandāśrama edn.).

उज्ज्वला — com. of हरदत्त on आपस्तम्बधर्मसूत्र (Kumbhakonam edn.).

कुल्लूक — Nirn. edn.

चतुर्ववर्ग० — चतुर्वर्गचिन्तामणि of हेमाद्रि (B.I. edn.)

चतुर्विंश० — चतुर्विंशतिमतसंग्रह (Benares Sanskrit Series).

दायभाग — (edition of 1829).

परा० मा० — पराशरमाधवीय (Bombay Sanksrit Series).

म० पा० — मदनपारिजात (B. I. Series).

मिता० — मिताक्षरा of विज्ञानेश्वर.

मेधा० — com. of मेधातिथि on मनु (Mr. Gharpure's edn.).

वि. र० — विवादरत्नाकर (B.I. edn.).

विश्व० — commentary of विश्वरूप on याज्ञवल्क्य (published by Pandit T. Ganapati Sastri).

वीर० — वीरमित्रोदय.

शङ्खस्मृति — The collection of *smṛtis* by M.N. Dutt, Vol. I. (Calcutta 1908).

स्मृतिच० — स्मृतिचन्द्रिका (Mr. Gharpure's edition).

हरदत्त — com. on गौतमधर्मसूत्र (Ānandāśrama edn.).

हार० — हारलता (B.I. edn.).

[For a more elaborate discussion on the *Śaṅkha-Likhita Dharmasūtra*, ***vide*** Dr. P.V. Kane's *History of Dharmaśāstra*, Vol. I/I, pp. 136 to 142. Dr. Kane has utilised the matter of this article in the above volume and added some new points. This paper is originally published in the *ABORI*, Vol. VII, pp. 101-28, 1926 and text in Vol. VIII (pp. 93-132), 1927 and has inspired the present editor to restore the *Ṛṣyaśṛṅga-Smṛti*, ***vide*** *The Mysore Orientalist*, Vol. XIV, pp. 64-77. ***Also see*** S.G. Moghe's *Studies in Dharmaśāstra*, pp. 65-80.]

S. G. Moghe

The Text

1. **शङ्खलिखितौः**— आम्नायः स्मृतिधारकः।

2. **शङ्खः**— तत्र वेदमूलाः स्मृतयः।

3. **शङ्खः** — स्मृतिर्धर्मशास्त्राणि तेषां प्रणेतारो मनुयमदक्षविष्णवङ्गिरोबृहस्पत्युशन-आपस्तम्बगौतमसंवर्तात्रिहारीतकात्यायनयशङ्खलिखितपराशरव्यासशाता-तपप्रचेतोयाज्ञवल्क्यादयः।

4. **शङ्खलिखितौः**— रागद्वेषाग्निदग्धानां मग्नानां विषयाम्भसि।
चिकित्सा सर्वशास्त्राणि व्याधीनामिव भेषजम्।।

5. **शङ्खलिखितौः**— वेदा वै विप्रकीर्णत्वाद्दुर्ज्ञेया धर्मसाधनम्।
सुबोधात्तत्समर्था हि ब्रह्मणा विहिता श्रुतिः।।
श्रुतिस्मृत्युदितान्धर्मान् मानवास्तान् पृथक्पृथक्।
कुर्वतः प्राप्नुयुर्धर्मन्यथा नरके गतिः।।
श्रौतं स्मार्तं क्रियावाक्यं हेतुभिर्यो विघातयेत्।।
असच्छास्त्रमुपाश्रित्य स ज्ञेयः शिष्टनिन्दितः।।

6. **शङ्खः** — तत्र धर्मलक्षणानि। देशः काल उपायो द्रव्यं श्रद्धा पात्रं त्याग इति समयः तेषु धर्मोदयः साधारणः। अन्यथा विपरीतः।

7. **शङ्खः** — देश आर्यो गुणवान् प्रागस्तादर्वागुदयाद् यावदुच्चा गिरयो यावत्पुण्याः सरितः प्राक्सिद्धत्वाद्देशः सनातनः पुण्यः। कृष्णमृगो वा यावद्विचरति

---

1. तन्त्रवार्तिक, p. 139.
2. स्मृतिच०, I., p. 2.
3. स्मृतिच०, I, p. I. (omitting the words स्मृति. . . णेतारः); वीर० (परिभाषा०, p. 16) gives the same names but the order is different in some cases; चतुर्वर्ग० Vol. I., p. 527, attributes to शङ्खलिखित।
4. चतुर्वर्ग०, Vol. II, part I, p. 23.
5. चतुर्वर्ग०, Vol. II, part I, p. 24.
6. विश्व० on या० I.6; अपरार्क (या० I.6) has the words from देशः and reads 'इति समस्तेषु धर्मोदयः साधारणो न्याय्योन्यथा विपरीतः'; चतुर्वर्ग० Vol. II, part I, p. 25 reads समस्तेषु. वीर० (परिभाषाप्रकाश, p. 57).
7. विश्व० (on या० I.2.) has the words देश . . . दयात् and पुण्यः कृष्णो वा... सारः स्यात् compare वसिष्ठ I. 8 and 13; बौ० ध० सू०, I. 1.25 and 28.

तावदाचारः स्यात्। प्राक्सिन्धुसौवीराद्दक्षिणेन हिमवतः पश्चात्काम्पिल्या उदक् पारियात्रादनवद्यं ब्रह्मवर्चसं सर्वेषामतोन्यदेशजातिकुलधर्माणामन्वयाः।

8. **शङ्खः** — कृष्णमृगो यावद्विचरति तावदार्यावर्तः स्यात्।

9. **शङ्खः** — श्रुतिविरोधे त्रैविद्यसमवायेषु निर्णयः।
यथावलेपं शास्त्रतस्तेनुब्रूयुः।

10. **शङ्खः** — एतानि ब्राह्मणोधिकुरुते स च वृत्तिं दर्शयतीतरेषाम्।

11. **शङ्खलिखितौः** — पाकयज्ञा हविर्यज्ञाः सोमसंस्थास्तथैव च।
संस्कारा ह्यग्निहोत्रान्ता अग्निहोत्रं तु जुह्वतः।।
संस्कारैः संस्कृतः पूर्वैरुत्तरैरनुसंस्कृतः।
नित्यमष्टगुणैर्युक्तो ब्राह्मणो ब्रह्मलौकिकः।।
ब्राह्मं पदमवाप्नोति तस्मान्न च्यवते पुनः।

12. **शङ्खलिखितौः** — इन्धनोदकाग्निकाष्ठ-तृणोपलपुष्पफलपर्णादिनिष्वपचयं दैवतीर्थाभिगमनं गृहकोष्ठप्रवेशनं पथि शस्त्रधारणमसंबद्धमासनं प्रस्तुतेष्वनिवारणं असद्वामश्चेति शिलोकष्पदतोधोग्यराशिग्रहणमग्रोत्सर्गप्रसववृद्धिकर्षापणशुल्कनदीतीरेष्वनुपरोधनं परस्त्रीसंभाषणं राजस्त्रीदर्शनं राज्ञा समासनं व्यतिक्रमणं च कोपात्सर्वमर्हति ब्राह्मणः।

13. **शङ्खलिखितौः** — नार्तवे दिवा मैथुनं ब्रजेत्। क्लीबा अल्पवीर्याश्च दिवा प्रजायन्ते अल्पायुषश्च।

14. **शङ्खयाज्ञवल्क्यौः** — षष्ठेष्टमे वा सीमन्तः।

---

8. म० पा०, p. 12; स्मृतिच०, I, p. 8.

9. विश्व० on या०, I. 9.

10. मिता० on या०, I. 3 (एतानि refers to विद्यास्थानानि), वीर० (संस्कारप्रकाश, p. 512) omits वृत्तिम्.

11. सुबोधिनी on (याज्ञ०) मिताक्षरा, II.4 and in the बालंभट्टी; स्मृतिच०, I., p. 13 quotes from संस्कारैः. . . पुनः as from शङ्ख and explains पूर्व as गर्भाधानादयः and उत्तर as पाकयज्ञादयः.

12. वि० र०, p. 660.

13. स्मृतिच०, I, p. 15.

14. चतुर्वर्ग०, Vol. III, Part 2, p. 734; याज्ञ०, I.11.

15. **शङ्खः** — गर्भस्पन्दने सीमन्तोन्नयनं यावद्वा न प्रसवः।

16. **शङ्खलिखितौ**: — प्रसूते जातकर्म यवपिष्टमधुसर्पिर्भिर्मन्त्रवत्प्राशनं तस्य सुवर्णान्तर्हितयानामिकया मेधाधिकं ब्राह्मणस्य करोति एवमितरयोः।

17. **शङ्खः** — कुमारप्रसवे नाभ्यामच्छिन्नायां गुडतिलहिरण्यवस्त्रगोधान्यादि-प्रतिग्रहेष्वदोषस्तदहस्त्वेके कुर्वत इति।

18. **शङ्खः** — सर्वेषां सकुल्यानां द्विपदचतुष्पदधान्यहिरण्यानि दद्यात्।

19. **शङ्खः** — आशौचे तु व्यतिक्रान्ते नामकर्म विधीयते।

20. **शङ्खलिखितौ** — दशम्यामुत्थाप्य पिण्डवर्धनं पितॄणां तन्न सान्निध्यमिति श्रुतेः।

21. ब्रह्मणे चाहुतिं पूर्वे पितॄननुमान्य तदहरेव नामकरणं कुर्याद्वेवता-नक्षत्रादिसंबद्धं पिता नाम कुर्यादन्यो वा कुलवृद्धश्चतुरक्षरं द्व्यक्षरं वा घोषवदाद्यन्तस्थं पुंसामीकारान्तं स्त्रीणामेवं कृते नाम्नि शुचि तत्कुलं भवतीति।

22. **शङ्खः** — अयुग्माक्षरमाकारान्तं स्त्रियै तद्विहितमपि।
कुलदेवतासंबद्धं पिता नाम कुर्यादिति।

23. **शङ्खः** — चतुर्थे मासि कर्तव्यं बालस्यादित्यदर्शनम्।

---

15. स्मृतिच०, I, p. 17; नि० सि०; चतुर्विंश०, p. 7.

16. वीर० (संस्कारप्रकाश, p. 193).

17. म० पा०, 354; मेधा० (मनु, 5.62) reads वस्त्रप्रावरणगोधान्यप्रतिग्रहेष्वदोषस्तदहरित्येके; परा० मा०, 1.2, p. 213 follows मेधा०; वीर० (संस्कारप्रकाश, p. 199) reads गुर्वर्थे कुर्वतः and so does हारलता, p. 28.

18. स्मृतिच०, I., p. 20; चतुर्विंश०, p. 8.

19. म० पा०, 356; कुल्लूक (मनु, 2.30); compare शङ्खस्मृति, 2.2.

20-21. म० पा०, 256; स्मृतिच० (I., p. 21) has दशम्या . . . नामकरणं and reads 'पिण्ड-विवर्धनं' and ब्रह्मणे हुत्वाहुतीः' and स्मृतिच० (I., p. 20). has कुलदेवतानक्ष . . . कुलवृद्धः and ईकारान्तः स्त्री . . . भवति; परा० मा०, I. 2. pp. 24, 26; compare महाभाष्य, Vol. I, p. 38, 'दशम्युत्तरकालं पुत्रस्य जातस्य नाम विदध्याद् घोषवदा-द्यन्तरन्तस्थमवृद्धं त्रिपुरुषानूकमनरिप्रतिष्ठितम्' etc.

22. म० पा०, 357; मिता० (या०, I.12) has the second.

23. स्मृतिच०, I., p. 22, compare शङ्खस्मृति, 2.4.

24. **शङ्खः** —संवत्सरेन्नप्राशनमर्धसंवत्सर इत्येके।

25. **शङ्खलिखितौ** — तुतीये वर्षे चूडाकर्म विधीयते।
द्वितीये वा तृतीये वा कर्तव्यं श्रुतिचोदनात्।।

26. तृतीये चूडाकर्म पञ्चमे वा।

27. **शङ्खयाज्ञवल्क्यौः** — चूडाकर्म यथाकुलम्।

28. **शङ्खः** — पयोयवाग्वामिक्षाहाराः क्रमशस्त्रयाणामुपनद्यनाद्धि गर्भाधानादिषु संस्कारेषु दश दश विप्रा भोज्याः।

29. **शङ्खलिखितौ** — नोन्मत्तमूकान् संस्कुर्यात्।

30. **शङ्खः** —मन्त्रवर्जे शूद्रस्य।

31-32. **शङ्खलिखितौ** — गर्भाष्टमे ब्राह्मणमुपनयेत्। राजन्यमेकादशे द्वादशे वैश्यम्।

33. **शङ्खमनुव्यासाः** — गर्भाष्टमे वै कुर्वीत ब्राह्मणस्योपनायनम्।

34. **शङ्खः** — वसन्तो ग्रीष्मः शरदिति कालाः।

35. **शङ्खः** — कृष्णरुरुवस्तान्युत्तरीयाणि।

36. (a) **शङ्खलिखितौः** — बिल्वपालाशखादिराश्वत्थपैलवौदुम्बरा दण्डाः केशललाटवक्त्रान्ताः।

---

24. स्मृतिच० (I., p. 22); अपरार्क on या० 1.11-12; म० पा०, p. 360.

25-26. म० पा०, 361; स्मृतिच०, I., p. 23 has the last adding वर्षे after तृतीये; चतुर्विंश० has तृतीये वर्षे . . . वा.

27. चतुर्वर्ग०, Vol. III, part 2, p. 743; compare शङ्खस्मृति, 2.5, याज्ञ०, I.12.

28. अपरार्क (या०, I.14).

29. उज्जवला (आप०, I.1.1.9).

30. विश्वरूप on या०, I. 13.

31-32. चतुर्वर्ग०, Vol. III, Part 2, p. 745.

33. चतुर्वर्ग०, Vol. III, Part I, p. 112; compare शङ्खस्मृति, 2.5, मनु., 2.36.

34. विश्व० on याज्ञ०, I.14; *vide* बौ० ध० सू०, I.2.11.

35. स्मृतिच०, I, p. 29; compare गौ० ध०, I.16 and बौ०, I.2.15 for almost same words.

36. (a) वीर० (संस्कारप्रकाश, p. 437); *vide* गौ०, I.25 and बौ० ध० सू०, I.2.16 for almost same words.

36. (b) **शङ्खः** — केशावधिललाटनासतुल्याः प्रोक्ताः क्रमेण।

37. **शङ्खः** — प्रयतः काल उत्थाय स्नातो हुतहुताशनः।
कुर्वीत प्रणतो भक्त्या गुरूणामभिवादनम्।।

38. **शङ्खः** — भृतकाध्यापको यस्तु स उपाध्याय उच्यते।

39. **शङ्खलिखितौ**: — द्वादशद्वादश वर्षाणि वा प्रतिवेदं यावद् ग्रहणं वा वेदस्य तावत् ब्रह्मचर्यमाचरेत्।

40. **शङ्खः** — नोदकुम्भहस्तोभिवादयेन्न भैक्षं चरन्न पुष्पाज्यादिहस्तो नाशुचिर्न जपन्न देवपितृकार्ये कुर्वन्न शयानः।

41. **शङ्खः** — न स्नानेन न होमेन नैवाग्निपरिचर्यया।
ब्रह्मचारी दिवं याति स याति गुरुपूजनात्।।

42. **शङ्खलिखितौ** — न मातापित्रोरन्तरमिच्छेत्पुत्रः कामं मातुरेवानुब्रूयात्। सा हि धारिणी पोषणी च। न पुत्रः प्रतिमुच्येतान्यत्र सौत्रामणीयागाज्जीवन्नृणान्मातुरेवमत्याज्या माता तथा पिता। सपिण्डा गुणवन्तः सर्व एवात्याज्याः। यस्त्यजेत्कामादपतितान् स दण्डं प्राप्नुयाद्द्विशतम्।

43. **शङ्खलिखितौ** — अथ मान्याः माता पिता पितुर्भार्या ज्येष्ठो भ्राता भगिनी ज्येष्ठः श्यालः पितुः सखा गुरुराचार्यः पितृव्यमातुलश्वस्रूःश्वशुरवृद्धाः।

---

36. (b) स्मृतिच०, I, p. 30.

37. स्मृतिच०, I, p. 32. This is शङ्खस्मृति, 3.2.

38. स्मृतिच०, I, p. 34; this is शङ्खस्मृति, 3.1; compare मनु०, II.141.

39. चतुर्वर्ग०, Vol. III, Part 2, p. 779; compare गौ०, 2. 51-53 and बौ० ध०, 1, 2.2 and 4.

40. मिता० on याज्ञ०, III.293, स्मृतिच०, I., p. 39, which reads पुष्पान्नहस्तः; म० पा०, p. 961; वीर० (संस्कारप्रकाश, p. 464) reads कार्यं कुर्वन्न परिषन्मध्ये स्वैरवाक्; compare बौ०, I. 2.32.

41. स्मृतिच०, I, p. 44; *see* शङ्खस्मृति, 5.9.

42. वीर० (संस्कारप्रकाश, p. 479) has only up to ०णान्मातुः and reads गच्छेत् for इच्छेत्; वि० र०, 357; स्मृतिच० (I, p. 35) has the words न पुत्रः . . . मातुः and attributes them to शङ्ख; compare मनु, 8.389.

43. वीर० (संस्कारप्रकाश, p. 470).

44. **शङ्खः** — न वेदमनधीत्यान्यां विद्यामधीयीत। अन्यत्र वेदाङ्गस्मृतिभ्यः।

45. **शङ्खः** — अष्टम्याः प्रदोषे (अधीयीत)।

46. **शङ्खः** — उपाध्याये राजनि च श्रोत्रिये च मृते सब्रह्मचारिणि चन्द्रार्कयो राहुदर्शने शक्रध्वजप्रपतने चाचार्ये च मृते त्रिरात्रम्।

47. **शङ्खः** — निर्घातभूमिवेगोल्कापातदिग्दाहपांशुशोणितमांतास्थिक-सदधिलाजगौरवर्षेषु स्वस्त्ययनं कृत्वाभ्यञ्जनाक्रुष्टवान्तश्रमदुःस्वप्नदर्शनेष्वेकोद्दिष्टसूतकमृतकेष्वाद्यं प्रायश्चित्तं कृत्वा ब्राह्मगमनेष्ट्यादीनि दत्वानुज्ञाप्याधीयीरन्।

48. **शङ्खः** — अष्टम्यां प्रदोषे।

49. **शङ्खः** — ब्राह्मे मुहूर्ते तूत्थाय मूत्रपुरीषोत्सर्गं कुर्यात्।

50. **शङ्खः** — वाग्यतोवगुण्ठिताशिरा भूमिमन्तर्धाय मेहेत्।

51. **शङ्खलिखितौ** — नानन्तर्वासा न निर्वासाः कुर्यात्।

52. **शङ्खः** — नानुदको नामृत्को नापरिवेष्टितशिराः।

53. **शङ्खः** — मेहने मृत्तिकाः सप्त लिङ्गे द्वे परिकीर्तिते।
एकस्मिन्विंशतिर्हस्ते द्वयोर्ज्ञेया चतुर्दश।।
तिस्रस्तु मृत्तिका देया कर्तुं वै नखशोधनम्।

---

44. स्मृतिच०, I, p. 48; कुल्लूक on मनु, II.168.

45. वीर० (संस्कारप्रकाश, p. 538).

46. चतुर्वर्ग०, Vol. III, Part 2, p. 756; स्मृतिच० (I, p. 57) has the words राहु . . . त्रिरात्रम् compare गौ० ध० सू०, 16.22, मनु, 4. 110, याज्ञ०, I. 44.

47. चतुर्वर्ग०, Vol. III, Part 2, p. 762.

48. चतुर्वर्ग०, Vol. III, Part 2, p. 759.

49. अपरार्क (या०, I.98).

50. विश्व० on या०, I.16.

51. वीर० (आह्निकप्रकाश, p. 37).

52. स्मृतिच०, I, p. 90.

53. स्मृतिच० (I, p. 93) reads तु चतुर्गुणम्; म० पा०, 46 reads अपाने for मेहने; अपरार्क (या०, I.17) has the first verse; *vide* शङ्खस्मृति, 18.20-23.

तिस्रस्तु पादयोर्ज्ञेया शौचकामस्य सर्वदा।
शौचमेतद् गृहस्थानां तथा गुरुनिवासिनाम्।
द्विगुणं स्याद्वनस्थानां यतीनां त्रिगुणं स्मृतम्।।
मृत्तिका तु समुद्दिष्टा त्रिपर्वी पूर्यते यया।

54. **शङ्खः** — अङ्गुष्ठमूलस्योत्तरतः प्रागग्रायां रेखायां ब्राह्मं तीर्थे प्रादेशिन्यङ्गुष्ठयोरन्तरा पित्र्यं कनिष्ठिकातलयोरन्तरा प्राजापत्यम्। पूर्वेणाङ्गुलिपर्वणि दैवम्।

55. **शङ्खलिखितौः** — कमण्डलुमुपस्पृश्य प्रक्षाल्य पाणिपादौ चाचम्येशानं मनसा ध्यायेत्।

56. **शङ्खः** — उद्धृत्य परिपूताभिरभिद्रवेक्षिताभिरक्षाराभिरनधिश्रिताभिरफेनाभिरबुद्बुदाभिः।

57. **शङ्खः** — ततोऽङ्गुलिचतुष्केण स्पृशेन्मूर्धानमादितः।
तर्जन्यङ्गुष्ठयोगेन स्पृशेन्नेत्रद्वयं पृथक्।।
मध्यमानामिकाभ्यां तु स्पृशेन्नासापुटे क्रमात्।
अङ्गुष्ठेन कनीयस्याः कर्णौ संयोगतः स्पृशेत्।
तर्जन्यङ्गुष्ठयोगेन नाभिं हृदि तलं स्पृशेत्।।

58. **शङ्खः** — स्नानभोजनकालेष्वाचान्तः पुनराचामेत्।

59. **शङ्खः** — काशहस्तस्तु नाचामेत्कदाचिद्वेधशङ्कया।

60. **शङ्खलिखितौ** — मूत्रपुरीषष्ठीवनादिषु शुक्तवाक्याभिधानेषु च पुनरुपस्पृशेत्।

---

54. परा० मा०, I.1, p. 235; स्मृतिच०, I, p. 96 has up to प्राजापत्यम्; मेधा० (मनु, 2.59) reads, 'अङ्गुष्ठस्याधरतः प्रागग्रायाश्च रेखाया . . . कनिष्ठिकान्तरालयोः कायं पूर्वेणाप्रमङ्गुलीनां दैविकम्.' Compare बौ० ध०, I.5.12-13 and वसिष्ठ, 3.26.

55. वीर० (आह्निक०, p. 61).

56. विश्व० (याज्ञ०, I.20) has the first two words only; वीर० (आह्निक, p. 68); compare बौ० ध०, I.5.14 and वसिष्ठ, 3.31; *vide* 459 below.

57. म० पा०, 55.

58. आचारमयूख.

59. आचारमयूख, (p. 16).

60. वीर० (आह्निक, p. 108).

61. **शङ्खः** — अद्भिः समुद्धृताभिस्तु हीनाभिः फेनबुद्बुदैः।
वह्निना च न तप्ताभिरक्षताभिरुपस्पृशेत्।।

62. **शङ्खः** — दन्तवद्दन्तलग्नेषु रसवर्जमन्यत्र जिव्हाभिमर्शनात्।

63. **शङ्खलिखितौः** — नोद्धतकुहकैः सहैकत्र तिष्ठेत्।

64. **शङ्खलिखितौः** — भार्याः कार्याः स्वजातीयाः श्रेयस्यः सर्वेषां स्युरिति पूर्वकल्पः।
ततोनुकल्पः चतस्रो ब्राह्मणस्यानुपूर्व्येण तिस्रो राजन्यस्य द्वे वैश्यस्यैका शूद्रस्य।

65. **शङ्खः** — ब्राह्मणी क्षत्रिया वैश्या ब्राह्मणस्य प्रकीर्तिता।
क्षत्रिया चैव वैश्या च क्षत्रियस्य प्रकीर्तिता।।
वैश्यैव भार्या वैश्यस्य शूद्रा शूद्रस्य कीर्तिता।

66. **शङ्खलिखितौ** — तत्र सवर्णः सवर्णाय विदितायैव नग्निकां दद्यात्स ब्राह्मः।

67. **शङ्खलिखितौः** — गोमिथुनेन वस्त्रयुगलेन वार्षः सर्वेष्वलंकारः स्त्रीधनं च देयम्।

68. **शङ्खलिखितौ** — सप्ताद्यन्तयोरात्मानं च प्राजापत्यः पञ्चार्षः त्रीन्दैव उत्तरेषु क्रियाप्राधान्यम्।

69. **शङ्खः** — दारानाहरेत्सदृशानसमानार्षेयानसंबन्धानासप्तमपञ्चमात्पितृमातृ-बन्धुभ्यः।

---

61. स्मृतिच०, I, p. 96; परा० मा०, I. 1, p. 236 reads अक्षाराभिः. This verse is शङ्खस्मृति, 9.6.

62. अपरार्क (या० I.195); स्मृतिच० (I, p. 101) reads जिह्वास्पर्शनात्; compare गौ०, 1.41-43 for almost same words, बौ० ध०, I.5.20 and वसिष्ठ, 3.41.

63. म० पा०, 121.

64. दायभाग (p. 210, ed. of 1829).

65. दायभाग, p. 212 (ed. of 1829); compare शङ्खस्मृति, 4.7-8.

66. वीर० (संस्कारप्रकाश, p. 848); compare बौ० ध०, 4.1.12.

67. वीर० (संस्कारप्रकाश, p. 851).

68. वीर० (संस्कारप्रकाश, p. 865).

69. उज्ज्वला (आप०, II.5.11.16); compare याज्ञ०, I.53.

70. **शङ्खः** — विन्देत विधिवद्भार्यामसमानार्षगोत्रजाम्।
मातृतः पञ्चमीं चापि पितृतस्त्वथ सप्तमीम्।।

71. **शङ्खः** — पञ्चमीं वोभयतः।

72. **शङ्खलिखितौ** — इषुं गृह्णाति राजन्या। प्रतोदं वैश्या। दशान्तं शूद्रा। ब्राह्मणस्तु सवर्णायाः पाणिं गृह्णीयात्।

73. **शङ्खः** — शुद्धा भर्तुश्चतुर्थेह्नि अशुद्धा देवैपत्रयोः।
दैवे कर्मणि पैत्रे च पञ्चमेहनि शुध्यति।।

74. **शङ्खः** — पुत्रपौत्रप्रतिष्ठस्य बह्वपत्यस्य जीवतः।

75. **शङ्खः** — ब्राह्मणेन क्षत्रियायामुत्पादितः क्षत्रिय एव भवति। क्षत्रियेण वैश्यायामुत्पादितो वैश्य एव भवति। वैश्येन शूद्रायामुत्पादितः शूद्र एव भवति।

76. **शङ्खः** — क्षत्रियवैश्यानुलोमान्तरोत्पन्नजो रथकारस्तस्येज्यादानोपनयनसंस्कार-क्रिया अश्वप्रतिष्ठारथसूत्रवास्तुविद्याध्ययनवृत्तिता च।

77. **शङ्खः** — नानुक्ता गृहान्निर्गच्छेत्। नानुत्तरीया। न त्वरितं व्रजेत्। न पर-पुरुषमभिभाषेतान्यत्र वणिक्प्रव्रजितवृद्धवैद्येभ्यः। न नाभिं दर्शयेत्। आ गुल्फाद्वासः परिदध्यात्। न स्तनौ विवृतौ कुर्यात्। न हसेदनपावृतम्। न भर्तारं न तद्बन्धून्वा विद्विषेत्। न गणिकाधूर्ताव्यभिचारिणीप्रव्रजितेक्षणि-कामायामूलकुहककारिकादुःशीलादिभिः सहैकत्र तिष्ठेत्। संसर्गेण हि चारित्र्यं दुष्यतीत्यादिशन्ति।

---

70. वीर० (संस्कारप्रकाश, p. 704); compare शङ्खस्मृति, 4.1.

71. विश्व० on या०, I.53.

72. परा० मा०, I.2., p. 98; compare मनु, 3.44 for almost same words.

73. हारलता, p. 70.

74. विश्व० on या०, I.78.

75. मिता० on याज्ञ०, I. 91; अपरार्क has same with slight variations. Contrast with this बौ० ध०, I.8.6, मनु, 10.6.

76. मिता० on याज्ञ०, I.95; अपरार्क.

77. मिता० (या० I.87) reads हसेदप्रावृता and ०धूर्ताभिसारिणी०; अपरार्क (या० 1-83), म० पा० (p. 195) has same passage and reads द्विष्यात् for विद्विषेत् and '०मायामूलकुहककारूकारिका०'.

78. **शङ्खलिखितौ:** — स्त्री परानुव्यक्तवक्त्रा बहिर्निष्क्रामेत्। नानुत्तरीया परिधावेत्। नानुत्सवे गन्धमाल्याभरणानि विकृतानि वासांसि बिभृयात्। न परपुरुषमभिभाषेत। अन्यत्र बालकप्रव्रजितवृद्धेभ्यः। न नाभिं दर्शयेत्। कुलवधूरागुल्फं वासः परिदध्यात्। न स्तनौ विवृतौ कुर्यात्। न हसेतानावृतम्।

79. **शङ्खलिखितौ:** — न गणिकाधूर्त्तचारिणीक्षणिकामायाविनीकुहकशीला-विप्लुताभिः सहैकत्र तिष्ठेत्। संसर्गेण हि चारित्र्यं दुष्येत। न भर्तुः प्रतिकूलमाचरेत्। न प्रकीर्णभाण्डभोजनीयोपस्करद्रव्या नोत्तानखट्वासन-पादुका स्यात्।

80. **शङ्खः** —तिस्रः कोट्योर्धकोटी च यानि लोमानि मानुषे।
तात्वत्कालं वसेत्स्वर्गे भर्तारं यानुगच्छति।।

81. **शङ्खः** —मृते भर्तरि या नारी समारोहेद्धुताशनम्।
सारुन्धतीसमाचारा स्वर्गलोके महीयते।।

82. **शङ्खलिखितौ:** — अप्रियशीलां पुरुषद्वेषिणीमननुकूलां चाधिविन्देत।

83. **शङ्खः** — साध्वाचारा न तावत्स्यात्स्नातापि स्त्री रजस्वला।
यावत्प्रवर्तमानं हि रजो नैव निवर्तते।।
रोगेण यद्रजः स्त्रीणामत्यर्थं तु प्रवर्तते।
अशुच्यो नैव तास्तेन येन वैकारिकं हि तत्।।

84. **शङ्खः** — तिस्रः पुनर्भ्वश्चतस्रः स्वैरिण्यः।

85. **शङ्खलिखितौ:** — तत्र पूर्वा पूर्वा जघन्या तासामपत्यानामृक्थपिण्डोदकयज्ञेषु यो विकल्पः स मातुरेव गुणवत्तया व्याख्यातः।

---

78. स्मृतिच०, II, p. 249-50; वि० र० 430.

79. स्मृतिच०, II, p. 249-50 reads 'चारिणी मायाविनी'; वि० र० 431.

80. (Quoted as from शङ्ख and अङ्गिरस् in मिता० on या०, I. 86). This is the same as पराशर, 4.32.

81. परा० मा०, II. 1., p. 54.

82. वीर० (संस्कारप्रकाश p. 872).

83. चतुर्वर्ग०, Vol. III, Part 1, p. 804.

84. विश्व० on याज्ञ०, I. 67.

85. वि० र०, 452 (about पूनर्भू and स्वैरिणी).

86. **शङ्खः** — बालवृद्धमत्तोन्मत्तोपहतदेहमाराक्रान्तस्त्रीस्नातकप्रव्रजितेभ्यः। अथ ब्राह्मणायाग्रे पन्था देयो राज्ञ इत्येके। तच्चानिष्टं गुरुर्ज्येष्ठश्च ब्राह्मणो राजानमतिशेते तस्मै पन्थाः।

87. **शङ्खः** — तुषकेशपुरीषभस्मास्थिश्लेष्मनखलोमान्यप्सु न निक्षिपेत्। पादेन पाणिना वा जलं नाभिहन्यात्।

88. **शङ्खः** — एतैरेव गुर्णैयुक्तं धर्मार्जितधनं तथा।
याजयेत सदा विप्रो ग्राह्यस्तस्मात्प्रतिग्रहः।।

89. **हारीतशङ्खलिखितयमाः** — यज्ञियाः समिध आहृत्य संमार्जनोपलेपनोब्दोधनसमूहनसमिन्धनपर्यग्निकरणपरिक्रमणोपस्थानहोमस्तोत्रनमस्कारादिभिरग्निं परिचरेत्। नाग्निमधितिष्ठेत्। न पद्भ्यां कर्षेत्। न मुखेनोपधमेत्। नापश्चाग्निं च युगपद्धारयेत्। नाजीर्णमुक्तो नोच्छिष्टो वाभ्यादध्यात्। विविधैर्हविर्विशेषैरामग्रेयैरहरहरग्निं समिन्धेत्। आमन्त्र्य गच्छेत्। आहृत्य निवेदयेत् तन्मनाः। शरीरोपरमान्ते ब्रह्मणः सायुज्यं गच्छति।

90. **शङ्खलिखितौ** — आहारं मैथुनं निद्रां संध्याकालेषु वर्जयेत्।
कर्म चाध्यापनं चैव तथा दानप्रतिग्रहौ।।

91. **शङ्खः** — नानियुक्तोग्रासनं गच्छेत्। नाग्रासनस्थः प्रथममश्नीयात्। नाधिकं दद्यान्न प्रतिगृह्णीयात्।

92. **शङ्खलिखितौ** — ब्रह्मतीर्थेनाचामेत्।

93. **शङ्खलिखितौः** — हृदयंगाभिरद्भिर्ब्राह्मणः शुचिः। कण्ठगाभिः क्षत्रियः। तालव्यामिर्वैश्यः। स्त्री शूद्रः स्पर्शान्तिकाभिः।

---

86. मिता० on या०, I.117; स्मृतिच०, I, p. 40 reads बालवृद्धगात्रापहतदेह and goes on up to प्रवजितेभ्यः; compare मनु०, II.138-39, बौ० ध० सू०, II.3.50, गौ०, 6.21-22, आप० ध०, II.5.11.5-6, वसिष्ठ, 13.58-60.

87. मिता० on या०, I.137.

88. म० पा०, 217.

89. परा० मा०, I.2, p. 49-50; चतुर्विंश०, p. 47; compare आप० ध०, II.5.12.8-9 and I.5.15.20 for some of these *sūtras*.

90. परा० मा०, I.1, p. 194.

91. अपरार्क (या०, 1.107); स्मृतिच०, (1, p. 227) has the *sūtra* नाग्रासन०.

92. चतुर्वर्ग०, Vol. III, Part 1, p. 990.

93. चतुर्वर्ग०, Vol. III, Part 1, p. 985; compare मनु०, 2. 62, वसिष्ठ, 3.31-34, बौ० ध० I.5.18.

94. **शङ्खः** — विप्रः शुध्यति हृद्गाभिः कण्ठगाभिस्तु भूमिपः।
तालुगाभिस्तथा वैश्यः शूद्रः स्पृष्टाभिरन्ततः।।

95. **शङ्खलिखितौ** — न तिष्ठन्न प्रणतो नाङ्गुलिभिर्न मुखशब्दं कुर्वन्नाधौतपादो नायज्ञोपवीती न मुक्तशिखः (आचामेत्)।

96. **शङ्खः** —प्राजापत्येन तीर्थेन त्रिः प्राश्नीयाज्जलं शुचिः।

97. **शङ्खलिखितौ** — त्रिः प्राश्य द्विरुन्मृज्य शिरश्चक्षुः श्रोत्रं घ्राणं हृदयं मूर्धानं चालभेत।

98. **शङ्खः** — प्रातः संक्षेपतः स्नानं शौचार्थं तु तदिष्यते।
मन्त्रैस्तु विधिनिष्पाद्यं माध्याह्ने तु सविस्तरम्।।

99. **शङ्खलिखितौः** — अनश्नन्ननग्नः स्नायात्। नाप्सुमेहेत। नोद्घर्षणं कुर्यात्। न पादेन पाणिना वा जलमभिहन्याद्यस्मादापो वै सर्वा देवताः। न स्रवन्तीं वृथातिकामेदनवसिच्य। अमेध्योदकं परिहरेत्। नाल्पोदके स्नायान्न समुद्रमवगाहेत। न नदीषु नदीं ब्रूयात्। न पर्वतेषु पर्वतान्।

100. **शङ्खः** — स्नानं तु द्विविधं प्रोक्तं गौणमुख्यप्रभेदतः।
तयोस्तु वारुणं मुख्यं तत्पुनः षड्विधं भवेत्।।
नित्यं नैमित्तिकं काम्यं क्रियाङ्गं मलकर्षणम्।
क्रियास्नानं तथा षष्ठं षोढा स्नानं प्रकीर्तितम्।।
अस्नातस्तु पुमान्नार्हो जप्याग्निहवनादिषु।
प्रातःस्नानं तदर्थं तु नित्यस्नानं प्रकीर्तितम्।।

---

94. चतुर्वर्ग०, Vol. III, Part 1, p. 975.

95. चतुर्वर्ग०, Vol. III, Part 1, p. 977; compare बौ० ध०, I.5.15.

96. चतुर्वर्ग०, Vol. III, Part 1, p. 991.

97. चतुर्वर्ग०, Vol. III, Part 1, p. 995; compare बौ० ध०, I.5.21, वसिष्ठ, 3.26-28, मनु, 2.60.

98. चतुर्वर्ग०, Vol. III, Part 1, p. 888.

99. वीर० (आह्निकप्रकाश, p. 167) stops at ०गाहेत; स्मृतिच०, I, p. 129 ascribes to शङ्ख alone the words नाल्पोदके . . . गाहेत; चतुर्वर्ग०, Vol. III, Part 1, p. 863 reads आमग्नो अनग्नः.

100. अपरार्क (या० 1-100) has all except the first; the first two occur in म० पा०, p. 236; स्मृतिच० (I, p. 110) up to क्रियास्नान and p. 128 for the verse स्नातस्य वह्नितप्तेन; परा० मा०, I.1.268-69.

चण्डालशवयूपादि स्पष्ट्वाऽस्नातां रजस्वलाम्।
स्नानार्हस्तु यतः स्नाति स्नानं नैमित्तिकं हि तत्।।
पुष्य (ष्य) स्नानादिकं यत्तु दैवज्ञविधिचोदितम्।
तद्धि काम्यं समुद्दिष्टं नाकामस्तत्प्रयोजयेत्।।
जप्तुकामः पवित्राणि अर्चिष्यन्देवताः पितॄन्।
स्नानं समाचरेद्यस्तु (त्तु) क्रियाङ्गं तत्प्रकीर्तितम्।।
मलापकर्षणं नाम स्नानसमभ्यङ्गपूर्वकम्।।
मलापकर्षणार्था तु प्रवृत्तिस्तस्य नान्यथा।।
सरःसु देवखातेषु तीर्थेषु च नदीषु च।
क्रियास्नानं समुद्दिष्टं स्नानं तत्र क्रिया मता।।
तत्र काम्यं तु कर्तव्यं यथावद्विधिचोदितम्।
नित्यं नैमित्तिकं चैव क्रियाङ्गं मलकर्षणम्।
तीर्थाभावे तु कर्तव्यमुष्णोदकपरोदकैः।
स्नातस्य वह्नितप्तेन तथैव परवारिणा।
शरीरशुद्धिर्विज्ञेया न तु स्नानफलं लभेत्।
अद्भिर्गात्राणि शुध्यन्ति तीर्थस्नानाद्भवेत्फलम्।।
सरःसु देवखातेषु तीर्थेषु च नदीषु च।
स्नानमेव क्रिया यस्मात्स्नानं पुण्यतमं स्मृतम्।।

101. **शङ्खः** — प्रातःस्नानं प्रशंसन्ति दृष्टादृष्टकरं हि तत्।
सर्वमर्हति शुद्धात्मा प्रातःस्नायी जपादिकम्।।
अलक्ष्मीः कालकर्णी च दुःस्वप्नाद्दुर्विचिन्तितम्।
याम्यं हि पातनाद्दुःखं नित्यस्नायी न पश्यति।
नित्यस्नानेन पूयन्ते अपि पापकृतो नराः।।

102. **शङ्खः** — रथ्याकर्दमवर्षासु प्रविश्य ग्रामसंकरम्।
जङ्घयोर्मृत्तिकास्तिस्रः पादयोर्द्विगुणास्ततः।।

103. **शङ्खः** — क्रियास्नानं प्रवक्ष्यामि यथावद्विधिपूर्वकम्।
मृद्भिरद्भिश्च कर्तव्यं शौचमादौ यथाविधि।।

---

101. म० पा०, 61-2.

102. म० पा०, 257.

103. स्मृतिच० (I, p. 127); परा० मा०, I.1, p. 274-275 for some of these; म० पा०, 270-1; all these verses occur in the शङ्खस्मृति, eighth chapter.

जले निमग्नस्तून्मज्ज्य उपस्पृश्य यथाविधि।
तीर्थस्यावाहनं कुर्यात्तत्प्रवक्ष्याम्यतः परम्।।
प्रपद्य वरुणं देवमम्भसां पतिमूर्जितम्।
याचेत देहि मे तीर्थे सर्वपापापनुत्तये।।
सान्निध्यमस्मिंस्तोये तु स्थीयतां मदनुग्रहात्।
रुद्रान्प्रपद्ये वरदान्सर्वानप्सुषदस्त्वहम्।।
सर्वानप्सुषदश्चैव प्रपद्ये प्रणतः स्थितः।
देवमप्सुषदं वह्निं प्रपद्ये त्वनिसूदनम्।।
आपः पुण्याः पवित्राश्च प्रपद्ये शरणं तथा।।
रुद्राश्चाग्निश्च सर्पाश्च वरुणश्चाप एव च।
शमयन्त्वशुभं पापं रक्षन्तु च सदा शुभम्।।
इत्येवमुक्त्वा कर्तव्यं ततः संमार्जनं कुशैः।
आपो हि ष्ठेति तिसृभिर्यथावदनुपूर्वशः।।
हिरण्यवर्णा इति च ऋग्भिश्च तिसृभिस्तथा।
शं नो देवीरीति तथा शं न आपस्तथैव च।।
इदमापः प्रवहतेत्येवं सर्वमुदीरयन्।।
एवं संमार्जनं कृत्वा छन्द आर्षे च दैवतम्।
अघमर्षणसूक्तस्य संस्मरेत्प्रयतः सदा।।
ततोम्भसि निमग्नस्तु त्रिः पठेदघमर्षणम्।
प्रपद्यान्मूर्धनि तथा महाव्याहृतिभिर्जलम्।।

104. **शङ्खः** — तीर्थं प्राप्यानुषङ्गेण यस्तत्र स्नानमाचरेत्।
स्नानजं फलमाप्नोति तीर्थयात्राश्रितं न तु।।
तृणां पापकृतां तीर्थं पापप्रशमनं भवेत्।
यथोक्तफलदं तीर्थे भवेच्छुद्धात्मनां तृणाम्।।

105. **शङ्खलिखितवसिष्ठाः** — सर्ववेदपवित्राणि वक्ष्याम्यहमतः परम्।
येषां जपैश्च होमैश्च पूयन्ते नात्र संशयः।।
अघमर्षणं देवकृतं शुद्धवत्यस्तरत्समाः।

104. स्मृतिच०, I, p. 132.

105. वीर० (आह्निकप्रकाश, p. 319). These are six verses found in the शङ्खस्मृति (10th chap.) and also in वसिष्ठ ध० सू०, 28-10-15. One of them अघमर्षणं देवकृतं occurs in बौ० ध० सू०, 4.3.7.

कूष्माण्ड्यः पावमान्यश्च दुर्गा सावित्र्यथैव च ।।
अभीषङ्गा पदस्तोमाः सामानि व्याहृतीस्तथा ।।
भारुण्डानि च सामानि गायत्रं रैवतं तथा ।
पुरुषव्रतं च भासं च तथा देवव्रतानि च ।
ब्लिङ्गा बार्हस्पत्यं च वाक्सूक्तं मध्वृचस्तथा ।।
शतरुद्रियमथर्वशिरस्त्रिसुपर्णं महाव्रतम् ।
गोसूक्तं चाश्वसूक्तं च इन्द्रशुद्धे च सामनी ।।
त्रीण्याज्यदोहानि रथन्तरं च अग्निव्रतं वामदेव्यं बृहच्च ।
एतानि गीतानि पुनन्ति जन्तूञ् जातिस्मरत्वं लभते य इच्छेत् ।।

106. **शङ्खः** – इति वेदपवित्राण्यभिहितानि । एतेभ्यः सावित्री विशिष्यते । नाघमर्षणात् परतरमन्तर्जले न व्याहृतिभ्यः परं होमे न सावित्र्याः परं जप्ये ।

107. **शङ्खः** – कुशबृस्यां समासीनः कुशोत्तरायां वा हस्तोपयामैर्वा कुशपवित्रपाणिरुदङ्मुखः सूर्याभिमुखो वाक्षमालामादाय देवतां ध्यायञ्जपं कुर्यात् । सुवर्णमणिमुक्ताफलस्फटिकपद्माक्षेन्द्राक्षपुत्रजीवकानामन्यतमादक्षमालां कुर्यात् कुशग्रन्थिकृतां वा हस्तोपयामैर्वा गणयेत् । आदौ देवतामार्षं छन्दश्च संस्मरेत् । ततः सप्रणवा व्याहृतीरादावावर्त्य गायत्रीमावर्तयेत् । अथास्याः सविता देवता । ऋषिर्विश्वामित्रो गायत्री च्छन्दः । ओंकारस्य प्रणवाख्या । ओं भूः । ओं भुवः । ओं स्वः । ओं महः । ओं जनः । ओं तपः ओं सत्यमिति व्याहृतयः । ओं आपो ज्योती रसोमृतं ब्रह्मभूर्भुवः स्वरोमिति शीर्षम् ।

108. **शङ्खलिखितौ** – पवित्रं धर्मशास्त्रमप्रतिरथं मध्ये गायत्रीमनुश्राव्य (जपेत्) ।

---

106. स्मृतिच०, I, p. 144 has the words from नाघमर्षणात्...जप्ये; वीर० (आह्निकप्रकाश, p. 312); *vide* शङ्खस्मृति, II.1.

107. अपरार्क (या०, 1-23) and स्मृतिच० (I, p. 148 and 230) for the first, latter omitting the words हस्तोपयामैर्वा; the सूत्र occurs in शङ्खस्मृति 11th chap.; परा० मा०, I, p. 303; वीर० (आह्निकप्रकाश, p. 312).

108. चतुर्वर्ग०, Vol. III, Part I, p. 1072 (अप्रतिरथं सामेति भाष्यकारः। आशु शिशान इत्येतद्वादशर्चमित्यन्ये).

109. **शङ्खः** — स्वरवर्णपदैर्वाक्यं शुद्धमावर्तयेज्जपन्।
न कम्पयेच्छिरो ग्रीवां दन्तान्नैव प्रदर्शयेत्।

110. **शङ्खलिखितौः** — उभाभ्यामपि हस्ताभ्यां प्राङ्मुखो यज्ञोपवीती प्रागग्रै कुशैर्देवतातर्पणं देवतीर्थेन कुर्यात्।

111. **शङ्खः** — दर्भाः कृष्णाजिनं मन्त्रा ब्राह्मणाश्च विशेषतः।
अयातयामान्येतानि नियोज्यानि पुनः पुनः।।

112. **शङ्खः** — कुशालाभे द्विजश्रेष्ठः काशैः कुर्वीत यत्नतः।
तर्पणादीनि कर्माणि काशाः कुशसमाः स्मृताः।।

113. **शङ्खः** — अमावास्यासु न च्छिन्द्यात्कुशांस्तु समिधस्तथा।
सर्वत्रावस्थिते सोमे हिंसायां ब्रह्महा भवेत्।।

114. **शङ्खः** — गृहे त्वेकगुणं जप्यं नद्यादौ द्विगुणं स्मृतम्।
गवां गोष्ठे दशगुणमग्न्यगारे शताधिकम्।।
सिद्धक्षेत्रेषु तीर्थेषु देवतानां च संनिधौ।
सहस्रशतकोटीनामनन्तं विष्णुसंनिधौ।।

115. **शङ्खः** — अमावास्या तु सोमेन सप्तमी भानुना सह।
चतुर्थी भूमिपुत्रेण सोमपुत्रेण चाष्टमी।।
चतस्रास्तिथयस्त्वेतास्तुल्याः स्युर्ग्रहणादिभिः।
सर्वमक्षयमत्रोक्तं स्नानदानजपादिकम्।।

116. **शङ्खः** — स्नातः कृतजप्योन्तर्जानुरुदङ्मुखो दिव्येन तीर्थेन देवानुदकेन तर्पयेत्। अर्थ तर्पणविधिः। भगवन्तं शेषं तर्पयामि। ततः कालाग्निरुद्रं

---

109. स्मृतिच०, I. 149.

110. परा० मा०, I.1, p. 352; ascribed to लिखित by अपरार्क (या० I.101) who reads संवृताङ्गुष्ठकाभ्यां after हस्ताभ्याम्; *vide* म० पा०, p. 291 also.

111. स्मृतिच०, I, p. 107.

112. स्मृतिच०, I, p. 109.

113. स्मृतिच०, I, p. 126.

114. स्मृतिच०, I, p. 150.

115. स्मृतिच०, III, p. 345.

116. चतुर्वर्ग०, Vol. III, Part 1, pp. 950-55; वीर० (आह्निकप्रकाश, p. 356 ff.); compare बौ० ध०, 2.3.15-29 for a similar passage on तर्पण.

श्वेतवराहमजितं रुक्मभौमं शैलभौमं नीलभौमं रक्तभौमं पीतभौमं श्वेतभौमं कृष्णभौमामिति पातालसप्तकम्। जम्बूद्वीपं शाकद्वीपं कुशद्वीपं कौञ्चद्वीपं शाल्मलिद्वीपं प्लुक्षद्वीलपं पुष्करद्वीपमिति द्वीपसप्तकं, लोकालोकाख्यं पर्वतं स्वधानामानं शंपदं केतुमन्तं हिरण्यरोमाणमिति कल्पस्थायिनो लोकालोकपालान् ततो लवणोदकं क्षीरोदकं घृतोदकं दध्युदकं रसोदकमिक्षुरसोदक स्वादूदकमिति समुद्रसप्तकं सागरचतुष्कं, शृङ्गवन्तं श्वेतं नीलं मेरुं माल्यवन्तं गन्धमादनं निषधं हेमकूटं हिमवन्तमिति महापर्वतान्, महेन्द्रं मलयं सह्यं शुक्तिमन्तमृक्षवन्तं विन्ध्यं परियात्रकमिति सदा कुलपर्वतान् कैलासमैनाकमुखांश्च, पर्वतांश्च बिन्दुसराप्रमुखानि सरांसि सप्तप्रवाहां गङ्गां त्रिलोकप्रवाहिनीं गङ्गाम्, सप्तसरस्वतीं यमुनां प्रथमं पुष्करं द्वितीयं पुष्करं तृतीयं पुष्करं प्रयागं नैमिषं गयाशीर्षं सर्वतीर्थानि सर्वप्रस्रवणानि सर्वाः सरितस्तु इन्द्रतीर्थमश्वत्थप्रमुखान् वनस्पतीन् यवप्रमुखान् ओषधीन् मानसोत्तराख्यं पर्वतं लोकपालांस्तु इन्द्रं शचीं वज्रमैरावतं मातलिं चित्रसेनप्रमुखान् गन्धर्वाप्सरसः मुदोनामाप्सरसः शुनोनामाप्सरसः असुरोनामाप्सरसः भारानामाप्सरसः पृष्टमोनामाप्सरसः ऊर्जोनामाप्सरसः अग्निसन्तां स्वाहां अग्नीधं यमं धर्मं श्रियं सत्यं तपः सयज्ञं दक्षिणां दीक्षां ब्रह्मचर्यं व्यवसायं धर्मराजानं दण्डं पिङ्गलं कालपाशौ आयुधं स्वर्गं मृत्युं चित्रगुप्तं यमपुरुषान् श्यावशबलौ विरूपाक्षं नैर्ऋतं धर्मप्रधानान् दैत्यान् दानवान् विद्याधरान् यक्षान् राक्षसान् पिशाचान् रोगान् ज्वरं रोगाधिपं आरोग्यं वरुणं गौरीर्नागान् वासुकिमनन्तं सर्पान् वनस्पतीन् वायुं शिरां प्राणापानसमानोदानव्यानान् इन्द्रियाणि इन्द्रियार्थान् जीवं सोमं नक्षत्राणि वर्तमानं नक्षत्रं पितॄन् आभासुरं बर्हिषदोग्निष्वात्तान् क्रव्यादान् तत्तद्रूपान् आज्यपान् सुकालिनः महादेवं पार्वतीं सेनानीं स्कन्दं विशाखं स्कन्दवहान् बालग्रहान् स्कन्दपार्षदान् रुद्रपार्षदान् भूतानि भौमान् रुद्रान् अन्तरिक्षान्रुद्रान् विद्यारूद्रान् सर्वगतान् रुद्रान् मातृयोगीश्वरीं देवपत्नीर्देवमातृगणान् धराधिपान् विनायकं सितस्मितं शालकटङ्कटौ कूष्माण्डं राजपुत्रान् धर्मसन्धं कामं गतिं निद्रां क्षुधं अदितिं आपत्तिं नियतिं कीर्तिं प्रज्ञां घृतिं मेधां क्षान्तिं रुचिं श्रद्धां वाणीं सरस्वतीं दक्षं दाक्षायणीं प्रजापतीन् सनकं सनन्दनं सनातनं सनत्कुमारं क्रतुं पितॄन् ब्रह्मऋषीन् देवर्षीन् राजर्षीन् ऋषिकान् ऋषिपत्नीं ऋषिपुत्रान् गायत्रीमुष्णिहमनुष्टुभं बृहतीं पङ्क्तिं जगतीं स्वच्छन्दांसि गरुडमरुणं

हव्यजातं सुरभिं दिङ्नागान् वैश्रवसं धन्वतरिं भुवननागान् दिव्यनागान् विश्वकर्माणं वैश्रवणमृद्धिं नलकूबरं रेवतं शङ्खपद्मौ नहुषपुत्रं तत्पत्नीं तत्प्रजां काश्यपं तत्पत्नीं तत्प्रजां धनदं तत्पत्नीं तत्प्रजां प्रजापतिं तत्पत्नीं तत्प्रजां चन्द्रं तत्पत्नीं तत्प्रजां अरिष्टनेमिं तत्पत्नीं तत्प्रजां कृशानुं जयामजामस्त्राणि शस्त्राणि शास्त्राणि ऋग्वेदं यजुर्वेदं सामवेदमथर्ववेदमितिहासपुराणं धनुर्वेदं गान्धर्ववेदमायुर्वेदं कुलवेदं ज्योतिषं शिक्षां कल्पं व्याकरणं निरुक्तं छन्दोविचितिं धर्मशास्त्रं भारतं मनुं विष्णुं यमं वसिष्ठं नारदं दक्षं संवर्तं शातातपं पराशरमापस्तम्बमौशनसं कृष्णद्वैपायनं कात्यायनं बृहस्पतिं गौतमं शङ्खं लिखितं हारीतमत्रिं याज्ञवल्क्यम्, अथ भगवन्तं धर्ममुत्तानपादं यज्ञं नारायणं नासत्यं वरुणार्यमणौ संवत्सरं मित्रमिन्द्राग्नी मरीचिकश्यपौ ध्रुवमगस्त्यं धातारं मार्तण्डं रामं वाल्मीकिं महाकल्पं मन्वन्तरं वर्तमानम्, इन्द्रमोजस्विनं स्वायम्भुवं स्वारोचिषौत्तमं तामसं रैवतं चाक्षुषं महातैजसं वैवस्वतमर्कं सावर्णं ब्रह्मसावर्णं रुद्रसावर्णं दक्षसावर्णं धर्मसावर्णं रौच्यं भौत्यं युगं वर्तमानं संवत्सरं वर्तमानमयनं वर्तमानमृतुं वर्तमानं मासं वर्तमानं पक्षं वर्तमानमादित्यं सोमं बुधं जीवं शुक्रं शनैश्चरं राहुं केतुमृक्षाणि वर्तमानं दिवसं रात्रिसन्ध्ये किंपुरुषान् सर्वाणि भूतानि देवान् वरान् देवानुगान् ओं एकज्योतिषं त्रिज्योतिषं चतुर्ज्योतिषमेकशक्र द्विशक्रं त्रिशक्रं इन्द्रं गात्यादसं नभं शङ्खपितं संमितं सितमृतजितं सत्यजितं सुषेणं, अतिमित्रवन्मित्रं पुरुषमित्रं धृतं धर्तारं विधर्तारं धरण ध्रुवं विधातरमीदृक्षमेतादृक्षं सदृक्षं प्रतिसदृक्षममृताशिनं प्रीतिनं शुगदृक्षं सभवमतिं धर्तारमुखं धनिभीममतियुक्तमृक्षपादं सहं द्युतिं वपुराधृक्षवासं कामं जयं विजयमित्येकोनपञ्चाशतं मरुतो भुवनं भावनं पर्जन्यं स्वजनं क्रतुं वसुं मूर्धानं राजं वास्तवं प्रणवमाप्यायनमृक्षमिति द्वादश भृगून् मनुं मन्वन्तरं प्राणायामं चित्तिं छयं मयं हंसं नरनारायणं विभुं प्रभुमिति द्वादश साध्यान् सवितारं धातारं मित्रमर्यमणं पूषणमंशं त्वष्टारं विवस्वन्तं मित्रं विष्णुं वरुणं भगमिति द्वादशादित्यान् अपावकं सूर्यं निकृतिं खमजैकपादमहिर्बुध्नं धूमकेतुं कलापिनमेकादश रुद्रान आत्मानमजमनीम् ऋक्षं दमं प्राणं हविष्मन्तं गरिष्ठं ऋतं सत्यमिति द्वादशाङ्गिरसः क्रतुं दक्षं वसुं सत्यं कालं कामं धुरिं रोचनं माद्रवं पुरुरवसमिति दश विश्वान्देवान्, धवं ध्रुवं सोममापमनलमनिलं प्रत्यूषं प्रभासमित्यष्टौ वसून् नासत्यं दस्रमित्यश्विनौ, एतान् नरगणान् सानुचरान् स्वायम्भुवं सावित्रीं सर्वान् देवान् सतीं देवीं लक्ष्मीं

धरामनिरुद्धं प्रद्युम्नं सङ्कर्षणं वासुदेवं भूलोकं भुवर्लोकं स्वर्लोकं महर्लोकं जनोलोकं तपोलोकं सत्यलोकं ब्रह्माण्डं पृथ्वीमपो वह्निं वायुमाकाशं मनः शुद्धिमासनमव्यक्तं पुरुषं तर्पयामि।

इदं चान्ते प्रत्यृचै पुरुषसूक्तेनाञ्जलीन् दद्यात् पुष्पाञ्जलिं च भक्त्या। अथ कृतापसव्यो दक्षिणामुखोन्तर्जानुः पित्र्येण तीर्थेन पितॄन् यथाश्रद्धं यथाप्रकाशमुदकं दद्यात्। सौवर्णेन पात्रेण राजतेनौदुम्बरेण खड्गपात्रेण वा शङ्कुनाप्युदकं पितृतीर्थं स्पृशन् दद्यात्। पित्रे पितामहाय प्रपितामहाय मात्रे पितामह्यै प्रपितामह्यै मातामहाय प्रमातामहाय वृद्धप्रमातामहाय मातामह्यै प्रमातामह्यै वृद्धप्रमातामह्यै च आसप्तमात् पुरुषात् पितृपक्षे यावतां नाम जानीयात् पितृपक्षाणामुदकतर्पणं कृत्वा।

गुरूणां कुर्यात्। गुरूणां कृत्वा मातृपक्षाणां कुर्यात्। मातृपक्षाणां कृत्वा संबन्धिबान्धवानां कुर्यात्। तेषां कृत्वा सुहृदां कुर्यात्। भवति चात्र वचनम्

विना रूप्यसुवर्णेन विना ताम्रतिलेन च।
विना दर्भैश्च मन्त्रैश्च पितॄणां नोपतिष्ठते॥
सौवर्णराजताभ्यां तु खड्गेनौदुम्बरेण वा।
दत्तमक्षय्यतां यानि पितॄणां तु तिलोदकम्।
हिमेन सह यद्दत्तं क्षीरेण मधुनाथवा।
तदप्यक्षय्यतां याति पितॄणां तु तिलोदकम्॥

117. **शङ्खः** — सौवर्णेन पात्रेण राजतेन औदुम्बरेण खड्गपात्रेण वा शङ्कुनाप्युदकं पितृतीर्थं स्पृशन् दद्यात्।

118. **शङ्खलिखितौ** — आसप्तमात्तु पुरुषात् पितृपक्षे यावतां तु नाम जानीयात् तावतां पितृपक्षाणामुदकतर्पणं कृत्वा गुरूणां कुर्यात्। गुरूणां कृत्वा मातृपक्षाणां कुर्यात्। मातृपक्षाणां कृत्वा तत्संबन्धिबान्धवानां कुर्यात्। तेषां कृत्वा सुहृदां कुर्यात्।

119. **शङ्खलिखितौः** — नेष्टकाचिते पितॄंस्तर्पयेत्। वापीतडागोदपानेषु सप्त पञ्चत्रीन् वा पिण्डानुद्धृत्य देवपितॄंस्तर्पयेत्।

---

117. चतुर्वर्ग०, Vol. III, Part 1, p. 921. This occurs above.

118. चतुर्वर्ग०, Vol. III, Part 1, p. 928. This occurs above in No. 116.

119. वीर० (आह्निकप्रकाश, p. 172); स्मृतिच० (III, p. 385) has the first *sūtra*.

120. **शङ्खः** — उदकेनोदकं कुर्यात्पितृभ्यस्तु कदाचन।
उत्तीर्य च शुचौ देशे कुर्यादुदकतर्पणम्।।

121. **शङ्खः** — स्नातः सन् तर्पणं कृत्वा पितृणां तु तिलाम्भसा।
पितृलोकमवाप्नोति प्रीणाति च यथा पितॄन्।।

122. **शङ्खः** — आब्रह्मस्तम्बपर्यन्तं जगत्तृप्यत्विति क्रमात्।
जलाञ्जलित्रयं दद्यादेतत्संक्षेपतर्पणम्।।

123. **शङ्खः** — एवं यः सर्वभूतानि तर्पयेदन्वहं द्विजः।
स गच्छेत्परमं स्थानं तेजोरूपमनामयम्।।

124. **शङ्खः** — उभयत्र स्थितैर्दर्भैः समाचमति यो द्विजः।
सोमपानफलं तस्य भुक्त्वा यज्ञफलं भवेत्।।
ग्रन्थिर्यस्य पवित्रस्य न तेनाचमनं भवेत्।
आचामेद्यस्तु मोहाच्च यथा भोक्ता तथा तु सः।।

125. **शङ्खलिखितौः** — स व्रती बहिः संध्यामुपासीत।

126. **शङ्खः** — पूर्वो संध्यां जपेत्तिष्ठन्नासीनः पश्चिमां तथा।

127. **शङ्खः** — प्रातःसंध्यां सनक्षत्रां मध्यमां स्नानकर्मणि।
सादित्यां पश्चिमां संध्यामुपासीत यथाविधि।।

128. **शङ्खः** — चन्दनकुङ्कुमकर्पूरमृगमदजातीफलवर्जमनुलेपनं समादद्यात्।

129. **शङ्खः** — शङ्खचक्राद्यङ्कनं च तुलसीदलभक्षणम्।

---

120. स्मृतिच०, I, p. 192.
121. स्मृतिच०, I, p. 196.
122. म० पा०, 64.
123. म० पा०, 296.
124. म० पा०, 239-40.
125. वीर० (आह्निकप्रकाश, p. 260).
126. स्मृतिच०, I, p. 151; *vide* शङ्खस्मृति, 9, 19.
127. स्मृतिच०, I, p. 185.
128. स्मृतिच०, I, p. 201.
129. आचारमयूख (p. 37).

यः कुर्यान्नियतं भक्त्या स याति परमां गतिम् ।।
नान्यं देवं नमस्कुर्यान्नान्यं देवं निरीक्षयेत् ।
चक्राङ्कितः सदा तिष्ठेद्यद्भक्तः पाण्डुनन्दन ।

130. **शङ्खलिखितौः** — शेषभुङ् महायज्ञानहरहर्निर्वपेदापन्नः शाकोदकेभ्यः ।

131. **शङ्खः** — पञ्च सूना गृहस्थस्य चुल्ली पेषण्युपस्करः ।
कण्डनी चोदकुम्भश्च तस्य पापस्य शान्तये ।।
पञ्चयज्ञविधानं तु गृही नित्यं न हापयेत् ।

132. **शङ्खलिखितौः** — अत ऊर्ध्वं देवयज्ञः सर्वेषामुपदिश्यते । आश्रमधर्माविरोधेन प्रतिनियतानामोषधीनां कोद्रवचणकमाषमसूरकुलत्थोद्दालकवर्जं निर्वपणीयम् । तण्डुलान्वा प्रातः पत्न्यै दद्यात् । स्वयं वाधिश्रियेत् । सुसंमृष्टगृहद्वारोपलेपनधूपजपप्रयतो नियतः सायं प्रातरन्नादावश्यकानि कुर्यात् । अग्नये जातवेदसे स्वाहा इत्यग्नौ, तूष्णीं द्वितीयाम्, उदु त्यं जातवेदसमित्यादित्यमुपतिष्ठेत, ब्रह्मणे नम इति ब्रह्मस्थले बलिं हरेत् । सोमायेत्युपकुम्भे, वायव इति वास्तुगृहे गृहपतय इति गृहद्वारे, प्रजापतय इति गर्भगृहे, शं नो देवीरित्यग्निकार्ये, दिक्पतिभ्यस्तत्पुरुषेभ्य इति प्रतिदिशं, नक्षत्रदेवताभ्योन्तरिक्षे, सर्वतः पशूनां पतये, नमो देवेभ्य इति प्रागुदीच्याम्, ब्रह्मस्थले स्वधा पितृभ्य इति दक्षिणेन निवाप्य गोदोहमात्रं कालमन्वाचक्षतेतिथिम् ।

133. **शङ्खलिखितौः** — गोदोहनमात्रं कालमन्वाकाङ्क्षेत् । अतिथिः श्रोत्रियो देवव्रती यतिधर्मा नैष्ठिकः समानवृत्तिर्योन्यो वागच्छेत् तस्मिन्काले तमर्चयित्वाश्नीयात् । कुशवृत्तेरपि ब्राह्मणोनश्नन् सुकृतमादत्ते पर्यश्नतः पूजां कुर्वन्ति ।

वयोवर्णविद्यातपःसंपन्नाय पाद्यमर्घमाचमनीयमन्नविशेषांस्तस्मै शक्तितो दद्यात् । सहासीत प्रदोषेनुज्ञाप्य शयीत पूर्वं प्रतिबुध्येत प्रस्थितमनुव्रजेत् । समेत्य न्यायतो निवर्तेत वेद्युद्यानारामसभाप्रपातडागदेवगृहमहागमस्थाननदीनामन्यतमस्मिंस्तं प्रदक्षिणं कुर्यात् वाचमुत्सृज्य पुनर्दर्शनायेति ।

---

130. वीर० (आह्निकप्रकाश, p. 388); at p. 395 occur the words अहरहः पञ्चयज्ञान्निर्व०.

131. स्मृतिच०, I, p. 208; *vide* शङ्खस्मृति, 5.1-2.

132. वीर० (आह्निकप्रकाश, pp. 394 and 404).

133. वीर० (आह्निकप्रकाश, pp. 442-43); compare गौ०, 5.30 and 34.

134. **शङ्खः** — सहासीत प्रदोषेनुज्ञाप्य शयीत पूर्वे प्रतिबुध्येत प्रस्थितमनुव्रजेत्। समभ्यनुज्ञातो निवर्तेत।।

135. **शङ्खलिखितौः** — नाब्राह्मणोतिथिर्ब्राह्मणस्य।श्रोत्रियाय गुणवते आतिथ्यम्। राजन्यवैश्याभ्यां मित्रवत्। शूद्रायानृशंस्यार्थमातिथ्यं यथावत्।

136. **शङ्खलिखितौः** — कृशरं पायसं यावं दधि मधु कृष्णाजिनानि शूद्रेभ्यो न दद्यान्नोपाकृतं किंचित्।

137. **शङ्खः** — यदि बहूनां नाशक्नुयादेकस्मै शीलवते दद्याद्यः प्रथममुपागतः स्याच्छ्रोत्रियस्तस्मै दद्यात्।

138. **शङ्खः** — इष्टिभिः पशुबन्धैश्च चातुर्मास्यैर्यजेत्तु यः।
अग्निष्टोमादिभिर्यज्ञैर्यजेत च स इष्टवान्।।
अग्निहोत्रं तपः सत्यं वेदानां चैव पालनम्।
आतिथ्यं वैश्वदेवं च इष्टमित्यभिधीयते।।
एकाग्निकादौ यत्कर्म त्रेतायां यच्च हूयते।
अन्तर्वेद्यां च यद्दानमिष्टं तदभिधीयते।।
रोगिणां परिचर्या च पूर्तमित्यभिनिर्दिशेत्।

139. **शङ्खः** — नापणीयमन्नमश्नीयात्।

140. **शङ्खः** — अपूपाः सक्तवो धानास्तक्रं दधि घृतं मधु।
एतत्पण्येषु भोक्तव्यं भाण्डलेपो न चेद्भवेत्।।

141. **शङ्खः** —आदित्या वसवो रुद्रा ब्रह्मा चैव पितामहः।
मण्डलान्युपजीवन्ति तस्मात्कुर्वीत मण्डलम्।।

---

134. अपरार्क (या०, 1.113).

135. वीर० (आह्निकप्रकाश, p. 452); compare गौ०, 5.39-42 for similar words.

136. चंतुर्वर्ग०, Vol. I, p. 54.

137. स्मृतिच०, I, p. 217.

138. चतुर्वर्ग०, Vol. I, pp. 19-20.

139. कुल्लूक on मनु, 5.129; मेधा० (मनु, 5.128) has आपणीयान्यभक्ष्याणि (if it is a quotation); गोविन्दराज (मनु, V.129).

140. अपरार्क (या०, I. 165-167); म० पा०, p. 337.

141. स्मृतिच०, I, p. 221; म० पा०, p. 328 has the second verse.

चतुष्कोणं द्विजाग्र्यस्य त्रिकोणं क्षत्रियस्य तु।
मण्डलाकृति वैश्यस्य शूद्रस्याभ्युक्षणं स्मृतम्।।

142. **शङ्खः** — अशूद्रात्तु धनं भिक्षेत्संर्वं दद्याच्च भिक्षितम्।

143. **शङ्खः** — अनध्यायेष्वधीयानाः शौचाचारविवर्जिताः।
शूद्रान्नरसपुष्टाङ्गाः ब्राह्मणाः पङ्क्तिदूषकाः।।

144. **शङ्खः** — गृहाश्वरथभूम्यर्थे गवार्थे च विशेषतः।
श्रोत्रियेणापि भोक्तव्यं शूद्रान्नं तु यमोब्रवीत्।।

145. **शङ्खलिखितौः** — गा रक्षेत। तास्वपीतासु न पिबेन्न तिष्ठन्तीषूपविशेन्न स्वयमुत्थापयेच्छनैरार्द्रशाखया सपलाशया पृष्ठतो हन्यान्न तीर्थे न विषमे नाल्पोदकेवतारयेद् बालवृद्धरोगार्तश्रान्त उपासीत शक्तितः प्रतिकारं कुर्याद्गवामेष धर्मोन्यथा विप्लवः।

146. **शङ्खः** — तिलमुद्गमाषयवगोधूमादीनां सस्यमुष्टिग्रहणेषु न दोषः पथिकानाम्।

147. **शङ्खः** — उच्छिष्टलेपनं स्पर्शे प्रक्षाल्यान्येन वारिणा।
भोजनान्ते नरः स्नात्वा गायत्रीं त्रिशतं जपेत्।।

148. **शङ्खः** — त्रैवार्षिकाधिकान्नस्तु पिबेत्सोममतन्द्रितः।
इष्टिं वैश्वानरीं कुर्यात्तथैवाल्पधनो द्विजः।।

149. **शङ्खः** — सहस्रं भोजयेत्सोमे ब्राह्मणानां शतं पशौ।
चातुर्मास्येषु सर्वेषु शतं पर्वणि पर्वणि।।

---

142. स्मृतिच०, I, p. 160; compare मनु०, 11.24 and याज्ञ०, I.127.

143. अपरार्क (या०, I. 222-4); स्मृतिच० (III, p. 402). This is शङ्खस्मृति, 13.4.

144. अपरार्क (या०, 1.168).

145. स्मृतिच०, I, p. 170; परा० मा०, I.1, p. 477 reads रोगार्तानां शक्तितः प्रतिकारं कुर्यादन्यथा विप्लवः।

146. स्मृतिच०, I, p. 176.

147. चतुर्विंश०, p. 167.

148. स्मृतिच०, I, p. 159; अपरार्क (या०, I, 125). This is शङ्खस्मृति, 5.15-16; compare, मनु०, 11.39-40.

149. स्मृतिच०, I, p. 159.

150. **शङ्खलिखितौ:** — सुरां पिबन्ति त्रिदशाः सा चापेया द्विजातिभिः।
हरन्ति वित्तं यत्सिद्धा न ह्यसिद्धेन विद्यते।।

151. **शङ्खः** — एषामन्नभोजनेष्वतिकृच्छ्रः।

152. **शङ्खः** — वृथाकृसरसंयावपायसापूपमांसाशनमाहिताग्निः कृत्वा प्राजापत्यं चरेत्। त्रिरात्रमितरेषाम्।

153. **शङ्खलिखितौ** — तिलदधिक्षौद्रलवणलाक्षामद्यमांसकृतान्नस्त्रीपुरुषहस्त्यश्ववृषभगन्धरसकृष्णाजिनसोमोदकात्सद्यः पतति ब्राह्मणः।

154. **शङ्खः** — सर्वासां द्विस्तनीनां क्षीरमभोज्यमजावर्जम्।

155. **शङ्खः** — महिषं गव्यमाज्यं च भक्ष्यं क्षीरेषु निर्दिशेत्।

156. **शङ्खलिखितौ:** — त्रयाणामपि वर्णानां पूर्वरात्रे प्रजागरः।

157. **शङ्खलिखितौ:** — न विशीर्णखट्वायां नान्यवर्णोपवेशितायामनभ्युक्ष्य न भूतयक्षग्रहायतनेषु न श्मशानवृक्षशाखासु न पर्वणि रभसोत्सवे वा।

158. **शङ्खलिखितौ:** — पुत्रानुत्पाद्य संस्कृत्य वेदमध्याप्य वृत्तिं विधाय दारैः संयोज्य गुणवति पुत्रे कुटुम्बमावेश्य कृतप्रस्थानलिङ्गो वृत्तिविशेषाननुक्रामेत्। क्रमशो यायावराणां वृत्तिमुपास्य वनमाश्रयेदुत्तरायणे पूर्वपक्षे।

159. **शङ्खः** — गृहस्थस्तु यदा पश्येद्वलीपलितमात्मनः।

---

150. स्मृतिच०, I, p. 73.

151. अपरार्क (या०, 1. 161-4).

152. विश्व० on या०, I.172.

153. स्मृतिच०, I, p. 180; compare मनु, 10.88-93, याज्ञ०, III.40.

154. चतुर्वर्ग०, Vol. III, Part I, p. 571.

155. स्मृतिच०, III, p. 423; चतुर्वर्ग०, Vol. III, Part 1, p. 57 ascribes to शङ्खलिखित and reads क्षीरं तु निर्दशम्।

156. वीर० (आह्निकप्रकाश, p. 555).

157. वीर० (आह्निकप्रकाश, p. 557).

158. परा० मा०, I.2, p. 140; विश्व० (याज्ञ०, I.127) has only अत ऊर्ध्वं पुत्रानुत्पाद्य and then क्रतु (कृत?) प्रस्थान०. . . नुक्रमः श्रेयान् याया . . . वार्तामुपास्य वनमाश्रयेत्।

159. म० पा०, 364: This is whole of chap. 6 of शङ्खस्मृति.

अपत्यस्यैव चापत्यं तदारण्यं समाश्रयेत्।।
पुत्रे दारान्विनिक्षिप्य तथा वानुगतो वने।
अग्नीनुपाचरेन्नित्यं वन्यमाहारमाहरेत्।।
यदाहारो भवेत्तेन पूजयेत्पितृदेवताम्।।
तेनैव पूजयेद्विद्वानतिथिं समुपागतम्।।
ग्रामादाहृत्य वाश्नीयादष्टौ ग्रासान् समाहितः।
स्वाध्यायं च तथा कुर्याज्जटाश्च विभृयात्तथा।।
तपसा शोषयेन्नित्यं स्वकं चैव कलेवरम्।
आर्द्रवासास्तु हेमन्ते ग्रीष्मे पञ्चतपास्तथा।।
प्रावृष्याकाशशायी च नक्ताशी च सदा वसेत्।
चतुर्थकालिको वा स्यात् षष्ठकालिक एव वा।।
कृच्छ्रैर्वापि नयेत्कालं ब्रह्मचर्यं च पालयेत्।
एवं नीत्वा वने कालं द्विजो ब्रह्माश्रमी भवेत्।। इति।

160. **शङ्खः** — ऊर्ध्वं वार्षिकाभ्यां नैकस्थानवासी।

161. **शङ्खलिखितौः** — वनवासादूर्ध्वे शान्तस्य परिणतवयसः कामतः परिव्रजनमेवाग्निमात्मन्यारोप्य व्यपगतभयलोभमोहक्रोधशोकद्रोहमदमत्सरकलत्रस्योचितवेदनावस्थितमनसः श्रद्धाद्यनियतं भवति तस्मात्तदहरेवोपासीत यदहरेव संन्यसेत् सर्वारम्भपरिग्रहानुत्सृज्य।

162. **शङ्खलिखितौः** — आत्मयाजिनां शरीरस्याद्भिर्मृद्भिश्च ज्ञानेन बुद्धेः तपसा पापानां सन्तानजानां मातृपितृकाणां दोषाणां यमनियममन्त्रव्रतोपवासादिभिः (शुद्धिः)।

163. **शङ्खः** — मलसंयोगजं तज्जं यस्य येनोपहन्यते।
तस्य तच्छोधनं प्रोक्तं सामान्यं द्रव्यशुद्धिकृत्।।

164. **शङ्खः** — उष्णोदकेन कांस्यस्य सीसस्य त्रपुणस्तथा।

---

160. मिता० on याज्ञ०, III.58.

161. चतुर्वर्ग०, Vol. III, Part 2, p. 809; कुल्लूक (on मनु, 6.33) has only the words वन . . . वयसः परिव्राज्यम्.

162. चतुर्वर्ग०, Vol. III, Part 1, p. 792.

163. अपरार्क (या०, 1.183); म० पा०, p. 451 has सामान्यद्रव्य० while अपरार्क reads. मलं संयोग० and शोषणं for शोधनम्.

164. अपरार्क (या०, 1.183); *vide* शङ्खस्मृति, 16.3-4 for the first verse.

क्षारेण शुद्धिं कांसस्य लोहस्य च विनिर्दिशेत्।।
लोहानां दाहनच्छुद्धिर्भस्मना गोमयेन वा।
दहनात्खननाद्वापि शैलानामम्भसापि वा।।
काष्ठानां तक्षणाच्छुद्धिर्मृद्गोमयजलैरपि।।

165. **शङ्खः** — सूतिकोच्छिष्टभाण्डस्य सुरामद्यहतस्य च।
त्रिःसप्तमार्जनाच्छुद्धिर्न तु कांसस्य तापनम्।।

166. **शङ्खलिखितौः** — कर्षणमुपलेपनमद्भिरभ्युक्षणं कालो दाहश्च भूमेः (शुद्धिः)

167. **शङ्खलिखितौः** — चमसानामद्भिर्यज्ञसोमैकशौचमध्वरेषु चमसवद् यतिपात्राणां यतिसमयपात्राणं भस्मोदकेन घर्षयेत्।

168. **शङ्खलिखितौः** — सर्वेषामापो मृदरिष्टकेङ्गुदबिल्वतण्डुलसर्षपकल्कक्षारगोमूत्रगोमयादीनि शौचद्रव्याणि संहतानां प्रोक्षणमित्येके।

169. **शङ्खलिखितौः** — बालस्त्रीपरिगतान्यगारेषु दुष्यन्ति धूमाग्निरजांसि वाय्वीरितानि विप्रुषः छाया मक्षिका इति स्पर्शे मेध्याः।

170. **शङ्खः** — शयनासनयानानां संहतवच्छौचम्।।

171. **शङ्खः** — द्रव्यहस्त उच्छिष्टो निधायाचामेत्।
अद्भिरभ्युक्ष्य द्रव्यं शुध्यति।

172. **शङ्खः** — रागद्रव्याणि प्रोक्षितानि शुचीनि।

173. **शङ्खलिखितौः** — अहतानां प्रोक्षणमिति।

---

165. अपरार्क (या०, 1.183); म० पा०, p. 448.

166. चतुर्वर्ग०, Vol. III, Part I, p. 822.

167. चतुर्वर्ग०, Vol. III, Part I, p. 815.

168. चतुर्वर्ग०, Vol. III, Part 1, p. 817.

169. चतुर्वर्ग०, Vol. III, Part I, p. 839; अपरार्क on याज्ञ० (I.193) has the words धूमाग्नि . . . रितानि शुद्धानि.

170. अपरार्क (या०, I.184); म० पा०, p. 455.

171. विश्व० on याज्ञ०, I. 195; स्मृतिच० (I, p. 103) reads निधायाचम्य अभ्युपेक्ष्य तद्द्रव्यम्; compare गौ०, I, 27, बौ०, I.5.22-24; वसिष्ठ, 3.43 and मनु०, 4.143.

172. मिता० on या०, I.186.

173. म० पा०, च० 455.

174. **शङ्खः** — मृद्भस्मगोमूत्रक्षारोदकैश्चेलानां चेलवद्धान्यानां पक्ष्मचामरचर्म-तृणवालवेत्रवल्कलादीनाम्।

175. **शङ्खः** — चेलानामुत्स्वेदनं प्रक्षालनं तन्मात्रच्छेदो वा।

176. **शङ्खः** — कारुहस्तः शुचिस्तथा कराः। तद्द्रव्याणि प्रोक्षितान्यभ्युक्षितानि शुचीनि। आकरजानामभ्यवहरणीयानां घृतेनाभिघारितानां पुनः पचनम्। एवं स्नेहानां स्नेहवद् रसानां संहतानामद्भिर्द्रव्याणामुत्पवनं शुष्काणामुद्धृतदोषाणां संस्कारः परिप्लावितानां दोषाणां ततस्त्यागः।

177. **शङ्खः** — नारीणां चैव वत्सानां शकुनीनां शुनां मुखम्।
रतौ प्रस्रवणे वृक्षे मृगयायां सदा शुचि।।

178. **शङ्खः** — ब्रह्मक्षत्रविशां चैव संकृत् संमार्जनाच्छुचिः।
चतुर्थेन तु यद्भुक्तं चतुर्भिर्यत्र मार्जनम्।।
अग्नौ प्रक्षिप्य गृह्णीयादद्धस्तौ प्रक्षाल्य यत्नतः।
गोशृङ्गेण तु संसृष्टं तत्पात्रं शुचितामियात्।।

179. **शङ्खः** — तैजसानां कुणपरेतोमूत्रपूरीषोपहतानामावर्तनमुल्लेखनं भस्मनं वा त्रिःसप्तकृत्वः परिमार्जनम्।

180. **शङ्खः** — कृष्णशकुनिमुखावसृष्टं निर्लिखेच्छ्वापदमुखावसृष्टं पात्रं न प्रयुञ्जीतेति।

181. **शङ्खः** — घृतदधिपयस्तक्राणामपवरकभाण्डे स्थितानामदोषः।
आधारदोषे तु नयेत्पात्रात् पात्रान्तरं द्रव्यम्।

---

174. विश्व० on या०, I. 195; अपरार्क on या०, I.187 reads 'चैलानां मृद्भस्म . . . दकैः' and 'पक्षचामर . . . वल्कवेत्रजानां च०'.

175. विश्व० on याज्ञ०, I.182.

176. विश्व० on या०, I.186 has the words कारुहस्त . . . स्नेहवद् द्रवाणाम्; अपरार्क (या०, I.187) reads the first two *sūtra*s as कारु . . . करात्तद्द्रव्याणि प्रोक्षितानि' (omitting the last two words); मिता० has अभ्यवहार्यीणां . . . रसानाम्; चतुर्वर्ग०, Vol. III, Part 1, p. 827 attributes to शङ्खलिखित.

177. अपरार्क (या०, I.187); *vide* शङ्खस्मृति, 16.16.

178. म० पा०, 448; अपरार्क (या० I.183) has first line.

179. विश्व० on या०, I.190; मेधा० (मनु, 5.111) reads कुणपरुधिररेतो०.

180. म० पा०, p. 446.

181. परा० मा०, II, p. 145; अपरार्क (या०, I.190) reads आकरमाण्ड०.

घृतं तु पायसं क्षीरं तथैवेक्षुरसो गुडः।
शूद्रभाण्डस्थितं तक्रं तथा मधु न दुष्यति।।

182. **शङ्खः** — कुसुम्भकुङ्कुमानां च और्णकार्पासयोस्तथा।
प्रोक्षणात् कथिता शुद्धिरित्याह भगवान्यमः।।

183. **शङ्खः** — श्रपणं घृततैलानां प्लावनं गोरसस्य तु।
भाण्डानि प्लावयेदद्भिः शाकमूलफलानि च।।
सिद्धमन्नं तथा सर्पिः क्षीरं च दधि चाम्बु च।
एतेषामवलीढानां तेजसा शुद्धिरिष्यते।।
काकमार्जारनकुलसर्पमूषकपक्षिभिः।
संस्कृतं तु यदा ह्यन्नमवलिह्यते केनचित्।।
सुवर्णवर्णताम्रोल्कैर्गोवाले रजतेन वा।
स्पृष्टमेकतरेणापि भोज्यं घ्रातमजेन वा।।

184. **शङ्खः** — रथ्याकर्दमतोयेन ष्ठीवनाद्येन वा त्वथ।
नाभेरूर्ध्वं नरः स्पृष्टः सद्यः स्नाने शुध्यति।।

185. **शङ्खलिखितौ**: — धर्मेण वित्तमादाय पितृभ्यो दद्यात्।

186. **शङ्खलिखितौ**: — पिता पितामहश्चैव तथैव प्रपितामहः।
भूयस्तत्रैव जायन्ते तदहर्वेदयन्ति च।।
तस्मात्स दिवसः पुण्यः पितृणां प्रीतिवर्धनः।

187. **शङ्खमनुशातातपाः** — कुर्यादहरहः श्राद्धमन्नाद्येनोदकेन वा।
पयोमूलफलैर्वापि पितृभ्यः प्रीतिमावहन्।।

188. **शङ्खः** — पितुः पुत्रेण कर्तव्या पिण्डदानोदकक्रिया।
पुत्राभावे तु पत्नी स्यात्पत्न्यभावे तु सोदरः।।

---

182. परा० मा०, II, p. 185. This is शङ्खस्मृति, 16.11-12.

183. अपरार्क (या०, 1.190).

184. मिता० (या०, III.80) and स्मृतिच० (I, p. 119); अपरार्क (या०, 1.197 and 3.29). This is शङ्खस्मृति, 16.18.

185. चतुर्वर्ग०, Vol. III, Part 1, p. 524.

186. चतुर्वर्ग०, Vol. III, Part 1, p. 325-26.

187. वीर० (आह्निकप्रकाश, p. 432); *vide* शङ्खस्मृति, 12.3, मनु०, III.82.

188. स्मृतिच०, III, p. 335; अपरार्क (या०, I.217-18).

189. **शङ्खः** — भार्यापिण्डं पतिर्दद्यात् भर्त्रे भार्या तथैव च।
श्वश्र्वादेश्च स्नुषा चैव तदभावे तु सोदरः।।

190. **शङ्खः** — अन्वष्टकां तथा मातृश्राद्धं चैव मृताहनि।
एकोद्दिष्टं तथा भुक्त्वा स्त्रीषु नान्यत्पृथग्भवेत्।।
पित्रादित्रयपत्नीषु भोज्या मातृः प्रति द्विजाः।
स्त्रीणामेव तु तद्यस्मान्मातृश्राद्धमिहोच्यते।।

191. **शङ्खः** — भोजयेदथवाप्येकं ब्राह्मणं पङ्क्तिपावनम्।
दैवे कृत्वा तु नैवेद्यं पश्चात्तस्य तु निर्वपेत्।।
म्लेच्छदेशे तथा रात्रौ संध्यायां च विशेषतः।
न श्राद्धमाचरेत्प्राज्ञो म्लेच्छदेशं न च व्रजेत्।।

192. **शङ्खः** — गोगजाश्वादिवृक्षेषु कृत्रिमायां तदा भुवि।
न कुर्याच्छ्राद्धमेतेषु पारक्याशुचिभूमिषु।।

193. **शङ्खः** — प्रौष्ठपद्यामतीतायां मघायुक्तां त्रयोदशीम्।
प्राप्य श्राद्धं न कर्तव्यं मधुना पायसेन च।।
प्रजामिष्टां यशः स्वर्गमारोग्यं च धनं तथा।
नृणां श्राद्धे सदा प्रीताः प्रयच्छन्ति पितामहाः।।

194. **शङ्खः** — वाराणस्यां कुरुक्षेत्रो भृगुतुङ्गे हिमालये।
नर्मदाबाहुदातीरे सर्वमानन्त्यमश्नुते।।
गङ्गाद्वारे प्रयागे वै नैमिषे पुष्करे तथा।
सन्निहत्य गयायां च दत्तमक्षय्यतां व्रजेत्।।

---

189. हारलता, p. 175 reads श्वशुरादेः and तदभावे द्विजोत्तमः; म० पा०, p. 403.

190. अपरार्क (या०, 1.217-8); स्मृतिच० (III, p. 369) reads अन्वष्टक्यां तथा वृद्धौ मातुः श्राद्धमृता०.

191. अपरार्क (या०, 1.226-30); स्मृतिच० (III, p. 405) has the first line; *vide* शङ्खस्मृति, 13.10 for the first and 14.4 for the second.

192. चतुर्विंश०, p. 121; स्मृतिच०, III, p. 385 has the first half and reads गजाश्व-नदीपृष्ठे.

193. स्मृतिच०, III, p. 368; *vide* शङ्खस्मृति, 14.6-7.

194. स्मृतिच०, III, p. 386; परा० मा०, 1.2, p. 304.

195. **शङ्खः** — सकृन्निर्वा विकिरं कुर्यात्।

196. **शङ्खः** — गन्धमाल्यधूपाच्छादनसिद्धोपहारैः पिण्डं निर्वपेत्।

197. **शङ्खः** — उपवीतं कटौ कृत्वा कुर्याद्गात्रानुलेपनम्।
एकवासाश्च योऽश्नीयान्निराशाः पितरो गताः।।
उग्रगन्धीन्यगन्धीनि चैत्यवृक्षोद्भवानि च।
पुष्पाणि वर्जनीयानि रक्तवर्णानि यानि च।
जलोद्भवानि देयानि रक्तान्यपि विशेषतः।
धूपार्थे गुग्गुलुं दद्याद् घृतयुक्तं मधूत्कटम्।।

198. **शङ्खलिखितौः** — जन्मशरीरलक्षणगुणोपेतान् ब्राह्मणानुपनिमन्त्रयेत् श्वोद्य वा श्राद्धमाचरिष्य इति।

199. **शङ्खलिखितौः** — अथ पाङ्क्तेया वेदवेदाङ्गवित्पञ्चाग्निरनूचानः सांख्ययोगोपनिषद्धर्मशास्त्रविच्छ्रोत्रियस्त्रिणाचिकेतस्त्रिमधुस्त्रिसुपर्णी ज्येष्ठसामगः।
सांख्ययोगोपनिषद्धधर्मशास्त्राध्यायी वेदपरः सदाग्निको मातृपितृशुश्रूषुर्धर्मशास्त्ररतिः।

200. **शङ्खः** — षडङ्गवित् त्रिसौपर्णो बह्वृचो ज्येष्ठसामगः।
त्रिणाचिकेताः पञ्चाग्निर्ब्राह्मणाः पङ्क्तिपावनाः।।
ब्रह्मदेयानुसंतानो ब्रह्मदेयाप्रदायकः।
ब्रह्मदेयापतिर्यश्च ब्राह्मणाः पङ्क्तिपावनाः।
यजुषां पारगो यश्च साम्नां यश्चातिपारगः।
अथर्वशिरसोऽध्येता ब्राह्मणाः पङ्क्तिपावनाः।।
नित्यं योगपरो विद्वान् समलोष्टाश्मकाञ्चनः।
ध्यानशीलो यतिर्विद्वान् ब्राह्मणाः पङ्क्तिपावनाः।।

---

195. मेधा० (मनु०, 3.244).

196. मेधा० (मनु०, 3.216).

197. अपरार्क (या०, 1.234); स्मृतिच० (III, p. 434 and 454) has all the lines; *vide* शङ्खस्मृति, 13.14-15, 17 for the verses उग्रगन्धी० etc.

198. चतुर्वर्ग०, Vol. III, Part 1, p. 1132.

199. चतुर्वर्ग०, Vol. III, Part 1, p. 391.

200. चतुर्वर्ग०, Vol. III, Part 1, p. 399; परा० मा०, I.2, p. 342; *vide* शङ्खस्मृति, 13.5-8 with slight variations.

201. **शङ्खलिखितौ:** — अनृक् तस्करो राजभृत्यो वृक्षारोपकवृत्तिर्गरदोग्निदः श्वागणिकः शूद्रोपाध्यायो बन्दी घाण्टिको देवलः पुरोहितो नक्षत्रादेशवृत्तिर्ब्रह्मपुरुषो मद्यपो ब्रह्मविक्रयी कितवः कूटकारको मानुषपशुविक्रयिणश्चेत्यपाङ्क्तेयाः।

202. **शङ्खलिखितौ:** — न वै दुष्टान् भोजयेत्। दुश्चर्मकुनखिकुष्ठिश्चित्रिश्यावदन्ता ये चान्ये हीनातिरिक्ताङ्गास्तानपि वर्जयेत्।

203. **शङ्खलिखितौ:** — प्रयतोपराह्णे शुचिः शुक्लवासा दर्भेषु तिष्ठन् स्वागतमिति ब्रूयात्।

204. **शङ्खलिखितौ:** — पाद्यार्घ्याचमनीयोदकानि दत्त्वा ब्राह्मणानुपसंगृह्योपवेशयेदासनमन्वालभ्य।

205. **शङ्खलिखितौ:** — देवादिश्राद्धमात्मानं च रक्षन्ति पितॄणामग्रे नियुक्ताः पूर्वमुपवेशिताः।

206. **शङ्खलिखितौ:** — ब्राह्मणाननुज्ञाप्य पितॄनावाहयिष्यामीत्युशन्तस्त्वेति आवाह्य।

207. **शङ्खः** — अजस्य दक्षिणे कर्णे पाणौ विप्रस्य दक्षिणे।
अप्सु चैव कुशस्तम्बे अग्निं कात्यायनोब्रवीत्।।
रजते च सुवर्णे च नित्यं वसति पावकः।

208. **शङ्खः** — यद्येकजाता बहवः पृथक्क्षेत्राः पृथग्जनाः।
एकपिण्डाः पृथक् शौचाः पिण्डस्त्वावर्तते त्रिषु।।

---

201. चतुर्वर्ग०, Vol. III, Part 1, p. 492.

202. चतुर्वर्ग०, Vol. III, Part 1, p. 468.

203. चतुर्वर्ग०, Vol. III, Part 1, p. 1181.

204. चतुर्वर्ग०, Vol. III, Part 1, p. 1177.

205. चतुर्वर्ग०, Vol. III, Part 1, p. 1196.

206. चतुर्वर्ग०, Vol. III, Part 1, p. 1259.

207. अपरार्क; चतुर्वर्ग०, Vol. III, Part 1, p. 1344; the first and third lines are लिखितस्मृति, 31 (Ānandāśrama collection).

208. विश्व० and मिता० on या०, 1.53; मेधा० on मनु०, 5.60; म० पा०, p. 140 reads पृथग्गोत्राः.

209. **शङ्खः** — उदक्प्लवमुदीचां तद्दक्षिणां दक्षिणाप्लवम्।
उत्तरे कृतसंयुक्तान्पूर्वाग्रान्विन्यसेत्कुशान्।।

210. **शङ्खः** — इष्टिश्राद्धे क्रतुदक्षौ संकीर्त्यौ वैश्वदेविके।
नान्दीमुखे सत्यवसू काम्ये तु धुरिलोचनौ।।
पुरूरवार्द्रवौ चैव पार्वणे समुदाहृतौ।
नैमित्तिके कालकामावेवं सर्वत्र कीर्तयेत्।।

211. **शङ्खः** — नाम चैव तथोत्पत्तिर्न विज्ञेया द्विजातयः।
श्लोकमेते पठेयुस्ते ब्राह्मणानां समीपगाः।
आगच्छन्तु महाभाग विश्वेदेवा महाबलाः।
ये अत्र विहिताः श्राद्धे सावधाना भवन्तु ते।।

212. **शङ्खलिखितौः** — अपसव्यं वासोयज्ञोपवीते कृत्वा तिलैरवकीर्य सर्वसुरभितिलोन्मिश्रपात्रेषूदकं कृत्वा शं नो देवीरिति।

213. **शङ्खः** — त्रीण्येव पात्राणि सतिलकुशगन्धोदकानि।

214. **शङ्खलिखितौः** — पवित्रान्तर्हितेषु ब्राह्मणहस्तेषूदकं निनयेत्।

215. **शङ्खलिखितौः** — गन्धमाल्यधूपैरलंकृत्य ब्राह्मणान् सघृतमन्नमनुज्ञाप्य दर्भैर्दक्षिणाग्रैरग्निं परिस्तीर्य जुहुयात्। अग्नये कव्यवाहनाय स्वाहा सोमाय पितृमते स्वाहा।

216. **शङ्खलिखितौः** — अङ्गुष्ठमुपयम्येदं विष्णुरिति जानू निषद्य भूमौ पितॄन्ध्यायन्मनसा।

217. **शङ्खलिखितौः** — गायत्रीमनुश्राव्य तृप्ताञ्ज्ञात्वा स्वादितमिति पृष्ट्वाशेषमन्न-

---

209. म० पा०, p. 268.

210. चतुर्विंश०, p. 149; परा० मा०, I.2, p. 403.

211. स्मृतिच०, III, p. 444.

212. चतुर्वर्ग०, Vol. III, Part 1, p. 1278.

213. चतुर्वर्ग०, Vol. III, Part 1, p. 1281.

214. चतुर्वर्ग०, Vol. III, Part 1, p. 1290.

215. चतुर्वर्ग०, Vol. III, Part 1, p. 1310 and pp. 1353-54; म० पा०, 589.

216. चतुर्वर्ग०, Vol. III, Part 1, p. 1378.

217. चतुर्वर्ग०, Vol. III, Part 1, p. 1392 and p. 1406.

मनुज्ञाप्य प्रकृतान्नविकिरं कुर्यात् ।स्वधां वाचयित्वा विष्टरांस्त्रीन्निदध्यात् त्रीण्येवोदपात्राणि सतिलानि सपवित्राणि मृण्मयाश्ममयौदुम्बराणि वा धूपगन्धमाल्यादर्शप्रदीपाञ्जनादीनि चोपहरेत्सर्वान्नप्रकारमादाय पिण्डा-न्निदध्यात् ।

218. **शङ्खः** – दर्भैर्दक्षिणाग्रैरग्निं परिस्तीर्य जुहुयात् । जानू निषद्य भूमौ पितॄन् ध्यायन् मनसा ततस्तिलैर्मांसैः शाकैर्यूषैः कृसरपायसापूपैर्लाजैर्मधुना घृतेन दध्ना पयसा च प्रभूतमिष्टतोऽन्नं दद्यादनसूयुः । ब्राह्मणाश्वाश्नन्तो न गुणदोषानभिदध्युर्नान्योन्यं संस्पृशेयुर्नान्योन्यं प्रशंसेयुः। अन्नपानं प्रभूतमिति न ब्रूयुः । न विकृतं ब्रूयुः अन्यत्र हस्तसंज्ञानात् । यावत्सोष्मान्नं तावदश्नन्ति पितरः अन्यत्र मूलफलपानेभ्यः । पवित्रपाणिर्दर्भेष्वासीनो मधुवातीयं जपेत् । पवित्रं धर्मशास्त्रम् ।

219. **शङ्खः** – उष्णमन्नं द्विजातिभ्यः श्रद्धया विनिवेदयेत् ।
अन्यत्र फलपुष्पेभ्यः पानकेभ्यश्च पण्डितः ।।

220. **शङ्खः** – आम्रान्पालेवतानिक्षून् मृद्वीकां च व्यदाडिमम् ।
विदार्याश्च भचुण्डांश्च श्राद्धकालेपि दापयेत् ।।
द्राक्षां मधुयुतां दद्यात्सक्तून शर्करया सह ।
दद्याच्छ्राद्धे प्रयत्नेन शृङ्गाकटकशेरुकान् ।।

221. **शङ्खः** – लाजान्मधुयुतान्दद्यात्सक्तूञ्शर्करया सह ।
दद्याच्छ्राद्धे प्रयत्नेन शृङ्गाटकगवेधुकम् ।।

222 **शङ्खलिखितौः** – माहिषं चाजमौरभ्रं मार्ग रौरवमेव च ।
भक्ष्यमांसं समुद्दिष्टं यत्र वै पार्षतं स्मृतम् ।।
वराहाश्च तथा भक्ष्या महारण्यनिवासिनः ।

---

218. विश्व० on या०, I. 236; चतुर्वर्ग०, Vol. III, Part 1, p. 605 has the words ततस्तिलै . . . न्नं दद्यात् with slight variations.

219. अपरार्क (या०, 1.237); कुल्लूक (on मनु, 3.236) reads फलमूलेभ्यः; *see* शङ्खस्मृति, 13.12 for first half.

220. परा० मा०, I.2, p. 370; *vide* शङ्ख, 13.21-22.

221. अपरार्क (या०, I.257-58).

222. स्मृतिच०, III, p. 429; चतुर्वर्ग०, Vol. III, Part 1, p. 579.

223. **शङ्खः** — तित्तिरं च मयूरं च लावकं च कपिञ्जलम्।
वार्ध्रीणसं वर्तकं च भक्ष्यानाह यमः सदा।।

224. **शङ्खः** — राजीवाः सिंहतुण्डाश्च सशल्काश्च तथैव च।
पाठीनरौहितौ चापि भक्ष्या मत्स्येषु कीर्तिताः।।

225. **शङ्खः** — अग्नौकरणशेषेण यदन्नमभिधारयेत्।
तस्मिंस्तु प्राशिते दद्याद्यदन्यत्प्रकृतं भवेत्।।

226. **शङ्खः** — श्राद्धपङ्क्तौ तु भुञ्जानो ब्राह्मणो ब्राह्मणं स्पृशेत्।
तदन्नमत्यजन्भुक्त्वा गायत्र्यष्टशतं जपेत्।
हुङ्कारेणापि यो ब्रूयाद्धस्ताद्वापि गुणान्वदेत्।
भूतलाच्चोद्धरेत्पात्रं मुञ्चेद्धस्तेन वापि तत्।।
प्रौढपादो बहिःकक्षो बहिर्जानुकारोथ वा।
अङ्गुष्ठेन विनाश्नाति मुखशब्देन वा पुनः।।
पीतावशिष्टं तोयादि पुनरुद्धृत्य वा पिबेत्।
खादितार्धे पुनः खादेन्मोदकानि फलानि वा।।
मुखेन वा धमेदन्नं निष्ठीवेद्भाजनेपि वा।
इत्थमश्नन् द्विजः श्राद्धं हत्वा गच्छत्यधोगतिम्।।

227. **शङ्खः** — श्राद्धे नियुक्तान्भुञ्जानान्न पृच्छेल्लवणादिषु।
उच्छिष्टाः पितरो यान्ति पृच्छतो नात्र संशयः।।
बाहुः पतति दातुर्वै जिह्वा भोक्तुस्तु भिद्यते।

228. **शङ्खलिखितौः** — तत्रापेयान्यभक्ष्याणि वर्जयेदमेध्यपतितचण्डालपुक्कसरज-
स्वलाकुणपकुष्ठिसंस्पृष्टानि।

229. **शङ्खः** — भीतावगीतरुदिताक्रन्दितावघुष्टक्षुधितपरिभुक्तविस्मितोन्मत्ता-
वधूतराजपुरोहितान्नानि वर्जयेत्। न पापीयसोन्नमश्नीयान्न द्विःपक्वं न

---

223. स्मृतिच०, III, p. 428; चतुर्वर्ग०, Vol. III, Part 1, p. 577.

224. कुल्लूक on मनु, 5.16; *vide* शङ्खस्मृति, 17.25.

225. अपरार्क (या०, I.239-40).

226. स्मृतिच०, III, p. 448; परा० मा०, I.2, p. 425.

227. स्मृतिच०, III, p. 469; परा० मा०, I.2, p. 425.

228. चतुर्वर्ग०, vol. III, part 1, p. 614.

229. मिता० on याज्ञ०, I.165 and I.167; स्मृतिच०, III. p. 419 for न पर्युषित

शुक्तं न पर्युषितमन्यत्र रागखाण्डवचुक्रदधिगुडगोधूमयवपिष्टविकारेभ्यः।
अमेध्यपतितचाण्डालपुल्कसरजस्वलाकुनखिकुष्ठिसंस्पृष्टान्नं वर्जयेत्।

230. **शङ्खलिखितौः** — विद्विषाणस्य नाश्नीयाद् ब्रह्मविद्यापकारिणः।
श्राद्धसूतगणान्नानि परिभूतानि यानि च।।

231. **शङ्खः** — दधि वर्ज्यं न शुक्तेषु यच्चान्यद्दधिसंभवम्।
सपक्षं भक्ष्यं स्यात् सर्पिर्युक्तमिति स्थितम्।।

232. **शङ्खः** — कृष्णजाजीनिभं चैव शीतपाकी तथैच च।
वर्जयेल्लवणं सर्वं तथा जम्बूफलानि च।।
अवर्जिता च रुदितं तथा श्राद्धेषु वर्जयेत्।

233. **शङ्खः** — नाद्याच्छ्राद्धनिषिद्धं तु भक्ष्यभोज्यादिकं द्विजः।

234. **शङ्खलिखितौः** — आपो रूपरसगन्धवत्यः परिशुद्धा जीवचर्मकरण्डैरन-
भ्युद्गताः। भूमिगता मेध्या यत्र गौर्वितृषा भवेत्।

235. **शङ्खः** — उमासूत्रं (ऊर्णा?) तु दातव्यं कार्पासमथवा नवम्।
दशां विवर्जयेत्प्राज्ञो यद्यप्यहतवस्त्रजाम्।।

236. **शङ्खः** — आद्यं श्राद्धमशुद्धोपि कुर्यादिकादशेऽहनि।
कर्तुस्तात्कालिकी शुद्धिरशुद्धः पुनरेव सः।।

विकारेभ्यः; वीर० (आह्निकप्रकाश, p. 504) has the first *sūtra* with slight variations and (p. 520) reads last as तत्रापेयान्यभक्ष्यणि च वर्जयेदमेध्यपतित० . . . स्पृष्टानि and (p. 521) reads the second as नापणीयमन्नमश्नीयात् न द्विः पक्वं etc. वीर० ascribes all three to शङ्खलिखित; चतुर्वर्ग० (Vol. III, Part 1, p. 614 and p. 779) ascribes the *sūtra* नापणीयमन्नमश्नीयात् . . . विकारेभ्यः and मीतावगीत वर्जयेत् to शङ्खलिखित.

230. चतुर्वर्ग०, Vol. III, Part 1, p. 779.

231. स्मृतिच०, III, p. 419.

232. स्मृतिच०, III, p. 415; परा० मा०, I.2, p. 377 reads कृष्णाजाजीं त्रिडं चैत्र and अवक्षुवाकरुदिनम्.

233. स्मृतिच०, III, p. 418.

234. चतुर्वर्ग०, Vol. III, Part 1, p. 619.

235. स्मृतिच०, III, p. 476; म० पा०, p. 602, शङ्खस्मृति, 13.15-16.

236. मिता० (या०, I.256); अपरार्क; म० पा०, p. 613.

237. **शङ्खः** — सद्यः शौचेपि दातव्यः प्रेतस्यैकादशेहनि।
स एव दिवसस्तस्य श्राद्धशय्यासनादिषु।।

238. **शङ्खः** — मातुः सपिण्डीकरणं कथं कार्यं भवेत्सुतैः।
पितामह्यादिभिः सार्धं सपिण्डीकरणं स्मृतम्।।

239. **शङ्खः** — अमावस्या क्षयो यस्य प्रेतपक्षेथवा यदि।
सपिण्डीकरणादूर्ध्वं तस्योक्तः पार्वणो विधिः।।

240. **शङ्खः** — अमायां तु क्षयो यस्य प्रेतपक्षेथवा पुनः।
पार्वणं तस्य कर्तव्यं नैकोद्दिष्टं कदाचन।।

241. **शङ्खलिखितौः** — पत्नी वा मध्यमं पिण्डं आग्रियादार्तवस्नातेत्युच्यते।

242. **शङ्खः** — घृतेन दीपो दातव्यस्तिलतैलेन वा पुनः।
वसामेदोद्भवं दीप प्रयत्नेन विवर्जयेत्।।

243. **शङ्खलिखितौः** — न गृध्नुपरिवारः स्यात्कामं गृध्नो राजा प्रेयान्न हंसपरिवारो न हंसो गृध्नुपरिवारः। परिवाराद्धि दोषाः प्रादुर्भवन्ति। तेलं विनाशाय। तस्मात्पूर्वमेव तत्परिवारं लिखेत् श्रुतशीलान्वयोपपन्नम्।।

244. **शङ्खलिखितौः** — राजा दीर्घदर्शी महोत्साहः शक्तिमाननसूयुर्भक्तबलस्त्यागी शरण्यः सर्वभूतानां संविभक्तः सत्यवागमत्सरी गम्भीरोमर्षणो बुधस्तेजस्वी प्रतिविधानकुशलोदीर्घसूत्रो दक्षः क्षमावान् लक्ष्यज्ञो देशकालद्रव्यप्रयोगसंग्रहनिमित्तज्ञानकुशलो गूढमन्त्रप्रचारसंवृतरन्ध्रः पररन्ध्रज्ञो दृढप्रहारी लघुहस्तो जितस्थानासनहिमातपो जितकामरागद्वेषलोभमत्सरः प्रजाभिरामो दीनानुग्रहकर्ता ब्राह्मणेष्वन्नप्रदाता श्रीयशोर्थी।

---

237. म० पा०, 623; चतुर्विंश०, p. 176.

239. अपरार्क (या०, 1.225).

240. परा० मा०, I.2, p. 416.

241. स्मृतिच०, III. p. 486; compare मनु०, 3.262, मत्स्यपुराण, 16.53-54.

242. मिता० on या०, I.231; स्मृतिच० (III, p. 435) reads दातव्यस्त्ववाप्यौषधी. रसैः; *vide* शङ्खस्मृति, 13-16 for first line.

243. वीर० (राजनीतिप्रकाश, p. 185); विश्व० on या०, I.305 has the words न हंसो गृध्रपरिवारः कामं तु गृध्रो हंसपरिवारः स्यात् (from शङ्ख).

244. वीर० (राजनीतिप्रकाश, p. 116).

245. **शङ्खलिखितौ:** — राजा स्वाधीनवृत्तिरात्मप्रत्ययकोशः स्वयं कृत्यानुदर्शी विप्रस्वनिवृत्तधिवरं भद्राणि पश्यति।

246. **शङ्खलिखितौ:** — स्वपक्षे परपक्षे च स्थानवृद्धिक्षयाश्रयः।
स्थानादीनां विभागश्च काले द्रव्यार्थसंग्रहः।।

247. **शङ्खलिखितौ:** — दद्याद्दानमर्चयित्वा ब्राह्मणाय। निमित्तपूर्वं शेषेभ्यः। कृपणातुरानाथव्यङ्गविधवाबालवृद्धानौषधावसथाशनाच्छादनैर्बिभृयात्।

248. **शङ्खलिखितौ:** — राजन्यवैश्यावप्यजीवन्तौ राजानमुपतिष्ठेयाताम्। तावुभौ शक्तितः संविभक्तावुपकुर्याताम्। स्वस्वधर्मानुष्ठानेन शिल्पिनः कारवश्च शूद्राः।

249. **शङ्खलिखितौ:** — राज्ञः शङ्खपटहतूर्येण प्रस्वापोत्थानम्।

250. **शङ्खलिखितौ:** — राज्ञः प्रत्यहं घृतान्वीक्षणं मङ्गलदर्शनं कपिलाप्रदानं स्वलंकृतस्य संभाषणं वैद्यदर्शनम्।

251. **शङ्खलिखितौ:** — सर्वेषां राजकुलरक्षणं कोशपरिपालनं गोब्राह्मणपरित्राणं सांपरायिकं क्रियासाधारणत्वादनुजीविनां विशेषेण चारप्रतिचारौ मन्त्रप्रणिधयश्च सर्पाः तत्प्रयोजनत्वात्प्रत्यक्षा वृत्तिस्तस्य राज्ञो भवेत्। एकान्ततो हि दोषाः। तस्माद् भृत्यपक्षाः क्रोधलोभमानभयदोषोपहताः संलपिता विमानिताभ्याख्याता दानमानस्थानव्यपरोपिता हृतसर्वस्वाः स्वदोषोपहतादयः सततं प्रत्यवेक्षितव्याः। धर्मार्थविषयेष्वेतेषां यतेत। स्वविषयाश्रावः परविषयभेदः सामादिभिरुपायैर्मन्त्रज्ञेषु मन्त्रकर्म दण्डकर्म कर्मकरेषु वीरा महत्स्वात्मनि च धर्मनित्याः संग्रहेष्वलुब्धाः प्रत्यन्तेषु मौलाः शुचयोर्थकृत्येषु अन्येषु यथानुरूपं नियोज्याः।

---

245. वीर० (राजनीतिप्रकाश, p. 134).
246. वीर० (राजनीतिप्रकाश, p. 135).
247. वीर० (राजनीतिप्रकाश, p. 138).
248. वीर० (राजनीतिप्रकाश, p. 141).
249. वीर० (राजनीतिप्रकाश, p. 154).
250. वीर० (राजनीतिप्रकाश, p. 158).
251. वीर० (राजनीतिप्रकाश, p. 186).

252. **शङ्खलिखितौ**: — वाहनयोधानां सततमन्वीक्षणं, प्रतिमासं द्वैसौवर्णिकीवृत्तिः षाण्मास्यं स्मरणं चातुर्मास्यं वा, स्वर्यातेषु दानमनुक्रोशो विदितेष्वनुप्रदानम्, कुलचारित्रशीलविद्यालक्षणगुणाधिकेषु संमानं प्रयुञ्जीत।

253. **शङ्खलिखितौ**: — राजक्रतुरेवाश्वमेधस्तं नासार्वभौमः प्रतिपादयितुमर्हति। अश्वमेधेन यक्ष्य इति परविषयमभियायाद्देशकालशक्तिसंपन्नः प्रभूतयवसेन्धनोदकाविच्छिन्नसांपरायिकः पथि संविहितसर्वोपकरणो दुर्गासारामात्यदेशदण्डाकन्दाद्यगुणविधिज्ञः पर्षदं प्रति नववान् विदितमध्वानं हितमनुकामेत्। यथा भूमिभागस्तथा विनियोगः श्रेयान्। पानभोजनोपनिवेशस्थानशङ्काप्रतिविधानकुशलो भूपतिरवहितः शत्रुणा सह युध्येत्।

254. **शङ्खः** — न पानीयं पिबन्तं न भुञ्जानं नोपानहौ मुञ्चन्तं नावर्माणं सवर्मा न स्त्रियं न करेणुं न वाजिनं न सारथिं न दूतं न ब्राह्मणं न राजानमराजा हन्यात्।

255. **शङ्खलिखितौ**: — न वैष्टिकं जाङ्गिकं क्षेत्रद्रव्यापहरणं पुष्पमूलप्रचयनं स्वयमर्जितप्रवेशनं निष्क्रमणप्रवेशनेष्वनिवेदनं स्कन्धब्राह्मेषु शुल्को गणसमयश्रेणीपूगचरणव्यवहारनिष्ठा स्वामिनः परिज्ञातारोऽन्यत्र राजाभिद्रोहात्। नगरनिवासिनां विप्रेतराणामपि परिग्रहा अनपराधाः।

256. **शङ्खः** — धर्मस्थानं प्राच्यां दिशि तच्चाग्न्युदकैः समवेतं स्यात्।

257. **शङ्खः** — पैत्रं विनाप्यागमेन पूर्वपुरुषाभ्यां भुक्तं लभेत्।

258. **शङ्खलिखितौ**: — अदण्ड्यौ मातापितरौ स्नातक पुरोहितौ परिव्राजकवानप्रस्थौ जन्मकर्मश्रुतशीलशौचाचारवन्तश्च एते हि धर्मप्रतिकरा राज्ञः स्त्रीबालवृद्धास्तपस्विनस्तेभ्यः क्रोधं नियच्छेत्।

---

252. वीर० (राजनीतिप्रकाश, p. 252).

253. वीर० (राजनीतिप्रकाश, p. 402).

254. मिता० on या०, I.326.

255. वि० र०, 662.

256. स्मृतिच०, II, p. 19.

257. स्मृतिच०, II, p. 73.

258. स्मृतिच० (II, p. 126) and परा० मा०, III.1, p. 206 have the words आदण्ड्यौ . . . चारवन्तश्च; वि० र०, 628.

259. **शङ्खः** — त्रयाणां वर्णानां धनापहारवधबन्धनक्रिया विवासनाङ्ककरणं ब्राह्मणस्य।

260. **शङ्खलिखितौ**: — येन येनाङ्गेनापराधं कुर्यात्तत्तदस्य च्छेत्तव्यमन्यत्र ब्राह्मणात्।

261. **शङ्खलिखितौ**: — सर्वत्र त्रयाणां वर्णानां धनहारकारावधबन्धाः क्रियासु चोपरोधः। महत्स्वपि पातकेषु विवासोङ्ककरणं ब्राह्मणस्य। प्रायश्चित्तानि वा शोधनम्। अपीड्यो हि ब्राह्मणः।

262. **शङ्खलिखितौ**: — शिल्पिनः कारवः शूद्रास्तेषां व्यभिचारेष्वपि शिल्पोपकरणानि रक्षेत। तुलामानप्रतिमानसमुत्थानि वणिक्पथानां, क्षेत्रबीजभक्तगोशकटकर्षणद्रव्याणि कर्षकाणां, वाद्यभाण्डालङ्कारवासांसि रङ्गोपजीविनाम्, गृहशयनालङ्कारवासांसि वेश्यानां, शस्त्राणि चायुधोपजीविनां सर्वेषां कारणद्रव्याणि नाहार्याणि, राज्ञाधर्मिकेण हि पुरुषाः पापबहुलाश्वाविधेयाश्च भवन्ति तेभ्यः पापांशभाग्राजा, तस्मान्नाधनान्नानुपकरणान् कुर्यात्तन्मूला हि वृत्तिर्भवति। वृत्तिमूलो हि निवासः। तैर्निवसद्भिः स्फीतं राष्ट्रमित्युच्यते।

263. **शङ्खलिखितौ**: — चतुर्विंशतिरेकनवतिः प्रथमसाहसः द्विशतं पञ्चशतं चैव मध्यमसाहसः षट्शतं सहस्रं चोत्तमः। यथासारापकारम्।

264. **शङ्खः** — असाक्षिप्रणिहिते दिव्यम्। अथवा मित्रैः सज्जनैरात्मानं ना शोधयेदेव। स चेद्दण्ड्योऽर्थिनां चार्थं दापयेत्।

265. **शङ्खः** — दिव्यं नाम तुलारोहणं विषाशनमप्सुप्रवेशो लोहधारणमिष्टापूर्तप्रदानमन्यांश्च शपथान्कारयेत्।

---

259. मिता० on या०, II.81; स्मृतिच०, II, p. 124 (त्रयाणामपि and वधक्रियाविवासनाङ्ककरणे); compare गौ०, 12.44.

260. व्य० म०

261. वि० र०, 634; परा० मा०, III.1, p. 208 reads त्रयाणामपि वर्णानामपहारवधबन्धक्रिया विवासनं धिक्करणं; compare बौ० ध० सू०, I.10.17-18 अवध्यो वै ब्राह्मणः सर्वापराधेषु। ब्रह्महत्या...स्तप्तेनायसा ललाटेङ्कयित्वा विषयान्निर्धनम्। and कौटिल्य 'सर्वापराधेष्वपीडनीयो ब्राह्मणः' (IV. 9.83).

262. वि० र०, 696.

263. वि० र०, 664.

264. अपरार्क (या० 2.269).

265. अपरार्क (या०, 2.95); परा० मा० reads तुलाधारणं and अग्निप्रवेशः.

266. **शङ्खलिखितौ:** — अथ सप्ताश्वत्थपर्णान्तरितं षोडशपलमग्निवर्णं लोहपिण्डमञ्जलिनादाय सप्तमर्यादां गच्छेत्।

267. **शङ्खलिखितौ:** — सदसच्च त्वमेव वरुण उभयोः प्रतिष्ठितः त्वयि सत्यं त्विदं देव वरुण त्वमेव तद् ब्रूहि वरेण्य तदादिशस्त्वा।

268. **शङ्खलिखितौ:** — स यद्येकपुत्रः स्याद् द्वौ भागावात्मनः कुर्याद् द्विपदचतुष्पदेषु रूपमधिकम्। वृषभो ज्येष्ठाय गृहं यवीयसे अन्यत्र पितुरवस्थानात्।

269. **शङ्खः** — द्वौ भागौ पितुः द्वावेवौरसस्य त्रयः क्षेत्रजपुत्रिकापुत्रयोः एकैकमितरेषाम्।

270. **शङ्खलिखितौ:** — पितर्यशक्ते कुटुम्बव्यवहारान् ज्येष्ठः प्रतिकुर्यादन्यतरो वा कार्यज्ञस्तदनुमतो न त्वकामे पितरि रिक्थविभागो वृद्धे विपरीतचेतसि दीर्घरोगिणि वा ज्येष्ठ एव पितृवदर्थान्पालयेदितरेषाम्। रिक्थमूलं हि कुटुम्बमस्वतन्त्राः पितृमन्तो मातर्यप्येवमवस्थितायाम्।

271. **शङ्खलिखितौ:** — अत ऊर्ध्वं रिक्थभागो न जीवति पितरि पुत्रा रिक्थं विभजेरन् यद्यपि स्यात्पश्चादधिगतं तैरनर्हा एव पुत्राः। अर्थधर्मयोरस्वातन्त्र्यात्।

---

266. स्मृतिच०, II, p. 112; व्य० म०; वीर०.

267. वीर०, p. 270 (वरुणाभिमन्त्रणमन्त्र in जलदिव्य).

268. वि० र०, pp. 465-66 and also 475; अपरार्क (या०, II, 114) has the words यद्येकपुत्रः ... कुर्यात् and attributes them to शङ्खः; दायभाग (p. 81) explains एकस्य पुत्रः एकपुत्रः औरसः; स्मृतिच०, II, p. 261.

269. विश्वरूप on याज्ञ०, II.136 (पिण्डदोंशहरः etc.).

270. वि० र०, p. 460; दायतत्त्व, p. 31; म० पा०, p. 647 reads from अकामे up to रोगिणि च (omitting) दीर्घ; the दायभाग omits कुटुम्ब before व्यवहारान् and reads अनन्तरो for अन्यतरो; स्मृतिच०, II, p. 258 refers पितर्यशक्ते . . . अनुमतेन to शङ्खलिखित and the words न त्वकामे रोगिणि च to शङ्ख, rads अमन्तरो . . . दनुमतेन; वि० र० reads कुटुम्बस्य व्यवहारं and अनुमतेन; अपरार्क has अकामे . . . रोगिणि वा and ascribes it to शङ्ख; compare कौटिल्य, III.5.60 अनीश्वराः पितृमन्तः स्थितपितृमातृका पुत्राः.

271. वि० र०, 456; स्मृतिच० (II, p. 254) has the passage from न जीवति and attributes the passage to शङ्ख; so does परा० मा०, III.2, p. 479.

272. **शङ्खलिखितौ:** — कामं वसेयुरेकतः संहता वृद्धिमाचक्षीरन्।

273. **शङ्खः** — पूर्वनष्टां च यो भूमिमेकश्चेदुद्धरेच्छ्रमात्।
यथाभागं भजन्त्यन्ये दत्त्वांशं तु तुरीयकम्।।

274. **शङ्खलिखितौ:** — जीवति वा पितरि रिक्थभागोऽनुमतः प्रकाशं वा मिथो वा धर्मतः।

275. **शङ्खलिखितौ:** — अन्यवर्णस्त्रीषु जातानां दायादर्धार्धहानिर्वर्णक्रमेण।

276. **शङ्खलिखितौ:** — विभज्यमाने दायेभ्यः स्वकन्यालंकारं वैवाहिकं स्त्रीधनं च कन्या लभते।

277. **शङ्खलिखितौ:** — न शूद्रापुत्रोर्थभागी यदेवास्य पिता दद्यात्स एवास्य भागः। तस्य गोमिथुनं चापरं दद्यात्कृष्णायसं कृष्णधान्यं तिलवर्जम्।

278. **शङ्खलिखितौ:** — न वास्तुविभागो नोदकपात्रालङ्कारोपयुक्तस्त्रीवाससाम् अपां प्रचाररथ्यानां विभागश्चेति प्रजापतिः।

279. **शङ्खः** — भ्रातॄणामप्रजाः प्रेयात्कश्चिच्चेत्प्रव्रजेत वा।
विभजेरन्धनं तस्य शेषास्तु स्त्रीधनं विना।।

---

272. वि० र०, 458.

273. दायतत्त्व, p. 29 says 'एतद्वचनं स्मृतिमहार्णवकामधेनुपारिजातप्रभृतिष्वलिखिनादयुक्तमेवेति रत्नाकरः। तन्न दायभागमिताक्षराप्रभृतिधृतत्वात्।'; म० पा०, p. 684 reads तु for च, लभन्ते for भजन्ति; दायभाग, p. 202. तु यो for च यो, एक एवोद्धरेत्, दत्वा भागं तुरीयकरम्; मिता० on याज्ञ०, II.119 reads पूर्वे नष्टां तु, क्रमात् for श्रमात्, लभन्ते for भजन्ति.

274. स्मृतिच० (II, p. 260) reads रिक्थविभागः, वि० र०, 463.

275. वि० र०, 531.

276. स्मृतिच० (II, p. 269) reads दायाद्ये कन्यालं०; वि० र०, 495; परा० मा०, III.2, p. 511 reads दाये कन्यालङ्कारमेव हि वैवाहिकं च लभते; compare बौ०, II.2.44.

277. वि० र०, p. 536; मेधा० (मनु०, 9.155) reads only न... स एव तस्य भागे गोमिथुनं त्वपरं दद्युः.

278. दायतत्व, p. 26; व्य० म० reads न वास्तुविभागो नोदपात्रालङ्कारोपयुक्तवाससाम्। दायभाग, p. 201 reads '०रानुपयुक्तस्त्री०' and प्रचारार्थानां, वि० र०, p. 503 reads ०कारानुयुक्त० and प्रचारवर्त्मनामविभागश्चेति प्रजापतिः.

279. वि० र०, p. 603, which reads प्रम्रियेत for प्रव्रजेत, भरणं चास्य, ०तरासु तत्. म० पा०, 680 omits या तस्य... मतः; विश्व० (या०, II, 139-40) has the first verse but does not attribute it to शङ्ख and reads भ्रातरः for शेषास्ते.

भरणं वास्य कुर्वीरन्स्त्रीणामाजीवनक्षयात्।
रक्षन्ति शय्यां भर्तुश्चेदाच्छिन्द्युरितरासु च।।
या तस्य दुहिता तस्याः पित्रंशो भरणे मतः।

280. **शङ्खः** — गोत्रभागविभागार्थे सन्देहे समुपस्थिते।
गोत्रजैश्चापरिज्ञाते कुलं साक्षित्वमर्हति।।

281. **शङ्खलिखितयमाः** — पिता पितामहश्चैव तथैव प्रपितामहः।
जातं पुत्रं प्रशंसन्ति पिप्पलं शकुना इव।।
मधुमांसेन खड्गेन पयसा पायसेन वा।
एष दास्यति नस्तृप्तिं वर्षासु च मघासु च।।

282. **शङ्खलिखितपैठीनसयः** — यत्र क्वचन जातेन पिता पुत्रेण नन्दति।
तन चानृणतां याति पितॄणां पिण्डदेन वै।।

283. **शङ्खलिखितविष्णुवशिष्ठहारीताः** —
पुत्रेण लोकाञ्जयति पौत्रेणानन्त्यमश्नुते।
अथ पुत्रस्य पौत्रेण ब्रध्नस्याप्नोति विष्टपम्।।

284. **शङ्खलिखितौः** — अग्निहोत्रं त्रयो वेदा यज्ञाश्च शतदक्षिणाः।
ज्येष्ठपुत्रप्रसूतस्य कलां नार्हन्ति षोडशीम्।।
पुत्रपौत्रप्रतिष्ठस्य बहुपुत्रस्य जीवतः।
अक्षुण्णवेदयज्ञस्य हस्तप्राप्तं त्रिविष्टपम्।।

285. **शङ्खलिखितौः** — पितॄणामनृणो जीवन् दृष्ट्वा पुत्रमुखं पिता।
स्वर्गी सुतेन जातेन तस्मिन् संन्यस्य तदृणम्।।

286. **शङ्खलिखितौः** — ब्राह्मणस्तु सवर्णायाः पाणिं गृह्णीयात् तस्यां पितामहानां तनवोऽनुसूयन्ते पुत्रोपचारेणात्मानं संमन्त्रयेत्। एवं ह्याह अङ्गादङ्गादित्यादि। आधत्त पितरो गर्भे कुमारं पुष्करस्रजम्। यथेह पुरुषस्यात्मा तथा

---

280. दायतत्व, p. 31; दायभाग, p. 359.
281. दायभाग (p. 105); चतुर्वर्ग०, Vol. III, Part 1, p. 202.
282. वि० र०, 584.
283. वि० र०, 585; दायभाग, p. 249 attribute it to शङ्ख, मनु, विष्णु, वसिष्ठ and हारीत.
284. वि० र०, 584-85; दायभाग (p. 249) has the first and reads यज्ञाश्चैव तदक्षिणाः.
285. दायभाग, p. 249.
286. वि० र०, p. 554-55.

त्वमभिजायसे। आत्मा पुत्र इति प्रोक्तः पितुर्मातुरनुग्रहात्। पुन्नाम्नस्त्रायते यस्मात्पुत्रस्तेनासि संज्ञितः।।

287. **शङ्खलिखितौ:** — क्षेत्रिकस्याविज्ञानेन यद्बीजं प्रकीर्यते तत्क्षेत्रिकस्यैव।

288. **शङ्खलिखितौ:** — नियतं क्षेत्रिणामपत्यमिति च वेदवादो मातुरपत्यमित्येके ऋषयो वदन्ति द्व्यामुष्यायणमनुमन्त्रयत इति। वसिष्ठकश्यपयोर्जलगत-योरुदवासादुत्तीर्य एकः प्रजामुत्पादयत्यविज्ञानो लोकानाम्। एवं तयोर्द्विधा सन्तानः। यस्मात्कुलधर्मपरिग्रहरिक्थपिण्डोदकानि चैकतः कृत्वा परक्षेत्रोत्पन्ना अपि प्रयच्छन्ति।

289. **शङ्खलिखितौ:** — मन्त्रसंस्कारकर्तुरपत्यमित्याङ्गिरसो बीजिक्षेत्रिकयोरनुमते तद्बीजं प्रकीर्यते तद्द्विधा शस्यमित्युशनाः।

290. **शङ्खलिखितौ:** — पुत्रिका पुत्रवदिति प्राचेतसः। तस्यापत्यं पुत्रिकासुतो मातामहपितामहाभ्यां पिण्डदः।
पुत्रदौहित्रयोर्लोके न विशेषोस्त्यनुग्रहे।
तस्मात्तु संशयान्नेहोपेयादभ्रातृकां स्त्रियम्।।

291. **शङ्खलिखितौ:** — षट्सु दायादेषु विकल्पः। औरसः क्षेत्रजः पुत्रिकापुत्रः पौनर्भवः कानीनो गूढोत्पन्नश्चेति षट्पुत्रा बन्धुदायादाः पितृपितामहाना-मेकगोत्राः रिक्थपिण्डौ सापिण्ड्यं च। तेषामर्थं दशधा कुर्यात् द्वौ भागौ पितुर्द्वावौरसस्य त्रीन् क्षेत्रजपुत्रिकापुत्रयोरेकैमितरेषाम्।

292. **शङ्खलिखितौ:** — श्रेयसः श्रेयसोभावे पापीयान्रिक्थमर्हति।

293. **शङ्खलिखितपैठीनसियमाः** — अथापुत्रस्य स्वर्यातस्य भ्रातृगामि द्रव्यं तद्भावे मातापितरौ लभेतां पत्नी वा ज्येष्ठा सगोत्रशिष्यसब्रह्मचारिणः।

---

287. वि० र०, 583.

288. वि० र०, 581.

289. वि० र०, 557.

290. वि० र०, 559-60.

291. वि० र०, 547.

292. वि० र०, 552.

293. विश्व० (या०, II.139-40); स्मृतिच० (II, p. 305); मिता० and अपरार्क (या०, II, 136) ascribe it to शङ्ख and read only up to ज्येष्ठा वा पत्नी; विश्व० and मिता० read स्वर्यातस्य त्त्वपुत्रस्य . . . पितरौ हरेयातां; दायभाग (p. 238); उज्ज्वला (आप० ध०, II, 6.13.2) reads लभेयाताम्; हरदत्त on गौ० ध०, 28.25 reads हरेताम्.

294. **शङ्खः** — अकृत्वा प्रेतकार्याणि प्रेतस्य धनहारकः।
वर्णानां यद्वधे प्रोक्तं तद्व्रतं नियतश्चरेत्।

295. **शङ्खलिखितौः** — प्रेतायाः पुत्रिकायास्तु न भर्ता द्रव्यमर्हति।

296. **शङ्खः** — स्वयं शुल्कं वोढा।

297. **शङ्खलिखितौः** — समं सर्वे सोदर्या द्रव्यमर्हन्ति कुमार्यश्च।

298. **शङ्खलिखितौः** — स्त्रीधनं कन्या लभते तदपत्यस्य च द्रव्यं कन्याभागः।

299. **शङ्खलिखितौः** — अपपात्रितस्य रिक्थपिण्डोदकानि निवर्तन्ते।

300. **शङ्खलिखितौः** — परिषद्गामि वा श्रोत्रियद्रव्यं न राजगामि न हार्यं राज्ञा देवब्राह्मणसंस्थितं सनिक्षेपोपनिधिक्रमागतं न बालस्त्रीधनानि। एवं ह्याह। न हार्यं स्त्रीधनं राज्ञा तथा बालधनानि च। नार्याः षडागमं वित्तं बालानां पैतृकं धनम्॥

301. **शङ्खलिखितौः** — रक्षेद्राजा बालानां धनान्यप्राप्तव्यवहाराणां श्रोत्रियवीर-पत्नीनां प्रहीणस्वामिकानि राजगामीनि भवन्ति।

302. **शङ्खः** — तत्र चेदनुप्राप्ते सवने ऋत्विङ्म्रियेत तस्य सगोत्रोथ शिष्यो वा तत्कार्यमनुपूरयेत्। अथ चेदबान्धवस्ततोन्यमृत्विजं वृणुयात्।

303. **शङ्खलिखितौः** — अथ ऋत्विजि वृत्ते पश्चादन्यं वृणुयात्पूर्ववृतस्यैव दक्षिणा पश्चाद्वृतः किञ्चिल्लभेत। प्रवसेच्चेत्तत्कालं निमित्तं वा अपेक्ष्य यक्ष्य-

---

294. दायतत्त्व, p. 20.

295. दायभाग, p. 276.

296. वि० र०, p. 521.

297. दायभाग, p. 127; हरदत्त on गौ० ध०, 28.22 reads मातृकं द्रव्यमहाः स्त्रीकुमार्यश्च.

298. वि० र०, 561.

299. स्मृतिच० (II, p. 270) reads आवपातिकस्य (?); वि० र०, 486.

300. वि० र०, 598.

301. वि० र०, 598-99.

302. स्मृतिच०, II, p. 188 (about संभूयसमुत्थान); वि० र० (p. 117) attributes it to शंङ्खलिखित and reads म्रियेत तत्र किं कार्यमिति जिज्ञासा तस्य सगोत्रः etc.

303. वि० र०, 120; स्मृतिच० (II, p. 188) has the words अथ . . . ल्लभेत.

माणस्तकालमुदीक्षेत नान्तरा यजेत स्यादात्ययिको वा तं क्रतुं समापयेत्। प्रोष्य प्रत्यागतश्च किञ्चिल्लभेत। अथ चेत्प्रतिषिद्धः प्रवसेत्कामप्दनुप्राप्ते साने ऋत्विक् शतं दण्ड्यः स एव वा दुष्टः तस्य ऋत्विक्कुलोपाध्यायः। एवं व्याधितपतितोन्मत्तप्रहीणप्रध्वस्तेषु संप्रसादकरणमृत्विक्षु। कामाच्चेदपतितं याज्यं त्यजेदृत्विक् प्राप्नुयाद्द्विशतं दण्डम्। याज्यश्चैव तदेवाप्नुयात्त्यागे ऋत्विजोऽपतितस्य। कामं पतितमश्रोत्रियं त्यजेद्याज्यं चाभिशस्तमदातारम्।

304. **शङ्खलिखितौ:** — रात्रौ चरन्ति गौः पञ्च माषान्दिवा त्रीन्मुहूर्ते माषं ग्रामे त्वदण्डः।

305. **शङ्खलिखितौ:** — सर्वेषामेव वत्सानां माषं महिषी दश खरोष्ट्रं षोडश अजाविकं चतुरः।

306. **शङ्खः** — छागवृषभा अनिर्दशाहा गावः शस्यापबाधे न दण्डमाप्नुयुः।

307. **शङ्खलिखितौ:** — क्षुद्रपशवः सर्वथा अनिवार्याः, अश्वतरगजवाजिनश्चादण्ड्याः अवश्याः शनैरपवार्याः।।

308. **शङ्खलिखितौ:** — मार्गक्षेत्रे वृतिः कार्या यामुष्ट्रो नावलोकयेत् नाश्वशूकरावन्तरं विन्देताम्।

309. **शङ्खलिखितौ:** — गृहक्षेत्रयोर्विरोधे सामन्तप्रत्ययः सामन्तविरोधे अभिलेख्यप्रत्ययः अभिलेख्यविरोधे ग्रामनगरवृद्धश्रेणिप्रत्ययः ग्रामनगरवृद्धश्रेणिविरोधे दशवर्षभुक्तमन्यत्र राजविप्रस्वात्।

310. **शङ्खलिखितौ:** — मार्गक्षेत्रे पथि विसर्गो राजमार्गरथपरिवर्तनं पूर्वमर्यादास्थापनं तोरणगृहरथ्यान्तरेषु त्रिपदं देवराजायतनेषु यथेष्टम्।

---

304. वि० र०, 234; स्मृतिच० (II, p. 212) reads ग्रासे for ग्रामे.

305. वि० र०, 235.

306. वि० र०, 240.

307. वि० र०, 241.

308. वि० र०, 233.

309. वि० र०, 208.

310. वि० र०, 220; स्मृतिच० (II, p. 235) has the words मार्ग... विसर्गः.

311. **शङ्खलिखितौ:** — क्षेत्रमर्यादाभेदे अष्टशतं सीमातिक्रमणे अष्टसहस्रं क्षेत्रोदकाहरणे अष्टशतम्।

312. **शङ्खलिखितौ:** — यथाकाल उत्तमवर्णाक्षेपे तत्प्रसादो दण्डस्त्रयो वा कार्षापणाः शुक्तवाक्याभिधानेऽप्येवमेव। तथा सवर्णव्यतिक्रमे द्वादश कार्षापणाः यथारूपविशिष्टाक्षेपे विशिष्टस्य चतुर्विंशतिः।

313. **शङ्खलिखितौ:** — तथाधिकृतान्गुरून् विप्रांश्च निर्भर्त्सनं ताडनं गोमयानुलेपनं खरारोहणं दर्पहरो दण्डो वा।

314. **शङ्खलिखितौ:** — आक्रोशे ब्राह्मणः क्षत्रियस्य शतं दण्ड्यः शतार्धे वैश्यस्य पञ्चविंशतिं शूद्रस्य।

315. **शङ्खलिखितौ:** — प्रहारोद्यमे षट्पञ्चाशन्निपातने तद्द्विगुणम्।

316. **शङ्खलिखितौ:** — कूटशासनप्रयोगे राजशासनप्रतिषेधे कूटतुलामानप्रतिमानव्यवहारे शारीरोऽङ्गच्छेदो वा।

317. **शङ्खलिखितौ:** — अन्नादे भ्रूणहा मार्ष्टि पत्यौ भार्यापचारिणी।
गुरौ शिष्यश्च याज्यश्च स्तेनो राजनि किल्विषम्।।

318. **शङ्खलिखितौ:** — सुवर्णरत्नापहरणे (शारीरोच्ङ्गच्छेदो वा)।

319. **शङ्खलिखितौ:** — वापीतडागोदपा (न) भेदमार्गरसद्रव्यदूषणे अदासीदाससंप्रदानकरणे (शारीरोंगच्छेदो वा)।

---

311. वि० र०, 223; स्मृतिच० (II, p. 236) has सीमा...सहस्रम्; परा० मा० III.2, p. 404 has सीमाव्यतिक्रमे त्वष्टसहस्रम्.

312. वि० र०, 248.

313. वि० र०, 250.

314. वि० र०, 261.

315. वि० र०, 263.

316. वि० र०, pp. 369 and 298.

317. चतुर्वर्ग०, Vol. III, Part 1, p. 781; this is same as मनु०, 8.317; compare आप० ध० सू०, I.8.19.15.

318. वि० र०, p. 324.

319. वि० र०, p. 365.

320. **शङ्खलिखितौ:** — तुलामानप्रतीमानव्यवहारार्घसंस्थापनं देशद्रव्यानुरूपं प्रत्ययितपुरुषाधिष्ठितम्।

321. **शङ्खलिखितौ:** — राजपुत्रापहारेऽष्टसहस्रं शारीरो वा दण्डः तत्कुलीनेष्वर्धे स्त्रीपुरुषयोश्च।

322. **शङ्खलिखितौ:** — हस्त्यश्वगोरथयानेषु राजपुत्रापहारवद्दण्डः। अजाविकेष्वर्धत्रयोदशपणा नकुलबिडालापहरणे कार्षापणः।

323. **शङ्खलिखितौ:** — अष्टशतं सीताद्रव्यापहरणे यथाकालम्।

324. **शङ्खलिखितौ:** — कृतकाष्ठाश्मकौलालचर्मवेत्रदलभाण्डेषु मूल्यात्पञ्चगुणस्त्रयो वा कार्षापणाः। एकचक्रापहरणे चत्वारिंशत्, शकटे त्वशीतिशतम्।

325. **शङ्खलिखितौ:** — अब्राह्मणो ब्राह्मणस्य समिदाज्येध्माग्निकाष्ठतृणोपलपुष्पफलमूलान्यपहरन् बलादविज्ञातो वा हस्तछेदनमाप्नुयात्। कुशकरकाग्निहोत्रद्रव्यापहारे प्रत्यक्षतोऽङ्गच्छेदः स्यात्, अप्रत्यक्षं यथाविदितोऽयं किल्बिषीति ब्राह्मणः खरयानमवाप्नुयात्। मूलमौण्ड्यमितरेषां खरयानमेव च।

326. **शङ्खलिखितौ:** — न मातापितरावनुक्रामेन्न गुरून्त्रयाणामतिक्रमेऽङ्गच्छेदः।

327. **शङ्खलिखितौ:** — प्रतिमारामकूपसंक्रमध्वजसेतुनिपानभङ्गेषु तत्समुत्थापनं प्रतिसंस्कारोष्टशतं च।.

328. **शङ्खलिखितौ:** — केशाकेशिसंग्रहणात् पारजायिक उल्काहस्तोग्निदः शस्त्रपाणिर्घातुको लोप्त्रहस्तश्चोरः।

---

320. वि० र०, 302; supply राज्ञा कार्यम्.

321. वि० र०, 318.

322. वि० र०, 318-19.

323. वि० र०, 324.

324. वि० र०, 327.

325. वि० र०, 329; मेधा० (मनु०, 8.334) has the words कुश...द्रव्यान्यपहरतोङ्गच्छेदः स्यात् and attributes them to शङ्ख. Mr. Gharpure is not right in printing the words सुलभेष्व...ह्रियमाणेषु as part of the quotation from शङ्ख.

326. वि० र०, 358.

327. वि० र०, 364.

328. स्मृतिच०, II, p. 95; परा० मा०, III.1, p. 119 reads ०ग्रहणात् पारदारिकः.

329. **शङ्खलिखितौ:** — सर्वेषां स्वदारनियमः स्वकर्मप्रतिपत्तिश्च। येन येनाङ्गेनापराधं कुर्यात् तत्तस्य छेत्तव्यमष्टसहस्रं वा दण्डोन्यत्र ब्राह्मणाददण्ड्यो हि ब्राह्मणः।

330. **शङ्खलिखितौ:** — अनिवेदितप्रवेशे तत्रोत्तममुत्तमायां विपर्यये मध्यमसाहसं प्रतिलोमैकान्तरावस्कन्दने सर्वस्वं वधो वा विपर्यये संनिरोधः सर्वस्वं वा।

331. **शङ्खः** — श्रेयसः शयनशायिनं राजा बद्ध्वा श्वभिः खादयेत् काष्ठैश्चैनां दहेत्।

332. **शङ्खलिखितौ:** — कन्यायामसकामायां व्यङ्गुलच्छेदो दण्डः। उत्तमायां वधो जघन्यस्य। समायां शुल्कमाभरणं च द्विगुणं स्त्रीधनं दत्वा प्रतिपाद्येत।

333. **शङ्खलिखितौ:** — यस्मिन् भावोर्पितः स्त्रीणामार्तवे तच्छीलं जनयन्ति यथा नीलवृषेण नीलवृषवत्सप्रभवः श्वेतेन श्वेत एव जायते एवं योनिरेव बलवती यस्माद्वर्णाः संकीर्यन्ते।

334. **शङ्खलिखितौ:** — कामचारिणीं मलिनां कुचेलां पिण्डमात्रोपजीविनीं निवृत्ताधिकारामधःशय्यां निरुद्धां निवासयेदत्यर्थव्यभिचरिणीम्।

335. **शङ्खलिखितौ:** — श्वः श्वः पचनभाण्डानामुपलेपनं सुसंमृष्टगृहद्वारोपलेपनं कृतशौचानुकूल्यदध्यक्षतदूर्वाप्रवालपुष्पकृतबलिकर्म श्वश्रूश्वशुराद्यभिवादनानन्तरं गृहावश्यकानि कुर्यात्। न देवभूतपतिभ्योऽग्रेऽश्नीयात्। न भर्तुरन्यत्र प्रतिकारौषधात्।

---

329. वि० र०, 387-388.

330. वि० र०, p. 390.

331. वि० र०, 396.

332. वि० र०, 402.

333. वि० र०, 441; स्मृतिच० (II, p. 251) has the words यस्मिन्...तच्छीलं जनयति; compare मनु०, 9.9.

334. स्मृतिच०, II, p. 242.

335. वि० र०, 429; स्मृतिच० (II, p. 251) has the portion श्वः . . . कुर्यात् with some omissions.

336. **शङ्खलिखितौ:** — न भर्तारं द्विष्याद्यद्यप्यष्ठीवलः स्यात्पतितोऽङ्गहीनो व्याधितो वा पतिर्हि देवता स्त्रीणाम्।

337. **शङ्खः** — न च व्रतोपवासनियमेज्यादानधर्मो वानुग्रहकरणं स्त्रीणामन्यत्र पतिशुश्रूषायाः। कामं तु भर्तुरनुज्ञया व्रतोपवासनियमादीनामभ्यासः स्त्रीधर्मः।

338. **शङ्खलिखितौ:** — न वै स्त्रीणां व्रतं न मन्त्रक्रिया न कार्यम्।

339. **शङ्खः** — न व्रतेनोपवासेन धर्मेण विविधेन च।
नारी स्वर्गमवाप्नोति प्राप्नोति पतिपूजनात्।।

340. **शङ्खः** — सुरालशुनपलाण्डुगृञ्जनकमांसान्यभक्ष्याणि विवर्जयेदाहारमयं हि शरीरं तन्मयत्वाद्ब्राह्मणः संकीर्यते, मातुरशितपीतादिभिर्गर्भः संभवति।

341. **शङ्खलिखितौ:** — सर्वासां प्रोषिते भर्तरि ब्राह्मणी चारित्र्यं रक्षेत्। इतरासां मातापितरौ अनन्तरो वा राजन्यो वा। प्रेङ्खाताण्डव-विहारचित्रदर्शनाङ्ग-रागोद्यानयानविवृतशयनोत्कृष्टपानभोजनकन्दुकक्रीडाधूपगन्धमाल्यालंकार-दन्तधावनाञ्जनादीनामस्वतन्त्राणां प्रोषितभर्तृकाणां कुलस्त्रीणाम-नारम्भः।

342. **शङ्खः** — दक्षिणामुखा अपोवतीर्य सकृदाप्लुत्य नोद्धर्षणं कुर्युः।

343. **शङ्खलिखितौ:** — उदकक्रिया कामं श्वशुरमातुलयोः शिष्ये सहाध्यायिनि राजनि च।

---

336. स्मृतिच०, II, p. 251; परा० मा०, II.1, p. 38 reads अशील and अर्थहीनः.

337. हरदत्त on गौ० ध०, 18.1 reads ०पवासैर्निय०; स्मृतिच०, II, p. 252, 291 (for last *sūtra*); परा० मा०, II, 1, p. 38 ascribes it to शङ्खलिखित.

338. चतुर्वर्ग०, Vol. III, Part 1, p. 847.

339. स्मृतिच०, II, p 252. It is शङ्खस्मृति, 5.8.

340. अपरार्क० (या०, 3, 256); म० पा०, p. 824; अपरार्क reads भक्ष्याण्याह रसमयं and म० पा० reads संकीर्तयेत्; स्मृतिच० (II.250) reads मांसादीन्यभक्ष्याणि च वर्जयेत् and पाताद्धि गर्भः; so does वि० र०, p. 437.

341. वि० र०, 439; स्मृतिच. (II, p. 253) reads ०धावनाञ्जनादर्शनप्रसाधनादीनामस्वत०.

342. विश्वरूप, on या०, III.3.

343. हारलता, p. 150.

344. **शङ्खलिखितौः** — प्रेतस्य बान्धवा यथावृद्धमुदकमवतीर्य नोद्धर्षयेरन् अपः प्रसिञ्चेरन् सकृत् प्रदक्षिणाभिमुखाः। राजन्यवैश्यावप्यपसव्यं वासो-यज्ञोपवीते कृत्वा असावेतत्ते इति।

345. **शङ्खलिखितः** — उत्तीर्य प्रेतस्पृष्टानि वासांस्युत्मृज्येतराणि परिधाय गृहद्वारे तस्मै प्रेताय पिण्डं दत्त्वा पश्चात् दूर्वाप्रवालान् गोमयमग्निं जलं वृषभं चालभ्य प्रविशन्तो घृतगौरसर्षपैर्मूर्धानमङ्गानि चालभेरन्।

346. **शङ्खः** — दूर्वाप्रवालमग्निं वृषभं चालभ्य गृहद्वारे प्रेताय पिण्डं दत्त्वा पश्चात्प्रविशेयुः।

347. **शङ्खः** — भूमौ माल्यं पिण्डं पानीयमुपलेपनं च दद्युः।

348. **शङ्खः** — समानाशौचसंपाते प्रथमेन समापयेत्।
असमानं द्वितीयेन धर्मराजवचो यथा।
मातर्यादौ परीतायामशुद्धौ म्रियते पिता।
पितुःशेषेण शुध्येत्तु मातुः कार्या तु पक्षिणी।।

349. **शङ्खः** — अनूढानां तु कन्यानां तथा वै शूद्रजन्मनाम्।
अनूढभार्यः शूद्रस्तु षोडषाद्वत्सरात्परम्।
मृत्युं समधिगच्छेत्तु मासात्तस्यापि बान्धवाः।
शुद्धिं समधिगच्छन्ति नात्र कार्या विचारणा।।

350. **शङ्खलिखितौः** — राज्ञां पुरोहितोमात्यः शुद्धिस्तस्य तदाश्रया।
शिष्यस्य पैतृकं शौचं गुरुरेव प्रपद्यते।।

---

344. हारलता, p. 147; अपरार्क (on या०, 3.5.) reads अवतीर्याप नाइत्यर्थयेरन्नपः प्रसिञ्चेरन् and कृत्वाञ्जलिनासावेतदुदकमित्युक्त्वा तस्मादुत्तीर्य प्रेत, etc.

345. हारलता, p. 154; अपरार्क (on या०, III.5) has वासांसि परित्यज्य परिदध्युरन्यानि.

346. अपरार्क (या०, 3.12-13); मिता० has ०वृषभौ वा only.

347. अपरार्क (या०, 3.16); म० पा०, p. 399 reads ०पानीयमुपलेष्वादद्युः, मिता० reads ०मुपले वा दद्युः.

348. हारलता, p. 65 reads शौचं प्रथमे; अपरार्क (या०, 3.20), परा० मा०, I.2, p 267 and I.2, p. 265; *vide* शङ्ख 15.10. for first verse.

349. हारलता, p. 48; अपरार्क (या०, 3.22) has the 2nd and 3rd lines; शङ्खस्मृति., 15.6-7.

350. हारलता, p. 104.

मातापित्रोरुपासीने न गुरुः प्रतिपद्यते।
पिण्डोदकं तु जनकगोत्रमेव प्रपद्यते।।

351. **शङ्खः** — दानं प्रतिग्रहो होमः स्वाध्यायः पितृकर्म च।
प्रेतपिण्डक्रियावर्जं सूतके विनिवर्तते।।

352. **शङ्खलिखितौः** — अथ चेदन्तरा प्रमीयेत जायेत वा शिष्टैरेव दिवसैः शुध्येत्।
अहःशेषे द्वाभ्याम्। प्रभाते तिसृभिः।

353. **शङ्खः** — मरणादेव कर्तव्यं संयोगो यस्य नाग्निना।
दाहादूर्ध्वमशौचं स्याद्यस्य वैतानिको विधिः।।

354. **शङ्खः** — अग्निहोत्रार्थे स्नानोपस्पर्शनात्तत्कालं शौचम्।

355. **शङ्खलिखितौः** — अथ शस्त्रानाशकाग्निरज्जुभृगुजलविषप्रमापणेष्वेवमेव (सद्यः शौचं)।

356. **शङ्खः** — बालस्त्वन्तर्दशाहे तु प्रेतत्वं यदि गच्छति।
सद्य एव विशुद्धिः स्यान्नाशौचं नैव सूतकम्।।

357. **शङ्खः** — प्राङ्नामकरणात्सद्यः शुद्धिः।

358. **शङ्खलिखितौः** — जननेप्येवं तत्र मातापितरावशुची मातेत्येके।

359. **शङ्खकार्ष्णाजिनीः** — अजातदन्तासु पित्रारेकरात्रम्।

360. **शङ्खः** — अजातदन्ते बाले तु सद्यः शौचं विधीयते।

---

351. हारलता, p. 26.

352. परा॰ मा॰, I.2. 266.

353. हारलता, p. 131.

354. मिता॰ on याज्ञ॰, III, 20; कुल्लूक (मनु॰, 5.84) attributes it to शङ्खलिखित and reads ॰स्पर्शनाच्छुचिः; परा॰ मा॰, I.2, p. 231 reads ॰होत्राद्यनुष्ठानार्थं स्नात्वोप॰; हारलता, p. 7, attributes to शङ्खलिखित and reads ॰स्पर्शनादेव पिता शुचिः.

355. हारलता, p. 113.

356. हारलता, p. 41.

357. मिता॰ (या॰, III, 20 and 23) reads शौचं for शुद्धिः; म॰ पा॰, 384.

358. हरदत्त on गौ॰ ध॰, 14.12; हारलता, p. 17 adds तेषां before तत्र.

359. परा॰ मा॰, I.2, p. 246.

360. अपरार्क (या॰, 3,23); शङ्खस्मृति, 15.4-5.

अहोरात्रात्तथा शुद्धिर्बाले तु कृतचूडके।।
तथैवानुपनीते तु त्र्यहाच्छुध्यन्ति बान्धवाः।

361. **शङ्खलिखतौः** — सपिण्डता तु सर्वेषां गोत्रतः साप्तपौरुषी।
पिण्डं चोदकदानं च शौचं चैव तदानुगम्।।

362. **शङ्खः** — कृच्छ्रपादः सपिण्डस्य प्रेतालंकरणे कृते।
अज्ञानादुपवासः स्यादशक्तौ स्नानमिष्यते।।

363. **शङ्खलिखितौः** — देशान्तरिते बाले चातीते सद्यः शौचम्। य ऊनत्रिवर्षः स्यादनुत्पन्नदन्तक इत्येके।

364. **शङ्खः** — देशान्तरगतं श्रुत्वा कल्याणं मरणं तथा।
यच्छेषं दशरात्रस्य तावदेवाशुचिर्भवेत्।।
अतीते दशरात्रे तु त्रिरात्रमशुचिर्भवेत्।

365. **शङ्खः** — अतीते सूतके स्वे स्वे त्रिरात्रं स्यादशौचकम्।
संवत्सरे व्यतीते तु सद्यः शौचं विधीयते।।

366. **शङ्खलिखितौः** — एकाहं कन्यायामूढायां पुनर्गोत्रतः पिण्डाशौचयोर्निवृत्तिः।

367. **शङ्खलिखितौः** — अन्यपूर्वासु भार्यासु कृतकेषु सुतेषु च।
तेषा चोपरते स्नानं नाध्यायो नोदकक्रिया।।

368. **शङ्खः** — अनौरसेषु पुत्रेषु भार्यास्वन्यगतासु च।
परपूर्वासु च स्त्रीषु त्रिरात्राच्छुद्धिरिष्यते।।

369. **शङ्खः** — काले शक्तितः शरीरं शोषयेद्यमनियममन्त्रोपवासादिभिः। कुश-

---

361. हारलता, p. 96; कूल्लूक on मनु०, 5.60 for first half.

362. मिता० (या०, III, 26 reads पदोऽसपिण्डस्य; म० पा०, 437.

363. हारलता, p. 38.

364. परा० मा०, I.2, p. 234 and 236; शङ्खस्मृति, 15.11-12.

365. हारलता, p. 35.

366. हारलता, p. 49.

367. हारलता, p. 81.

368. परा० मा०, I.2, p. 250; शङ्खस्मृति, 15.13.

369. अपरार्क (या०, 3.51).

चीरचर्मवल्कलवासा जटी कृष्णाजिनोत्तरीयो जलशयनपञ्चतपा-भ्रावकाशनियमपरः।

370. **शङ्खः** — अशुचित्वशुचित्वस्य प्रियाप्रियविपर्ययान्।
गर्भवासे च वसतिं पश्येन्मुच्येत नान्यथा।।

371. **शङ्खः** — प्राग्रात्रापररात्रेषु योगी नित्यमतन्द्रितः।
ध्यायेत्तु पुरुषं विष्णुं निर्गुणं पञ्चविंशकम्।।

372. **शङ्खः** — मनःसंयमनात्तज्ज्ञैधार्रणेति निगद्यते।

373. **शङ्खः** — यथा पृथिव्यां बीजानि रत्नानि निधयो यथा।
एवमात्मनि कर्माणि तिष्ठन्ति प्रभवन्ति च।।

374. **शङ्खलिखितौः** — कुम्भीपाक-रौरव-महारौरव-कूटशाल्मलि-शिलासंघात-वज्रकण्टकशयनान्यसिपत्रवनान्ययस्तुडाः पक्षिणः पूयशोणितकर्दमः केशकल्मलशैवालाः क्षारनद्यो ज्वलिताङ्गारकुण्डास्तप्तकरम्भवालुका निस्त्रिंशमुद्गरनिपाताःसूचिप्रतोदवेध्यःअल्पोदकाःसाग्निगर्ताःप्रदीप्तायः-पिण्डलोहकण्टकशयनानि नरकपञ्जराणि कालसूत्राणि तीक्ष्णाग्राश्च शूलाः श्यावशबलौ वज्रदंष्ट्रिणौ तप्तोदका वैतरणी एतेषु पच्यन्ते पापकर्मिणः।

375. **शङ्खलिखितः** — अत ऊर्ध्वं बहूनि वर्षसहस्राणि यमविषये कम्भीपाकरौरवादिषु स्थानेषु दुःखान्यनुभूयेह जातानामिमानि लक्षणानि भवन्तिः तद्यथा ब्रह्महा कुष्ठी गोघ्नश्चान्धोनेकरोगिणश्च।

376. **शङ्खलिखितौः** — सुवर्णस्तेयी कुनखी। वस्त्रापहारी श्वित्री। हिरण्यापहारी दद्रुणः।तैजसापहारी मण्डली।स्नेहापहारी क्षमामयी अजीर्णवानन्नापहारी। वागपहारी मूकः। गृध्रो देवद्रव्योपजीवकः। पाण्डुरोगी दीपहारी।

---

370. अपरार्क (या०, 3.62).

371. अपरार्क (या०, 3.63).

372. अपरार्क (या०, 3.198-201).

373. परा० मा० II.1, p. 11.

374. म० पा०, 684.

375. परा० मा०, II.2, p. 246.

376. परा० मा०, II.2, p. 263.

ब्राह्मणवृत्तिघ्नश्च दरिद्रः। कर्मफलविशेषेण कुब्जषण्ढपङ्गुदरिद्राश्च जायन्ते।।

377. ब्रह्महा कुष्ठी। तैजसापहारी मण्डली। देवब्राह्मणकोशकः खलतिः। गर-दाग्निदावुन्मत्तौ। गुरुं प्रतिहन्तापस्मारी। गोघ्नश्चान्धः धर्मपत्नीं मुक्त्वान्यत्र प्रवृत्तः शब्दवेधी प्राणिविशेषः। कुण्डाशी भगभक्तो देवब्राह्मणापहारी पाण्डुरोगी न्यासापहारी काणः। स्त्रीपण्योजीवी षण्ढः। कौमारपरत्यागी दुर्भगः। मिष्टैकाशी वातगुल्मी। अभक्ष्यभक्षको गण्डमाली। ब्राह्मणीगामी निर्बीजी। क्रूरकर्मा वामनो वस्त्रापहारी पतङ्गः शय्याहारी क्षपणकः शङ्खशुक्त्यपहारी कपाली। दीपाहारी कौशिकः। मित्रध्रुक् क्षयी मातापित्रोराक्रोशकः खण्डनकारक इति। **वृद्धगौतमः**। अनृतवाग्मुहुर्मुहुः संलग्नवाक्। जलोदरी दारत्यागी कूटसाक्षी श्लीपदी उच्छूनजङ्घचरणो विवाहविघ्नकर्ता छिन्नोष्ठः अवगोरणकर्ता छिन्नहस्तो पितृघ्नो मातृघ्नो वा नेत्रविकलः स्नुषागामी वातवृषणः स्थूलः चतुष्पथे मूत्रविसर्जने मूत्र-कृच्छ्री कन्यादूषकः षण्ढः ईर्षालुर्मशकः पित्रा विवदमानोऽपस्मारी न्यासापहारी अनपत्यो रत्नापहारी अत्यन्तदरिद्रो विद्याविक्रयी पुरुषः मृगः वेदविक्रयी द्वीपी बहुयाजको जलप्लवः अयाज्ययाजको वराहः अनिमन्त्रितभोजी वायसः मिष्टैकभोजी वानरः यत्रतत्राश्नन्मार्जारः कक्षवनदाही खद्योतो दारिकाचार्यो मुखविगन्धः पर्युषितभोजी कृमिः अदत्तादायी बलीवर्दो मत्सरी भ्रमरोऽग्न्युत्सादी मण्डलकुष्ठी शूद्राचार्यः श्वपाको गोहतो सर्पः स्नेहापहारी क्षयी अन्नापहारी अजीर्णी ज्ञाना-पहारी मूकः चाण्डालीपुक्कसीगमने अजगरः प्रव्रजितागमने मरुपिशाचः शूद्रागमने दीर्घकीटः सवर्णाभिगामी दरिद्रो जलहारी मत्स्यः क्षीरहारी बलाकः वार्धुषिकोऽङ्गहीनः अविक्रेयविक्रयी गृध्रो राजमहिषीगामी नपुंसको राजाकोशको गर्दभो गोगामी मण्डूकः अनध्यायेऽध्ययने शृगालः परद्रव्यापहारी परप्रेष्यो मत्स्यवधे गर्भवासीत्येके अनूर्ध्वगामिनः।

378. **शङ्खलिखितौ**: — वेश्यापहारी अद्रिसर्पः। परजलापहरी शिशुमारः।

---

377. म० पा०, 701-702; मिता० (या०, III.216) has the passage from ब्रह्महा to खण्डनकारकः with slight variations and ascribes the passage from अनृतवाक् to गौतम; compare 20th chap. of गौतमसंहिता० in M.N. Dutt's collection of texts and विष्णुध० सू० 44.11-43 and 45.3-31.

378. परा० मा०, II.2, pp. 259 and 269.

सस्यापहारी कपोतः। कव्यापहारी वायसः। ताम्रापहारी वल्गुलः। अपूपापहारी प्रेतः। शास्त्रापहारी जडः। छत्रापहारी कारण्डवः। गन्धापहारी पतङ्गः। ध्वजापहारी कृकलासः। शाकापहारी पशुः। शय्यापहार्यशयनः। पुष्पापहारी दुर्गन्धी। फलापहार्यफली। दीपापहारी कौशिकः। भूम्यपहारी नकुलाहिबिडालाखूनामन्यतमः। पर्वमैथुनी प्रमेही पुरुषव्याधिपीडितः। परदारगाम्यगुप्तदारः। गोष्ववकीर्णी दुश्चर्मा। खराभिगामो मूत्रमेही। सगोत्राभिगामी मद्यपस्त्रीगामा च श्लीपदी। मातृपितृभगिनीगाम्यबीजी। स्वदारादन्यत्र दीव्यतः केशाल्पत्वम्। गुरुतल्पगो दुश्चर्मा चण्डाल्यवकीर्णी कन्यादूषी सगोत्राभिगाम्यबीजी। धर्मपत्न्यामास्ये प्रवर्तकः खल्वाटः मातृभगिनीगाम्यवकीर्णी श्लीपदी वध्री मधुमेही च।

378a. **शङ्खः** — अत ऊर्ध्वं पतनीयानि।
निष्कृतिस्तेषां विहिता सद्‌भिरकामकृते।

379. **शङ्खः** — अकामकृते ब्रह्महा परिषदोऽनुमते खट्वाङ्गी गर्दभाजिनी मृन्मयपात्रपतितशिष्टान्नभोजी कपालचिह्नध्वजी स्वकर्म ख्यापयंश्चरेद्‌भैक्षमेककालाहारः शून्यागारपर्वतगुहानदीवृक्षमूलनिकेतनः। स एवं गोसहस्रं दत्वा द्वादशवर्षे शुद्धिमाप्नोति। अन्तरा वा ब्राह्मणं मरणान्मोचयित्वा गवां वा द्वादशानां परित्राणात् सद्य एवाश्वमेधावभृथे स्नात्वा पूतो भवति।

प्रायश्चित्तमुपासीनो वाग्यतस्त्रिरुपस्पृशेत्।
एकवासार्द्रवासाश्च लघ्वाशी स्थण्डिलेशयः।।
स्थानं वीरासनं मौनं मौञ्जी दण्डकमण्डलू।
भैक्षचर्याग्निकार्यं च कूष्माण्डीभिः सदा घृतम्।।

380. **शङ्खः** — अश्वमेधावभृथं गत्वा तत्रानुज्ञातः स्नातः सद्यः पूतो भवति।

378a. विश्वरूप on या०., III.237.

379. विश्वरूप on या०, III.237; मिता० (यो०, III.244) has the passage द्वादशे वर्षे पूतो भवति and the verse स्थानवीरासनी (on या०, III.243); अपरार्क (या०, 3.252; last sentence on या०, 3.244), म० पा०, p. 797 has the passage from द्वादशवर्षे with slight variations; *vide* No. 443 below.

380. मिता० on या०, III.244.

381. **शङ्खः** — ब्राह्मणो ब्राह्मणं घातयित्वा तस्य शिरः कपालमादाय तीर्थान्यनुचरेदात्मनः पापं संकीर्तयन् द्वादशे वर्षे शुद्धिमाप्नोति। अथाश्वमेधं पश्यति तस्य दर्शनादेव शुद्धिमाप्नोति।

382. **शङ्खः** — पूर्ववदमतिपूर्वे चतुर्षु वर्णेषु विप्रं प्रमाप्य द्वादश वत्सरान् षट् त्रीन् सार्धसंवत्सरं च व्रतान्यादिशेत् तेषामन्ते गोसहस्रं तदर्धं तस्यार्धं तदर्धं च तद्यात् सर्वेषां वर्णानामानुपूर्व्येण।

383. **शङ्खः** — एकपक्तङ्क्त्युपविष्टानां विषमं यः प्रयच्छति।
यश्चैवाश्नात्ययं सर्वः कुर्याद् ब्रह्महणि व्रतम्।।

384. **शङ्खः** — सुवर्णस्तेनः प्रकीर्णकेश आर्द्रवासा आयसं मुसलमादाय राजानमुपतिष्ठेदिदं मया पापं कृतमनेन मुसलेन मां घातयस्वेति। स राज्ञा शिष्टः सन्पूतो भवति।

385. **शङ्खलिखितौः** — (a) क्षुरेण शिश्नवृषणावुत्कृत्यानवेक्षमाणो व्रजेदिति
(b) गुरुतल्पगस्तप्तमायसं शयनमुपसंविशेत्। क्षुरेण वा शिश्नं सवृषणमुत्कृत्याञ्जलावाधाय नैर्ऋतीं दिशमनवेक्षमाणो व्रजेदाशरीरपातात् पूते भवति।

386. **शङ्खलिखितौः** — एवं मातुलानी-पितृष्वसृ-स्नुषा-भगिनी-दुहितृगमनेष्वाचार्यदुहितरि च।

387. **शङ्खः** — नित्यं त्रिषवणस्नायी कृत्वा पर्णकुटीं वने।
अधःशायी जटाधारी पर्णमूलफलाशनः।।

---

381. विश्वरूप on या०, III.237.

382. मिता० on या०, III.243 and on 267; म० पा०, p. 791 has the words from प्रमाप्य द्वादश etc.

383. हरदत्त on गौ० ध०, 23.26.

384. मिता० on या० III, 257; म० पा०, p. 827.

385. (a) मिता० (on या०, III, 259); म० पा० 836; compare वसिष्ठ 20.13; मनु०, 11.104.
(b) विश्वरूप on या०, III.254.

386. विश्वरूप on या०, III.254; परा० मा०, II.1, p. 317 reads मातृष्वसृ omits भगिनी and reads चान्द्रायणं after दुहितरि.

387. मिता०, (या०, III.259); हरदत्त on गौ० ध०, 23.11; अपरार्क (या०, 3.243); *see also* 3.259-60 for the second and last three lines; शङ्खस्मृति, 17.1-3.

ग्रामं विशेच्च भिक्षार्थी स्वकर्म परिकीर्तयन्।
एककालं समश्नीत वर्षे तु द्वादशे गते।
रुक्मस्तेयी सुरापश्च ब्रह्महा गुरुतल्पगः।
व्रतेनैतेन शुध्यन्ति महापातकिनस्त्विमे।।

388. **शङ्खः** — यागस्थं क्षत्रियं हत्वा वैश्यं हत्वा तु यागगम्।
एतदेव व्रतं कुर्यादात्रेयीविनिषूदकः।।

389. **शङ्खः** — (a) असुरामद्यपायी चान्द्रायणं चरेत्।

(b) सुरापोग्नितप्तमस्पृश्यमुदकं पिबेत्। स तेन निर्दग्धकायः शुद्धिमाप्नोति। ... अथवा बालचीरवासाः सुरापः खट्वाङ्गी गुरुतल्पगश्च ब्रह्महत्याव्रतमेव चरेयातां तौ तावता कालेन शुद्धिमाप्नुतः।

390. **शङ्खः** — पतितसंस्पृष्टो ह्यात्मानमुद्धरन्संवत्सरं तप्तकृच्छ्रं चरेत्। तथा पतितसंव्यवहारी। मित्रध्रुक्शरणागतघाती प्रतिरूपकवृत्तिर्जलशयन-पञ्चतपोभ्रावकाशानतिष्ठेद्धेमन्तग्रीष्मवर्षासु। मासं वा गोमूत्रयावकं पिबेयुरेवं शुध्यन्ति।

390a. **शङ्खः** — पतितो ह्यात्मानमुद्धरेत्। संवत्सरं तप्तकृच्छ्रमाचरेत्। कृतवापनः शुचिरपोभ्यवेयात् त्रिरेकार्द्रवासाः काष्ठमौनी वीरासनमासीत रात्रौ दिवा तिष्ठेद्युक्तोग्निकार्यपरः सावित्रीं सवनानुगां जपेत् स्वयं व्रतमभ्युपगम्य कुशचीरफलकवासा मौञ्जी मेखली दर्भपवित्रपाणिर्हविष्यं श्रपयेच्चरुं भैक्षमदुष्टं वा यात्रिकमश्नीयाद् द्वादशरात्रं चोपवासो ब्राह्मणतर्पणं गवाह्निकमित्येवं व्यवहार्योन्यथा पतितः शिष्टैरसंभाष्यः।

391. **शङ्खः** — राजा वा राजपुत्रो वा ब्राह्मणो वा बहुश्रुतः।
अकृत्वा वपनं तेषां प्रायश्चित्तं कथं भवेत्।।

---

388. परा० मा०, II.1, p. 99; शङ्ख, 17.4.

389. (a) मिता० on याज्ञ०, III.255;
(b) विश्वरूप on या०, III.248.

390. विश्वरूप (on या० III.252) reads हिरण्यस्तेन पतितसंव्यवहारी...वृत्तिरित्येते जलशयनं पञ्चतापमभ्रावकाशं चानुतिष्ठयुर्ग्रीष्मवर्षहिमन्तेषु; *vide* on या०, III.257, also; अपरार्क (या०, 3.261).

390(a). विश्वरूप on या०, III.237.

391. परा० मा०, II.1, p. 290.

केशानां रक्षणार्थाय दिगुणं व्रतमाचरेत्।
द्विगुणे व्रत आचीर्णे दक्षिणा द्विगुणा भवेत्।।

392. **शङ्खः** — ऊनैकादशवर्षस्य पञ्चवर्षात्परस्य च।
प्रायश्चित्तं चरेद्भ्रांता पिता वान्यः सुहृज्जनः।
अतो बालतरस्यास्य नापराधो न पातकम्।
राजदण्डो न तस्यास्ति प्रायश्चित्तं न विद्यते।।

393. **शङ्खः** — गोघ्नः पञ्चगव्याहारः पञ्चविंशतिरात्रमुपवसेत्सशिखं वपनं कृत्वा गोचर्मणा प्रावृतो गाश्वानुगच्छन् गोष्ठेशयो गां च दद्यात्।

394. **शङ्खः** — पादोनं शूद्रहत्यायामुदक्याग्रहणे तथा।
गोवधे तु तथा कुर्यात्परस्त्रीगमने तथा।।
औषधं स्नेहमाहारं दद्याद्गोब्राह्मणेषु च।
प्राणिनां प्राणवृत्त्यर्थं प्रायश्चित्तं न विद्यते।।

395. **शङ्खः** — यस्य यस्य तु वर्णस्य वृत्तिच्छेदं समाचरेत्।
तस्य तस्य वधे प्रोक्तं प्रायश्चितं समाचरेत्।।
अपहृत्य तु वर्णानां भूमिं विप्रः प्रमादतः।
प्रायश्चित्तं वधः प्रोक्तं ब्राह्मणानुमते चरेत्।।
गजाश्वस्यापहरणे मणीनां रजतस्य च।
धनापहरणे चैव कुर्यात्संवत्सरव्रतम्।।
तिलधान्यान्नवस्त्राणां शय्यानामामिषस्य च।
संवत्सरार्धं कुर्वीत व्रतमेतत्समाहितः।।
क्षुद्रान्पशूंश्चापहृत्य प्राजापत्यं समाचरेत्।
गुडकार्पासधान्यानि सर्पिर्लवणमेव च।।

---

392. मिता० on याज्ञ०, III. 243.

393. विश्वरूप on या०, III.262; मिता० on याज्ञ०, III.264 where it is ascribed to both शङ्ख and प्रचेतस्. हरदत्त on गौ० ध० सू० 22.18 does the same; अपरार्क reads गा अनुतिष्ठेद्गोष्ठे वसेद्गोप्रदानं च.

394. अपरार्क (या०, 3-264-65; on 3.288 the half verse पादं तु शूद्रहत्यायां occurs); मिता० has the half verse पादस्तु . . . क्यागमने तथा; शङ्खस्मृति, 17.9 for first verse.

395. अपरार्क (या०, 3.264-65); शङ्ख (17.13-16) has all verses except the last.

396. **शङ्खः** — ब्राह्मणोच्छिष्टाशने महाव्याहृतिभिरभिमन्त्र्यापः पिबेत् क्षत्रियोच्छिष्टाशने ब्राह्मीरसविपक्वेन त्र्यहं क्षीरेण वर्तयेत्। वैश्योच्छिष्टाशने त्रिरात्रोपोषितो ब्राह्मीं सुवर्चलां पिबेत्। शूद्रोच्छिष्टभोजने षड्रात्रमभोजनम्।

397. **शङ्खः** — परिवित्तिः परिवेत्ता च संवत्सरं ब्राह्मणगृहेषु भैक्षं चरेयाताम्। ज्येष्ठभार्यामनियुक्तो गच्छंस्तदेव कनिष्ठभार्यां च।

398. **शङ्खः** — परिवित्तिः परिवेत्ता च यया च परिविद्यते।
व्रतं संवत्सरं कुर्युर्दातृयाजकपञ्चमाः।।

399. **शङ्खः** — वैश्यायामवकीर्णः संवत्सरं ब्रह्मचर्यं त्रिषवणं चानुतिष्ठेत्। क्षत्रियायां द्वे वर्षे त्रीणि ब्राह्मण्यां वैश्यावत् शूद्रायां ब्राह्मणपरिणीतायाम्।

400. **शङ्खलिखितौ:** — गुप्तायां वैश्यायामवकीर्णः संवत्सरं त्रिषवर्णमनुतिष्ठेत्। क्षत्रियायां तु द्वे वर्षे ब्राह्मण्या त्रीणि वर्षाणि।

401. **शङ्खः** — स्वैरिण्यां वृषल्यामवकीर्णः सचैलस्नात उदकुम्भं दद्याद्ब्राह्मणाय वैश्यायां च चतुर्थकालाहारो ब्राह्मणान्भोजयेद्यवसभारं च गोभ्यो दद्यात्। क्षत्रियायां त्रिरात्रोपोषितो घृतपात्रं दद्यात्। ब्राह्मण्यां षड्रात्रोपोषितो गां दद्याद्गोष्ववकीर्णः प्राजापत्यं चरेत्। अनूढायामवकीर्णः पलालभारं सीसमाषकं च दद्यात्।

402. **शङ्खलिखितौ:** — रजस्वलाबधूतादिगमने त्रिरात्रोपवासो घृतप्राशनं च कुर्यात्।

---

396. मिता० on या०, III, 290; परा० मा०, II.1, p. 395.

397. मिता० on या०, III.265 and on 288 (where we have the whole); अपरार्क has the first *sūtra*.

398. परा० मा०, II.1, p. 49; शङ्खस्मृति, 17.43-44.

399. विश्वरूप on या०, III.254; मिता० on याज्ञ०, III.265; अपरार्क reads व्रवर्णमनुतिष्ठेत्; म० पा०, 887; हरदत्त on गौ० ध० स०, 22.30.

400. मिता० on या०, III.280; विश्वरूप on या०, III.254 with variations.

401. मिता० on या०, III.265. The same is attributed to शङ्खलिखित on III.280 where we read षण्ढायामवकीर्णः for अनुढायामव० परा० मा०, II.1, p. 332, attributes to शङ्खलिखित and omits यवसभारं . . . दद्यात्, reads यवाढकं for घृतपात्रं, and ब्राह्मण्यांत्र्यहमुपोष्य घृतपात्रं दद्यात्।

402. परा० मा०, II.1, p. 337.

403. **शङ्खः** — नास्तिको नास्तिकवृत्तिः कृतघ्नः कूटव्यवहारी मिथ्याभिशंसी इत्येते पञ्चसंवत्सरं ब्राह्मणगृहे भैक्षं चरेयुः। संवत्सरं धौतं भैक्ष्यमश्नीयुः। षण्मासान् वा गा अनुगच्छेयुः।

404. **शङ्खलिखितौः** — नास्तिकः कृतघ्नः कूटव्यवहारी ब्राह्मणवृत्तिघ्नो मिथ्याभिशंसी चेत्येते षड्वर्षाणि ब्राह्मणगृहेषु भैक्षं चरेयुः संवत्सरं धौतभक्षमश्नीयुः षण्मासान्वा गा अनुगच्छेयुः।

405. **शङ्खः** — धारयित्वा तुलां वक्रां विषमं कारयन्वणिक्।
सुरालवणमद्यानां कृत्वा क्षीरस्य विक्रयम्।।
लाक्षायाश्चैव मांसस्य कुर्यादर्धं महाव्रतम्।
विक्रेता प्राणिनामब्दं तिलस्य च तथा चरेत्।।

406. **शङ्खः** — अग्न्युत्सादी संवत्सरं प्राजापत्यं चरेद्गां दद्यादिति।

407. **शङ्खः** — पशुवेश्याभिगमने प्राजापत्यम्।

408. **शङ्खः** — तिर्यग्योनिषु गोवर्जं सचैलं स्नात्वौषधिभारं दद्याद्गोभ्यः। गोष्ववकीर्णः संवत्सरं प्राजापत्यं चरेत्।

409. **शङ्खलिखितौः** — (a) क्षुद्रजन्तूनामनस्थ्नामनसः प्रमापणे शूद्रवयोस्थिमतो सहस्रं प्रमाप्य शूद्रवधः।

शङ्ख — (b) मारुताः पशवो याज्ञा दैवीश्च मरुतो विशः।
वैश्यहत्याव्रतं कुर्यादतस्तेषां प्रमापणे।।

---

403. मिता० on या०, III.279 has first *sūtra* only; परा० मा०, II.2, p. 151 reads कूटव्यवहारी ब्राह्मणवृत्तिघ्नः.

404. मिता० on या०, III.286.

405. अपरार्क (या०, 3.267-68).

406. मिता०; अपरार्क (या० III.289) reads चान्द्रायणं for प्राजापत्यं; म० पा०, 879; परा० मा०, II.2, p. 108 reads अभ्युत्साही; शङ्ख, 11.23.

407. हरदत्त on गौ० ध० सू०, 22.36.

408. अपरार्क (या०, 3.267-68); परा० मा०, II.1, p. 341, reads स्नातो यवसाहारं गोभ्यो दद्यात्.

409. (a) परा० मा०, II.1.85.
(b) विश्वरूप on या०, III.262.

410. **शङ्खः** — पशून्हत्वा तथा ग्राम्यान्मासं कुर्याद्विचक्षणः।
अदत्तानां तथा दाने तदर्धं तु विधीयते।।
हत्वा द्विजस्तथा सर्वं जलेशयबिलेशयम्।

411. **शङ्खः** — अध्यस्य शयनं यानमासनं पादुके तथा।
द्विजः पलाशवृक्षस्य त्रिरात्रं तु व्रती भवेत्।।
क्षत्रियस्तु रणे सृष्टं दत्वा प्राणपरायणः।
संवत्सरं व्रतं कुर्याच्छित्वा वृक्षं फलप्रदम्।।
द्वौ विप्रौ ब्राह्मणाग्नी वा दम्पती गोद्विजोत्तमौ।।
अन्तरेण यदा गच्छेत् कृच्छ्रं सान्तपनं चरेत्।।
होमकाले तथा दोहे स्वाध्याये दारसंग्रहे।।
अन्तरेण यदा गच्छेद्द्विजश्चान्द्रायणं चरेत्।।

412. **शङ्खः** — (a) नीलीकाष्ठक्षतो विप्रः शुना दष्टस्तथैव च।
त्रिरात्रं तु व्रतं कुर्यात्पुंश्चलीदशनक्षतः।।

(b) नरवायसखरवानरश्वपुंश्चलीभिर्दष्टः समुद्रगां नदीं गत्वा प्राणायामशतं कृत्वा घृतप्राशनेन शुध्यति।

413. **शङ्खः** — आक्रोशानृतवादेषु एकरात्रमुपवासः।

414. **शङ्खलिखितौः** — कृच्छ्राणि द्विजातीनामेव नावरस्य कामं धर्मेप्सोः प्रतिषेधः।

414a. **शङ्खः** — अत ऊर्ध्वमुपपतनीयानि। कन्यादूषी सोमविक्रयी वृषलीपतिः कौमारदारत्यागी असुरामद्यपायी गोघ्नः शूद्रवधी गुरोः प्रतिहन्ता नास्तिकः कृतघ्नः कूटव्यवहारी वृत्तिघ्नो मिथ्याभिशंसी हिरण्यस्तेनः

---

410. अपरार्क (या०, 3.275); शङ्खस्मृति, 17.10-11.

411. म० पा०, 959; the second verse occurs in अपरार्क (या०, III.276) who reads रणे नष्टः प्रौढः प्राण०.

412. (a) अपरार्क (या०, 3.277).
(b) विश्वरूप on या०, III.272.

413. अपरार्क (या०, 3.285); परा० मा०, II.1, p. 459 reads आक्रोशेनृतवादेवा . . . रात्रं त्रिरात्रमुप०.

414. म० रा०, 780,

414(a). विश्वरूप on या०, III.229-36.

पतितसंव्यवहारी मित्रध्रुक् शरणागतघाती प्रतिकूलवृत्तिरित्येतान्यष्टादशैवोपपातकानि।

415. **शङ्खः** — कन्यादोषी सोमविक्रयी च कृच्छ्रमब्भक्षं चरेयाताम्।

416. **शङ्खः** — देवगृहप्रतिश्रयोद्यानारामसभाप्रपातडागपुण्यसेतुमुतविक्रयं कृत्वा तप्तकृच्छ्रं चरेत्।

417. **शङ्खलिखितौः** — पद्म-बिल्व-पलाशोदुंबर-कुशोदकान्येकैकमभ्यस्तानि पर्णकृच्छ्रः। समस्तान्येतानि त्रिरात्रेण पर्युक्तानि पर्णकूर्च इति।

418. **शङ्खः** — लशुनपलाण्डुगृञ्जनछत्राकनालिङ्कविड्वराहग्रामकुक्कुटनखरोममांसभक्षणे चान्द्रायणं कुर्यात्।

माहिष्यं गव्यमाजं च भक्ष्यं क्षीरेषु निर्दिशेत्।
भुक्त्वा परस्य तु क्षीरं मासं कुर्यात् व्रतं बुधः।।
अनिर्दशाहं गोक्षीरं माहिषं चाजमेव च।
गोश्च क्षीरं विवत्सायाः संधिन्याश्च तथा पयः।।
संधिन्यमेध्यभक्षाया भुक्त्वा पक्षव्रतं चरेत्।
क्षीराणि यान्यभक्षाणि तद्विकाराशने बुधः।।
सप्तरात्रं व्रतं कुर्याद्यदेतत्परिकीर्तितम्।

419. **शङ्खलिखितौः** — शृगालकुक्कुटदंष्ट्रिक्रव्यादवानरखरोष्ट्रगजवाजिविड्वराहगोमानुषमांसभक्षणे चान्द्रायणम्।

420. **शङ्खः** — भुक्त्वा चोभयतोदन्तांस्तथा चैकशफानपि।
औष्ट्रं गव्यं तथा जग्ध्वा षण्मासान् व्रतमाचरेत्।।

---

415. मिता० on या०, III.289; अपकरो reads कन्यादूषी and कृच्छ्रमंब्दम्.

416. मिता० on याज्ञ०, III.288.

417. म० पा०, 733.

418. मिता० has last three lines with slight variations; हरदत्त on गौ० ध०-सू०, 23.25; अपरार्क (या० 3.289); स्मृतिच० (III, p. 423) has the last verse; *vide* शङ्खस्मृति, 17, 29-30 for last two.

419. परा० मा०, II.1.368.

420. मिता० on या०, III.290.

421. **शङ्खः** — लशुनपलाण्डगृञ्जनविड्वराहग्रामकुक्कुटकुम्भीकभक्षणे द्वादशरात्रं पयः पिबेत्।

422. **शङ्खः** — मद्यभाण्डस्थितं तोयं पीत्वा सप्तरात्रं गोमूत्रं यावकं पीबेत्।

423. **शङ्खः** — बकबलाकाहंसप्लवचक्रवाककारण्डवगृहचटककपोतपारावतपाण्डुशुकसारिकारसटिष्टिभोलूकङ्करक्तपादचाषभासवायसकोकिलशाड्वलिकुक्कुटहारीतभक्षणे द्वादशरात्रमनाहारः पिबेद्गोमूत्रयावकम्।

424. **शङ्खः** — सर्वासां द्विस्तनीनां क्षीरसमोज्यमजावर्जम्।
क्षीराणि यान्यभक्ष्याणि तद्विकाराशने बुधः।
सप्तरात्रं व्रतं कुर्यात्प्रयत्नेन समाहितः।।

425. **शङ्खलिखितौः** — सर्वासां द्विस्तनीनां क्षीरप्राशनेऽजावर्जमेतदेव। (षड्रात्रमभोजनं चान्द्रायणं च)

426. **शङ्खः** — अपः सुराभाजनस्थाः पीत्वा पक्षं व्रती भवेत्।
मद्यभाण्डस्थिताः पीत्वा सप्तरात्रं व्रती भवेत्।।
पीतावशेषितं पीत्वा पानीयं ब्राह्मणः क्वचित्।
त्रिरात्रं त व्रतं कृर्याद् वामहस्तेन वा पुनः।।
मद्गुहंसं बकं काकं कोकिलं खञ्जरीटकम्।
मत्स्यादाश्च तथा मत्स्यान् बलाकाः शुकशारिके।।
चक्रवाकं प्लवं चैव मण्डूकं भुजगं तथा।
मासमेकं व्रतं कुर्याद्भूयश्चैव न भक्षयेत्।।
जलेचरांश्च जलजान्प्रतुदान्नखविष्किरान्।
रक्तपादाञ्जालपादान्सप्तरात्रं व्रतं चरेत्।।

---

421. मिता० on या०, I.176; अपरार्क; स्मृतिच० (III, p. 457) has the words from विड्वराह०; compare मनु, 5.14.

422. मिता० on या०, III, 255.

423. मिता० on या०, I.175; परा० मा०, II.1, p. 406 reads चक्रवाकखअरीटकाककारण्डवकटमारकचटकगृहकपोतशुक० रक्तपादजलपादभाष०, भासमदुशिशुमारनक्रमकरनिमितिर्मिगिलनकुलविडालसर्पमण्डूकमूषकवाल्मीकादिमांसभक्षणे द्वादशाहमनाहारः पिबेद्गा०.

424. अपरार्क (या०, 1.170); स्मृतिच० (III, p. 422) has the first line.

425. हरदत्त on गौ० ध०, 23.26.

426. अपरार्क (या०, 3.289); शङ्खस्मृति, 17.22-24 and 26 for last four.

427. **शङ्खः** — लोहितान्वृक्षनिर्यासान् व्रश्चनप्रभवांस्तथा।
भुक्त्वा ऋजीषपक्वं च त्रिरात्रं तु व्रती भवेत्।

428. **शङ्खः** — केवलानि च शुक्तानि तथा पर्युषितं च यत्।
ऋजीषपक्वं भुक्त्वा च त्रिरात्रं तु व्रती भवेत्।।

429. **शङ्खलिखितौः** — भुक्त्वा वार्धुषिकस्यान्नमवृत्तस्यासुतस्य च।
शूद्रस्य तु तथा भुक्त्वा त्रिरात्रं स्यादभोजनम्।।

430. **शङ्खः** — अमेध्यपतितचाण्डालपुल्कसरजस्वलावधूतकुणिकुष्ठिकुनखिंस-स्पृष्टानि भुक्त्वा कृच्छ्रं चरेत्।

431. **शङ्खः** — शुनोच्छिष्टं तु भुक्त्वान्नं मासमेकं व्रतं चरेत्।
काकोच्छिष्टं गवाघ्रातं भुक्त्वा पक्षं व्रती भवेत्।
दूषितं केशकीटैश्च मार्जारिर्दूषिकैस्तथा।
मक्षिकामष(श)कैश्चैव त्रिरात्रं तु व्रतं चरेत्।।
वृथाकृसरसंयावपायसापूपशष्कुलीः।
भुक्त्वा त्रिरात्रं कुर्वीत व्रतमेतत्समाहितः।।

432. **शङ्खः** — चान्द्रायणं नवश्राद्धे पराको मासिके स्मृतः।
पक्षत्रयोतिकृच्छ्रः स्यात्षण्मासे कृच्छ्र एव तु।।

आब्दिके पादकृच्छ्रः स्यादेकाहः पुनराब्दिके।
अत ऊर्ध्वं न दोषः स्याच्छङ्खस्य वचनं यथा।।

433. **शङ्खः** — त्रिरह्नि त्रिर्निशायां तु सवासा जलमाविशेत्।
एकवासा आर्द्रवासा वा लब्धाशीः स्थण्डिलेशयः।।

---

427. हरदत्त on गौ० ध० सू०, 23.26; शङ्ख, 17.31 for first half.

428. मिता० on या०, III.290.

429. परा० मा०, II.1, p. 379.

430. मि० on या०, III.290; अपरार्क; म० पा०, p. 934.

431. मिता० has the first verse; शङ्खस्मृति, 17. 44-46; अपरार्क (या०, 3.289); म० पा०, p. 934 for last.

432. मिता० on या०, III.290; अपरार्क; म० पा०, 942.

433. मिता० on या०, III.326.

434. **शङ्खः** — शूद्रान्नं ब्राह्मणो भुक्त्वा तथा रङ्गावतारिणः।
चिकित्सकस्य क्रूरस्य तथा स्त्रीशूद्रजीविनः।।

षण्ढस्य कुलटायाश्च तथा बन्धनरक्षिणः।
अभिशस्तस्य चोरस्य अवीरायाः स्त्रियास्तथा।।

चर्मकारस्य वैणस्य क्लीबस्य पतितस्य च।
कर्मारस्य तथा तक्ष्णो रजकस्य च वार्धुषेः।।

कदर्यस्य नृशंसस्य वेश्यायाः कितवस्य च।
गणान्नं गणिकान्नं च मृगजीविश्ववृत्तिनाम्।।
सैनिकान्नं सूतिकान्नं भुक्त्वा मासं व्रती भवेत्।

435. **शङ्खः** — अभिशस्तरजकपतितचाकिकतैलिकग्रामयाजकशूद्रसांवत्सरिक-
कुलिकसूवर्णकारचर्मकारकर्मारचित्रवृत्तिघोषकतन्तुवायरङ्गावतारिककूट-
मानकृच्छ्रौण्डिकवधजीविनृशंसात्मविक्रयिवार्धुषिक तारिक भगवृत्ति-
व्रात्यतस्करगणान्नभोजनेष्वतिकृच्छ्रं कुर्यात्।।

436. **शङ्खः** — शूद्रस्य सूतके भुक्त्वा षण्मासान्व्रतमाचरेत्।
वैश्यस्य तु तथा भुक्त्वा त्रीन्मासान् व्रतमाचरेत्।।
क्षत्रियस्य तथा भुक्त्वा द्वौ मासौ व्रतमाचरेत्।
ब्राह्मणस्य तथाशौचे भुक्त्वा मासं व्रती भवेत्।।

437. **शङ्खः** — दुःस्वप्नारिष्टदर्शनादौ घृतं सुवर्णं च दद्यात्।

438. **शङ्खः** — दिवा तु मैथुनं कृत्वा नग्नः स्नात्वा तथाम्भसि।
नग्नां परस्त्रियं दृष्ट्वा दिनमेकं व्रतं चरेत्।।

439. **शङ्खः** — अध्यास्य शयनं यानमासनं पादुके तथा।
पलाशस्य द्विजश्रेष्ठस्त्रिरात्रं तु व्रती भवेत्।।

---

434. परा० मा०, II.1, p. 384-85; शङ्ख, 17-36-39.

435. अपरार्क (या०, 3.289); परा० मा०, II.1, p. 385-386.

436. मिता० on या०, III.290; अपरार्क; शङ्ख, 17.39-41.

437. मिता० on या०, III.293.

438. अपरार्क (या०, 3.290); शङ्खस्मृति, 17.50.

439. अपरार्क (या०, 3.292); मिता० has the 1st, 3rd and 4th and last verses; *vide* शङ्ख, 17.48 for last.

क्षिप्त्वाऽग्नावशुचिद्रव्यं तदेवाम्भसि मानवः।
मासमेकं व्रतं कुर्यादुपाक्रुश्य तथा गुरुम्।।
द्वौ विप्रौ ब्राह्मणाग्नी च दंपती तौ द्विजोत्तमौ।
अन्तरेण यदा गच्छेत्कृच्छ्रं सान्तपनं चरेत्।।
होमकाले तथा दोहे स्वाध्याये दारसंग्रहे।
अन्तरेण यदा गच्छेद्विजश्चांद्रायणं चरेत्।।
दारान्नधनलाभानां बुद्ध्वा विघ्नं समाचरेत्।।
प्रत्येकं प्राकृतं कुर्याद्ब्रह्मचर्यं तु वार्षिकम्।।
पादप्रतापनं कृत्वा कृत्वा वह्निं तथाप्यधः।
कुशैः प्रमार्ज्य पादौ तु दिनमेकं भवेद् व्रती।।

440. **शङ्खः** — प्रेतस्य प्रैतकार्याणि अकृत्वा धनहारकः।
वर्णानां यद्वधे प्रोक्तं तदर्धं प्रयतश्चरेत्।।
अतिमानादतिक्रोधाद्भयादज्ञानतोऽपि वा।
तद्बध्नीयात्स्त्री पुमान्वा गतिर्येषां न विद्यते।।
पूयशोणितसंपूर्णे तमस्यन्धे सुदारुणे।
षष्टिं वर्षसहस्राणि नरकं पर्युपासते।।
गोभिर्हतं तथोद्बद्धं ब्राह्मणेन च घातितम्।
संस्पृशन्ति तु ये विप्रा अग्निदा गरदाश्च ये।।
अनुयातारोऽपि चान्ये ये चान्ये पाशछेदकाः।
सर्वे ते पापसंयुक्तास्तेषां वक्ष्यामि निष्कृतिम्।।
तप्तकृच्छ्रेण शुध्येत्तु कुर्याद्ब्राह्मणभोजनम्।
अनुडुत्सहितां गां च दद्याद्विप्राय दक्षिणाम्।।

441. **शङ्खः** — सुवर्णस्तेयकृद्विप्रो ब्रह्महा गुरुतल्पगः।
सुरापश्च विशुध्यन्ति लक्षजापान्न संशयः।।
हुता देवी विशेषेण सर्वकल्मषनाशिनी।
सर्वकामप्रदा देवी वरदा भक्तवत्सला।।
घृतयुक्तैस्तिलैर्वह्निं हुत्वा तु सुसमाहितः।।
पापात्मा लक्षहोमेन पातकेभ्यः प्रमुच्यते।
अभीष्टं लोकमाप्नोति तथा पापविवर्जितः।।

440. अपरार्क (या॰, 3.292); शङ्खस्मृति, 17.57 for first.

441. अपरार्क (या॰, 3.311); शङ्खस्मृति, II.5, 8, 11,12.

442. **शङ्खः** – स्वयं व्रतमभ्युपगम्य चीरवल्कलवासा अधःशायी।

443. **शङ्खः** – न्युप्य केशनखान्पूर्वं नद्यां स्नात्वा बहिर्निशि।
प्रत्येकं नियतं कालमात्मनो व्रतमादिशेत्।।

प्रायश्चित्तमुपसीनो वाग्यतस्त्रिरुपस्पृशेत्।
एकवासा आर्द्रवासा लघ्वाशी स्थण्डिलेशयः।।

स्थानं वीरासनं मौनं मौञ्जी दण्डकमण्डलू।
भैक्षचर्याऽग्निकार्यं च कूष्माण्डैर्जुहुयाद् घृतम्।।

तस्करश्वापदाकीर्णे बहुव्यालमृगे वने।
न व्रतं ब्राह्मणः कुर्यात्प्राणबाधाभयात्सदा।।

सर्वतो जीवितं रक्षेज्जीवन्पापं व्यपोहति।
व्रतैः कृच्छ्रैस्तथा दानैरित्याह भगवान्यमः।
शरीरं धर्मसंयुक्तं रक्षणीयं प्रयत्नतः।
शरीरात्स्रवते धर्मः पर्वतात्सलिलं यथा।।

444. **शङ्खः** – अभुक्त्वा प्रातराहारं ज्ञात्वा चास्य समाहितः।
सूर्याय देवताभ्यश्च निवेद्य व्रतमाचरेत्।।

अग्ने व्रतपते व्रतमालभे तत्ते प्रब्रवीमि तच्छकेयमेवं
वायो व्रतपते सूर्य व्रतपत इति व्रतमालभेत अग्न
व्रतपते व्रतमचारिषं तदशकं तत्ते प्रब्रूमस्तन्ते गोपाय।
एवं वायो व्रतपत इत्यादिना व्रतं विमुञ्चेत।

445. **शङ्खः** – एतदेव त्र्यहाभ्यहस्तं यतिसान्तपनं स्मृतम्।

446. **शङ्खः** – कृच्छ्रपादे वस्त्रदानं कृच्छ्रार्धे त्वर्धकाञ्चनम्।
पादम्बूने तु गां दद्यात् पूर्णे गोमिथुनं स्मृतम्।।

---

442. अपरार्क (या० स्मृ०, 3.300).

443. अपरार्क (या०, 312-13); म० पा०, p. 781 has the two verses तस्कर० and शरीरं; *vide* शङ्ख, 17.59-61 for last three.

444. अपरार्क (या०, 3.312-13). compare वसिष्ठध० for the मन्त्र 'अग्ने व्रतपते' *vide* वाज; सं०, I.5 and II.28.

445. मिता०; अपरार्क (या०, 3.314); म० पा०, p. 731.

446. परा० मा०, II.1, p. 265; शङ्ख, 18.29.

447. **शङ्खः** — देवगृहप्रतिश्रयोद्यानारामसभाप्रपातटाकपुण्यसेतुसुतविक्रयं कृत्वा तप्तकृच्छ्रं चरेत्।।

448. **शङ्खः** — बिसान्युदकसिद्धानि मासमश्नीत संयतः।
सकृद्वा सोदकं मासं कृच्छ्रो वारुण उच्यते।।

बिल्वैरामलकैर्वापि पद्माक्षैरथवा शुभैः।
मासेन लोके श्रीकृच्छ्रः कथ्यते द्विजसत्तमैः।।

गोपुरीषाद्यवान्नं च मासं नित्यं समाहितः।
व्रतं तु यावकं कुर्यात्सर्वपापानुत्तये।।

449. **शङ्खः** — अकामतस्तु यो विप्रश्चण्डालीं यदि गच्छति।
तप्तकृच्छ्रेण शुध्येत प्राजापत्यद्वयेन वा।।
कामतस्तु यदा विप्रश्चण्डालीं यदि सेवते।
चान्द्रायणेन शुध्येत प्राजापत्यद्वयेन य।।

450. **शङ्खलिखितौः** — क्रयविक्रयदुष्टभोजनप्रतिग्रहेष्वनादिष्टप्रायश्चित्तेषु सर्वेषु चान्द्रायणं प्राजापत्यं च।

451. **शङ्खः** — सर्वेषामवकृष्टानां वधे प्रत्येकं चान्द्रायणम्।

452. **शङ्खः** — आर्द्रामलकमात्रास्तु ग्रासा इन्दुव्रते स्थिताः।
तथैवाहुतयस्तत्र शौचार्थं चैव मृत्तिका।।

453. **शङ्खः** — एकवासो चरेद्भिक्षां स्नात्वा वासो न पीडयेत्।
गायत्र्या दशसाहस्रमाह्निकं जप उच्यते।।

---

447. परा० मा०, II.2, p. 131.

448. अपरार्क (या०, 3-322); म० पा०, p. 737 and p. 746 (last only); the last verse does not occur in अपरार्क; म० पा० reads विषान्यु० and सक्तुन्वा मोदकान्.

449. परा० मा०, II.1, p. 308.

450. परा० मा०, II.1, p. 461.

451. मिता० on या०, III.262; विश्वरूप on या०, III.258 reads सवषामन्योन्यापकृष्टवधे चान्द्रायणम्.

452. अपरार्क (या०,3.323); म० पा०, p. 742; अपरार्क reads ग्रासार्थे for शौचार्थम्.

453. म० पा०, 750.

454. **शङ्खः** — शतं जप्ता तु सावित्री महापातकनाशिनी।
सहस्रजप्ता तु तथा पातकेभ्यः प्रमोचिनी।।

दशसाहस्रजाप्येन सर्वकिल्बिषनाशिनी।
लक्षं जप्ता तु सा देवी महापातकनाशिनी।।

सुवर्णस्तेयकृद्विप्रो ब्रह्महा गुरुतल्पगः।
(सु!) परापश्च विशुध्यन्ति लक्षं जप्त्वा न संशयः।।

455. **शङ्खः** — तस्य गुरोर्बान्धवानां राज्ञश्च समक्षं दोषानभिख्याप्यानुभाष्य पुनः पुनराचारं लभस्वेति स यद्येवमप्यनवस्थितमतिः स्यात्ततोस्य पात्रं विपर्यस्येत्।

456. **शङ्खः** — ततोङ्गलिचतुष्केण स्पृशेन्मूर्धानमादितः।
तर्जन्यङ्गुष्ठयोगेन स्पृशेन्नेत्रद्वयं पृथक्।।

मध्यमानामिकाभ्यां तु स्पृशेन्नासापुटे क्रमात्।
अङ्गुष्ठेन कनीयस्याः कर्णौ संयोगतः स्पृशेत्।।
तर्जन्यङ्गुष्ठयोगेन नाभिं हृदितलं न्यसेत्।

457. **वृद्धशङ्खः** — तर्जन्यङ्गुष्ठयोगेन स्पृशेन्नासापुटद्वयम्।
मध्यमाङ्गुष्ठयोगेन संस्पृशेच्छ्रवणं ततः।।

अङ्गुष्ठस्थानामिकया योगेन श्रवणे स्पृशेत्।
कनिष्ठाङ्गुष्ठयोगेन स्पृशेत्सन्धिद्वयं (स्कन्धद्वयं!) नरः।।

नाभिं च हृदयं तद्वत् स्पृशेत्पाणितलेन तु।
संस्पृशेत्तु ततः शीर्षमयमाचमने विधिः।।

त्रिः प्राश्नीयाद् यदम्भस्तु प्रीतास्तेनास्य देवताः।
ब्रह्मा विष्णुश्च रुद्रश्च भवन्तीत्यनुशुश्रुम।।

गङ्गा च यमुना चैव प्रीयते परिमार्जनात्।

---

454. मिता० on या०, III.309; शङ्ख, 11.4-5 for first and last; वीर० (आह्निकप्रकाश, p. 312) has these and other verses from शङ्ख about गायत्रीजप and प्राणायाम.

455. मिता० on या०, III.295; compare गौ०, 20.2-7; मनु० XI.182-83.

456. स्मृतिच०, I, p. 98; चतुर्वर्ग०, Vol. III, part 1, p. 998 (with slight variations).

457. स्मृतिच०, I, p. 98 where immediately after the first three verses शङ्ख also is quoted in verse.

पादाभ्यां प्रीयते विष्णुर्ब्रह्मा शिरसि कीर्तितः।।

नासत्यदस्रौ प्रीयेते स्पृष्टौ नासापुटद्वये।
स्पृष्टे लोचनयुग्मे तु प्रीयेते शशिभास्करौ।।

कर्णयुग्मे तथास्पृष्टे प्रीयेते त्वनिलानिलौ।
स्कन्धयोः स्पर्शनादेवं प्रीयन्ते सर्वदेवताः।।

नाभिस्पर्शेन देवेशाः प्रीयन्ते चास्य नित्यशः।
संस्पृष्टे हृदये चास्य प्रीयन्ते सर्वदेवताः।।

मूर्ध्नि संस्पर्शनात्तस्य प्रीतस्तु पुरुषो भवेत्।
भूम्यम्बूत्सर्गतो गावो विष्टद्भिश्च चराचरम्।।

458. **बृहच्छंखः** – तर्जन्यङ्गुष्ठयोगेन स्पृशेन्नासापुटद्वयम्।
मध्यमाङ्गुष्ठयोगेन स्पृशेन्नेत्रद्वयं ततः।।

अङ्गुष्ठास्यानामिकाया योगेन श्रवणे स्पृशेत्।
कनिष्ठाङ्गुष्ठयोगेन स्पृशेत्स्कंधद्वयं ततः।।

नाभिं च हृदयं तद्वत्स्पृशेत्पाणितलेन तु।
संस्पृशेच्च तथा शीर्षमयमाचमने विधिः।।

459. **लिखितः** – उद्धृत्यपरीक्षिताभिरक्षाराभिरशृताभिरबुद्बुदभिरशूद्राशुद्ध्येकपाण्यावर्जिताभिराचामेत्।

460. **लिखितः** – यस्य चाग्नौ न क्रियते यस्य चान्नं न दीयते।
न तद्भोज्यं द्विजातीनां भुक्त्वा चोपवसेदहः।।

वृथा कृसरसंयावपायसापूपशष्कुलीः।
आहिताग्निर्द्विजो भुक्त्वा प्राजापत्यं समाचरेत्।।

461. **लिखितः** – भुक्त्वा वार्धुषिकस्यान्नमव्रतस्यासुतस्य च।
शूद्रस्य च तथा भुक्त्वा त्रिरात्रं स्यादभोजनम्।।

---

458. म० पा०, 54; चतुर्वर्ग०, vol. III, part 1, p. 999 attributes to वृद्धशङ्ख.

459. अपरार्क (या०, I.18); *vide* 56 above.

460. मिता० on या०, III.290; अपरार्क has the priest.

461. मिता० on या०, III.290; मद० पा०, p. 946 has the verse परवाक०.

परपाकनिवृत्तस्य परपाकरतस्य च।

अपचस्य तु भुक्त्वान्नं द्विजश्चान्द्रायणं चरेत्।
गृहीत्वाग्निं समारोप्य पञ्चयज्ञान्न निर्वपेत्।
परपाकनिवृत्तोसौ मुनिभिः परिकीर्तितः।।

पञ्च यज्ञांस्तु यः कृत्वा परान्नादुपजीवति।
सततं प्रातरुत्थाय परपाकरतस्तु सः।।
गृहस्थधर्मवृत्तौ यो ददाति परिवर्जितः।
ऋषिभिर्धर्मतत्त्वज्ञैरपचः संप्रकीर्तितः।।

462. **लिखितः** — छिद्राण्येतानि विप्राणां येनध्यायाः प्रकीर्तिताः।
छिद्रेभ्यः स्रवति ब्रह्म ब्राह्मणेन यदार्जितम्।
तत्काले तस्य रक्षांसि श्रियं ब्रह्म यशो बलम्।
सर्वमादाय गच्छन्ति वर्जयन्तीप्सितं फलम्।।

463. **लिखितः** — शुष्केणान्तर्जले चैव बहिरप्यार्द्रवाससा।
स्नानं दानं जपो होमो निष्फलं पितृतर्पणम्।।

---

462. स्मृतिच०, I, p. 61.

463. स्मृतिच०, I, p. 102; अपरार्क.

No. 110 is ascribed to लिखित and No. 56 also.

3

Asahāya, the Commentator of the Gautama-Dharmasūtra and the Nāradasmṛti

ASAHĀYA is one of those eminent and ancient commentators of the *Dharmaśāstra* whose works once famous are now not available. Dr. Jolly in his edition of *Nāradasmrti* (Bibliotheca Indica Series) has incorporated a portion of the *Bhāsya* of Asahāya as revised by Kalyāṇabhatta. Even this revised version extends only up to the middle of the fifth *adhyāya* of the *Nāradasmrti* The exact relation of Kalyāṇabhatta's labours to the original *bhāṣya* cannot be ascertained with precision from the words: *dṛṣtvāsahāyaracitam nāradabhāṣyaṁ kulekhakairbhrastam* I *kalyāṇena kriyate prāktanametadviśodhya punaḥ* I (first verse) and *iti asahāyanāradabhāṣye keśavabhaṭṭaprotsāhitakalyāṇabhaṭṭapariśo-dhita-vyavahāramātṛkāyāṁ prathamodhyāyaḥ* I (at the end of the first chapter of the Introduction). It is probable that Kalyāṇabhatta took very great liberties with the text of the *Bhāṣya* of Asahāya. On page 9, verse 15 *rājā satpurusah sabhyaḥ śāstram ganaka-lekhakau* the comment is *śāstraṁ manunāradaviśvarūpātmakam*. If this Viśvarūpa be the same as the commentator of the *Yājña-valkayasmṛti* (as is most likely), it is difficult to see how Asahāya could regard him as of almost equal authority with Manu and Nārada. Asahāya flourished earlier than Medhātithi, i.e., before AD 900 and was therefore either a contemporary of Viśvarūpa or even earlier than the latter. Viśvarūpa is another name of Sureśvarācārya, the famous pupil of the great Śaṅkarācārya. In the *Parāśara-Mādhava* (Vol. I, part I, page 57, Bombay Sanskrit Series) we read "*idam ca vākyaṁ* (viz. *āmre phalārthe nimitta* — *ĀpDhS*, I.7.20.3) *nityakarmaviṣayatvena vārtike viśvarūpācārya udājahāra āmre phalārthe ityādi hyāpastambasmrtervacah* I *phala-vattvaṁ samācaṣṭe nityānāmapi karmaṇām* I I"

The verse quoted occurs in the *Brhadāraṇyakopanisad-bhāṣya-vārtika* (I.I.97) of Sūreśvara. Therefore the *Parāśara-Mādhava* looked upon Viśvarūpa and Sūreśvara as indentical. In the *Purusārthaprabodha* of Brahmānanda-bhāratī composed in 1476 (probably of the Śaka era, MS. in the Bharu Daji collection in Bombay Royal Asiatic Society) we have the famous work *Niaskarmyasiddhi* ascribed to Viśvarūpa *ityevaṁ naiṣkarmyasiddhau brahmāṁśairbrahmavittamaiḥ* I *śrīmadbhirviśvarūpākhyairācāryaiḥ karunārnavaih* (folio 6). Therefore the reference to Viśvarūpa in the comment on the *Nāradasmṛti* is probably from the pen of Kalyānabhatta. The name of Kalyānabhaṭṭa is frequently quoted in the commentary itself (e.g., page 81 *tathā coktameva sāmānya-grāha-patra-laksanavicāraprakarane kalyānabhattena;* page 86, *yathoktaṁ trisastilekhya-prakaraṇa-kārakalyāna-bhaṭṭena;* page 89, *kalyāṇavaktaṁ ślokatrayamasti*), altogether it is difficult to separate Kalyanabhaṭṭa's handiwork from the original text of the *Bhāsya* of Asahāya.

The *Hāralatā* (B.I. edn.) of Aniruddha gives us the interesting information that Asahāya wrote a *bhāṣya* on the *Gautama-Dharmasūtra*. *gautamaḥ bāladeśāntaritapravrajitānāṁ sapindānāṁ sadayaḥ śaucam* (*GDhS*, 14.44) I *yatra mrto'śaucābhyantare na śrūyate taddeśāntaram tatra mṛto deśāntarita iti gautamabhāṣya-kṛtā'sahāyena vyākhyātam* I (*Hāralatā*, p. 35). In another place the *Hāralatā* quotes the *Gautama-Dharmasūtra* and the comment of Asahāya thereon, but expresses its disapproval of the views of Asahāya *gautamaḥ — pindanivṛttiḥ saptame pañcame vā* (*GDhS*, 14.12) *atrāsahāyavyākhyā-yadā pitrpitāmahaprapitāmahāstrayo jīvanti tadā prapitāmahādūrdhvaṁ tribhyaḥ pindadānam* I . . . *idaṁ tu vyākhyānam na śobhanaṁ pratibhāti* I (*Hāralata*, page 97)." These quotations make it clear that the author of the *Hāralatā* had the *bhāṣya* of Asahāya on the *Gautama-Dharmasūtra* before him. Aniruddha, the author of the *Hāralatā*, was the *guru* of Ballāla Sena of Bengal who commenced his work called *Adbhutasāgara* in Śaka 1090, i.e., AD 1168.

It appears that Asahāya wrote a commentary also on the *Manusmṛti*. In the *Sarasvatīvilāsa* (Foulke's edition) we read: *dharmavibhāgo manu-yājñavalkyādi-smṛtikārānāṁ tatsmṛti-vyākhyātṝnāmasahāya-medhātithi-vijñāneśvarāparārkāṇām nibandhṝṇāṁ candrikākārānāṁ ca saṁmata eva* (sec. 33). Here it will be noted that the order in which the four commentators are named requires that Asahāya was cited as a commentator of Manu. This conclusion is further corroborated by the fact that the *Vivādaratnākara* quotes with reference to the verse of Manu (9. 182, *bhrātṝṇāmekajātānāmekaścetputravānbhavet* I) the words of Asahāya *atra asahāyenoktaṁ puṁsāṁ sati brātṛje strīṇāṁ sapatnīputre ksetrajādayaḥ pratinidhayo na kartavyā iti* (page 583).

The foregoing discussion establishes that Asahāya composed *bhāsyas* on three of the most prominent works on *Dharmaśāstra*, viz the *Gautama-Dharmasūtra*, the *Manusmṛti* and the *Nāradasmrti*. It is a matter of profound regret that the commentaries of such an ancient writer upon these works that are of paramount authority in matters of law and usage should be lost to us. Great efforts must be made by those engaged in the search for Mss. to find out the lost works of Asahāya.

A few words may be said about the date of Asahāya. The Mitākṣarā while commenting upon Yājñavalkya (II.124 *bhaginyaśca nijādaṁśāddatvāṁśaṁ tu turīyakam*) quotes the views of Asahāya and Medhātithi and opposes them to those of Bhāruci and approves the views of Asahāya. *ato'sahāya-medhātithi-prabhṛtīnāṁ vyākhyānameva caturasraṁ na bhāruceḥ*. It is to be noted that some Mss. read *asmatsahāya*. This is due to the fact that the very name of Asahāya had been forgotten. It is curious that the Bālalambhattī explains the word *asahāya* as an attribute of Medhātithi and takes it in the sense of 'peerless'. Of all works on *Vyavahāra*, the *Sarasvatīvilāsa* quotes Asahāya most frequently. This shows that in the fifteenth or sixteenth century his works had not been lost altogether. Dr. Jolly expressed it as his opinion that Asahāya lived earlier than Medhātithi (*Tagore Law Lectures*, p. 5; ***vide*** *Sacred Books of the East*, Vol. 25, page VII also). His main reason was that both Vijñāneśvara and the *Sarasvatīvilāsa* place him before Medhātithi whenever authorities on topics of *Vyavahāra* are enumerated. Dr. Jolly does not appear to have been aware that Medhātithi actually mentions Asahāya by name in his *bhāṣya* on Manu (VIII.155 *adarśayitvā tatraiva* etc.'). Medhātithi flourished about AD 900, as he mentions Kumārila by name and appears to refer to the *bhāṣya* of Śaṅkarācārya on *Chāndogya Upaniṣad*, II.23.4 (on Manu II.83) and as he is regarded as an authority by the Mitāksarā (latter half of 11th century). Therefore Asahāya must have flourished before AD 850. How much earlier Asahāya lived it is difficult to say.

Some of the doctrines associated with the name of Asahāya may be stated here. It has been already shown above that Vijñāneśvara followed the views of Asahāya on the question of the right of sisters when their brothers separated. The *Vivādaratnākara* (p. 578) quotes the Prakāśa as referring to the views of Asahāya on the verse of Manu (9.198) *striyāstu yadbhavedavittaṁ pitrā dattaṁ kathaṁcan* |) that the special rule of succession laid down by Manu applies to all the *strīdhana* of a woman belonging to the kṣatriya or lower castes who has a co-wife of the brāhmaṇa caste, *pitrā dattamiti strīdhanamātro-palaksanamiti asahāya-medhātithiriti* (? *thī iti*) *prakāśakāraḥ* | The *Sarasvatīvilāsa* notes that Asahāya defined *dāya* in the same way as Vijñāneśvara did later on *asahāyavijñanayogiprabhṛtīnāṁ yatsvāmisambandhādeva nimittādanyasya svaṁ bhavati tddāya-śabdenocyata iti* | *tanna sahante bhārucyaparārkaprabhrtayah* (sec. 19). Asahāya seems to have held that as regards the succession to the *śulka* of a woman even step-brothers should be given something, though the major portion would go to full brothers *ataśca kanyāśulkavisaye sodarāsodaravibhāge'sodarānāmapi kiñcid deyamiti asahāya-vyākhyānamasahāyam*' (sec. 314). On the words of Yājñavalkya *bhaginyaśca nijādaṁśāddatvāṁśaṁ tu turīyakam* the *Sarasvatīvilāsa* tells us that the views of Asahāya, Medhātithi and Vijñāneśvara coincide (sec. 131 *etañca sarvamasahāya-medhātithivijñānayogipradīpikākārādīnāṁ mata eva*). According to Asahāya, the wealth of a childless brāhmana went to the teacher even before a fellow-student, then to the teacher's son and so on (*Sarasvatīvilāsa* sec. 608 *asahāyādayastu yonisambandhān-antaraṁ vidyāsambandhavaśādācāryagāmi tvetadaghnaṁ tadabhāve tatputragāmi tadabhāve tatpatnigāmi* etc.) It is worthy of note that in section 195 we have order *vijñāneśvarāsahāya-medhātithīnāmiyaṁ vyakhyā* I

[This paper is originally published in *JBORS*, Vol. VIII-II (pp. 120-24), 1922, Dr. P.V. Kane in his *History of Dharmaśāstra*, Vol. I/I, pp. 548-49 adds that Asahāya also seems to have written a Commentary on the *Manu-Smṛti*, as is evident from the *Sarasvatīvilāsa*, p. 465 and the *Vivādaratnākara*, p. 583. This text also indicates that Dr. Kane has made significant addition on this paper published in 1922] ***S.G. Moghe***

4

The Tantravārtika and the Dharmaśāstra Literature

THE *Tantravārtika* of the great *Mīmāṁsaka* Kumārilabhaṭṭa is, apart from its depth, subtlety and abstruseness, replete with information on various topics. Among other subjects it sheds a flood of light on the ancient *Dharmaśāstra* literature. As it is now generally agreed that Kumārilabhaṭṭa flourished about the middle of the eighth century AD,[1] the incidental notices of the *Dharmaśāstra* literature contained in the *Tantravārtika* are of great value for the understanding of the development and chronology of that literature. In the following pages an attempt is made to bring together important passages bearing on that literature contained in the *Tantravārtika*.

In considering the question how far certain practices like the *Holākā* festival are restricted to the eastern people or are prescribed for all Āryas, Kumārila starts the discussion whether the *Gṛhyasūtras* and the *Dharmasūtras*, like those of Gautama, are restricted as authoritative to particular Vedic schools or have authority in all schools.[2] Then he makes the following interesting observations — "The *Dharmaśāstras* of Gautama, Vasiṣṭha, Śaṅkha-Likhita, Hārīta, Āpastamba, Baudhāyana and others — which stand apart from the *Purāṇas*, the work of Manu (the *Manusmṛti*) and *Itihāsa* (i.e., the *Mahābhārata*)[3] — and the *Gṛhya* works are seen to be separately studied in distinct *caraṇas* (Vedic schools), as is the case with the

Prātiśākhyas. For example, the works of Gautama and Gobhila are accepted (i.e., studied) by the *Chandogas* (*Sāmavedins*); the Vasiṣṭha by the *Bahvṛcas* (*Ṛgvedins*); and the work of Śaṅkha-Likhita by the Vājasaneyins only; and the works of Āpastamba and Baudhāyana by the *Taittirīyas* only. In the same way, after exhibiting how the *Gṛhya* works are restricted as regards their study to separate (*caraṇas*) the following matter should be considered, viz. whether these works are authoritative (respectively) only in those *caraṇas* or whether all are authoritative in all schools."[4] The *siddhānta* view is that all are authoritative in all schools. It is to be noted that in the above passage, Kumārila mentions by name six *Dharmasūtras*. Out of these the *Dharmasūtras* of Gautama, Vasiṣṭha, Āpastamba and Baudhāyana have been already published. A Ms. of Hārīta's *Sūtra* has been found. The *Sūtra* of Śaṅkha-Likhita is yet to come to light."[4a]

Among the *Dharmasūtras* Kumārila quotes the work of Gautama more frequently than any other. In some cases Gautama is mentioned by name; in other cases his work is quoted simply as *Smṛti* or he is referred to as *Smṛtikāra*. There are at least a dozen quotations taken from the *Dharmasūtra* of Gautama. In one place Gautama is spoken of as Gautamācārya.[5] In another place it is said that practices opposed to Vedic tradition are declared by Gautama not to be binding.[6] As contrasted with the tenets of the Bauddhas, Gautama is said to be based on *Veda*.[7] Gautama allows a person to practise the vow of 'studenthood' either for twelve years or for 24, 36, or 48 years.[8] Two *Sūtras* of Gautama are quoted with slight variations.[9]

The *Sūtras* mentioned in the footnote below are quoted as *Smṛti*.[10] Some *Sūtras* are styled simply as *vacana* or *āgama*.[11] In a few places, though there is no *Sūtra* actually quoted, it appears as if the author has in mind the words of Gautama.[12] In one place Kumārila seems to be referring to an ancient reading of the *Dharmasūtra* of Gautama.[13]

The *Dharmasūtra* of Āpastamba is referred to in a few cases.

"Āpastamba has laid down that certain practices are allowed in certain countries, though they are prohibited in others."[14] In another place it is said that if a doubt arises, on account of the words of the *Āpastamba-Smṛti*, that the absolute prohibition of drinking (in some *Smrtis*) is counterbalanced, that doubt is removed by the direct Vedic injunction "therefore a brāhmana does not (should not) drink liquor." This seems to be a reference to the words of the *Dharmasūtra* of Āpastamba laying down that "one who drinks liquor should (by way of punishment) drink wine as hot as fire".[15]

The *Dharmasūtra* of Baudhāyana is referred to in one place as being in conflict with the words of Āpastamba. Āpastamba allowed certain practices in certain localities though they were opposed to Vedic tradition and declared that they were sinful in other countries.[16] This dictum of Āpastamba is refuted by Baudhāyana who cites only examples of sinful practices opposed to *Smṛti.*[17] Baudhāyana seems to be quoted in yet another place.[18]

There is in the present work at least one quotation from Śaṅkha-Likhita.[19] It is cited for showing that the word *āmnāya* is applied to *Smṛti* works also. It is noteworthy that the words quoted are not in prose but are a line of an *anustubh* stanza.

Quotations from other *Dharmasūtras* could not be identified, if they exist at all in the *Tantravārtika. Dharmasūtras* are said in one place to give instructions about the duties of the castes and estates and that, as the *dharmas* are mostly uniform, the *Dharmasūtras* agree with one another[20] and are called *Smṛti* equally with *Aṅgas*. The *dharmasūtrakāras* are also referred to in another place on the binding character of usages.[21]

The *Tantravārtika* stands in a special relation to the *Manusmṛti*. Whenever Kumārila speaks of *Smrtis*, that of Manu is uppermost in his mind.[22] He quotes it or refers to it even before the *Gautamadharmasūtra*.[23] He often refers to the *Manusmrti* as *Mānava*,[24] which latter word is found very often in the *Dharmasūtra* of Vasistha.[25] Over at least twenty verses are wholly or partly quoted from the extant *Manusmṛti.* The quotations are scattered over all the chapters from the first to the last.[26] In some cases the verses of Manu are not actually quoted though they are referred to in such a way that identification is quite easy.[27] A few verses or parts of verses quoted in the *Tantravārtika* as Manu's have not been traced.[28] It is remarkable that a verse which is treated in the editions of the *Manusmṛti* as interpolated, because it has not been commented upon by commentators like Medhātithi and Kullūka, is quoted in the *Tantravārtika.*[29] The text of Manu that Kumārila had before him was essentially the same as that we now have, and the *Manusmṛti* was, according to him, the highest authority on matters of *dharma.* It is not probable that this position could have been attained by the *Manusmṛti* in a century or two. Therefore the extant *Manusmṛti* must be several centuries older than AD 750. Modern scholars detect earlier and later portions in the *Manusmṛti.* Kumārila looks upon all parts of the extant *Smṛti* as equally authoritative. If we have to postulate two redactions of the *Manusmṛti*, then the earlier one, out of which the extant *Smṛti* could be said to have grown, must be placed centuries earlier than the date to which the extant *Manusmṛti* can be assigned. This conclusion is immensely strengthened by the fact that Śabarasvāmin, the ancient commentator of *Jaimini's Sūtras,* seems to have looked upon the extant *Manusmṛti* as an authoritative *Smṛti.* For example, in his *bhāsya* on the *Pūrvamīmāṁsā* (VI. 1.12) he says[30] "whatever is acquired by her (scil. the wife) in another manner must become the property of her husband and (an author of a *Smṛti*) declares, 'the wife, the slave and the son are all without wealth', etc." In another place he says "Manu and others have given directions." This is not the place to discuss the date of Śabara. But from his archaic style and from the relation in which he stands to Kumārila, it may be said that he is certainly not later than AD 500 and may be earlier by a few centuries.

Kumārila starts an extremely interesting discussion about *sadācāra.*[31] He quotes the *Sūtra* of Gautama (I.3) "transgression of *dharma* and also rashness are seen among the great" and then observes that many high personages such as Prajāpati, Indra, Vasiṣṭha, Viśvāmitra, Yudhisthira, Krsna-dvaipāyana, Bhīṣma, Dhṛtarāṣṭra, Vāsudeva and Arjuna were guilty of transgressing the Law and even people of his time do the same. He then sets out in detail how these high personages of old transgressed the Law and tries to explain away most of the transgressions. Some of his explanations are quite after the manner of modern scholars of comparative mythology. The charge brought against Kṛṣṇa-dvaipāyana is that, being a 'perpetual student', he produced offspring on the wives of Vicitravīrya. This is explained away on the ground that he was ordered to do so by the elders as also on the ground of his great *tapas*. Vāsudeva and Arjuna are blamed for having married Rukmiṇī and Subhadrā, who were respectively their maternal uncle's daughters, and for drinking *surā* (liquor).[32] As to the charge of drinking *surā* the answer is that *surā* which was produced by fermentation, etc., from food was forbidden to the three higher castes, but *madhu* (mead) and *sīdhu* (rum) were not forbidden to kṣatriyas and vaiśyas, and that as Vāsudeva and Arjuna were kṣatriyas and had only taken *madhu*, there is nothing wrong in their conduct.[33] As to the charge of marrying one's maternal uncle's daughter, the explanation is that in common parlance one's maternal aunt's son is also called brother and hence Subhadrā, though described as the sister of Vāsudeva, must have been the maternal aunt's daughter or the daughter of Kṛṣṇa's mother's paternal aunt's daughter (and so there is nothing wrong in Arjuna's marrying Subhadrā).[34] As to Vāsudeva's marriage with Rukmiṇī the reply is — "How can he who was an exemplar (lit. mirror) to all the worlds and who said elsewhere (in the *Bhagavadgītā,* III.21 and VI.11) "whatever a great man does, other people do the same; people follow what he looks upon as authoritative; and men in every way would follow in my path, — set up a practice that is forbidden?"

Kumārila then says that even in his day brāhmaṇa women of Ahicchatra and Mathurā drank *surā* (fermented liquor), that northern people gifted away, accepted and sold horses, mules, asses and animals with two rows of teeth and took food in the same plate with their wives, children and friends; while southern people married maternal uncle's daughter and took food seated on chairs and that both partook of food left or touched by friends and relatives, ate betel (*tāmbūla*) that had come in contact with men of all castes, did not ceremonially rinse the mouth after eating betel, put on clothes brought on the backs of asses and washed by washermen and did not stop intercourse with those who committed the great sins except brāhmana murder.[35]

It has been said above (note 4) that Kumārilabhaṭṭa looked upon *Purāṇa*s as authoritative works in the department of *Dharma*. The *Purāṇa*s he means are not those ancient works to which reference is made even in the *Upaniṣads*.[36] His remarks in other places show that he refers to the *Purāṇa*s that are now extant. In one place, among the topics of *Purāṇa*s he enumerates the divisions of the earth, the lineage of royal and other families, the measures of time and distance, and future history.[37] In another place he quotes a verse which occurs both in the *Viṣṇu Purāna* and the *Mārkandeya Purāṇa*.[38] He says that according to some by *svarga* is meant the top of Meru as established by reasoning in the *Itihāsa* (i.e., the *Mahābhārata*) and the *Purāṇas*.[39] In another place we are told that the *Purāṇa*s speak of the Bauddhas and others who will bring about the confusion of *Dharma* in the *Kali* age.[40] Thus it is beyond doubt that at least some of the extant *Purāṇas* existed in his day and were looked upon by him as authoritative in the province of *Dharma* equally with the *Smrti*s of Manu, Gautama and others. This irresistibly leads to the conclusion that some of the extant *Purāṇa*s were composed several centuries before AD 750.

The foregoing will, it is hoped, give some idea as to how a close study of the *Tantravārtika* will yield valuable results for the history of the *Dharmaśāstra* literature.

References

[This paper is originally published in *JBBRAS* (New Series) 1925, pp. 95-102] ***S.G. Moghe***

1. ***Vide*** Pathak, *JBBRAS*, 18, 217.
2. p. 179: देशधर्मानुदाहृत्य संप्रत्येतद्विचार्यते। किं व्यवस्थितमूलास्ते किं वैषां सर्वधर्मता।। . . . आद्यं सूत्रद्वयं यावदिदमप्यत्र चिन्त्यताम्। गृह्यगौतमसूत्रादिव्यवस्थासर्वगामिते।।
3. The idea is that the *Purāṇas*, the *Manusmṛti* and the *Mahābhārata* are *Dharmaśāstras*, but they are not, by their very form, restricted to any particular school as the works of Gautama and others were.
4. p. 179: पुराणमानवेतिहासव्यतिरक्तगौतमवसिष्ठशङ्खलिखितहारीतापस्तम्बबौधायनादिप्रणीतधर्मशास्त्राणां गृह्यग्रन्थानां च प्रातिशाख्यलक्षणवत्प्रतिचरणं पाठव्यवस्थोपलभ्यते। तद्यथा। गौतमीयगौभिलीये छन्दोगैरेव च परिगृहीते। वसिष्ठं बह्वृचैरेव शङ्खलिखितोक्तं च वाजसनेयिभिः। आपस्तम्बबौधायनीये तैत्तिरीयैरवं प्रतिपन्ने। इत्येवं तत्र तत्र गृह्यव्यवस्थाभ्युपगमादि दर्शयित्वा विचारयितव्यम्। किं तानि तेषामेव प्रमाणानि उत सर्वाणि सर्वेषामिति।

4a. ***See also*** the 'Sūtra of Śaṅkha-Likhita' restored by Dr. P.V. Kane and published in this volume, pp. 13 to 90.

5. p. 106: यथा च ततः शेषेण विशिष्टदेशजात्यादिमन्तो जन्म प्रतिपद्यन्ते इति स्वर्गफलकर्मणो निःशेषोपयोगादन्यफलस्य चान्यत्र व्यापारासंभवात्ततोन्येनेति वक्तव्ये ततः शेषेणेति गौतमाचार्येणोक्तम्। This is *Gautama DhS*, XI.29 (Ānandāśrama edn.).
6. p. 138: ननु गौतमेनाम्नायविरुद्धानामाचाराणामप्रामाण्यमुक्तम्। This refers to *Gautama DhS*, XI.20. This latter is quoted on p. 130 as the dictum of a *smṛtikāra*.
7. p. 117: न च तैर्वेदमूलत्वमुच्यते गौतमादिवत्।
8. p. 112: गौतमेनापि द्वादशवर्षाण्येकवेदब्रह्मचर्यं चरेदिति प्रथमकल्पमाशु गार्हस्थ्यप्रतिपत्त्यर्थमुक्त्वा द्वितीये कल्पे 'द्वादश प्रतिवेदं वा सर्वेषु' इत्यष्टाचत्वारिंशत्परिग्रह कृतः। This refers to *Gautama DhS*, II. 51-52.
9. p. 109: तथा गौतमेनाप्युक्तम् 'राज्ञांच कार्याविघातार्थं ब्राह्मणानां च स्वाध्यायानिवृत्त्यर्थम्'। ***Vide*** *Gautama DhS*, XIV.42-43.
10. *Gautama DhS*, XVI.43 (on p. 130); IX.4 (on p. 993); VIII.21 (on p. 1117); I.2 (on p. 143).
11. p. 136: मद्यं नित्यं ब्राह्मणस्येति वचनात्। This is *Gautama DhS*, II.25, where we read ब्राह्मणः; — द्वैपायनस्यापि गुरुनियोगात् 'अपतिरपत्यलिप्सुर्देवरादुस्प्रेरितादृतुमतीयादित्येवमागमात्'। p. 134 (***vide*** *Gautama DhS*, XVIII.4-5).
12. p. 142: नन्वेवं सति ब्राह्मणस्त्रीवधेपि पुंब्राह्मणवद् ब्रह्महत्यास्तीति यदात्रेय्यामेव केवलायां भ्रूणहत्याप्रायश्चित्तविधानं तन्नोपपद्यते। ***Vide*** *Gautama DhS*, XXII.12 or *ĀpDhS*, I.9.24.9.

13. p. 99: नन्वमेध्येन लिप्तस्य सा शुद्धिरभिधीयते। न लिप्तग्रहणं तत्र पाठेस्ति तु चिरन्तने।। अमेध्यस्यैवं यस्मात्पठन्ति। *Vide Gautama DhS*, I. 45.
14. p. 138: सर्वेषामेवमादीनां प्रतिदेशं व्यवस्थया। आपस्तम्बेन संहृत्य दुष्टादुष्टत्वमाश्रितम्।। This probably refers to *ĀpDhS*, II.6.15.1 or II.11.29.15.
15. *ĀpDhS*, I.9.25.3: सुरापोग्निस्पर्शां सुरां पिबेत्।
16. *Vide* note 14 above.
17. p. 139: आपस्तम्बवचनं तु बौधायनेन स्मृतिविरुद्धदुष्टाचारोदाहरणान्येव प्रयच्छता निराकृतम्। This refers to *BaudhāyanaDhS*, I.1.19-24 (Mysore edn.).
18. p. 993: तथा च स्मृतिः। न जीर्णमलद्वासाः स्यात् धारयेद्वैणवं दण्डं शुभे रौक्मे च कुण्डले। इत्यादि सूपपत्स्यते। Here the words धारये . . . कुण्डले seem to be an echo of *BaudhāyanaDhS*, II.3.28. Compare *Manu*, IV.34 and 36.
19. p. 139: स्मार्तधर्माधिकारे हि शङ्खलिखिताभ्यामुक्तं 'आम्नायः स्मृतिधारकः' इति।
20. p. 237: सर्वधर्मसूत्राणां वर्णाश्रमधर्मोपदेशित्वाद्धर्माणां चैकरूपप्रायत्वात्परस्परसंवादित्वं युक्तं . . . स्मृतित्वं त्वङ्गानां धर्मसूत्राणां चाविशिष्टम्।
21. *Tantravārtika*, p. 144.
22. e.g., pp. 69, 76, 115.
23. e.g. on p. 136: स्मृतिकाराश्च। आचारश्चैव साधूनां देशजातिकुलधर्माश्चाम्नायैर-विरुद्धाः प्रमाणम् — इति वेदविरुद्धानामाचाराणां सामान्यतः प्रामाण्यमनुमन्यन्ते। The first is *Manu*, II.6 and the second is *GautamaDhS*, XI.20; p. 195: प्रायेण मनुगौतमवसिष्ठादिप्रणीताः समानेष्वर्थेषु धर्मसंहता वर्तन्ते।
24. p. 642: वेदानधीत्य वेदौ वा इति मानवम्। p. 80: मानवेप्यभिहितं प्रत्यक्षमनुमानं च।
25. *VāsiṣṭhaDhS*, IV.5; III.2; XIII.16; XIX.37; XX.18.
26. *Manu* (Nirnayasagar edn.) I.21 (at p. 203); II.6 (at pp. 76, 128, 130, 143); II.7 (at p. 76); II.18 (at p. 143); II.44 (at p. 153); II.140 (at p. 178): II.125 (at p. 214); III.2 (at pp. 112 and 642); IV.61 (at p. 592); IV.138 (at p. 937); IV.178 (at p. 138); V.56 (at p. 111); VIII.57 (at p. 199); IX.182 (at p. 135); XI.28 and 30 (at p. 110); XI.93 and 95 (at p. 136); XI.96 (at p. 137); XII.95 (at p. 117); XII.105-6 (at p. 80).
27. p. 591: राज्यशब्दाभिधेयं परिपालनादि कर्म क्षत्रियस्येति मन्वादयः स्मरन्ति। This has in view *Manu*, I.89; p. 110: जग्धवानापदि ह्यार्तो विश्वामित्रः श्वजावनीम्। This refers to *Manu*, X.108.
28. p. 719: तथा च मनुनापि स्वर्गं लोकं गच्छन्नभिहितः-तेजोमूर्तिः पथर्जुनेति।; p. 241: यदपि मनुना पङ्क्तिपावनमध्ये वेदादेवोपलभ्योक्तं 'यश्च व्याकुरुते वाक्यं यश्च मीमांसतेध्वरम्' इति।; p. 110: तथा च मनुनाप्युक्तमापद्धर्मगतं प्रति। तत्रत्य-पापशेषाणामन्ते शौचं भविष्यति। कर्मणा येन केनेह मृदुना दारुणेन वा। उद्धरेद्दीन-मात्मानं समर्थो धर्ममाचरेत्।। इति।

29. p. 237: पुराणं मानवो धर्मः साङ्गो वेदश्चिकित्सितम्। इति हि तुल्यवत्प्रामाण्यकरणं (अङ्गानां)। This half verse occurs after *Manu*, XII.110.

30. एवं च स्मरति। भार्या दासश्च पुत्रश्च निर्धनाः सर्व एव ते। यत्ते समधिगच्छन्ति यस्य ते तस्य तद्धनम्।। This is *Manu*, IX. 416.

31. p. 127: सदाचारेषु हि दृष्टो धर्मव्यतिक्रमः साहसं च महता प्रजापतीन्द्रवसिष्ठविश्वामित्र-युधिष्ठिरकृष्णद्वैपायनभीष्मधृतराष्ट्रवासुदेवार्जुनप्रभृतीनां बहूनामद्यतनानां च।

32. p. 128: वासुदेवार्जुनयोः प्रतिषिद्धमातुलदुहितुरुक्मिणीसुभद्रापरिणयनम्। उभौ मध्वासवक्षीबौ इति सुरापानाचरणम्। The latter is a quotation from the *Udyogaparvan*, 59.1.

33. *See* pp. 136-37.

34. p. 137: यत्तु मातुलदुहितृपरिणयनं तयोस्तन्मातृस्वस्त्रीयादिसंबन्धव्यवधानेपि भ्रात्रादिव्य-व्यवहारादविरुद्धम्। यद्यपि वासुदेवस्वसेति सुभद्राख्याता तथाप्युत्पत्तौ बलदेववासु-देवयोरेकानंशायाश्च निजत्वान्वाख्यानान्मातृस्वस्रीया वा सुभद्रा तस्य मातृपितृस्वस्रीया-दुहिता वेति परिणयनाभ्युज्ञानाद्विज्ञायते। For वासुदेवस्वसा *vide Ādiparvan*, 219.17-8. [Dr. Kane treats these cases as examples of theological apologetics on the part of the *Mīmāṁsakas*. ***Vide*** *History of Dharmaśāstra*. Vol. V/II, pp. 1280-81 — ***S.G.M.***]

35. p. 128: The sale of horses, etc., was forbidden. Śabara on *Pūrvamīmāṁsā*, X.3.47 quotes a *Śruti:* न केसरिणो ददाति नोभयतोदतः प्रतिगृह्णाति।

36. e.g., *Chāndogya*, 7.1.2.

37. p. 79: एषैवेतिहासपुराणयोरप्युपदेशवाक्यानां गतिः। उपाख्यानानि त्वर्थवादेषु व्याख्यातानि। यत्तु पृथिवीविभागकथनं . . . किंचिद्वेदमूलम्। वंशानुक्रमणमपि . . . दर्शनस्मरणमूलम्। देशकालपरिमाणमपि . . . नुमानपूर्वकम्। भाविकथनमपि . . . वेदमूलम्।

38. p. 126: यथर्तावृतुलिङ्गानि नानारूपाणि पर्यये। दृश्यन्ते तानि तान्येव तथा भाति युगादिषु।। ***Vide*** *Viṣṇu Purāṇa*, I. 5.64 and *MārkaṇḍeyaP*, 48.44.

39. p. 244: [***Also see*** Dr. Kane's *History of Dharmaśāstra*, Vol. III, pp. 845-48 for Kumārila's explorations — ***S.G.M.***]

40. p. 127.

5

Passages from the Rājamārtaṇḍa on Tithis, Vratas and Utsavas

TO The *Journal of Oriental Research*, Madras, (Vol. XXIII for 1953-54) I contributed a lengthy paper (pp. 94-127) on 'King Bhoja and his works on *Dharmaśāstra* and Astrology'. Therein I referred to five works ascribed to Bhoja that are concerned with astrological matters in relation to *Dharmaśāstra*. Out of these five the most important is the *Rājamārtaṇḍa*. I pointed out that at least two hundred verses from the *Rājamārtaṇḍa* are quoted in the medieval digests (such as the *Kṛtyaratnākara*, the several *Kaumudīs* of Govindānanda and the *Tattvas* of Raghunandana) and expressed a hope that some young scholar would undertake to produce a critical edition of the text of the *Rājamārtanda*. As it contains 1462 verses it might be years before such an edition appears. Since the *Rājamārtaṇḍa* is one of the earliest extant *nibandhas** on such topics of *Dharmaśāstra* as *tīthis*, *vratas* and *utsavas* (which are matters to be discussed in the 5th and last volume of my *History of Dharmaśāstra*) I deemed it advisable to prepare a tentative edition of the portions of the *Rājamārtaṇḍa* (from three Mss. that I could secure) dealing with *tithis*, *vratas* and *utsavas*.

* The earliest published *nibandha* on *vratas* is the *Kṛtyaratnākara* (*Vratakāṇḍa*), which may be placed between AD 1110-30 and therefore the *Rājamārtaṇḍa* is about 60 to 80 years earlier than the former.

The three Mss are:

(A) The Ms of the *Rājamārtaṇḍa* in the Bhandarkar Oriental Institute at Poona, (D.C. Ms. No. 342 of 1879-80, described on p. 108 note 28 of the above-mentioned paper). It was copied in *Saṁvat* 1655, Caitra, i.e., in AD 1598 and is fairly old. It contains *pṛṣṭhamātrā*s.

(B) This and C are Mss of the *Rājamārtaṇḍa* deposited in the Oriental Institute, Baroda. Both these Mss contain *pṛṣṭhamātrā*s, but C appears to be the older of the two. They both agree very closely as the footnotes will show, though they frequently differ from A, and, if a guess may be hazarded, B is probably a copy of C or at least both had the same original before them. Both contain no date of copying. They may be briefly described as follows. B represents accession No. 9318, it has 75 folios with ten lines on each side of a folio, with about forty letters in each line. The handwriting is good but the scribe was probably indifferently acquainted with Sanskrit and it has a much smaller number of *pṛṣṭhamātrā*s than C or A.

(C) This is accession No. 3272. The folios are 27, but the last two are torn in two pieces. The two pieces of folio 26 are there but one piece of folio 27 is wanting. The corners of the last six folios are worn out and therefore the figures of the number of the folios after 21 cannot be made out. This Ms. has the largest number of *pṛṣṭhamātrā*s of all the three Mss. It is copied in a very small hand, the letters being clear enough, although the Ms. has a worn-out appearance. There are 17 lines on each side of a folio with about 65 letters in each line. The Ms. may be about 500 years old.

The principal Ms. is A. It has numbered the verses and I point out the folios in the notes where the verses cited here can be found. For ready reference the verses set out here are consecutively numbered by me. All the three Mss. are full of mistakes, but they serve to correct one another, I hope that I have been able to present a tolerably correct and readable text. The footnotes mention only important various readings. I have given a few references to some medieval digests wherein some of the verses occurring in the *Rājamārtaṇḍa* and contained in this communication are quoted. I have pointed out in the paper quoted above (pp. 113-14) and here also that the *Rājamārtaṇḍa* borrows many verses from other works without acknowledgement; even so some digests quote these borrowed verses as those of the *Rājamārtaṇḍa*.

षष्ठ्यामुपोष्य यः सम्यक् सप्तम्यामर्कमर्चयेत्।
स हव्यभाग् रुग्विमुक्तः फलं प्राप्नोति चेप्सितम्।।१।।

षष्ठ्यां यो नियतो भूत्वा सप्तम्यां विधिवद्रविम्।
सम्पूज्योपवसेत्सोपि मुमुक्षश्चेप्सितं लभेत्।।२।।

अष्टम्यां च चतुर्दश्यां यः शिवं संशितव्रतः।
मुमुक्षुः पूजयेन्नित्यं स लभेदीप्सितं फलम्।।३।।

एकादश्यामुपोष्याथ पक्षयोरुभयोरपि।
द्वादश्यामर्चयेद्विष्णुं स मुक्तिफलभाग्भवेत्।।४।।

The following abbreviations are used in this paper :

का० वि० = कालविवेक of जीमूतवाहन (B.I. Series)

क० त० = कृत्यतत्त्व of रघुनन्दन (Jivananda)

कृ० र० = कृत्यरत्नाकर of चण्डेश्वर (B.I. Series)

ति० त० = तिथितत्त्व of रघुनन्दन (Jivananda)

रा० मा० = राजमार्तण्ड (Ms. from Bhandarkar Institute)

व० क्रि० कौ० = वर्षक्रियाकौमुदी of गोविन्दानन्द (B.I. Series)

शु० का० = शुद्धिकौमुदी of गोविन्दानन्द (B.I. Series, 1905)

1. A स हव्यवाट् भुक्तिमुक्ती प्राप्नोति चेप्सितं फलम्। This occurs on folio 69b of A and is verse 1116. 1 and 2 are q. by का० वि०, pp. 418-19 (without name).

3. A omits (as a gap) words from पूजयेन्नित्यं in v. 3 to फलभाग्भवेत् (in 4).

4. This is q. by का० वि०, p. 430 (from पुराण).

त्रयोदश्यां नवम्यां यो देवीमिष्टां प्रपूजयेत्।
नियतात्माप्युपवसेल्लभते चेप्सितं फलम्।।५।।

एकादश्यष्टमी षष्ठी शुक्ला चैव चतुर्दशी।
पूज्याः परेण संयुक्ताः शेषाः पूर्वेण संयुताः।।६।।

एकादश्यष्टमी षष्ठी द्वितीया च चतुर्थिका।
चर्तुदश्यप्यमावास्या पूज्याः स्युरपरान्विताः।।६अ।।

युग्माग्निक्रतु (कृत?) भूतानि षण्मुन्योर्वसुरन्ध्रयोः।
रुद्रेण द्वादशी युक्ता चतुर्दश्या तु पूर्णिमा।७।।

प्रतिपद्यप्यमावस्या तिथ्योर्युग्मं महाफलम्।
एतद्व्यस्तं महादोषं हन्ति पुण्यं पुराकृतम्।।८।।

नागविद्धा तु या षष्टी भानुविद्धो महेश्वरः।
चतुर्दशी कामविद्धा तिस्रस्ता मलिनाः स्मृताः।।९।।

नागविद्धा तु या षष्टी रुद्रविद्धो दिवाकरः।
कामविद्धो भवेद्विष्णुरपूज्यास्ते तु वासराः।।१०।।

षष्ठ्येकादश्यमावास्या पूर्वविद्धा तथाष्टमी।
सप्तमी परविद्धा च नोपोष्यं तिथिपञ्चकम्।।११।।

नागविद्धा तु या षष्ठी सप्तम्या च तथाष्टमी।
दशमी चेशसंमिश्रा त्रयोदश्या चतुर्दशी।।१२।।

5&6. BC omits the verses (5 and 6) त्रयोदश्यां नवम्यां० and एकादश्यष्टमी०, verse 5 is q. from रा० मा० by व० कि० कौ० p. 24.

6अ. This is q. by का० वि०, p. 477 from शङ्करगीता which is the same as विष्णुधर्मोत्तर, I, chapters 52-65.

7. A reads °ग्निक्रतुभूतानि; BC read °ग्निक्रमभूतानि।

7-8. These are गरुडपुराण I.128.16-17 and अग्निपुराण 175.36-7; they are cited as from गृह्यपरिशिष्ट by का० वि०, p. 475, व० क्रि० कौ०, p. 3 and as निगम by अपरार्क (pp. 214, 246) and स्मृतिच० (II., p. 350).

9. This is q. by का० वि० 478 (from जाबालि).

11. BC ज्येष्ठ्यैकादश्यं तु मावास्य पूर्व०. This is q. by का० वि० p. 476, and व० वि० कौ० p. 27 (from स्कन्दपुराण).

12-3. BC दशम्येकादशीमिश्रा; BC काष्टकी श्रुतिः, Verses 12-13 are q. by का० वि० p. 478 (without name).

भूतविद्धाप्यमावास्या न पूज्या मुनिपुङ्गवैः।
उत्तरोत्तरविद्धास्ताः कर्तव्याः काठकी श्रुतिः।।१३।।

नागो द्वादशनाडीभिर्दिक् पञ्चदशभिस्तथा।
भूतोष्टादशनाडीभिर्दूषयत्युत्तरां तिथिम्।।१४।।

घटिकार्धं त्रिभागं वा स्वल्पं दूषयते तिथिम्।
पञ्चगव्यघटं पूर्णं सुराया बिन्दुको यथा।।१५।।

खर्वो दर्पस्तथा हिंस्रस्त्रिविधं तिथिलक्षणम्।
खर्वदर्पौ परौ कार्यौ हिंस्रं पूर्वत्र पूजयेत्।।१६।।

खर्वा दिनद्वये तुल्या दर्पा स्याद् वृद्धिगामिनी।
हिंस्रा सा तु तिथिर्ज्ञेया या भवेत्क्षयगामिनी।।१७।।

षण्मुहूर्ता न कर्तव्या या तिथिः क्षयगामिनी।
त्रिमुहूर्तापि कर्तव्या या तिथिर्वृद्धिगामिनी।।१८।।

यां तिथिं समनुप्राप्य उदयं याति भास्करः।
सा तिथिः सकला ज्ञेया दानाध्ययनकर्मसु।।१९।।

शुक्लपक्षे तिथिर्ज्ञेया यस्यामभ्युदितो रविः।
कृष्णपक्षे तु सा ज्ञेया यस्यामस्तमितो रविः।।२०।।

वर्धमानस्य पक्षस्य उदयात्पूज्यते तिथिः।
यदा पक्षः क्षयं याति तदा स्यादपराह्णकः।। २१।।

---

14. BC दूषयत्युत्तरं दिनम्, This verse is q. by का० वि०, p. 508.

15. BC त्रिभागं वा सा स्वल्पं. This is q. by का० वि० p. 478 (from स्मृतिसमुच्च्य), व० क्रि० कौ० p. 12. (from भविष्य).

16-7. BC read पूर्वा दिनद्वये (by mistake omitting some letters and running into the next verse) for पूर्वत्र पूजयेत्; खर्वा दिनद्वये (verse 16) is q. by का० वि०, p. 500 (from बौधायान), व० क्रि० कौ० p. 22 (from उशनस्).

18. A reads षण्मुहूर्तापि कर्तव्या. This is q. by का० वि०, p. 500 (from स्मृतिसमुच्चय).

19. A reads उदंय याति दिवाकरः (spoils the metre). This is q. by का० वि० p. 503 (from देवल०), which reads स्नानदानव्रतादिषु०।

20. This is q. by का० वि० p. 475 (no name), व० क्रि० कौ०, p. 16 (from विष्णुधर्मो०).

21. BC omit the half verse यदा . . . ह्णकः; this is q. by का० वि०, p. 474 (no name).

कृष्णपक्षे तु सा ज्ञेया यस्यामस्तमितो रविः।
व्रतोपवासस्नानादौ घटिकापि यदा भवेत्।।२२।।

उदये सा तिथिर्ज्ञेया श्राद्धादावस्तगामिनी।
दैवं कर्म तथा कार्यं यस्यामभ्युदितो रविः।।२३।।

सा तिथिः सकला ज्ञेया विपरीता तु पैतृकी।
दृष्टचन्द्रा सिनीवाली नष्टचन्द्रकला कुहूः।।२४।।

सिनीवाली सदा पित्र्ये दैवे तु कथिता कुहूः।
प्रतिपदा त्वमावास्या तिथ्योर्युग्मं महाफलम्।।२५।।

एतद्व्यस्तं महादोषं हन्ति पुण्यं पुराकृतम्।
भूतविद्धाप्यमावास्या प्रतिपन्मिश्रिताथवा।।२६।।

पित्र्ये कर्मणि विद्धापि ग्राह्या कुतपकालिकी।
घटिकैकाप्यमावास्या प्रतिपत्सु न चेत्तदा।।२७।।

भूतविद्धापि ग्राह्या . . . कुतपकालिकी।
घटिकैकाप्यमावास्या प्रतिपत्सु न चेत्तदा।।२८।।

भूतविद्धापि सा कार्या दैवे पित्र्ये च कर्मणि।
मुहूर्तमप्यमावास्या प्रतिपत्सु यदा भवेत्।।२९।।

तदा तमुत्तमं दैवं शेषं सर्वं हि पूर्ववत्।
तुलामकरमेषेषु कन्यायां मिथुने रविः।। ३०।।

---

22. A reads शुक्लपक्षे।

24-25. The two half verses दृष्टचन्द्रा and सिनीवाली सदा पित्र्ये are q. by का० वि० p. 355 (from जाबालि).

25-6. ABC all have the verse प्रतिपद . . . पुराकृतम्. But it has already occurred above (in verse 8).

27. A reads कुतपकालिनी।

28. A reads प्रतिपत्सु यदा भवेत्। तदा तमुत्तमं दैवं, skipping over four half verses. का० वि० p. 360 quotes the two halves घटिकैका and भूतविद्धा from बौधायन.

30. BC read तदा तमुत्तमं।

भूतविद्धाप्यमावास्या पूज्या भवति यत्नतः।
अमा वै सोमवारेण रविवारेण सप्तमी।।३१।।

चतुर्थी भौमवारेण विषुवत्सदृशं फलम्।
अमावास्या भवेद्वारे यदा भूमिसुतस्य वै।
जाह्नवीस्नानमात्रेण गोसहस्रफलं लभेत्।।३२।।

तिथिनिर्णयः।

शुक्ले वा यदि वा कृष्णे विष्णुपूजनतत्परः।
एकादश्यां न भुञ्जीत यदीच्छेत्स्वर्गसंस्थितिम्।।३३।।

एकाप्येकादशी शुक्ला वर्षवासरसंयुता।
उपोष्या सा महापुण्या अश्वमेधफलप्रदा।।३४।।

द्वादश्येकादशी यत्र तत्र संनिहितो हरिः।
कार्यस्तत्रोपवासस्तु संयतेन्द्रियधारिणा।।३५।।

कलाप्येकादशी यत्र परतो द्वादशी भवेत्।
तत्र क्रतुशतं पुण्यं त्रयोदश्यां तु पारणम्।।३६।।

एकादश्यां द्वादशी स्याच्छेषे चैव त्रयोदशी।
दिनक्षयेपि सा पूज्या यतीनामुत्तमा तिथिः।।३७।।

उपोष्या पारणप्राप्तौ न विन्देद्द्वादशीं यदि।
दशम्यापि हि विद्धा स्यादेकादश्येव पुण्यभाक्।।३८।।

---

31. The two halves तुलामकर० and भूतविद्धा in A are q. by का० वि० p. 383 (from हारीत).

32. This verse occurs on folio 70b-71a and is 1147. The passage from अमा वै . . . लभेत् is cited by व० क्रि० कौ० p. 9 (from भविष्य) with slight variations and by का० वि०, p. 492.

33. This begins on folio 71a and is verse 1148. This is q. by ए० त०, p. 39 (last पाद different) from श्रीपतिव्यवहारसमुच्चय।

35. B reads द्वादशी यत्र संनिहिते ह; C reads संनिहितो ह (omitting रिः).

36. BC read पारणे for पारणम्। This verse is q. by का० वि०, p. 440 (from ब्रह्माण्डपु०).

38. A reads उपोष्या पारणे प्राप्तौ।

दशम्येकादशीविद्धा गान्धार्या समुपोषिता।
तस्याः पुत्रशतं नष्टं तस्मात्तां परिवर्जयेत्।।३९।।

विद्धाप्येकादशी कार्या परतो द्वादशी भवेत्।
द्वादश द्वादशीर्हन्ति त्रयोदश्यां तु पारणे।।४०।।

दशम्यनुगता हन्ति द्वादशद्वादशीफलम्।
धर्मापत्यं धनायूंषि त्रयोदश्यां तु पारणे।।४१।।

एकादशी कलामात्रं द्वादशी तु क्षयं गता।
क्षीणा सा द्वादशी ज्ञेया तत्र नक्तं विधीयते।।४२।।

एकादश्यां यदा वृद्धिः पक्षयोरुभयोरपि।
तत्रोत्तरां यतिः कुर्यात् पूर्वामुपवसेद् गृही।।४३।।

दशम्यामेकभुक्तं तु मैथुनादिविवर्जितः।
एकादश्यां न भुञ्जीत यदीच्छेत्स्वर्गसंस्थितिम्।।४४।।

संक्रान्तौ रविवारेण ग्रहणे चन्द्रसूर्ययोः।
पारणं चोपवासं च न कुर्यात्पुत्रवान् गृही।।४५।।

संक्रान्तौ कृष्णपक्षे तु रविशुक्रदिने तथा।
एकादश्यां न कुर्वीत उपवासं च पारणम्।।४६।।

रविशुक्रदिने चैव संक्रान्त्यां च दिनक्षये।
पारणं चोपवासं च न कुर्यात्पुत्रवान् गृही।।४७।।

एकादश्यां यदा राम आदित्यस्य दिनं भवेत्।
उषोष्या सा महापुण्या पुत्रपौत्रप्रवर्धिनी।।४८।।

---

39. This is q. by का० वि०, p. 441 (from कूर्म), while कृ० र०, p. 635 quotes it as a स्मृति.

40. A repeats after first half 'तत्र क्रतुशत . . . मुत्तमा तिथिः' (verses 36-37) by mistake.

41. This is q. by का० वि०, p. 442 (with the words अत्र लिखन्ति).

42. BC एकादशी कालमात्रं.

44. BC reads स्वर्गसन्ततिम्.

46-47. B omits these two (probably because the words पुत्रवान् गृही) occur in verse 45 as well as in 47.

48. This is q. by का० वि०, 437 and व० क्रि० कौ० p. 59 (from विष्णुधर्मोत्तर).

शङ्खेनैव पिबेत्तोयं न भक्षेत् कूर्मसूकरौ।
एकादश्यां न भुञ्जीत पक्षयोरुभयोरपि।।४६।।

अह्नोराद्यन्तयोर्भुक्तमेकैकं मध्यतो द्वयम्।
चतुर्भुक्तानिषेधोऽयमुपवासविधिः स्मृतः।।५०।।

असत्यभाषणं द्यूतं दिवास्वापं च मैथुनम्।
एकादश्यां न कुर्वीत उपवासपरो नरः।।५१।।

असकृत्तोयपानेन ताम्बूलस्य च भक्षणात्।
उपवासो विनश्येत दिवास्वप्नाक्षमैथुनैः।।५२।।

कांसं(स्यं) मांसं मसूरं च चणकं कोरदूषकम्।
शाकं मधु परान्नं च वर्जयेदुपवसन् स्त्रियम्।।५३।।

कांसं(स्यं) मांसं सुरां क्षौद्रं लोभं वितथभाषणम्।
व्यायामं च व्यवायं च दिवास्वप्नमथाञ्जनम्।।५४।।

शिलापिष्टं मसूरं च द्वादशैतानि वैष्णवः।
द्वादश्यां वर्जयेन्नित्यं सर्वपापैः प्रमुच्यते।।५५।।

एकादश्यां निराहारो भूत्वा चैव परेऽहनि।
भोक्ष्येहं पुण्डरीकाक्ष शरणं मे भवाच्युत।।५६।। इत्येकादशीव्रतम्।

दिनाभिव्यापिनी कृष्णा शुक्ला चैव तु सप्तमी।
उपोष्या सा महापुण्या अश्वमेधफलप्रदा।।५७।।

---

50. This is q. by का० वि०, p. 498 (from पद्म).

51. This is q. by का० वि०, p. 452 (no name).

52. This is q. by व० क्रि० कौ०, p. 67 from विष्णुधर्म।

53. This is q. by का० वि०, p. 451 (without name) and by व० क्रि० कौ०, p. 62 (from गरुड).

53. A चणकं कोटकं तथा.

54-55. These are q. from कूर्म by का० वि०, p. 468 and from विष्णुरहस्य by व० क्रि० कौ०, pp. 63-64.

55. This verse is on folio 72a and is verse 1171.

56. A omits एकादश्यां . . . भवाच्युत. This verse occurs in *Nār*, I.23.15 and वराह, 39.32, q. by का० वि०, and व० क्रि० का० 60 (both from वराह).

57. BC reads दिनातिव्यापिनी. This begins on folio 72a and is verse 1172.

दिनाभिव्यापिनी षष्ठी सप्तम्यामष्टमी भवेत्।
षष्ट्यां सौरव्रतं कुर्यादष्टम्यामेव पारणम्।।५८।। इति सप्तम्यर्कव्रतम्।

वह्निस्कन्दपुरन्दरौ गणपतिर्लक्ष्मीर्यमौ भास्करो
वायुः पार्वतिका तथा वसुमती तोयाधिपः केशवः।
ब्रह्माशम्भुजिनादयः प्रतिपदारम्भे तिथौ शेरते
उत्तिष्ठन्त्यमुना क्रमेण वरदाः स्वे स्वे दिने पूजिताः।।५९।।

सर्वे देवाश्च तिथ्यादौ तिथ्यन्ते च महेश्वरः।
शक्रविष्णू तथा ऋक्षे आद्यन्ते च विबुध्यतः।।६०।।

आभाकासितपक्षेषु मैत्रश्रवणरेवती।
आदिमध्यावसानेषु शयनावर्तबोधनम्।।६१।।

मैत्राद्यपादे स्वपितीह विष्णुर्वैष्णव्यमध्ये परिवर्तते च।
पौष्णावसाने भुजगारिकेतुरुत्तिष्ठते मासचतुष्टयेन।।६२।।

विष्णुर्दिवा न स्वपिति न रात्री प्रतिबुध्यते।
द्वादशीऋक्षसंयोगात्पादयोगो न कारणम्।।६३।।

उत्थाने शयने चैव तद्वत्पार्श्वविवर्तने।
द्वादश्यामृक्षसंयोगात्पादयोगो न कारणम्।।६४।।

निशि स्वप्नो दिवोत्थानं सन्ध्यायां परिवर्तनम्।
पादयोगादन्यतिथौ द्वादश्यामृक्षसङ्गमात्।।६५।।

---

59. This occurs in folio 72a and is verse 1175 in A; but should be 1174 as the preceding verse is wrongly numbered 1174 and 1173 does not at all occur. It is q. by व० क्रि० कौ० 286 (from रा० मा०).

60. CB read शक्रविष्णू तथा रिक्षे; A reads शुक्रविष्णू तथा ऋत्रै (?).

61. A आभाकासितपक्षे तु.

63. CB read दिवा विष्णुर्न स्वपिति; BC read रिक्षसंयोगा न कारणम्. This is q. by व० क्रि० कौ० p. 283 from रा० मा० as दिवा स्वपिति नो विष्णु . . . द्वादश्यामेव कर्तव्यं पाद०, का० वि० p. 176 quotes it as in the text (विष्णुधर्मोत्तर).

64. A reads द्वादशीरिक्षसंयोगात्; C reads 'रिक्षसंयोगा . . . करणम्'.

65. A reads द्वादशमृक्षसङ्गमे.

मैत्रान्तस्य दिवाभागे द्वादश्यन्तसमायुतः।
तत्रापि शयनं विष्णोर्मैत्रे रात्रिसमायुते।।६६।।

रेवत्यन्तपदे रात्रौ प्राप्ते नारायणोत्सवे।
पादयोगमनादृत्य ऋक्षमेव प्रशस्यते।।६७।।

प्रबोधे वासरं प्राप्य शयनं वापि यामिनीम्।
न पादनियमस्तत्र न कालः परिवर्तने।।६८।।

पादयोगो यदा न स्यादृक्षेणापि तदा भवेत्।
रात्रौ स्वापं(पो?) दिवोत्थानं सन्ध्यायां परिवर्तनम्।।६९।।

रेवतीधिष्ण्यपर्यन्ते मेषे चन्द्रावलोकिते।
उत्तिष्ठन्तं हृषीकेशं योगनिद्रा विमुञ्चति।।७०।।

रेवत्यन्तो यदा रात्रौ द्वादश्यां न च संयुतः।
तदा प्रबुध्यते विष्णुर्दिनान्ते प्राप्य रेवतीम्।।७१।।

रेवत्यन्तो यदा रात्रौ गतः पादान्तरेवतीम्।
अपराह्णे तदा विष्णुर्योगनिद्रां विमुञ्चति।।७२।।

रेवत्यन्तो यदा रात्रौ द्वादश्यां च विनाशयेत्।
उभयोः प्राप्त्यभावेन सन्ध्यायां तु महोत्सवः।।७३।।

पौष्णे शेपेनाह्नि मैत्राद्ययामेपि शनौ निशि।
द्वादश्यां तु तदा कुर्यादुत्थानशयनं हरिः।।७४।।

इति विष्णुशयनोत्थानचिन्ता।

---

66. A reads द्वादश्यां न समायुतः.

68. BC read प्रबोधे वारेंसे प्राप्य.

69. BC पादयोगे यदा न; ABC रात्रौ स्वापं.

70. BC रेवतीरिक्षपर्यन्ते; ABC योगनिद्रां विमुञ्चति.

71. BC द्वादश्यां वा न संयुतः। का० वि०, p. 180 quotes this without name, but reads द्वादश्या च समायुतः

73. A उभयोरप्यभावेन; BC उभयोः प्राप्य भावेन.

74. BC पौषे शेषे; A जिनो निशि; first half is corrupt; A यदाकुर्यादुत्थानं शयनं; This occurs on folio 72b and is verse 1190.

A reads विष्णु(रु)त्थानशयनविधिः.

वामनशयनान्तरमसिततिथिः पञ्चमी या तु।
उत्थानं मनसाया मिथुनरवौ कर्कटे वापि।।७५।।

मधुरिपुशयनानन्तरमुत्थानं कृष्णपञ्चमी(मीं?) मुनयः।
प्राहुर्मनसायां (या?) वा मिथुने वा कर्कटे वार्के।।७६।।

सुप्ते क्षीराब्धिमध्ये सुरगणनमिते माधवे ध्वस्तदैत्ये
पञ्चम्यां कृष्णपक्षे दिवसपतियुते कर्कटे चैव नित्यम्।
कक्षे प्राग्भाद्रसंज्ञे शशिनि घटयुते मीनभे वामनस्य
तस्मिन्काले प्रबोधं व्रजति च महिता वन्दिता लोकवृन्दैः।।७७।।

सुप्ते पन्नगराजभोगशयनं संश्लिष्य लक्ष्मीपता–
वन्तर्धानपदं गते सुरगणे कृष्णे च पक्षे ध्रुवम्।
पञ्चम्यामथ पूर्वभाद्रपदभे भानौ कुलीरस्थिते
त्रैलोक्यस्य मनस्विनी जनहिता देवी समुत्तिष्ठते।।७८।।
इति मनसोत्थानम्।

वृषान्ते मिथुनस्यादावग्निदग्धं दिनत्रयम्।
अम्बुना सहितान्भानुः पन्नगानपि तापयेत्।।७९।। निर्गणनम्।

मृगशिरसि निवृत्ते रौद्रपादोम्बुवाची
अनुभवति च पृथ्वीं वर्जयेत् त्रीण्यहानि।
यदि वपति कृपणः क्षेत्रमासाद्य बीजं
न भवति फलभागो दर्शिते कर्मयोगे।।८०।।

रवौ रौद्रादिपादस्थे भूमेः सञ्जायते रजः।
तस्मात् दिनत्रयं यावद् बीजाधानं परित्यजेत्।।८१।।

चत्वारिंशल्लिप्तः षड्भागयुतो यदा रविर्भवति।
ज्ञेया तदाम्बुवाची शिवर्क्षपादस्थितो यावत्।।८२।।

---

76. All these Mss. read पञ्चमी मुनयः and मनसा यां वा.

78. This occurs on folio 73a and is v. 1194.
B omits मनसोत्थानम्.

80. In 3rd *pāda* the metre is spoilt. BC read दर्शितैः and A reads कामयोगे.

81. This is q. by व० क्रि० कौ० p. 284 from रा० मा० and by कृ० र० p. 193 (from ज्योतिष).

82. This is q. by व० क्रि० कौ०, p. 283 from रा० मा०

दिग्भागशून्यलिप्तो भवति रविर्यदा तदायं स्यात्।
भवति विनिर्गमकाले द्वितीयपादाश्रया रौद्रे।।८३।। अम्बुवाची।

वैशाखमासस्य तु या तृतीया नवम्यसौ कार्तिकशुक्लपक्षे।
नभस्यमासस्य तस्मिस्रपक्षे त्रयोदशी पञ्चदशी च माघे।।८४।।

भाद्रे कलिद्वापरमासि माघे त्रेता तृतीया नवमी कृते वा।
एता युगाद्याः कथिताः पुराणैरनन्तपुण्यास्तिथयश्चतस्रः।।८५।।

पानीयमप्यत्र तिलैर्विमिश्रं दद्यात्पितृभ्यः प्रयतो मनुष्यः।
श्राद्धं कृतं तेन समासहस्रं रहस्यमेतन्मुनयो वदन्ति।।८६।।

इति युगादयः।

नानादेशे महापुण्या अर्घदानक्रिया मुनेः।
अगस्त्यस्य सुरैः पूर्वं यथादिष्टं तथा शृणु।।८७।।

पुरा युगसहस्रं तु विष्णुर्वारुणिता मुने।
आराधितः प्रसादार्थं तस्मै प्रादाद्वरं हरिः।।८८।।

दक्षिणाशां पुरस्कृत्य गच्छ तिष्टस्व वारुणे।
हितार्थे सर्वलोकानां विधिं वक्ष्यामि यत्नतः।।८९।।

ये त्वां तत्र स्थितं भक्त्या नार्चयिष्यन्ति मानवाः।
संवत्सरकृतं पुण्यं मन्नियोगाद्भवेत्तव।।९०।।

---

83. A तदायं स्याः; BC रविर्यदा तदा तस्याः. This occurs on folio 73a and is verse 1199.

After this three verses on उपाकर्म are omitted in this place.

84. A reads वैशाखशुक्लस्य, This occurs in folio 73b and is verse 1203.

84. & 86. These are विष्णुपुराण, III.14.12-13; कृ० र०, p. 542 quotes 84-86 (except the half verse भद्रे . . . नवमी कृते वा) from विष्णुपुराण.

87. BC येणापुण्या and अर्घदान. This occurs in folio 73b and is verse 1206. अगस्त्यार्घदान extends over verses 1206-1228; व० क्रि० कौ०, pp. 341-42 quoted 14 vere from राजमार्तण्ड on अगस्त्यार्घदान, out of which only eight are found in the text presented here.

89. BC वानुणे; BC गेहेतोर्घे सर्व°.

ये त्वां सर्वविधानेन पूजयिष्यन्ति वारुणे।
श्वेतद्वीपं गमिष्यन्ति ते नरा मत्प्रसादतः।।९१।।

वेदवेदाङ्गविद्वांसो धनधान्यसुतान्विताः।
वारुणे ते भविष्यन्ति लोकेऽस्मिन्नर्घदास्तदा।।९२।।

एवं दत्तमगस्त्यस्य वरं देवेन चक्रिणा।
तस्य चार्घविधानं च कथ्यमानं मया शृणु।।९३।।

अप्राप्ते भास्करे कन्यां रात्रिभागिस्त्रिभिर्लवैः।
अर्घं दद्युरगस्त्याय ये वसन्ति महोदये।।९४।।

काशपुष्पमयीं रम्यां कृत्वा मूर्तिं तु वारुणे।
प्रदोषे विन्यसेत्तां तु पूर्णकुम्भे स्वलंकृते।।९५।।

कुम्भस्थं पूजयेत्तं तु पुष्पधूपविलेपनैः।
दध्यक्षतैर्बलिं दद्याद्रात्रौ कुर्यात्प्रजागरम्।।९६।।

प्रभाते तां समादाय यायात्पुण्यं जलाशयम्।
निशान्ते तां च विन्यस्य जलान्ते प्रतिमां मुनेः।।९७।।

अर्घं दद्यादगस्त्याय भक्त्या सम्यगुपोषितः।
पुष्पैर्मूलैः फलैर्मेध्यैः शारदैश्च सुगन्धिभिः।।९८।।

द्राक्षाखर्जूरकर्कन्धूनारिकेलादिभिः शुभैः।
पञ्चरत्नसमायुक्तं हेमरूप्यसमन्वितम्।।९९।।

सप्तधान्यसमायुक्तं दधिचन्दनमिश्रितम्।
अर्घपात्रं समादाय अर्घं दद्युर्द्विजातयः।।१००।।

अगस्त्यः खनमानः खनित्रैः प्रजामपत्यं बलमिच्छमानः।
उभौ वर्णावृषिरुग्रः पुपोष सत्या देवेष्वाशिषो जगाम।।१०१।।

---

91. BC यत्त्वा; BC अर्चयिष्यन्ति; ABC मप्रसादतः.

94. BC विभिर्दिनैः; महोदय is उज्जयिनी; का० वि० p. 291 explains it so; verses 26-27 are auoted by व० क्रि० कौ०, p. 341.

97. A जलाश्रयम्.

98. BC ससुगन्धिभिः.

101. BC बलमिच्छमानस्; A देवेष्वसिरवौ जगाम. This is ऋग्वेद, I.176.6. This is referred to in a verse 'अगस्त्यः खनमानेति पठेयुर्मन्त्रमुत्तमम्' q. from रा० मा०, by व० क्रि० का०, p. 341.

यथालाभकृतार्थास्ते सर्वे वर्णास्तु भक्तितः।
अर्घं दद्युरगस्त्याय शूद्रं (द्रे?) मन्त्रविधिस्त्वयम्।।१०२।।

काशपुष्पप्रतीकाश अग्निमारुतसम्भव।
मित्रावरुणयोः पुत्र कुम्भयोने नमोस्तु ते।।१०३।।

दत्त्वार्घं तु विधानेन नरः कुम्भोद्भवाय च।
त्यजेदगस्त्यमुद्दिश्य धान्यमेकं फलं रसम्।।१०४।।

ततोन्नं भोजयेद्विप्रान् घृतपायसमोदकैः।
गाः सुवर्णं च वासांसि तेभ्यो दद्याच्च दक्षिणाम्।।१०५।।

घृतपायसयुक्तेन पात्रेण सुगिताननम्। (स्थगिता०?)
सहिरण्यं च तं कुम्भं ब्राह्मणाय निवेदयेत्।।१०६।।

सप्त वर्षाणि दत्त्वार्घं विधानेन द्विजातयः।
देवान्महीं पशुं पुत्रान्धर्मारोग्यमवाप्नुयुः।।१०७।।

द्विजो यथालाभमुपाहितार्थः प्राप्नोति वेदांश्च सपुत्रपौत्रान्।
वैश्यश्च गां भूरिधनं च शूद्रो रोगक्षयं भूरिधनं च सर्वम्।।१०८।।

सत्पुत्रं लभते नारी दत्त्वार्घं विधिना मुनेः।
कन्या सत्पतिमाप्नोति धर्मारोग्यं पृथग्जनाः।।१०९।।

दत्त्वार्घं मुनिमुख्याय तोषयित्वा जनार्दनम्।
विष्णुलोकमवाप्नोति नरो नास्त्यत्र संशयः।।११०

इत्यगस्त्यार्धविधिः।

---

102. A तथालाभं; BC omit अर्घं; ABC read शूद्रं मन्त्र०.

103. All read कुम्भयोनि नमोस्तु. This is q. by व० क्रि० कौ०, p. 341 from रा० मा०

105. A भोजयेद्विद्वान्; verses 104-5 are quoted by व० क्रि० का०, pp. 341-42 from रा० मा०.

106. BC स्वदितवा (?) for last word of first half.

107. A omits the verse सप्तवर्षाणि . . . प्नुयुः. Verses 107-8 are q. by व० क्रि० कौ०, p. 342 from रा० मा० .

108. B omits letters after भूरिधनम्; A omits has letters after भूरि धनं च.

110-12. These occur on folio 74b and are verses 1228-30 in A; verses 111-12 are quoted by व० क्रि० कौ०, p. 320 from *Bhaviṣya* as included in रा० मा० along with 2 verses more, which the three Mss. do not contain. The two verses 111-12 are also from विष्णुरहस्य in का० वि०, p. 461.

श्रवणेन समायुक्ता मासि भाद्रपदे सिता।
द्वादशी सा महापुण्या नाम्ना तु विजया स्मृता।।१११।।

तस्यां स्नातो विधानेन सर्वतीर्थफलं लभेत्।
अर्चयित्वाच्युतं भक्त्या लभेत्पुण्यं दशाब्दिकम्।।११२।।

इति श्रवणद्वादशी।

अष्टमी कृष्णपक्षस्य रोहिणीऋक्षसंयुता।
भवेत्प्रौष्ठपदे मासि जयन्ती नाम सा स्मृता।।११३।।

जयन्त्यामुपवासं तु कृत्वा यश्चार्चयेद्धरिम्।
तस्य जन्मशतोद्भूतं पापं नाशयतेऽच्युतः।।११४।।

कौमारे यौवने बाल्ये वार्धके यदुपार्जितम्।
तत्पापं शमयेत्कृष्णस्तिथावस्यां सुपूजितः।।११५।।

रोहिणीसहिता कृष्णा मासि भाद्रपदेऽष्टमी।
अर्धरात्रादधश्चोर्ध्वं कलयापि यदा भवेत्।।११६।।

महापुण्यतमः कालो जयन्त्याख्यो हि स स्मृतः।
तत्र जातो जगन्नाथः कौस्तुभी हरिरीश्वरः।।११७।।

तमेवोपवसेत्कालं रात्रौ कुर्याच्च जागरम्।
एकाग्रेणैव भावेन विष्णोर्नामानुकीर्तनम्।।११८।।

अनघं वामनं शौरिं वैकुण्ठं पुरुषोत्तमम्।
वासुदेवं हृषीकेशं माधवं मधुसूदनम्।।११९।।

113-15. A कृत्वा भक्त्यार्चयेद्धरिं; this verse occurs on folio 74b verse 1231. Verses 113-40 deal with कृष्णजन्माष्टमी, though styled रोहिण्यष्टमी०. 113-15 are q. by व० क्रि० कौ० p. 299 (from भविष्य) and 114-15 are q. by का० वि० p. 494 from विष्णुरहस्य।

116-17. These are q. by व० क्रि० कौ०, p. 298 (from ब्रह्माण्ड) and 116 by का० वि०, p. 495.

118. While quoting this and the verses up to 129 the ति० त० (pp. 44-45) expressly states गरुडभविष्योत्तत्वचनानि राजमार्तण्ड-कृत्यचिन्तामणिधृतानि यथा। तमेवोपवसेत् कालम्।

119. Verses 119-23 are q. by व० क्रि० कौ०, p. 313 (from गरुड, I.131. 10-15).

वाराहं पुण्डरीकाक्षं नृसिंहं दैत्यसूदनम्।
दामोदरं पद्मनाभं केशवं गरुडध्वजम्।।१२०।।

गोविन्दमच्युतं कृष्णमनन्तमपराजितम्।
अधोक्षजं जगद्बीजं सर्गस्थित्यन्तकारणम्।।१२१।।

अनादिनिधनं विष्णुं त्रैलोक्येशं त्रिविक्रमम्।
नारायणं चतुर्बाहुं शङ्खचक्रगदाधरम्।।१२२।।

पीताम्बरधरं नित्यं वनमालाविभूषितम्।
श्रीवत्साङ्कं जगत्सेतुं श्रीपतिं श्रीधरं हरिम्।।१२३।।

प्रणमामि सदा देवं वासुदेवं जगत्पतिम्।
नामान्येतानि संकीर्त्य गत्यर्थं प्रार्थयेत्पुनः।।१२४।।

त्राहि मां सर्वलोकेश हरे संसारसागरात्।
त्राहि मां सर्वपापघ्न दुःखशोकार्णवात्प्रभो।।१२५।।

सर्वयज्ञेश्वर त्राहि पतितं मां भवार्णवे।
देवकीनन्दन श्रीश हरे संसारसागरात्।।१२६।।

त्राहि मां सर्वदुःखज्ञ रोगशोकार्णवाद्धरे।
दुर्वृत्तांस्त्रायसे विष्णो ये स्मरन्ति सकृत्सकृत्।।१२७।।

सोऽहं देवातिदुर्वृत्तस्त्राहि मां शोकसागरात्।
पुष्कराक्ष निमग्नोऽहं महत्यज्ञानसागरे।।१२८।।

त्राहि मां देवदेवेश त्वत्तो नान्योऽस्ति रक्षिता।।१२९।।
योगाय योगेश्वराय योगपतये योगसम्भवाय गोविन्दाय नमो नमः।।१३०।।
इति स्नानमन्त्रः।

---

121. A reads सृष्टिसंहारकारणम्.

122. A omits the verse 'अनादि . . . धरम्'.

124. A reads सञ्चिन्त्य for संकीर्त्य and प्रार्थयेत्ततः.

125. A reads रोगशोकार्णवाद्धरे. Verses 125-29 occur is व० क्रि० कौ०, pp. 313 (from गरुड I.131.17-20).

130. A reads ओं योगाय.

यज्ञाय यज्ञेश्वराय यज्ञपतये यज्ञसम्भवाय गोविन्दाय नमो नमः।।१३१।।
इत्यर्घमन्त्रः।

सोमायेति चन्द्रार्चनमन्त्रः। धर्मायेति होममन्त्रो घृततिलाभ्याम्। विश्वाय विश्वेश्वराय विश्वसम्भवाय गोविन्दाय नमो नमः। इति शयनमन्त्रः। सर्वाय सर्वेश्वराय सर्वपतये सर्वसम्भवाय गोविन्दाय नमो नमः। इति पारायणमन्त्रः।।१३२।। सर्वभूतायेति समाप्तिमन्त्रः।

अर्धरात्रेति योगोयं तारापत्युदये सदा।
नियतात्मा शुचिः शान्तः पूजां तत्र समाचरेत्।।१३३।।

फलपुष्पोपहारैश्च धूपदीपानुलेपनैः।
स्थण्डिले पूजयेद्देवं सचन्द्रां रोहिणीं तथा।।१३४।।

शङ्खे तोयं समादाय सपुष्पफलचन्दनम्।
जानुभ्यां धरणीं गत्वा चन्द्रायार्घं निवेदयेत्।।१३५।।

ततः स्तोत्रैश्च मन्त्रैश्च स्तुत्वा देवं जनार्दनम्।
गीतवादित्रनृत्यैश्च शेषं कालं यथामुखम्।।१३६।।

क्षीरोदार्णवसम्भूत अत्रिनेत्रसमुद्भव।
गृहाणार्घं शशाङ्कमं रोहिण्या सहितो मम।।१३७।।
इति चन्द्रार्घदानमन्त्रः।

बलभद्रश्च कृष्णश्च वासुदेवो (वसुदेवो?)थ रोहिणी।
देवकी च यशोदा च पूजनीया द्विजातिभिः।।१३८।।

अष्टम्यामथ रोहिण्यां न कुर्यात्पारणं क्वचित्।
हन्यात्पुरातनं कृत्स्नमुपवासार्जितं फलम्।।१३९।।

---

131. 131 and 132 occur in व० क्रि० कौ०, p. 311. All the prose passages in 130-32 occur in गरुडपुराण, I.131-4-5.

132. A reads ओं. सोमायेति च०.

B omits 'इति पारायणमन्त्रः'; A is corrupt and presents षामरणमन्त्रः; BC omit सर्व and read भूतायेति.

135. A reads जानुभ्यानवनिं गत्वा.

137. BC read क्षीरो . . . सम्भूतं अत्रि . . . द्रवम्.

139-40. These are q. by का० वि०, p. 493 (from भविष्य and विष्णु).

तिथिस्त्रयोदशं नक्षत्रं द्वादशैव तु।
तस्मात्प्रयत्नतः कुर्यात्तिथिभान्ते च पारणम्।।१४०।।
इति रोहिण्यष्टमीविधिः।

सिंहे रवौ सिते पक्षे हस्तादित्रिभसंयुता।
रुद्राणीप्रीतिदा ज्ञेया चतुर्थी हरितालिका।।१४१।।

करचित्रानिलर्क्षे तु हरौ सूर्ये चतुर्थिका।
हरिताडी तिथिः पुण्या पार्वतीप्रीतिदा सदा।।१४२।।

त्वाष्ट्रभे स्वातिभे वापि चतुर्थी हरितालिका।
भाद्रे मासि सिते पक्षे तिथीनामुत्तमा स्मृता।।१४३।।

भाद्रे मासि सिते पक्षे चतुर्थ्यां स्वातियोगतः।
करोति किल्बिषं घोरं दृष्टचन्द्रा न संशयः।।१४४।।
इति हरितालीचतुर्थी।

भाद्रपदे सिताष्टम्यामिन्द्रध्वजमिष्टदारुमयम्।
सम्पूज्य जागराद्यैः श्रवणेनोत्थापयेद्विधिवत्।।१४५।।

भाद्रे मासि सिते पक्षे दशमी मूलसंयुता।
समारोप्याढके शङ्कुं याम्यन्ते निशि पातयेत्।।१४६।।

सिंहं गते दिनकरे सितचारुपक्षे
हर्याद्यपादमुपसंनिहिते शशाङ्के।

140. Occurs on folio 75b verse 1255; verses 113-40 correspond to verses 1231 to 1255 (except 122) including the prose *mantras*.

141. A reads हरितालिका here and employs ह for ल in the next two verses. This and the following three verses occur on folio 75b and are verses 1256-59.

142. A reads हस्तचित्रा०. This and verse 144 are q. from रा० मा० by व० क्रि० कौ०, p. 318.

143. BC omit the half verse त्वाष्ट्र . . . हरितालिका; A reads 'तिथिः सैवोत्तमा स्मृता'.

144. A reads स्वातियोगिनी and reads 'जनस्य त्वभिशापाय मृगाङ्कस्य च दर्शनम्' for करोति . . . न संशयः.

145. From this to verse 177 in इन्द्रध्वजोत्थापनाविधिः and corresponds to verses 1260-92 on folios 76 and 77b of A.

146. BC reads समारोटके केशे सं (which is meaningless and corrupt).

उत्तिष्ठते त्रिदिवमन्दिरवन्द्यवृन्दो
याम्ये तनौ निशि निषीदति वज्रपाणिः।।१४७।।

श्रवणाद्ये भरण्यन्ते सिंहे चैव दिवाकरे।
ध्वजोत्थानं सुरेशस्य क्रमाद्विसर्जनं निशि।।१४८।।

द्वादशी हरिसंयुक्ता मासि भाद्रपदे सिता।
तस्यामुत्थापितं शक्रं भरण्यन्ते निपातयेत्।।१४९।।

तारापतौ त्रिदशदानवमन्त्रिभागे
सौम्यग्रहैर्नवमपञ्चमकण्टकस्थैः।
लग्नेषु दैत्यसचिवज्ञबृहस्पतीना-
मुत्थापनं शुभकरं भुवि वज्रपाणेः।।१५०।।

शशिनि शुभग्रहभवने कुर्यादिन्द्रध्वजोत्सवं सत्सु।
केन्द्रत्रिकोणगेषु प्रशस्तवेलाविलग्नेषु।।१५१।।

गुडपूपपायसाद्यैर्विप्रानभ्यर्च्य दक्षिणाभिश्च।
श्रवणेन द्वादश्यामुत्थाप्योऽन्यत्र वा श्रवणात्।।१५२।।

तत्र पताकाः श्वेता विजयाय भवन्ति रोगदा पीताः।
जयदा विचित्ररूपा रक्ता शस्त्रप्रकोपाय।।१५३।।

शक्रोत्सवं जयेच्छुः श्रवणेन द्वादशीसमेतेन।
विहितविलग्ने कुर्यात्तयोर्वियोगे पुनः श्रवणे।।१५४।।

श्रवणद्वादशीलाभयोगो यत्र न दृश्यते।
तत्र तु श्रवणे कुर्यादिन्द्रस्योत्थापनं नृपः।।१५५।।

---

147. BC read शितदायुपक्षे and याम्योततोमिशि निषादति॰. This is cited by का॰ वि॰, p. 295 (without name).

149. BC read भरण्यं निशि पातयेत्.

150. This is cited from ज्योतिःशास्त्र by का॰ वि॰ pp. 296-97.

151. BC read केन्द्रे त्रिकोणगेषु.

152. BC read गुडापूप. This is cited by का॰ वि॰, p. 294 from वराह (i.e. his बृहत्संहिता, 42.38).

153. This is same as बृहत्संहिता 42.27.

155. All three Mss. are corrupt here. A श्रवणद्वादश्यां भोगयोगो न विद्यते; B श्रवणद्वादशी भोगयोयत्र न दृश्यते; C श्रवणद्वादशी लोभ गयो यत्र न दृश्यते.

एकोऽपि जीवेन्दुजभार्गवाणां केन्द्रे यदि स्यादथवा त्रिकोणे।
उत्थानकाले त्रिदशाधिपस्य निहत्य दोषान् विजयं करोति।।१५६।।

केन्द्रे त्रिकोणे च शुभग्रहैश्च दुश्चिक्यलाभारिगतैश्च पापैः।
उत्पादयेद् देवगणाधिपूजां सौम्यग्रहाणामुदये स्वभे च।।१५७।।

अन्तकस्यादिमध्यान्तं यदि स्यादष्टमे दिने।
शक्रं विसर्जयेत्तत्र न विधिश्चाष्टमोपरि।।१५८।।

पातयेदष्टमे वाह्नि लोकपालं यमान्तिके।
निशायां सर्वसत्त्वानां करोति कुशलं भुवि।।१५९।।

नवमे तु दिने दृष्टो राज्ञां शक्रो भयप्रदः।
ततोऽनादृत्य याम्यान्तमष्टम्यां निशि पातयेत्।।१६०।।

अष्टम्याः परतः शक्रं याम्यान्तस्यानुरोधतः।
ये पश्यन्ति महीपालास्तेषां राष्ट्रं विनश्यति।।१६१।।

न भवति भरणीशेषं निशि सुरराजं विसर्जयेन्नृपतिः।
पौरपुरोहितयुक्तो याम्यसमेते निशान्ते च।।१६२।।

याम्यान्ततो देवपतेर्निशायां विसर्जनं शान्तिकरं नृपाणाम्।
दिवा कृतान्तान्तपदप्रसङ्गे निशावसाने भरणीभयोगे।।१६३।।

क्रव्यादकौशिकपोतककाककङ्कैः
केतुस्थितैर्महदुशन्ति भयं नृपस्य।
चापेन वापि युवराजभयं वदन्ति
श्येनोपि लोचनभयं नियतं करोति।।१६४।।

---

157. BC read ०रिगते च सौन्यैः; BC read ०मुदये शुभे च.

158. This is cited by का० वि०, p. 297 अन्तक stands for भरणी of which यम is presiding deity.

160. This is q. by व० क्रि० कौ०, p. 323 from रा० मा०.

161. BC read अक्रम्यान्तरशक्रं.

162. A reads भरणीं शेषं.

163. A reads भरणीभभागे.

164-5. All the three occur in का० वि०, p. 299 and they are the same as बृहत्संहिता 42.62-64.

छत्रभङ्गेपतने नृपमृत्युस्तस्करान्मधुकरोतिनिलीने।
हन्ति चाप्यथ पुरोहितमुल्का पार्थिवस्य महिषीमशनिस्था।।१६५।।

राज्ञीविनाशं पतिता पताका करोत्यवृष्टिं पिटकस्य पातः।
मध्यान्तमूलेषु च केतुभङ्गो निहन्ति मन्त्रिक्षितिपालपौरान्।।१६६।।

वज्रः शङ्कुच्छेदने बालपीडा राज्ञो मातुः पीडनं मातृकायाः।
यद्यत्कुर्युर्बालकाश्चारणाश्च तत्तत्तादृग्भावि पापं शुभं वा।।१६७।।

इन्द्रध्वजादर्शफलाद्विचित्रैर्विचित्रमालाकदलीक्षुदण्डैः।
सव्यालसिंहैः पिटकैर्गवाक्षैरलंकृतं दिक्षु च लोकपालैः।।१६८।।

अविरलजननादं मङ्गलाशीःप्रणामैः पटुपटहमृदङ्गैः शङ्खभेर्यादिभिश्च।
स्तुतिविहितवचोभिः पाठवद्भिश्च विप्रैरशुभरहितशब्दं केतुमुत्थापयेच्च।।१६९।।

फलदधिघृतलाजाक्षौद्रपुष्पार्घहस्तैः
प्रणिपतितशिरोभिस्तुष्टवद्भिश्च पौरैः।
स तु मणिमिव (? वृतमनिमिषमिव) भर्तुः केतुरीशः प्रजाना-
मरिनगरनताग्रं कारयेद् द्विड्वधाय।।१७०।।

नातिद्रुतं न च विलम्बितमप्रकम्प-
मध्वस्तसाम्यपिटकादिविभूषणं च।
तस्यामनिष्टमशुभं परतोऽन्यथा यत्।
तच्छान्तिभिर्नरपतेः शमयेत्पुरोधाः।।१७१।।

श्रवणाद्भरणीं यावत् पूजां कृत्वा विधानतः।

---

165. B छत्रभ्याङ्गपते नृप०, C छत्रस्याङ्गपते नृप०; BC read महिषीमशनिख.

166. A मध्याग्रमूलेषु and केतुभङ्गं निहन्ति; BC केतुबन्धभङ्गो निहन्ति.

167. A मात्रकायाः; BC मातृकायं.

168. This ocurs on folio 77a and is verse 1283 of A. It is the same as बृहत्संहिता 42.57 which reads छत्रध्वजा०.

169. BC omit प्रणामैः and read सुतविहित; A reads असुरविहितनष्टं; this is बृहत्संहिता 42.59.

170. A reads स्तोत्रवद्भिश्चपौरैः; BC प्रणपतित०; BC read कारयेद् विद्धया (?); A reads ०प्रकम्पविध्वस्त०; BC त्वानमिष्टमशुभं वदतोन्यथा यः.

170-1. These are बृहत्संहिता 42.60-61.

रात्रौ विसर्जयेद् देवं मन्त्रेणानेन पाण्डव।।१७२।।

सार्धं सुरासुरगणैः पुरन्दर शतक्रतो।
उपहारं गृहीत्वेमं महेन्द्रध्वज गम्यताम्।।१७३।।

विसर्जनात् प्राक् पूजा अनेन मन्त्रद्वयेन-
एह्येहि सर्वामरसिद्धसाध्यैरभिष्टुतो वज्रधरामरेश।
समुच्छ्रितस्त्वं श्रवणाद्यपादे गृहाण पूजां भगवन्नमस्ते।।१७४।।

वज्रहस्त सुरारिघ्न बहुनेत्र पुरन्दर।
रक्षार्थं सर्वसत्त्वानां पूजेयं प्रतिगृह्यताम्।।१७५।।

नमस्ते देव देवेश सहस्राक्ष नमोस्तु ते।
आखण्डल नमस्तुभ्यं पुष्टिं देहि श्रियं स्थिराम्।।१७६।।

कीर्तिं धृतिं तथा विद्यां मेधां देहि यशः सदा।
आरोग्यं देहि देवेश धनधान्यादिकं तथा।।१७७।।
इति इन्द्रोत्थापनविधिः।

मासि भाद्रेपदे चैव पुष्येनो(?णो)त्सर्जनं सदा।
उपाकर्म ततः कुर्यान्नक्षत्रे सूर्यदैवते।।१७८।।

छन्दोगा मिलिताः कुर्युः प्रातरूत्सर्गिकां क्रियाम्।
अपराह्ने ह्युपाकर्म पुष्यहस्तर्क्षयोर्द्वयोः।।१७९।। इति उपाकर्म।

आर्द्रायां बोधयेद्देवीं मूलेन प्रतिपूजयेत्।
उत्तरेणार्चनं कृत्वा श्रवणेन विसर्जयेत्।।१८०।।

---

172. A श्रवणाभरणींयावत्; BC श्रवणभरण्योर्यावत्; 172, 173, 175 occur in का० वि०, p. 296.

173. BC सार्धं शुक्र (शक्र?) सुरगणैः.

177. This occurs on folio 77b and is verse 1292. These are 33 verses on इन्द्रध्वजोत्थापन.

178. BC ०र्जनं तथा and उपाकर्म पुण्यहस्तर्क्षयोर्द्वयोः These two Mss. by mistake compress two verses into one. This occurs on folio 77b and is verse 1293.

179. After this there are 32 verses on श्राद्ध (in A, verses 1295-1326 in folios 77 & 78) that are omitted here.

179. This is q. by व० क्रि० का०, p. 375 from नन्दिकेश्वरपुराण.

180. This occurs on folio 78b verse 1327. Verses 180-88 are concerned with दुर्गोत्सव, occur on folios 78b and 79a and are verses 1327-35.

मूलेन प्रतिपूजयेद्भगवतीं चण्डांशुचण्डाकृति-
मष्टम्यामुपवाससंयतधिया भक्त्या समाराधयेत्।
नानापाशवमद्यमांसरुधिरैः कृत्वा नवम्यां बलिं
नक्षत्रं श्रवणं तिथिं च दशमीं संप्राप्य संप्रेषयेत्।।१८१।।

सप्तम्यां मूलयोगे प्रथमपदगते पत्रिका पूजनीया
ह्यष्टम्यां रात्रिभागे कृतनियमविधौ यज्ञकर्म प्रदिष्टम्।
नानाजीवाभिघातस्तिथिरथ नवमी रौद्रदृष्टिस्वरूपा
संप्राप्ते वैष्णवान्ते नियमकृतविधिः प्रेषयेत्तां दशम्याम्।।१८२।।

मूलं प्राप्य प्रथमचरणेऽभ्यर्चनं चण्डिकायाः
कृष्णाष्टम्यामशनरहितैस्त्यक्तनिद्रैः सुपूजाम्।
प्रातःकाले पशुबलिविधिं स्नानदानं नवम्यां
निर्माल्यं तु श्रवणदशमी वासवाकयुक्तिः(?)।।१८३।।

ऋक्षत्रये च मूलादो सप्तम्यामाश्विने सिते।
चण्डिकामुपहारैश्च पूजयेद्राष्ट्रवृद्धये।।१८४।। दुर्गोत्सवः।

कुर्याज्जागरमष्टव्यां नवम्यां विधिवद्बलिम्।
दशम्यां बलवृद्धयर्थं कुर्यान्नीराजनं नृपः।।१८५।।

उमाया नवमी प्रोक्ता हरस्य तिथिरष्टमी।
द्वयोरेका महापुण्या उमामाहेश्वरी स्मृता।।१८६।।

अष्टम्यां पूजितो रुद्रो नवम्यां शक्तिरुच्यते।
द्वयोर्योगे तु संप्राप्ते पूजायां तु महाफलम्।।१८७।।

---

181. The third पाद is quoted in ति० त०, p. 82. BC नाना ह्यासवमद्य०. Verse 181 is q. by का० वि० p. 515 as कात्यायनीश्लोक.

183. A सपूजां; BC सुपुञ्जाम्; BC ०कालो पशुवधबलिं; the last six latters at the end are corrupt; A reads वासवाक्य-युताः; BC read as above. The whole verse is q. by ति० त० on p. 86 reading 4th पाद as 'दशमीं ह्यात्मकर्क्षेषु जह्यात्'.

184. This occurs in का० वि०, p. 516 (from ज्योतिःशास्त्र).

185. BC read ज्जीवारमष्टम्यां.

186. BC reads ०मोहश्वरी तथा.

187. B reads अष्टम्यां शक्तिरुच्यते (omitting eight letters); BC ०र्योगेतिसंप्राप्ते and सुमहाफलम्.

उत्सवविधिं च विततं बलिं च नीराजनं च बलवृद्ध्यै।
आश्वयुजेष्टम्यादिषु कुर्वीत यथाक्रमं नृपतिः।।१८८।।
इति नीराजनविधिः।

कौमुदी यक्षरात्रिश्च कौमुदी फाल्गुनी तथा।
वासन्तिकेति विज्ञेया देशस्य महिमा स्मृता।।१८९।।

आश्विने मासि पौर्णमास्यामक्षैर्जागरणं निशि।
कौमुदी सा समाख्याता कार्या लोकैर्विभूतये।।१९०।। कोजागरः।

सिते पक्षे यदा भानुस्तुलां समधिरोहति।
उत्तिष्ठत्यग्रतो विष्णुः पश्चात्प्रेतचतुर्दशी।।१९१।।

दिनाधिपे भूततिथौ तुलायां चित्राभयुक्ते दिवसे कुजस्य।
एतेषु कामान्प्रवदन्ति नूनं यदार्धरात्रं कथितं पुराणे।।१९२।।

कृतयोगे भौमवारे चैत्रे कृष्णचतुर्दशी।
न हि प्रेतत्वमाप्नोति नरो रुद्रालयेस्थितः।।१९३।।

तुलायां वृश्चिके वापि उपस्थिते दिवाकरे।
प्रेतपक्षकुरः (?) कार्यः कन्यायां न कदाचन।।१९४।।

कुजवारसमायुक्ता कृष्णा चैव चतुर्दशी।
नक्तं चित्रानुसंयुक्ता महापुण्यतमा स्मृता।।१९५।।

वियुक्ता भौमवारेण चित्रभेन तथैव च।
तिथिरेव सदा पुण्या नात्र कार्या विचारणा।।१९६।।

पूज्य कृष्णचतुर्दश्यां चित्राङ्गारतुलान्विताम्।
उपोष्य लीयते पापो हेतुकेश्वरसंनिधौ।।१९७।।

---

189. This occurs on folio 79a and is verse 1336.

190. There is faulty metre in first half. This is q. by का० वि० 223 and 403 (without name), reading आश्विने पौर्णमास्यां च चरेज्जागरणं which makes the verse regular; व० क्रि० कौ० p. 453 quotes (from लिङ्गपुराण).

191. This is on folio 79a verse 1338; B omits the words from नहि प्रेतत्व . . . to समायुक्ता, probably because the copyist's eye travelled from the word चतुर्दशी in verse 193 to the same word in verse 195.

196. BC read नात्र कार्ये विचारणम्.

197. BC रात्रौ कृष्ण० for पूज्य कृष्ण०.

शिवे शूले तटे कन्यां वालखिल्यैः पुनर्भुवि।
स्नात्वा तु त्रिदिवं यान्ति ये मृतास्तेऽपुनर्भुवाः।।१९८।।
इति प्रेतचतुर्दशी।

अमावास्यां तुलादित्ये लक्ष्मीर्निद्रां विमुञ्चति।
तस्मिन् शुक्ले सदा विष्णुस्तुलायामथ वृश्चिके।।१९९।।

चित्रायां चित्रभानुर्विचरति सवितुर्वासुदेवा यदा वा
यावन्नाम्भोनिधिजलशयने योगनिद्रां जहाति।
भास्वन् पिष्टप्रदीप प्रतिहर रजनीघोरसान्द्रान्धकारे
तस्मिल्लँक्ष्मीः प्रबोधं व्रजति भगवति(?ती) सौख्यहेतुर्नराणाम्।।२००।।

तौलिस्थे तरणौ निशान्तसमये प्राप्ते गतेन्द्रातिथा-
वासन्ने मृगलाञ्छने शुभविधौ पिष्टप्रदीपाम्बुजैः।
कृत्वा गन्धनिवेद्यवाद्यरुचिरैः कल्हारपुष्पार्चिता
वन्द्या सा सुखरात्रिका नरपतेः दुःस्वप्नपापापहा।।२०१।।
इति सुखरात्रिः।

सुखरात्रिपरे चैव द्वितीया या सिता भवेत्।
तस्यां भातृद्वितीयायां भोजयेद् भ्रातरं स्वसा।।२०२।।

कार्तिके शुक्लपक्षस्य द्वितीयायां युधिष्ठिर।
यमो यमुनया पूर्वं भोजितः स्वगृहागतः।।२०३।।
इति भ्रातृद्वितीया।

कार्तिके मासि या दीपं दद्यादुद्दिश्य देवताम्।
पितरं वा दिने तस्य सदा तस्य फलं लभेत्।।२०४।।

---

198. BC बालखिल्ये पुनर्भवम्। This occurs on folio 79b and is verse 1345 in A.

199. BC तस्मात् शुक्ले; BC अक्ष्यां (लक्ष्यां?) निद्रां. This occurs on folio 76b and is verse 1346. This verse is quoted as माण्डव्य's in कालविवेक, pp. 196, 403.

200. BC read वसुदेवे यदा; BC यावन्नाम्भो जलनिधिशयने; the first two quarters are in different metres and 2nd line is metrically faulty.

201. A गतेन्द्रे तथा वासन्ने; BC पुष्पप्रदीपाम्बुजैः.

202. A द्वितीया सा सिता भवेत्.

203. This is quoted by का० वि०, p. 405 (from व्यास) and व० क्रि० कौ०, p. 477 (from भविष्य).

204. A पितरं वाजपेयस्य सदा भवेत्. This occurs on folio 80a and is verse 1351. This and verses 205, 206, 208 are quoted with अथ लिखन्ति in का० वि०, p. 326.

घृतेन दीपं प्रज्वाल्य तिलतैलेन वा पुनः।
दीर्घायुर्वपुषा युक्तश्चक्षुषा न च हीयते।।२०५।।

दीपदानपरो नित्यं ज्ञानदीपेन दीप्यते।
स्फुटबुद्धीन्द्रियश्चापि न कदापि विमुह्यति।।२०६।।

भवेदूर्ध्वगतिर्दीपो न कदाचिदधोगतिः।
दातापि दीप्यते चैव न तिर्यग्गतिमाप्नुयात्।।२०७।।

दीपं ददाति यो नित्यं देवतायतनेषु च।
चतुष्पथेषु विप्रेषु रूपवान्सुभगो भवेत्।।२०८।।

ज्वलमानं तथा दीपं हरेन्निर्वापयेन्न च।
दीपहर्ता भवेदन्धस्तमो गतिहतः प्रदः(?)।।२०९।।

दामोदराय नभसि तुलायां लोलया सह।
प्रदीपं ते प्रयच्छन्ति नमोऽनन्ताय वेधसे।।२१०।।

इत्याकाशदीपः।

कार्तिकाद्या द्विभा मासाः फाल्गुनस्तु त्रिभिः (भः?) स्मृतः।
अन्तोपान्ते त्रिभिर्मासैः कार्तिकादिव्यवस्थया।।२११।।

सौरो मासो विवाहादौ यज्ञादौ सावनो मतः।
प्रतिसंवत्सरश्राद्धे मासश्चान्द्रमसः स्मृतः।।२१२।।

अतः सावनमानेन मासाश्चान्द्रेण कीर्तिताः।
मासाः सौरेण मानेन नक्षत्रेण च नाडिकाः।।२१३।।

---

206. A न कदाचिदपि मुह्यति (wrong metre); B omits by mistake (copyist's eye travles further) ज्ञान . . . मुह्यति, the next verse and one quarter of the verse next to it.

209. BC ०स्तमोह गतिता प्रभुः.

210. This occurs on folio 80a and is verse 1357.

211. A फाल्गुनस्तु द्विभः स्मृतः and कार्तिक्यादि०.

212. This is on folio 80a verse 1359. The two verses 212 and 213 are in reverse order in BC. 213 occurs in का० वि० 395 (without name) reading आब्दिके पितृकार्ये च.

तुलामकरमेषेषु प्रातःस्नायी भवेत्सदा।
हविष्यं ब्रह्मचर्यं च महापातकनाशनम्।।२१४।।

यदीच्छेद्विपुलान् भोगान् चन्द्रसूर्यग्रहोपमान्।
कार्तिके सकले मासे प्रातःस्नायी भवेत्सदा।।२१५।।

इति कार्तिकस्नानादिचान्द्रसौरसावनादिविधिः।

वृश्चिकस्थे सहस्रांशौ मृगशीर्षभसंयुते।
पौर्णमास्यां प्रदोषे तु देवतामर्चयेत्सदा।।२१६।।

माघे शुक्लचतुर्थ्यां तु वरमाराध्य च श्रियम्।
पञ्चम्यां कुन्दकुसुमैः पूज्या कौन्दी समृद्धये।।२१७।।

वरचतुर्थीपञ्चम्यौ।

पौर्णमास्यो भवन्त्यन्याः कामं नक्षत्रयोगतः।
माघ एव तु माघी स्यान्मकरस्थे दिवाकरे।।२१८।।

श्रवणे स्याद्यदा भानुः पित्र्ये चैव निशाकरः।
महामाघी तदा ज्ञेया इति प्राह बृहस्पतिः।।२१९।।

माघे मासि रटन्त्यापः किञ्चिदभ्युदिते रवौ।
ब्रह्मघ्नं वा सुरापं वा कं पतन्तं पुनीमहे।।२२०।।

माघस्नानं महापुण्यं सर्वपापप्रणाशनम्।
ऋषयस्तेन धर्मेण प्राप्ता ब्रह्म सनातनम्।।२२१।।

इति माघस्नानम्।

214-15. BC omit 1 verses from हविष्यँ . . . प्रातःस्नायी भवेत्सदा by mistake (the eye having travelled from the first occurrence of प्रातःस्नायी भवेत्सदा in verse तुलामकर०). Verse 214 is quoted from भविष्य by व० क्रि० कौ०, p. 240 and from राजमार्तण्ड by क० र०, p. 149.

215. This occurs in का० वि०, 327 (without name) reading प्रातःस्नायी भवेन्नित्यं द्वौ मासौ माघफाल्गुनौ, but noticing the 2nd half as a various reading. A reads ०सौरश्रावणादिविधिः.

217. This is q. by व० क्रि० का० p. 498 (without name). It occurs on folio 80a and is verse 1364.

218. BC कामनक्षत्रयोगतः. Verses 218-21 are on folio 80b and are verses 1365-68.

219. CB पञ्च चैव निशाकरः.

220. BC ब्रह्मघ्नमपि चाण्डालं कं०; व० क्रि० कौ० 490 ascribes this verse to भविष्य; 220-21 are verses q. by का० वि०, p. 328 (without name).

सूर्यग्रहणतुल्या हि शुक्ला माघस्य सप्तमी।
तस्यामुदयवेलायां स्नात्वा पापैः प्रमुच्यते।।२२२।।

जननी सर्वभूतानां सप्तमी सप्तसप्तिका।
सप्तव्याहृतिके देवि नमस्ते सूर्यमण्डले।।२२३।।

यद्यज्जन्मकृतं पापं मया सप्तसु जन्मसु।
तन्मे रोगं च शोकं च माकरी हन्तु सप्तमी।।२२४।।

इति माघसप्तमी।

शुक्लाष्टम्यां तु माघस्य दद्याद्भीष्माय यो जलम्।
संवत्सरकृतं पापं तत्क्षणादेव नश्यति।।२२५।।

वैयाघ्रपद्यगोत्राय सांकृतिप्रवराय च।
अपुत्राय ददाम्येतत्सलिलं भीष्मवर्मणे।।२२६।।

इति भीष्माष्टमी।

फाल्गुने पौर्णमास्यां तु पटवासविलासिका।
ज्ञेया फाल्गुनिका सा च कार्या लोकैर्विभूतये।।२२७।।

फाल्गुनीऋक्षसंयुक्ते कुम्भस्थे च दिवाकरे।
रथस्थं स्कन्दमालोक्य मुच्यते ब्रह्महत्यया।।२२८।।

स्कन्दतीर्थे नरः स्नात्वा मौनं कृत्वा शिखिध्वजम्।
स्थानं प्रदक्षिणीकृत्य मुच्यते ब्रह्महत्यया।।२२९।।

---

222. First half is quoted by व० क्रि० कौ०, p. 499 (from भविष्य), by क० र०, p. 509 (without name) and का० वि०, p. 385 (without name).

223. A सर्वलोकानां; B omits सप्तसप्तिका.

223-24. These are quoted by क० र०, p. 509 (without name).

225. A मुच्यते for नश्यति. This occurs on folio 80b and is verse 1372. Verses 225-26 are q. by का० वि० p. 423 (without name), व० क्रि० कौ०, p. 503 (from भविष्योत्तर).

BC read भीष्मशर्मणे; A सातनुप्रवराय (शान्तनु?).

227. This is q. by का० वि०, p. 352 from लिङ्गपुराण and it reads 2nd पाद as 'सदा बालविलासिनी'.

228-9. Both these are marked as verse 1375 in A.

संयोगे द्वादशीपुष्ये कुम्भस्थे च दिवाकरे।
महापुण्यात्मके काले पूज्यो(ज्या?) ब्रह्महरीश्वरौ(राः?)।।२३०।।

कुम्भे-तिग्ममयूखमालिनि निशानाथोपगूढे गुरौ
द्वादश्यां विधिवद्विधाय विविधां पूजां हरेः श्रद्धया।
सर्पिः प्राश्य हविष्यमच्युतकथां शृण्वन् व्यपोहत्यघं
द्वादश्यां विधिरेष पुण्यदतमः कार्यो बुधैः सर्वदा।।२३१।।

द्वादश्यां शुक्लपक्षे शशिनि गुरुयुते कुम्भसंस्थे खरांशौ
कृत्वा पूजां सुरारेर्विधिविहितहविः प्राशयेन्मन्त्रपूतम्।
पुष्यं घिष्ण्यं न चेत्स्यात् तदपि विधिरयं वासुदेवस्य कृत्स्नं
द्वादश्यामेव कुर्यान्नहि भवति विधिर्द्वादशीमन्तरेण।।२३२।।

इति पुष्यद्वादशी।

चैत्रे मासि सिताष्टम्यामशोककुसुमैर्बुधः।
अर्चयेन्मन्मथं देवमशोकार्थं च सर्वदा।।२३३।।

त्वामशोक हराभीष्ट मधुमाससमुद्भव।
पिबामि शोकसन्तप्तो मामशोकं सदा कुरु।।२३४।।

अशोककलिकाश्चाष्टौ ये पिबन्ति पुनर्वसौ।
चैत्रे मासि सिताष्टम्यां न ते शोकमवाप्नुयुः।।२३५।। इत्यशोकाष्टमी।

भूतदिने मनुजानां क्रीडारससङ्कुलो नृपतिः।
मन्मथतिथिसंयुक्ता कर्तव्या च चैत्रावलिका।।२३६।।

रात्रौ त्रयोदशीं प्राप्य उद्याने कृत्रिमे शुभे।
सरतिं मन्मथं स्थाप्य क्रीडयेदपरेऽहनि।।२३७।।

---

230. BC read संयोगे; BC पुष्यो.

231. BC read पुष्यविगमे for पुण्यदतमः.

232. A कुम्भयुक्ते; A भवति कदा द्वादशी० This occurs on folio 80b and is marked as verse 1377.

233. A अर्चयेन्मृन्मयं.

234-35. These are q. by का० वि०, p. 422 from लिङ्गपुराण.

236. BC भूतंशिते मनुजानां; A संङ्कलो नृपतेः; BC नृपते; A कर्तव्या सा चैत्रा०; BC कर्तव्या सा च चैत्रा० This is on folio 81a and is verse 1381 in A.

237. A प्राप्य for स्थाप्य.

मधौ मासि सिते पक्षे कामक्रीडे (डा?) तिथित्रये।
तस्मात् त्रयोदशीविद्धा भवेत्पूज्या चतुर्दशी।।२३८।।

क्रीडाकालविनिर्मुक्ता कामविद्धा चतुर्दशी।
क्रीडार्थं च महादेवं मन्मथं तत्र कारयेत्।।२३९।।

इति चैत्रावली।

धवलितकलशन्यस्ता रक्तपताकान्विता स्नुही भवने।
चैत्रासितभूततिथौ पापरूजं दूरतो धत्ते।।२४०।।

इति चैत्रवारिकदानम्।

ज्येष्ठे संवत्सरे चैव ज्येष्ठमासस्य पूर्णिमा।
ज्येष्ठाभेन यदा युक्ता महाज्यैष्ठी प्रकीर्तिता।।२४१।।

ऐन्द्रे शशी गुरुश्चैव प्राजापत्ये रविस्तथा।
पूर्णिमा ज्येष्ठमासस्य महाज्यैष्ठी भवेत्तदा।।२४२।।

माससंज्ञे यदा ऋक्षे चन्द्रः सम्पूर्णमण्डलः।
गुरुणा याति संयोगं सा तिथिर्महती स्मृता।।२४३।।

महामाघी प्रयागे तु नैमिषे फाल्गुनी तथा।
शालग्रामे महाचैत्री एताः पुण्यतमाः स्मृताः।।२४४।।

गङ्गाद्वारे च वैशाखी ज्यैष्ठी तु पुरुषोत्तमे।
आषाढी कनखले चैव केदारे श्रावणी तथा।।२४५।।

महाभाद्री बदर्यां तु कुब्जायां च महाश्विनी।
पुष्करे कार्तिकी कान्यकुब्जे मार्गी सदा स्मृता।।२४६।।

237-38. These are q. fom रा० मा० by व० क्रि० कौ०, p. 530.

240. इति चैत्रावस्तिकदानम् (? चैत्रावलिक०). This verse occurs in folio 81a, verse 1985. It occurs in का० वि०, p. 471 (without name).

241. BC संवत्सरे. This is quoted by व० क्रि० का०, p. 79 from रा० मा० reading from the ज्येष्ठ०.

242. It is q. by व० क्रि० कौ०, p. 78 from रा० मा० (reading गुरुवारेण for ज्येष्ठमासस्य).

243. This is q. by का० वि०, p. 346 (from भारत) and व० क्रि० कौ०, p. 77 (reading विष्णुधर्मोत्तर, I. 52-65).

244. The following three verses are q. by का० वि० p. 351 (without name) occur no folio 81a and are verses 1389-92.

245. A वैशाखी.

अयोध्यायां महापौषी एताः स्युः सुमहाफलाः।
स्नानं ह्येतेषु कर्तव्यं मानवैः पुष्टिकांक्षिभिः।।२४७।।

वृषराशिस्थिते सूर्ये शुक्लपक्षे चतुर्दशी।
प्रोक्ता रुद्रार्चनायैवं(व?) सा चम्पकचतुर्दशी।।२४८।।

ज्येष्ठे मासि चतुर्दश्यां सावित्रीव्रतमुत्तमम्।
अवैधव्याय कुर्वन्ति स्त्रियः श्रद्धासमन्विताः।।२४९।।
इति सावित्रीव्रतम्।

वृषराशिस्थिते सूर्ये शुक्लपक्षे चतुर्थिका।
पञ्चतपा तु सा ज्ञेया पाषाणा चाभिधीयते।।२५०।।
इति पाषाणचतुर्थी।

ज्येष्ठे मासि सिते पक्षे षष्ठी चारण्यसंज्ञिता।
व्यजनैककरास्तस्यां रटन्ति विपिने स्त्रियः।।२५१।।
इत्यरण्यषष्ठी।।

ज्येष्ठशुक्लदशम्यां तु हस्तयोगेन जाह्नवी।
हरते दशपापानि तस्माद् दशहरा स्मृता।।२५२।।

यां काञ्चित्सरितं प्राप्य दद्याद् दर्भतिलोदकम्।
हरते दशपापानि तस्माद् दशहरा स्मता।।२५३।।

---

247. A स्युः स महाफलम्; BC एताः सुसुमहाफलाः. This occurs on folio 81a and is verse 1392.

248. A सा च चम्यक् चतुर्दशी. Verses 248-49 are q. by क० र०, p. 192 from रा० मा० and occur on folio 81a, verses 1393-94.

249. BC ज्येष्ठासिते चतुर्दश्यां. व० क्रि० कौ० p. 260 quotes this verse from रा० मा० but reads ज्येष्ठऽसितचतुर्दश्यां and add one more verse not found in the Mss. consulted viz. ज्येष्ठे कृष्णचतुर्दश्यां सावित्रीमर्चयन्ति याः। वटमूले सोपवासा न ता वैधव्यमाप्नुयुः।।

251. BC व्यञ्जनैककरास्तस्या०. This occurs on folio 81b and is verse 1396. This is q. by कृ० र०, p. 185, व० क्रि० कौ० 279, कृ० त० 430 as from रा० मा०, but व० क्रि० कौ०, p. 279 and कृ० त० add two more verses from रा० मा० which do not occur in the Mss. consulted.

252. BC हरेद्रै दश. This and the verses up to 260 occur on folio 81b and are verses 1397-1405. This is q. by व० क्रि० कौ०, p. 279 from भविष्य.

253. A दुर्भ्रतिलाक्षतैः. कृ० र०, p. 137 quotes the first half as a गौड़वाक्य and का० वि०, p. 400 from स्कन्द.

ज्येष्ठे मासि सिते पक्षे दशम्यां भौमवासरे।
अवतीर्णा यता गङ्गा हस्तर्क्षे च सरिद्वरा।।२५४।।

ज्येष्ठे शुक्लदशम्यां तु भवेद्भौमदिनं यदि।
ज्ञेया हस्तर्क्षसंयुक्ता सर्वपापहरा तिथिः।।२५५।।

परद्रव्येष्वभिध्यानं मनसानिष्टचिन्तनम्।
वितथाभिनिवेशश्च त्रिविधं कर्म मानसम्।।२५६।।

पारुष्यमनृतं चैव पैशुन्यं चापि सर्वतः।
असम्बद्धप्रलापश्च वाङ्मयं स्याच्चतुर्विधम्।।२५७।।

अदत्तानामुपादानं हिंसा चैवाविधानतः।
परदारोपसेवा च शारीरं त्रिविधं स्मृतम्।।२५८।।

एतानि दश पापानि प्रशमं यान्तु जाह्नवि।
स्नातस्य मम ते देवि जलैर्विष्णुपदोद्भवैः।।२५९।।

विष्णुपादार्घसम्भूते गङ्गे त्रिपथगामिनि।
धर्मद्रवीति विख्याते पापं मे हर जाह्नवि।।२६०।।

इति दशहरा।

रविसङ्क्रमणे पुण्ये यो न स्नातीह मानवः।
सप्तजन्मान्तरं रोगी दुःखभागी सदा भवेत्।।२६१।।

---

255. व० क्रि० कौ०, p. 280 quotes this from ब्रह्मपुराण.

256. BC मानसं त्रिविधं स्मृतम्.

256-58. These are cited by का० वि०, pp. 401-2 (without name), व० क्रि० कौ०, pp. 280-82 (from काशीखण्ड).

259. A हर त्वं मम जाह्नवि. This is cited from काशीखण्ड by व० क्रि० कौ०, p. 281.

260. B ०पादार्थसम्भूते; A त्रिपदगामिनि; this is quoted by कृ० त०, p. 431 (without name).

261. This is q. from रा० मा० by व० क्रि० कौ०, p. 214, का० वि०, p. 381 (from भगवतीपुराण), कृ० र०, p. 617 (from देवीपुराण). This and verses up to 268 occur on folio 81b and are verses 1406-13.

संक्रान्त्यां यानि दानानि हव्यकव्यानि मानवैः।
तानि तेषां ददात्यर्कः सप्तजन्म पुनः पुनः।।२६२।।

संक्रान्तिसमयः सूक्ष्मो दुर्लक्ष्यश्चापि स क्षणः।
तस्य योगादधश्चोर्ध्वं त्रिंशन्नाड्यस्तु कीर्तिताः।।२६३।।

अहःसंक्रमणे पुण्यमहः कृत्स्नं प्रकीर्तितम्।
रात्रिसंक्रमणे पुण्यं दिनार्धं स्नानदानयोः।।२६४।।

अर्धरात्रदधस्तस्य दिनार्धस्योपरि क्रिया।
ऊर्ध्वं संक्रमणे भानोरुदयात्प्रहरद्वयम्।।२६५।।

सम्पूर्णे चार्धरात्रे तु भानुः संक्रमते यदा।
पुण्यकालं प्रयत्नेन प्रभाते मनुरब्रवीत्।।२६६।।

निरंशः सविता यत्र तद्दिने स्नानमाचरेत्।
दानं चाप्यक्षयं प्रोक्तमंशकं प्राप्य निष्फलम्।।२६७।।

निरंशेन यदा भानुः पूर्वापरदिनद्वये।
पूजयेद्वासरं पूर्वमपरं पुण्यवर्जितम्।।२६८।।

निशार्धे वलिते भानौ निरंशं चेद् दिनद्वयम्।
पूर्वे त्वहनि कर्तव्यं स्नानदानजपादिकम्।।२६९।।

सम्पूर्णे चार्धरात्रे तु भानुः संक्रमते यदा।
तदा दिनद्वयं पुण्यं मुक्त्वा मकरकर्कटौ।।२७०।।

---

262. BC read संक्रान्त्यां यानि हव्य० (omitting by mistake the word दानानि) तानि तस्या ददात्यर्कः; का० वि०, p. 381 quotes this from भगवतीपुराण, कृ० र०, p. 617 (from शातातप).

264. This is q. by का० वि०, p. 387 (without name) and ति० त०, p. 144 remarks that it is cited in कालविवेक.

265. व० क्रि० कौ०, p. 218, quotes this from रा० मा० but reads ०धश्चेत्स्यात्तस्मिन्नेवाह्नि क्रिया and भानोरपरेऽहनि तत्क्रिया; ति० त०, p. 142 says that this verse is cited by भोजराज and चिन्तामणि; so it probably refers to रा० मा०.

266. BC पुन्यकालं प्रियन्नेन for पुण्यकालं &c.

269. BC निशार्धो बलिते; BC पूर्णे त्वहनि. This occurs on folio 82a and is verse 1414.

270. BC भानुः संक्रमणे यदा.

रात्रौ संक्रमिते भानौ विषुवत्यगते दिने।
या याः संनिहिता नाड्यस्तास्ताः पुण्यतमाः स्मृताः।।२७१।।

अतीतानागते पुण्ये ये तूदग्दक्षिणायने।
उपरागे तु तत्काले व्यतीते विषुवद्द्वये।।२७२।।

अयने विषुवे द्वे च चतस्रः षडशीतयः।
चतस्रो विष्णुपद्यश्च संक्रान्त्यो द्वादश स्मृताः।।२७३।।

मृगकर्कटसंक्रान्ती हे उदग्दक्षिणायने।
विषुवती तुलामेषे गोलमध्यगताः पराः।।२७४।।

मिथुनमीनधनुःकन्याः षडशीतिरुदाहृताः।
वृषवृश्चिककुम्भेषु सिंहे विष्णुपदी स्मृता।।२७५।।

विषुवन्मेषतुलायामयनं मकरे रवौ कुलीरे च।
षडशीतिर्द्विशरीरे (? ०शीतिर्द्विश०) विष्णुपदी च स्थिरे राशौ।।२७६।।

अयने कोटिगुणं पुण्यं लक्षं विष्णुपदीफलम्।
षडशीतिसहस्रं च षडशीत्यां स्मृतं बुधैः।।२७७।।

शतमिन्दुक्षये दानं सहस्रं तु दिनक्षये।
विषुवे शतसाहस्रं व्यतीपाते त्वनन्तकम्।।२७८।।

---

272. BC पुण्ये द्वे तूदग्दक्षिणायने.

A adds after the verse अतीतानागते . . . विषुवद्द्वये; one verse and a half viz. भविष्यत्यवने पुण्यमतीते चोत्तरायणे। मृगकर्कटसंक्रान्ती द्वे उदग्दक्षिणायने। ग्रहोपरागतत्काल (?) मतीते विषुवद्द्वये, which are verses 1418-19.

273. This is on folio 82a and is verses 1419-1420.

273-75. This are q. by का० वि०, p. 380 (from ज्योतिःशास्त्र) and by व० क्रि० कौ०, p. 204 (from अग्निपुराण).

274. A विषुवती तुले मेषे गोले मध्य०.

275. This is on folio 82a and corresponds to 1421-22.

277-78. Are q. by व० क्रि० कौ०, p. 214 from रा० मा० (reads आकामावैष्वनन्तकम्) and by का० वि०, pp. 381-82 from ज्योतिःशास्त्र.

278. A विपुवे शतसहस्रं च . . . नन्दकम्; BC व्यतीपाते त्वनन्तरम्।

शरदि विषुवे रात्रौ हेमन्ते च यदा दिवा।
उभयोः सस्यवृद्धिः स्याद्विपर्यासो विपर्यये।।२७६।।

मेषं याति यदा दिवा दिनपती रात्रौ तलां गच्छति
द्योतन्ते धनधान्यवस्त्रनिचयैः सम्यक्प्रजाः पूजिताः।
साधूनामुदयस्तदा वसुमती सस्यैः समग्रा भवेद्
राजानोऽपि परस्परं प्रियतमा मुञ्चन्ति वैराण्यपि।।२८०।।

समं संक्रमते भानुर्गरदादिकरणेषु च।
आदिद्वये सूपविष्ट ऊर्ध्वश्चैव ततो द्वये।।२८१।।

दुर्भिक्षरोगसम्पत्ती ऊर्ध्वं संक्रमते रविः।
समः (सुप्तः?) करोति कल्याणमुपविष्टः समं फलम्।।२८२।।

मृते जन्मनि संक्रान्तौ ग्रहणे सूर्यचन्द्रयोः।
अस्पर्शस्पर्शने चैव न स्नायादुष्णवारिणा।।२८३।।

इति संक्रान्तिनिर्णयः।

एकस्मिन्सावने त्वह्नि तिथीनां त्रितयं यदा।
तदा दिनक्षयः प्रोक्तस्तत्र साहस्रिकं फलम्।।२८४।।

त्र्यहस्पृग्दिवसश्चैव महापुण्यतमः स्मृतः।
तिथित्रयस्य संस्पर्शात् त्र्यहस्पृक् स उदाहृतः।।२८५।।

दिनेऽयने पर्वणि प्रातःकाले शशाङ्कसूर्यग्रहणे युते च।
धर्मं विदध्याद् विषुवद्वये च यत्तस्य पुंसोऽक्षयधर्मकोषः।।२८६।।

इति दिनक्षयः।

---

279. A ०पर्यायासे विपर्ययम्; BC विपर्यायासो विपर्ययम्.

280. BC साप्ते संक्रसते भानु०. The second half is very corrupt in all three Mss. The text is conjectural.

282-6. These occur on folio 82a and are verses 1428-32.

282. is quoted by व० क्रि० कौ०, p. 211 from रा० मा०

283. This is quoted by व० क्रि० का०, p. 214 from वराह.

284-5. These two are q. from रा० मा० by शु० कौ०, p. 214.

285. This is cited by का० वि०, p. 332 from भगवतीपुराण (probably the same देवीपुराण), but reads 4th पाद as तत्र दत्तमनन्तकम्.

286. BC शशाङ्कसूर्यग्रहणायनद्वये.

[This paper is published in *ABORI* 36, pp. 306-39, 1956. In *Jyotiṣa-maṇimālā* of *Keśavadaivajña* (Ms. No. 409 in the Descriptive Catalogue of Sanskrit manuscripts prepared by Prof. G.V. Devasthali, a portion from the *Rājamārtaṇḍa* of Bhoja is found copied] *S.G. Moghe*

6

The Meaning of 'Ācāryāḥ'

IN several works inspired by a study of the *Arthaśāstra* of Kauṭilya the views put forward as those of the *ācārya*s are supposed to have been held by the teacher of Kauṭilya himself. For instance, Prof. K.V. Rangaswami Aiyangar in his recent work *Rājadharma* states on p. 91 "Kauṭilya cites the views of his teacher to whom he shows reverence in Hindu style by referring to him not by name, but by the word *ācārya* in the honorific plural as many as thirty-nine times[1] and each citation is for the purpose of dissenting from the teacher's views." It is proposed in this article to examine the correctness of his opinion by reference to the usage of writers and works earlier and later than Kauṭilya.

The word *ācārya* is derived by the *Āpastambadharmasūtra*[2] (I.1.1.13 and 15) as '*ācārya* is he from whom he (the pupil) gathers the (knowledge) of religious duties; he (as if) gives birth to him (the pupil) through (the transmission of) Vedic learning'. Gautama (*Dharmasūtra*, I.10-11) states 'He is the *ācārya* who performs the *upanayana* of a pupil and teaches him the *Veda*'. *Manu*, II.140, *Vasiṣṭha*, II.4 and III.21, define *ācārya* in similar terms. Therefore the first meaning of the word *ācārya* is 'teacher of the *Veda*' (in the case of a pupil).

Another sense arose from this meaning of the word. The founder of a *śāstra* or any great teacher of any *śāstra* is called *ācārya* by subsequent writers. For examiple, Patañjali[3] when dealing with the two *vārtikas* '*bhave* and *proktādayaśca taddhitāḥ*' states that the *ācārya* (meaning Pāṇini) first composed the *sūtra* — *tatra bhavaḥ* (IV. 3.53) and then composed the *sūtra* — *tena proktam* (IV.3.101) and that *ācāryas* after first composing individual *sūtras* do not give them up. On the *vārtika* — *siddhe śabdārtha-sambandhe*, Patañjali[4] speaks of the *vārtikakāra* as *ācārya*. There are numerous places in the *Mahābhāṣya* where the epithet *ācārya* is applied to Pāṇini or to the *Vārtikakāra* according to the exigencies of the discussion (e.g. vol. I, p. 481, vol. II, p. 163, II.349, 359 for its application to the *Vārtikakāra*). Neither Pāṇini nor Kātyāyana is deemed by any one to be the teacher of Patañjali.

Śabara in his *bhāṣya* on Jaimini, III.4.13 states the view of the *ācārya* that[5] "the base and the termination together convey the sense of the termination and further that the *ācāryas* lay down in such *sūtras* as *kartari śap* (Pāṇini, III.1.68) that the termination denotes the agent or the object." Here the word *ācārya* is applied to Patañjali and the same word (in the plural) is applied to Pāṇini. In the same context a little later on Pānini is styled *sūtrakāra* and Patañjali simply *ācārya*.

Some passages from very ancient works where the word *ācāryāḥ* occurs may now be profitably set out. The *Aitareya Āraṇyaka* (III.2.6) states[6] that the *ācāryas* held that 'these *Saṁhitās* should not be imparted to one who is not a pupil, nor to one who does not stay (with the teacher) for a year, nor to one who may not or will not himself be an expounder.' Here by the word *ācāryāḥ* Sāyana does not understand the direct teacher of him, whoever he may be, that had the revelation of the *Āraṇyaka*, but 'great men who are endowed with the qualities of an *ācārya*' Similar rules about imparting some esoteric lore occur elsewhere also (without *ācāryāḥ* being added).

In the *Nirukta* there is a discussion[7] about Vaiśvānara 'Then who is Vaiśvānara? The *ācāryas* say that he is the (fire) in the intermediate regions, since (the Vedic sage) praises him on account of his action of sending down rain. The ancient *Yājñikas* hold that Vaiśvānara is the Sun and Śākapūṇī holds that he is this (terrestial) fire only'. Yāska does not state his own view, but as Śākapūṇi's opinion is placed last he most probably approved of that view. It is well-known that Yāska names numerous predecessors and also quotes the views of several schools of Vedic exegesis such as the *Nairuktas*, *Naidānas*, *Vaiyākaraṇas*, *Aitihāsikas*. It is very natural to hold that Yāska refers to his predecessors on the subject by the word *ācāryāḥ*. The two commentators Durga and Maheśvara support this view.

The *Hārīta Dharmasūtra*[8] as quoted by Aparārka (p. 221) states "a man should therefore be pure and should take a proper (requisite) and limited quantity of food. The *ācāryas* say 'purity of mind results when there is purity in the food taken'." The words quoted as voicing the view of the *ācāryas* are found in the *Chāndogya Upaniṣad*, VII.26.2. Therefore it follows that Hārīta is quoting the view of the inspired teachers of the *Upaniṣads* and it is impossible to hold that he is stating the view of his own teacher only.

In the discussion about *āśramas* the *Gautama Dharmasūtra* (III.36)[9] states 'But the *ācāryas* prescribe one *āśrama* only, because the order of householders is explicitly enjoined (in the *Vedas*).' Haradatta explains the word *ācāryāḥ* as 'all teachers'. Maskarin also holds that the word *ācāryāḥ* means 'Some teachers'. The same *sūtra* occurs in the *Baudhāyana Dharmasūtra* (II.6.29). If by *ācāryāḥ* the writer's own teacher is meant, then we shall have to suppose that the teachers of both Gautama and Baudhāyana held the view mentioned or that both had the same teacher. It is possible that Baudhāyana borrows Gautama's words. Even in that case it is not probable that Baudhāyana would have borrowed that *sūtra* if in his opinion it embodied merely the view of one single and so far obscure teacher of Gautama. But if in Baudhāyana's opinion *ācāryāḥ* meant 'some or many predecessors' he may naturally quote the very words of Gautama. In another place Gautama[10] (IV.18) states the view of *ācāryas* that the descendants of *anuloma* marriages 'reach another *varṇa* owing to the superiority or inferiority (of the male or female in each generation) in the seventh or fifth generation'. Here also Maskarin understands that it is the view of some *ācārya*s (and not of the teacher of Gautama) that is referred to.

It is well-known that Pāṇini mentions by name at least ten predecessors, viz. Āpiśali, Kāśyapa, Gārgya, Gālava, Cākravarmaṇa, Bhāradvāja, Śākaṭāyana, Śākalya, Senaka, Sphoṭāyana. He also refers to eastern and northern grammarians and in two places to *ācārya*s (VII.3.49, VIII.4.52). It is often said by the commentators[11] of Pāṇini that the individual authors are named only to show respect (*pūjārtham*) and not for the purpose of showing dissent from their views. No commentator says that by *ācāryāṇām*, Pāṇini refers to his own teacher. The *sūtra* — *dīrghādācāryāṇām* (VIII.4.52) comes after two *sūtra*s expressly mentioning Śākaṭāyana and Śākalya. Therefore it is reasonable to suppose that by the word *ācāryāṇām* Pāṇini refers to some teachers other than the two expressly named. The Kāśikā comments *dīrghād-uttarasya ācāryāṇām matena na dvitvam bhavati.* It does not say that the word is employed in the plural to show respect and its way of commenting shows that the *sūtra* refers to the view of some *ācārya*s. On *dīrghādācāryāṇām*, the *Nyāsa* states that the word *ācāryāṇām* is mentioned *pūjārtham*. Granting that it is so, it does not follow that it is the teacher of Pāṇini that is referred to. If by the word *ācāryāṇām* Pāṇini refers to his teacher and that too *pūjārtham*, there is no adequate reason why the teacher should be referred to only twice among thousands of *sūtra*s, particularly when some predecessors life Śākalya (I.1.1.16, VI.1.127, VIII.3.19, VIII.4.51) and Śākaṭāyana (III.4.111, VIII.3.18. VIII.4.50) are named three or four times. Therefore it must be held that Pāṇini refers to his predecessors generally by the word *ācāryāṇām*.

The *Śāntiparvan* (59) describes how Brahmā composed a vast work on the four *puruṣārtha*s and states that the *ācārya*s speak of four vices arising from *kāma*, viz., hunting, gambling, drinking wine and women, which were proclaimed by Brahmā in his work.[12] Here it is impossible to hold that *ācāryāḥ* refers to the teacher of the author of the *Mahābhārata*. Manu (VII.50) speaks of the same four vices.

The *Kāmasūtra* of Vātsyāyana is a work that, though some centuries later than the Kauṭilya, is quite similar in style, method and outlook to the Kauṭilya. Vātsyāyana informs us that several *ācārya*s like Cārāyaṇa, Suvarṇanābha, Gonardīya wrote on individual topics of the *Kāmaśāstra*, that the latter as a complete *śāstra* had become well-nigh lost, that he put into a small compass all the topics dealt with in works on distinct topics like those of Dattaka and in the comprehensive work of Bābhravya and composed the *Kāmasūtra*.[13] It is important to note that he refers to eight predecessors (mentioned in I.1.10-17) as *ācārya*s (I.1.18) and names no teacher from whom he learnt the *Kāmaśāstra*. The *Kāmasūtra* several times states the views of *ācārya*s and dissents from them. For example, the view of *ācārya*s was that as sexual desire was observed even in lower animals and as it is a constant tendency, no useful purpose is served by propounding a *śāstra* dealing with sexual desire. Vātsyāyana dissents from this view.[14] Here, as the com. *Jayamaṅgalā* rightly explains, the word *ācāryāḥ* refers to great teachers on *dharma, artha* and *mokṣa*. It is impossible to hold that *ācāryāḥ* here at least contains a reference to Vātsyāyana's own teacher on *Kāmaśāstra*, who, if one really existed, could not have told his disciple that the *śāstra* the latter was going to study was purposeless. Another view of the *ācārya*s[15] viz., that as women have no *adhikāra* nor ability (or opportunity) for the study of *śāstra*, no purpose is served by giving directions in this *śāstra* that are meant exclusively for women, is controverted by Vātsyāyana. Here also *ācāryāḥ* can hardly stand for his own teacher. In *Kāmasūtra*, II.1.70 he employs the word *ācāryāḥ* to convey the view of all writers on Erotics.[16]

Another example may be cited from a much later but famous writer. Varāhamihira (6th century AD) tells us, in the last chapter of his *Bṛhat-jātaka*, that he learnt astrology from his father (verse 9), that he received knowledge from the Sun, the sages (like Vasistha) and his father and then does obeisance to former expounders (verse 10). In his *Bṛhatsaṁhitā* (105.6) he has the same verse as *Bṛhat-jātaka*, 28.10 and asserts that in composing his *śāstra* he has not discarded the works of former *ācāryas*. In the *Bṛhatsaṁhitā* (chap. V) Varāhamihira refutes the view of those who hold that Rāhu is the cause of eclipses, states in a concise manner the real cause of solar and lunar eclipses (V.8) and remarks that the *ācāryas* that had a divine perception thus declared the real cause of eclipses and that *śāstra* states the real truth to be that Rāhu is not the cause of eclipses.[17] We find from the Āryabhaṭīya (Golapāda 37), the *Sūrya-siddhānta*, IV.6 and other works more ancient than Varāhamihira that they give the same explanation of eclipses as Varāha does. The words *śāstra-sadbhāva* and *divyadṛgbhir-ācāryaiḥ* cannot refer to his teacher of *Jyotisa* who was his father Ādityadāsa and in whose name no *śāstra* has come down to us and who has never been mentioned by any known commentator as an author.

It is not necessary to multiply examples of the use of the word *ācāryāḥ* from medieval and later writers.

A few striking passages where the views of *ācāryas* are combated by Kauṭilya may now be examined. Kauṭilya remarks[18] (I.4). "The *ācāryas* say 'The king desirous of maintaining the orderly government of the world should always have the rod of punishment ready: there is no such means of bringing beings under control as *daṇḍa*.' Kauṭilya's view is that this is not so. Since one whose rod of punishment is severe causes beings to turn away from him &c. The words of Manu, VII.102 (first *pāda*) are the same as the first part of the passage quoting the views of the *ācāryas*. Therefore here Kauṭilya is animadverting against the views now represented by Manu, and not merely the views of his own teacher.

In another place Kauṭilya (III.7)[19] starts a very important topic. "The *ācāryas* hold that (the child of) seed sown in the wife of another belongs to the owner of the field. Others say 'the mother is like bellows; the child belongs to him from whose seed the child is born; Kauṭilya holds that it belongs to both."

This subject exercised the minds of writers centuries before Kautilya. Gautama (18.9-13) mentions all the three views. *ĀpDhS*, II.6.13.6 expressly says that according to a *Brāhmaṇa* text the son .longs to him from whose seed he is born. The same three views are found in Manu, IX.50-53 and Vasiṣṭha, XVII.6-8, while Yājñavalkya, II.127 holds the same view as Kauṭilya does. The *Ādiparvan* 104 (6) states that one view was that the child of *niyoga* belonged to the husband. Vide *History of Dharmaśāstra*, Vol. II, part I, p. 605. Śaṅkha-Likhita state that according to the Vedic view the child belongs to him who is the owner of the wife, that according to Āṅgirasa the child belongs to him who had married the woman with Vedic *mantra*s and that according to Uśanas it belongs to both if it is produced on the wife of another with the mutual agreement of the husband and the person appointed.[20] We know from the Kauṭilya that among the schools on Politics there were two, viz. the Bārhaspatya and the Auśanasa. Śaṅkha-Likhita probably refer to the works of Bṛhaspati and Uśanas in the above passage. The very fact that Kauṭilya employs the word *apare* with regard to the second view leads irresistibly to the conclusion that in *ācaryāḥ* he refers to the view of *eke* and not to that of his teacher. If it is once accepted that in the above two passages *ācāryāḥ* does not refer to the teacher of Kauṭilya, then it will have to be presumed, until the contrary is proved, that Kauṭilya must have followed a uniform practice and in all other places he employs the word in the sense of 'some teachers'. The other numerous places where the views of *ācārya*s are cited and controverted cannot be discussed here for limitations of space. There is a further argument. It is somewhat difficult to understand why, if Kauṭilya employs the plural *ācāryāḥ* to show veneration for his teacher, he should have so many times, so vehemently and emphatically dissented from that honoured teacher, while he expresses dissent from seven predecessors only once and from others, only a few times. Later writers whenever they have to differ from the views of their father or teacher use very mild and halting expressions, e.g. *vide* Nīlakaṇṭha in his *Srāddha-mayūkha* (quoted in my

Introduction to the text of the *Vyavahāra-mayūkha*, p. XXXVII, n. 1).[21]

The foregoing discussion, it is hoped, establishes that *ācāryāḥ* in Kauṭilya should not be taken as referring to the author's teacher, but to previous great writers, since the usage of ancient writers and the traditional interpretation of such eminent commentators, as Durga, Haradatta, Maskarin, Sāyaṇa and others, is quite clear on the point.

References

[This paper is first published in *ABORI*, 23, pp. 206-13, 1942. Dr. Kane has made a passing reference to this article in his *History of Dharmaśāstra*, Vol. I/I, p. 209, ***Also see*** the discussion on p. 233 of the same volume. It may be noted here that in the Volume I, published in 1930, there is no reference to this article and it is but natural.] *S.G. Moghe*

1. Kauṭilya cites the *ācārya*s at least 54 times and not *39 times* only.
2. यस्माद्धर्मानाचिनोति सं आचार्यः। स हि विद्यास्तं जनयति। आप० ध०, I.1.1.13 and 15; तद्यस्मात्स आचार्यः। वेदानुवचनाच्च। गौ०, I.10-11.
3. पुरस्तादिदमाचार्येण दृष्टं भवे तद्धित इति तत्पठितम्। तत उत्तरकालमिदं दृष्टं प्रोक्तादयश्च तद्धिता इति तदपि पठितम्। न चेदानीमाचार्याः सूत्राणि कृत्वा निवर्तयन्ति। महाभाष्य (ed. by Kielhorn, Vol. I, p. 12) Similar words occur in several places, e.g., Vol. III, p. 393.
4. माङ्गलिक आचार्यो महतः शास्त्रौघस्य मङ्गलार्थं सिद्धशब्दमादितः प्रयुङ्क्ते। महाभाष्य, Vol. I, p. 7.
5. प्रकृतिप्रत्ययौ प्रत्ययार्थं सह ब्रूत इत्याचार्योपदेशात् कर्ता शब्दार्थः कर्म चेत्यवगम्यते। कर्तरि शप् कर्मणि यगिति प्रत्ययार्थं कर्तारं कर्म च समामनन्त्याचार्याः। तस्माच्छब्दार्थः कर्ता कर्म चेति। उच्यते। नाचार्यवचनात्सूत्रकारवचनाद्वा शब्दार्थो भवति। प्रत्ययादसौ गम्यते। शबरभाष्य on जैमिनि, III.4.13. The words प्रकृतिप्रत्ययौ . . . ब्रूतः occur in the *Mahābhāṣya* on *vārtika* 2 on Pāṇini, III.1.67 (महाभाष्य, Vol. II, p. 58). That Śabara refers to passages of the *Mahābhāṣya* in several places will be shown in another paper.
6. ता एताः संहिता नानत्वेवासिने प्रब्रूयान्नासंवत्सरवासिने नाप्रवक्त्र इत्याचार्याः। ऐतरेयारण्यक, III.2.6; compare बृह० उप०, VI. 3.12. एतं नापुत्राय वानन्तेवासिने वा ब्रूयात्।

7. तत्को वैश्वानरो मध्यम इत्याचार्या वर्ष कर्मणा ह्येनं स्तौति . . . अथासावादित्य इति पूर्वे याज्ञिकाः। . . . अयमेवाग्निर्वैश्वानर इति शाकपूणिः। — निरुक्त, VII.22-23.
8. हारीतः। . . . तस्माच्छुचिर्यथार्थपरिमिताहारः स्यात्। आहारशुद्धौ सत्त्वशुद्धिरित्याचार्याः। — अपरार्क, p. 221.
9. ऐकाश्रम्यं त्वाचार्याः प्रत्यक्षविधानाद्गार्हस्थ्यस्य। गौतम, III.35; ऐकाश्रम्यं त्वाचार्या अप्रजनत्वादितरेषाम्। बौ० ध० सू०, II. 6.29; वैखानसस्योक्त्वा इदानीमेकीयमतेनाश्रम-बाधपक्षं वक्तुकाम आह। ऐका०। गार्हस्थ्यमेवाचार्या इच्छन्ति। मस्करिभाष्य on गौतम. The words अप्रजनत्वादितरेषाम् occur in गौतम, III.3.
10. बर्णान्तरगमनमुत्कर्षापकर्षाभ्यां सप्तमे पञ्चमे वाचार्याः। गौतम, IV.18; पञ्चमेनैव युगपरिवर्तनेन वर्णान्तरगमनं भवतीति केचिदाचार्या वर्णयन्ति। मस्करिभाष्य. For detailed explanation, *vide History of Dharmaśāstra*, Vol. II, part I, pp. 62-64.
11. Even Patañjali on Pāṇini, I.2.25 (तृषिमृषिकृशेः काश्यपस्य) states that Kāśyapa is mentioned for showing respect 'काश्यपग्रहणं किमर्थम्। काश्यपग्रहणं पूजार्थम्। वेत्येव हि वर्तते।' महाभाष्य, vol. I, p. 201.
12. मृगयाक्षास्तथा पानं स्त्रियश्च भरतर्षभ।
कामजान्याहुराचार्याः प्रोक्तानीह स्वयम्भुवा।। — शान्तिपर्व, 59.60
vide also प्रागेवोक्तस्तु दोषोयमाचार्यैर्नृपसेविनाम्। — शान्ति०, 82.83
13. एवं बहुभिराचार्यैस्तच्छास्त्रं खण्डशः प्रणीतमुत्सन्नकल्पमभूत्। तत्र दत्तकादिभिः प्रणीतानां शास्त्रावयवानामेकदशत्वात्, महदिति च बाभ्रवीयस्य दुरध्येयत्वात् संक्षिप्य सर्वमर्थमल्पेन ग्रन्थेन कामसूत्रमिदं प्रणीतम्। — कामसूत्र, I.1.18-19 (ed. in Kashi S. Series).
14. तिर्यग्योनिष्वपि तु स्वयं प्रवृत्तत्वात्कामस्य नित्यत्वाच्च न शास्त्रेण कृत्यमस्तीत्याचार्याः। . . . सा चोपायप्रतिपत्तिः कामसूत्रादिति वात्स्यायनः। — कामसूत्र, I.2.21 and 23.
15. योषितां शास्त्रग्रहणस्याभावादनर्थकमिह शास्त्रे स्त्रीशासनमित्याचार्याः। प्रयोगग्रहणं त्वासां प्रयोगस्य च शास्त्रपूर्वकत्वादिति वात्स्यायनः। — कामसूत्र, I.3.4-5.
16. प्राप्नुवन्त्याशु ताः प्रीतिमित्याचार्या व्यवस्थिताः।। — कामसूत्र, II.1.70· 'सर्वेषामेतदेव मतमव्यभिचारित्वात्।' — जयमङ्गला.
17. एवमुपरागकारणमुक्तमिदं दिव्यदृग्भिराचार्यैः। राहुरकारणमस्मिन्नित्युक्तः शास्त्रसद्भावः।
— बृहत्संहिता, V. 13.
18. तस्माल्लोकयात्रार्थी नित्यमुद्यतदण्डः स्यात्। न ह्येवंविधं वशोपनयनमस्ति भूतानां यथा दण्ड इत्याचार्याः। नेति कौटिल्यः। तीक्ष्णदण्डो हि भूतानामुद्वेजनीयः। मृदुदण्डः परिभूयते। यथार्हदण्डः पूज्यः। कौटिल्य, I.4; compare मनु, VII.102-103; नित्यमुद्यतदण्डः स्यान्नित्यं विवृतपौरुषः। . . . नित्यमुद्यतदण्डस्य कृत्स्नमुद्विजते जगत्। Almost the same verses occur in शान्तिपर्व, 140.7-8.
19. परपरिग्रहे बीजमुत्सृष्टं क्षेत्रिण इत्याचार्याः। माता भस्त्रा यस्य रेतस्तस्यापत्यमित्यपरे। विद्यमानमुभयमिति कौटिल्यः। — अर्थशास्त्र, III.7; compare आदिपर्व, 74.110 भस्त्रा

माता पितुः पुत्रो येन जातः स एव सः। . . . रेतोधाः पुत्र उन्नयति नरदेव यमक्षयात्। . . .; *vide also* आदिपर्व 95.30-31.

20. नियतं क्षेत्रिणामपत्यामिति वेदवादः . . .। शङ्लिखितौ quoted in विवादरत्नाकर, p. 581; This passage is quoted on page No. 61 of this volume as no. 288 of the शंखलिखित-धर्मसूत्र restored by Dr. Kane. 'मन्त्रसंस्कारकर्तुरपत्यमित्याङ्गिरसो बीजिक्षेत्रिकयोरनुमते तद्बीजं प्रकीर्यते तद् द्विधा शस्यमित्युशनाः। – शङ्लिखितौ quoted in विवादरत्नाकर, p. 537.

21. अत्र कुलद्वयेपि चोच्छिन्ने स्त्रीभिः कार्या नृपक्रिया इति वाक्ये स्त्रीग्रहणं भार्या-परमित्यभिप्रेत्य मातुलाद्यभावे आसुरादिविवाहोढा क्रियाकारिणीति तातचरणाः। प्रमाणं त्वत्र न जाने।

7

The Mahābhārata Verses and Very Ancient Dharmasūtras and Other Works

THE authenticity of the text of the *Mahābhārata* and the age of its composition are very baffling problems. The critical edition of the *Mahābhārata* undertaken by the Bhandarkar Oriental Research Institute at Poona will make as near an approach to the original text of the *Mahābhārata* as the manuscript material at present available renders it possible. But the time when the original *Mahābhārata* was composed will probably remain an insoluble puzzle. That the *Mahābhārata* or the original work out of which the present text of the epic grew must have been composed at least before 500 BC is indicated by several considerations. In the following paper several verses are set out which occur in the *Mahābhārata* and also in such ancient works as the *Mahābhāṣya* of Patañjali and in the ancient *Dharmasūtras* of Āpastamba, Baudhāyana, Vasiṣṭha. Although the age of these and other *Dharmasūtras* cannot be ascertained with any certainty most scholars are agreed that these at any rate were composed some centuries before the Christian era. In the case of the *Mahābhāṣya* it is conceded by almost all scholars that it was composed about the middle of the second century BC. Baudhāyana, Vasistha and Viṣṇu together contain about two hundred verses which are also found in the *Manusmrti*. The latter work contains several hundred verses which also occur in the *Mahābhārata*. The latter two matters are not dealt with here since their examination will require a lengthy treatment. The verses cited below will be arranged in groups and in alphabetical order (in each group).

A. Verses found in the *Mbh* and also in the *MBhā*

(1) **ऊर्ध्वं प्राणा ह्युत्क्रामन्ति यूनः स्थविर आयति।**
प्रत्युत्थानाभिवादाभ्यां पुनस्तान्प्रतिपद्यते।।

This occurs in *MBhā*, VII. III, p. 58; in the *Anuśāsana* 104.64-65 and also in Manu, II.120.

(2) **कालः पचति भूतानि कालः संहरते प्रजाः।**

This is found in *MBhā*, Vol. II, p. 167 and in *Strīparva*, 2.24.

(3) **तपः श्रुतं च योनिश्च एतद् ब्राह्मणकारकम्।**
तपःश्रुताभ्यां यो हीनो जातिब्राह्मण एव सः।

This is quoted in the *MBhā*, Vol. I, p. 411 and Vol. II, p. 363. The first half is *Anuśāsana*, 121.7 (where we read °*yoniścāpyetad brāhmaṇyakāraṇam*) and the second half is—

त्रिभिर्गुणैः समुदितो ततो भवति वै द्विजः।

(4) **दूरादावसथान्मूत्रं दूरात्पादावसेचनम्।**
दूराच्च भाव्यं दस्युभ्यो दूराच्च कुपितादगुरोः।।

This occurs in *MBhā*, Vol. I, p. 457. The first half is found in Manu, IV.151, the second being—

उच्छिष्टान्ननिषेकं च दूरादेव समाचरेत्।

and in the *Anuśāsana*, 104.82 which reads—

उच्छिष्टोत्सर्जनं चैव दूरे कार्यं हितैषिणा।

B. Verses found in the *Mbh* and *ĀpDhS*

(5) **अभावे भूमिरुदकं तृणानि कल्याणि वागित्येतानि**
वै सतोऽगारे न क्षीयन्ते कदाचनेति।

This is *ĀpDhS*, II.2.4.14. The words *etāni . . . kadācana* from one half of an *Anuṣṭubh*. The first part appears to be a close paraphrase of *tṛṇāni . . . sūnṛtā*. That this is a quotation in Āpastamba follows from the word *iti* at the end. Manu, III.101, *Vanaparva*, 2.54, *Udyoga*, 36.24 have the verse—

तृणानि भूमिरुदकं वाक्चतुर्थी च सूनृता।
एतान्यपि सतां गेहे नोच्छिद्यन्ते कदाचन।।

Vanaparva, 2.54 and *Udyoga*, 36.24 read *satāmetāni geheṣu no*°. *VaDhS*, 13.61 has—

तृणभूम्यग्न्युदकवाक्सूनृतानसूयाः
सतां गृहे नोच्छिद्यन्ते कदाचन।

It will be seen that *VaDhS*, adds *agni* and *anasūyā* to the words of the verse in the *Māhābhārata*.

(6) **यदेकरात्रेण करोति पापं कृष्णं वर्णं ब्राह्मणः सेवमानः।**
चतुर्थकाल उदकाभ्यवायी त्रिभिर्वर्षैस्तदपहन्ति पापम्।।

This is *ĀpDhS*, I.9.27.11 and *BaudDhS*, II.1.59. This is *Śānti*, 165.29 (*niṣkṛṣṭavarṇam* and *sthānāsanābhyām viharam vratī sa tribhir varṣaiḥ śamayedātmapāpam*). Manu, XI.178 (which is same as *Viṣṇu Dharmasūtra*, 53.9 and Parāśara, VII.8-9) is a concise paraphrase of the same.

(7) **राज्ञः पन्था ब्राह्मणेनासमेत्य समेत्य तु ब्राह्मणस्यैव पन्थाः।**

This half verse is *ĀpDhS*, II.5.11.5-6 and is *Vanaparva*, 133.1. Manu, II.139 is only a concise statement of the same.

(8) **रेतोधाः पुत्रं नयति परेत्य यमसादने।**
तस्माद् भार्यां रक्षन्ति बिभ्यन्तः पररेतसः।।

This is one of the three verses quoted by *Āp.DhS*, II.6.13.6 and also occurs in *Baudh.DhS*, II.2.40. *Ādiparva*, 74.111 reads—

रेतोधाः पुत्र उन्नयति नरमेव यमक्षयात्।
भरस्व पुत्रं दुष्यन्त मावमंस्थाः शकुन्तलाम्।।

The same verse occurs again in *Ādiparva*, 95.31 where it is quoted as an *Ānuvaṁśa śloka*. So all (*Āp.DhS*, *Baudh.DhS* and

Mbh) probably borrowed from or adapted a common source.

C. Verses Common to *BaudhDhS* and *Mbh*

(9) नित्योदकी नित्ययज्ञोपवीती नित्यस्वाध्यायी वृषलान्नवर्जी ।।
ऋतौ च गच्छन्विधिवच्च जुह्वन्न ब्राह्मणश्च्यवते ब्रह्मलोकात् ।।

This is *Baudh.DhS*, II.2.1 (*SBE*, Vol. XIV, p. 224) and *Va.DhS*, VIII.17 (where the reading in 2nd *pāda* is *patitānnavarjī*). This is the same as *Udyogaparva*, 40.25 which reads *patitānnavarjī* and *satyam bruvan gurave karma kurvan na brā . . . lokāt.*

पन्था देयो ब्राह्मणाय गवे राज्ञे ह्यचक्षुषे ।
वृद्धाय भारतप्ताय गर्भिण्यै दुर्बलाय च ।।

This is *Baudh.DhS*, II.3.57 (*SBE*, Vol. XIV, p. 243) and *Anuśāsanaparvan*, 104.25 (which reads °*gobhyo rājabhya eva ca*).

(10) स्तुवतो दुहिता त्वं वै याचतः प्रतिगृह्णतः ।
अथाहं स्तूयमानस्य ददतोऽप्रतिगृह्णतः ।।

This is quoted in *BaudhDhS*, II.290 (*SBE*, Vol. XIV, 237) as a *gāthā* from the dialogue of the daughters of Uśanas and Vṛṣaparvan (viz. Devayānī and Śarmiṣṭhā). It is remarkable that the same verse occurs in *Ādiparva*, 78.10 in the same dialogue where the verse reads—

याचतस्त्वं हि दुहिता स्तुवतः प्रतिगृह्णतः ।
सुताहं स्तूयमानस्य ददतोऽप्रतिगृह्णतः ।।

If one may hazard a conjecture the form of the verse in *Ādiparva* looks more ancient and the verse in *BaudhDhS* an improved version, since the two halves of the verses in the *Ādiparva* do not show the same sequence of the actions of praising, begging and accepting in it, while in the verse as seen in *Baudh.DhS* they are so seen. In *Ādiparva*, 78.34 the words are *stuvato duhitā nityam . . . gṛhṇataḥ* I *aham tu stūyamānasya*, etc.

D. Verses Common to *Va.Dhs* and *Mbh*

(11) अग्नेरपत्यं प्रथमं सुवर्णं भूर्वैष्णवी सूर्यसुताश्च गावः ।

तासामनन्तं फलमश्नुवीत यः काञ्चनं गां च महीं च दद्यात्।

This is *Va.DhS*, 28.16. It is also *Vanaparva*, 200.28 where the third *pāda* is *lokāstrayastena bhavanti dattā* and the fourth has *gāśca*. It is remarkable that this verse occurs in many comparatively ancient inscriptions and is attributed to Vyāsa in some of them. For example, in the Rajim plate of Tīvaradeva (Gupta inscription, No. 81) this verse occurs, the third *pāda* being *dattāstrayastena bhavanti lokāḥ*. In *EI.*, Vol. VI, p. 285 at p. 293 (the Dantivarma plate of *śaka* 789) the verse is ascribed to Vyāsa and also in the Baloda plate of Tīvaradeva (*EI*, Vol. VII, p. 105); ***vide also*** *EI*, Vol. XI, p. 37 (plate of Indrarāja III, dated *saka* 836) and p. 173 (Khariar copper-plate of Mahāsudeva). In *EI*, Vol. VI, at p. 294 and in *EI*, Vol. IX, p. 37, the third *pāda* is *lokatrayam tena bhaveddhi dattam yaḥ*, etc.

(12) उद्वाहकाले रतिसंप्रयोगे प्राणात्यये सर्वधनापहारे।
विप्रस्य चार्थे ह्यनृतं वदेयुः पञ्चानृतान्याहुरपातकानि।।

This is *VaDhS*, 16.36. In the *Ādiparva*, 82.16 we have a similar verse:

न नर्मयुक्तं वचनं हिनस्ति न स्त्रीषु राजन्न विवाहकाले।
प्राणात्यये सर्वधनापहारे पञ्चानृतान्याहुरपातकानि।।

Here two *pāda*s are the same in both, though their positions differ. In *Śānti*, 165.30 we read *na narmayuktamanrtam hinasti . . . kāle | na gurvartham nātmano jīvitārthe pañcā°*.

E. Miscellaneous

(13) त्वमग्ने सर्वभूतानामन्तश्चरसि पावक।
साक्षिवत् पुण्यपापेभ्यो ब्रूहि सत्यं कवे मम।।

This is *Yājñavalkya-smṛti*, II.104. This is the same as *Ādiparva*, 5.27 where the last *pāda* reads *°pāpeṣu satyam brūhi kave vacaḥ* and there is *nityadā* for *pāvaka*. It looks as if *Yājñavalkya-smrti* twisted the words in the *Ādiparva* to suit the context of his section on fire ordeals.

(14) मयि जीवति यत्तातः केशग्रहमवाप्तवान्।
कथमन्ये करिष्यन्ति पुत्रेभ्यः पुत्रिणः स्पृहाम्।।

This is *Venīsaṁhāra*, III.27. It is the same as *Droṇaparva*, 195.9-10. It appears somewhat strange that Bhatta Nārāyaṇa bodily took over a stanza in his drama from the *Mahābhārata*.

(15-19) तलवद् दृश्यते वयोम खद्योतो हव्यवाडिव।
न तलं विद्यते व्योम्नि न खद्योते हुताशनः।।

न सा सभा यत्र न सन्ति वृद्धा वृद्धा न ते ये न वदन्ति धर्मम्।।
नासौ धर्मो यत्र नो सत्यमस्ति न तत्सत्यं यच्छलेनानुविद्धम्।।

नग्नो मुण्डः कपालेन परद्वारे बुभुक्षितः।
अमित्रान्भूयसः पश्येद्यः साक्ष्यमनृतं वदेत्।।

यां रात्रिमधिविन्ना स्त्री यां चैवाक्षपराजितः।
यां च भाराभितप्ताङ्गो दुर्विवक्ता स तां वसेत्।।

अश्वमेधसहस्रं च सत्यं च तुलया घृतम्।
अश्वमेधसहस्रात्तु सत्यमेव विशिष्यते।।

These five verses occur in the *Nārada-smṛti* (ed. by Jolly, *Vyavahāramātṛkā* 72, *sabhālakṣaṇa* 18, *ṛṇādāna* 202, 203, 211). They are respectively *Śānti*, 111.66, *Udyoga*, 35.58, *Udyoga*, 35.31-32 (but the first *pāda* of 32 is *nagare pratiruddhaḥ san bahirdvāre bubhukṣitaḥ*), *Ādi*, 74.103. The last also occurs in *Anuśāsana*, 72.29 and *Śānti*, 162.26. These five do not occur in Manu.

A few tentative conclusions may be set out from the above somewhat meagre material. We know from the *Śatapatha Brāhmaṇa* (*SBE*, Vol. 44, pp. 98, 369) that even in its days *Itihāsa* was spoken of as *Veda* and the same *itihāsa* was recited in the *Aśvamedha* sacrifice on the nights called *pāriplava*. In the oldest *Upaniṣads* like *Chāndogya* (III.4.1 and 2, VII.1.2 and 4, VII.2.1, VII.7.1) *Itihāsa-Purāṇa* is mentioned.[1] From the manner in which *Itihāsa-Purāna* is mentioned it follows that *Itihāsa-Purāṇa* was a body of literature almost as sacred as the four *Veda*s and held to be almost as ancient. In the *Brhadāraṇyaka Upanisad* (II.4.10, IV.1.2 and IV.5.11) also *Itihāsa* and *Purāṇa* are practically given the same status as the four *Vedas*. What the *Itihāsa* and *Purāṇa* of those days contained cannot be ascertained. Those works are irretrievably lost. Śaṅkarācārya had the insight to see that in the passages of the *Upanisads* *itihāsa* and *Purāṇa* could not refer to the *Mahābhārata* and the *Purānas* that were extant in his day and so he explains (on *BṛUp*, II.4.10) *Itihāsa* as *Brāhmaṇa* passages (e.g., *Śatapatha*, XI.5.1) such as the dialogue of Urvaśī and Purūravas, and *purāṇa* as such cosmological accounts as 'In the beginning this world was non-existent'. It seems that there were in the times of the oldest *Upaniṣads* probably two works closely connected that contained historical, legendary and cosmological matters. When such ancient works as the *ĀpDhS* refer to *purāṇa* (in the singular) they probably refer to the *Purāṇa* that was intended by the *Chāndogya Upaniṣad* or its subsequent recast and that they quote the verses from that very ancient work. It is equally possible that there was originally one work called *Itihāsa-Purāṇa* and that subsequently it was split up into two (*itihāsa* and *purāṇa*) and later into several *itihāsa*s and *purānas*. The *Taittirīya Āraṇyaka* (II.9-10) mentions *itihāsa*s and *Purāṇa*s after the *Brāhmaṇa*s. This is probably a later interpolation in that work. The *Nirukta* (in I.16 and XII.10) speaks of *aitihāsika*s and frequently says 'They tell the following story' (*tatra itihāsam . . . ācakṣate*). It probably refers to the ancient work called *itihāsa*. *Patañjali* (*Mahābhāṣya*, Vol. II, p. 234) derives the words *aitihāsika* and *paurānika*. Therefore it may be conjectured that the *itihāsa* of the *Upaniṣad* period was gradually incorporated into what became the *Mahābhārata* and the *Purāṇa* of that period was expanded into the several *Purāṇa*s of later days. Therefore the original kernel of the *Mahābhārata* was the *itihāsa* mentioned in the *Śatapatha Brāhmaṇa* and the *Upaniṣad*s and that the *Dharmasūtra*s present a few of the verses contained in that ancient work, which were retained in the next version of the *itihāsa* and so are found even now. The fact that several hundred verses occur in the *Mahābhārata* as well as in the *Manusmrti* and the *Dharmasūtra*s is to be explained as due to the same family (probably of the Bhṛgus) having devoted itself to the cultivation of the *Itihāsa-Purāna* and *Dharmaśāstra* literature. The *Manusmrti* originally might have contained verses in the *Triṣṭubh* metre, but subsequently when the final redaction was made about the beginning of the Christian era, there was a uniform employment of the *Anuṣṭubh* metre. It is due to this that in ancient *Dharmasūtras* like Vasiṣṭha verses in the *Triṣṭubh* metre are quoted as *Mānava-ślokas* (as in *VaDhS*, 19.37). The exact relationship of the extant *Mahābhārata* and the extant *Manusmrti* is however a subject that cannot be dealt with here.

References

[This paper is published in *Thomos Commemoration Volume*, pp. 128-33, 1939]. **S.G. Moghe**

1. स होवाचर्ग्वेदं भगवोध्येमि . . . आथर्वणं चतुर्थमितिहासपुराणं पञ्चमं वेदानां वेदम्।
— छा०, VII.1.2;
नाम वा ऋग्वेदो . . . आथर्वणश्चतुर्थ इतिहासपुराणः पञ्चमो वेदानां वेदः।
— छा०, VII.1.4.
2. एव वा अरेऽस्य महतो भूतस्य निश्वसितमेतद्यदृग्वेदो यजुर्वेदः सामवेदोऽथर्वाङ्गिरस इतिहास-पुराणं विद्या उपनिषदः etc. — बृह० उप०, II.4.10.

8

The Dvaitanirṇaya

THE *Dvaitanirṇaya* or *Dharma-dvaitanirnaya* is a work composed by Śaṅkarabhaṭṭa. The author was a very erudite *Mīmāṁsaka* and belonged to a very learned family of Benares *pandits*. His father Nārāyanabhaṭṭa was a very pious and learned man. It is related that, when the Mussulmans razed the temple of Viśveśvara at Benares to the ground, no rain fell for a long time and that, being afraid of the severe drought, the Mussulmans implored Nārāyanabhatta to propitiate Viśeśvara and agreed to re-build the temple of the god even if a little rain moistened their withering crops. Nārāyaṇabhatta propitiated Viśveśvara and then it rained copiously. Nārāyaṇabhaṭṭa was given the title of Jagadguru and was declared to be entitled to precedence over all brāhmaṇas at *Mantrajāgaras*. The latter distinction still continues in the family. Nārāyaṇabhaṭṭa is the author of the *Prayogaratna*, the *Tristhalīsetu* and several other important works. Śaṅkarabhaṭṭa was the father of Nīlakaṇṭha, the famous author of the *Vyavahāramayūkha* and other *Mayūkhas*. In all his works, Nīlakaṇṭha quotes with the greatest respect his father's views. For a thorough understanding of several passages in the *Vyavahāramayūkha* and the other works of Nīlakaṇṭha, a study of the *Dvaitanirnaya* is quite indispensable. In the following lines is given a brief account of the *Dvaitanirṇaya* taken from a Ms. in the Deccan College Collection (No. 109 of 1895-1902).

In the beginning there are eight introductory verses that are rather mutilated. They can be almost restored with the help of some passages that occur in the body of the work itself and by conjectural filling up of gaps. The first three are in the nature of benedictory stanzas. The author offers his salutations to Ganeśa, Rāma and the Sun. Then he refers to his father Nārāyaṇabhaṭṭa as fond of *Mīmāṁsā* and as equally favoured by Sarasvatī and Lakṣmī. In the fifth verse he refers to himself as *mimāṁsādvaitasāmrājyanītijñaḥ*. In the 6th and 7th verses he declares that he carefully studied Medhātithi, Aparārka, Smrtyarthasāra, Kālādarśa, Candrikā (i.e., *Smṛticandrikā* of Devaṇabhaṭṭa), Hemādri, Mādhava, Nrsiṁha and the *Tristhalīsetu* of his father.[1] In the last verse he says that he will abide by the views of Southern writers.[2]

The object of the work is to consider the doubts that arise on matters of ceremonial usages and rites to be performed on various days in the year and on matters of impurity on births and deaths and to give decisive opinions one way or the other. This may be illustrated by taking a few examples. The first topic treated of in the work is that of *Navarātra*. It may so happen that the first *tithi* of Āśvina begins on a certain day after a few *ghaṭī*s of the *amāvāsyā* of Bhādrapada and ends the next day a few *ghatī*s after sun-rise. The *Navarātravrata* is to be begun on the *pratıpadā*. Therefore a doubt arises whether it is to be begun on that day on which *pratipadā* is conjoined with *amāvāsyā* or on that day when it is joined to the second *tithi* of Āśvina. The *Nṛsiṁhaprasāda* and the *Durgāvatīprakāśa* are in favour of the first view and the *Paraśurāmaprasāda* is in favour of the latter. Śaṅkarabhaṭṭa establishes, after a great deal of acute reasoning and application of the rules of *Mīmāṁsā* that the latter is the proper view to hold. To take another instance; the question arises whether in the *Prauṣṭhapadī* (*Bhādrapada*) *Śrāddha*, the maternal grandfather is to be included along with paternal ancestors or not. The *Kālādarśa* favours inclusion, while other writers are opposed to that view. The author decides that the maternal ancestors are not to be included. Another interesting topic may be cited here as an example. The *Smrti*s lay down that what is promised to one by way of a gift should not be given to another. Supposing that the injunction is disobeyed, then the question arises whether (1) only the giver incurs sin, but ownership in the thing given does arise with respect to the recipient, or whether (2) the giver incurs no sin, but ownership does not pass, or whether (3) the giver incurs sin and ownership also does not pass to the donee. The *Siddhānta* view established by Śaṅkarabhaṭṭa is the last. Among the other topics for discussion are the following: *Pañcamīdvaitanirṇaya* (whether *paraviddhā* or *pūrvaviddhā*), *Kṛṣṇajanmāṣṭamīvratanirṇaya, Ekādaśīvedha, Caturdaśīdvaitanirṇaya, Śivarātrivarata, Sāvitrīvrato, Upākarma-nirṇaya, Holākānirṇaya* (*phālgunīpaurṇimā pūrvaviddhā paraviddhā vā grāhyā*), *Grahaṇadvaitanirṇaya, Saṁnipātāśaucanirṇaya*[4] (numerous doubts in connection with impurities on births and deaths are here dealt with). *Sapiṇḍīkaraṇakālanirṇaya, Piṇḍadā-nādhikārinirṇaya, Sāpiṇḍyanirṇaya.*

In all these discussions the authors most frequently quoted are Hemādri and Mādhava. On some matters he agrees with Hemādri and refutes Mādhava, while on others he approves of Mādhava's views and discards those of Hemādri. For example, he follows Hemādri in *Sāvitrīvrata-paurṇamāsīvipratipatti* in preference to Mādhava, while he prefers Mādhava to Hemādri in *Śivarātrivratanirṇaya, Pañcamīdvaitanirṇaya, Paurṇamāsīrūpaparvagatagrahaṇadvaitanirṇaya.* He refers to the views of Vijñaneśvara wth great respect, though much less frequently than those of Hemādri or Mādhava. He speaks of Vijñāneśvara as the foremost among the writers of *Nibandha*s.[4] But in a few places he finds fault with him also.[5] At the beginning and end of many of the topics selected for discussion he gives a verse or two eulogising himself and his efforts in arriving at the truth in the din of controversy.

The *Dvaitanirṇaya* was a very useful work in former times as it authoritatively dispelled doubts about religious rites and observances that were very dear to the heart of the people. In these days when the old order of things is undergoing a marvellous change and an entirely new mental attitude is being evolved, the *Dvaitanirnaya* may appear to be a more or less uninteresting performance. A modern critical student may regret that so much learning, acumen and subtlety should have been expended upon trivialities and on matters that are of evanescent interest But a modern critic must bear in mind that Śaṅkarabhaṭṭa was writing for his time and that in appraising the value of his work we must not be too severe on him for not having anticipated the needs of today. One is really struck by his mastery of the *Mīmāṁsā* and his skilful employment of some of the *Mīmāṁsānyāyas*. He very frequently refers to the following maxims: *Ardhajaratīya, Upasaṁhāranyāya, Śākhāntaranyāya, Sāmānyaviśesanyāya, Sāvakāśaniravakāśanyāya, Vidhiśesa, Kalpanālāghava.*

Some of the *sūtras* and *adhikarananaṇas* of Jaimini frequently referred to are: *sandigdheṣu vākyaśeṣāt* (*PūMīSūtra*, I.4.29); *tārtīyanyāyena datto dhāvati nakhāni kṛtanti ityādivat phalisaṁskāratayā vikalpenopavāsādīnāmaṅgatvāvasāyāt* (*PūMīSūtra*, III.7.6); *ekasya tūbhayatve saṁyogaprthaktvamiti cāturthikanyāyena dadhivadubhayārthatvaṁ mene* (IV. 3.5-7); *yathā hi ṣaṣṭhe ayajñiyā vai māṣāścanakāh kodravāśceti niṣedho vrīhyādiniyamenaiva māsādivyāvrtto vyarthaḥ san pratinidhitvena nisedhatītyuktam* (VI. 3.20); *bahūnāṁ syātsadharmatvamiti nyāyena saṁkocākhyabādhasyāyogāt* (*PūMīSūtra*, XII.2.22).

Among the authors and works mentioned by name are the following: *Agni Purāṇa,* Atri (verse), Anantabhaṭṭa, author of *Kālanirnaya* Aparārka, *āpastambīya* (verse) Āśvalāyana (*Gṛhyasūtra*), Ujjavalā (commentary of Haradatta on *Āpastama Dharmasūtra*) Ṛṣyaśṛṅga, *Aitareya-Brāhmana-bhāṣyakāra, Karka, Karmapradīpa* (of *Kātyāyana*) Kātyāyana, *Kālanirṇaya,*[6] *Kālanirnayadīpikā, Kālādarśa* (as quoting Vijñānayogī) *Kālikā Purāṇa*, Kārṣṇajini, Kumārila (also as Bhaṭṭapādāḥ), *Garuda Purāṇa*, Gobhila (*Grhyasūtra*), *Ślokagautama, Candrikā* (*Smṛticandrikā*), *Caturviṁśatimata, Jābāli,* Jātūkarṇya, *Jyotiḥparāśara, Toḍarānanda, Ḍāmarakalpa, Tantraratna* (of Pārthasārathi), *Trikāṇḍamandana, Trimśat-ślokī, Tristhalīsetu, Daśaślokī, Durgāvatiprakāśa, Durvāsas, Drāhyāyaṇasūtraṁ, Devī Purāna, Devī Rahasya, Dhvani-bhāṣyakāra, Dharmapravrtti, Dhaumya, Nāgarakhanda, Nāradīya Purāna, Brhannāradīya,*

Nārāyṇnaṇapravrtti (on *Āśvalāyanagṛhya*), *Nṛsiṁhaprasāda, Nyāyasudhā, Padma Purāṇa Paddhatikāra, Parāśarasmrti Brhatparāśara, Paraśurāmaprasāda, Pārthasārathi, Purānasamuccaya, Prthvīcandrodaya, Paithīnasi, Pracetas, Bṛhatpracetas, Prajāpati, Pratāparudranibandha* (*Sarasvatīvilāsa*?), *Prayogapārijāta, Baudhāyana* (both prose and verse), *Brahama Purāṇa, Brahmavaivarta, Bhaiviṣyottara, Bhāradvājasūtra, Bhṛgu* (not *Manusmṛti*), Maṇḍaṇa, *Madanapārijāta, Madanaratna, Manusmṛti, Mādhavācārya* (author of *Kālanirṇaya* and *Parāśaramādhvīya*), *Mārkaṇḍeya Purāṇa, Medhātithi, Maitrāyaṇīyaparisista, Yajñatantrasuddānidhi, Bṛhaddyam, Rāmacandrācārya* (described as *Śabdaśāsanābhijñataraiḥ*), *Rāmāṇḍārabhāṣya, Vāmana Purāṇa Vāyu Purāṇa,* Vijñāneśvara, *Viṣṇudharma, Viṣṇurahasya,* Vyāsa, *Śāstradīpikā, Śāṭyāyani, Śātātapa, Śuddhiviveka, Śūlapāṇi, Ṣaṭatriṁśanmata, Saṁgraha, Sumantu,* Bhaṭṭasomeśvara (author of *Nyāyasudhā*), *Skanda Purāna, Smṛticandrikā, Smrtimahārṇava, Smrtisaṁgraha* (probably the name as *Saṁgraha* above), *Smṛtiratnāvali, Smrtyarthasāra,* Hardatta (as author of *Mitāksarā on Gautamadharmasūtra*), Hari (author of *Vākyapadīya, Hārīta, Laghuhārīta, Hiraṇyakeśīsūtra*), Hemādri.

It is not yet settled beyond controversy whether Haradatta, the author of commentaries on the *Dharmasūtras* of Āpastamba and Gautama, is identical with Haradatta, the author of the celebrated grammatical work *Padamañjarī.* Śaṅkarabhatta refers to Haradatta, the commentator of the *Dharmasūtras* and without marking any distinction speaks of Haradatta as expounding a *Kārikā* of Hari.[7] This induces one to think that, in the opinion of Śaṅkarabhatta, Haradatta, the author of a commentary on Gautama, was also a profound Grammarian. The quotation from Haradatta is found in *Padamañjarī* and as Śaṅkarabhaṭṭa makes no difference between the two Haradattas, it may safely be inferred that according to him they are identical.

It appears that Śaṅkarabhaṭṭa's son, Dāmodarabhaṭṭa, wrote a *pariśista* to the *Dvaitanirṇaya.*[8] Śaṅkarabhaṭṭa seems to have commented on the *Śāstradīpikā* of Pārthasārathi.[9] We read in the *Saṁskāramayūkha*, edited by the son of Nīlakantha, that the editors' grandfather (Śaṅkarabhaṭṭa) wrote a work called *Śāstradīikā-prakāśa*.

One topic of great interest to modern students of Hindu Law deserves notice here. In most works on adoption a passage attributed to Śaunaka is cited, *viz. dauhitro bhāgineyaśca śūdrasyāpi ca dīyate*. Some interpret this passage as declaring that only a śūdra can adopt his sister's or daughter's son and not a person belonging to the three other castes. Others interpret it as meaning that a brāhmaṇa may adopt a daughter's or sister's son, but that, if available, a śūdra must prefer a daughter's or sister's son to any one else. Śaṅkarabhaṭṭa approves of the latter view. In the *Vyavahāramayūkha*, Nīlakaṇṭha refers to his father's exposition of this subject and follows it.

References

[This paper is published in *ABORI*, Vol. 3, pp. 67-72, 1921. ***Also see*** references to the *Dvaitanirṇaya* in Dr. Kane's *History of Dharmaśāstra*, Vol. I/I and II, pp. 546, 746, 938 and Vol. III, pp. 683 and 878 and 122n, 944n. ***Also see*** S.G. Moghe's *Studies in the Pūrva-Mīmāṁsā* (pp. 193-204). Ajanta Publications, Delhi, 1984, for Nīlakaṇṭha and Śaṅkarabhaṭṭa. The *Dvaita-Nirṇaya* is published under *Dharmaśāstra Grantha-Mālā* No. 28 by J.R. Gharpure in Bombay, 1943.] ***S.G. Moghe***

1. These verses are मेधातिथेश्चापरार्कविज्ञानेश्वरयोस्तथा! (विज्ञानेश्वरयोगिनो:?) स्मृत्ययसारकर्तुश्च कालादर्शकृतस्तथा।। चन्द्रिकाकार-हेमाश्ध्योर्माधव . . . नृसिंहयोः (मधिवार्युनृ०)। गुरोश्च त्रिस्थलीसेतुकर्तुर्ज्ञात्वा मतानि वै।।
2. दाक्षिणात्त्यमते स्थित्वा धर्मद्वैतेषु निर्णयम्।
   तनुनेऽसौ विगाह्यैव नावमान्यः कथंचन।।
3. 'त्रिरात्रशावमध्ये दशाहसूत्याशौचपाते किं शेषेण शुद्धिर्न वेति तथा दशाहसूत्याशौचन-वमाहोरात्रे त्र्यहशावाशौचपाते किं पूर्वेण शुद्धिर्न वेति'.
4. 'सर्वनिबन्धकृद्वरिष्ठेन विज्ञानेश्वरयोगिना'.
5. e.g. हेमाद्रिस्तु अग्न्याधानपक्षे दक्षिणाग्नावेव अग्नौकरणहोमं मिताक्षराकारमतं दूषयित्वा सिद्धान्तितवान्। तत्र हेमाद्रिमतमेव सम्यग्न विज्ञानेश्वरमतमिति नः प्रति-भाति।

6. There are several works bearing the name कालनिर्णय. In one place we have अनन्तभट्टकालनिर्णयेऽपि and in another place we read 'हेमाद्रितात्पर्यवेत्तुभिःकालनिर्णयकारैःसामान्यत उक्तम्'।
7. 'तदुक्तं हरिणा-गुणक्रियायां स्वातन्त्र्यात् प्रेषणे कर्मतां गतः। नियमात्कर्मसंज्ञायाः स्वधर्मणाभिधीयते।। अस्यार्थो हरदत्तेन विवृतः.
8. अस्मत्सुतदामोदारभट्टकृतेऽस्मत्कृत-द्वैतनिर्णयस्य परिशिष्टे दत्ताक्षतायाःकन्यायाः पुनर्दानं परस्य चेति कलिनिषेधव्याख्याने उक्तम्।
9. 'इत्यादि बहुदूषणैरयं पक्षोऽस्माभिर्मातुलकन्यापरिणयस्य दुराचारत्वमुपपादयद्भिः शास्त्रदीपिकांशे निरस्तः'।

9

Vedic Mantras and Legends in the Purāṇas

IT is stated that Vyāsa composed the *Mahābhārata* and the *Purāṇa*s for the benefit of women, śūdras and *dvija*s (that were so only by birth) who could not or did not study the *Veda*. The rites, ceremonies, usages and religious views on which most of the *Purāṇa*s lay emphasis are often different from the Vedic tradition. But it should not be supposed that the *Purāna*s ignore the Vedic heritage. On the contrary the *Purāṇa*s try hard to build on the foundations of the Vedic tradition. It is proposed in this paper to illustrate this briefly from a few passages of the *Brahma Purāṇa*, which heads the lists of *Purāṇa*s at least from the eleventh century AD, if not earlier. When Yājñavalkya, I.3 enumerates the *vidyāsthāna*s commencing with *Purāṇa*, the Mitākṣarā explains *Purāṇa* as *brahmādi*. In the lists of *Purāṇa*s contained in many *Purāṇa*s, the *Brahma Purāṇa* is placed at the head, while the *Vāyu* (104.3) enumerates the *Matsya* as the first.[1]

The *Brahma Purāṇa* quotes in several places Vedic verses and texts (without accents) and also makes use of Vedic legends for the glorification of certain holy places described by it. This shows that, though the *Veda* could not be studied by th śudras and women in the orthodox manner from a teacher, the authors of the *Purāṇa*s had no objection to women and śūdras listening to Vedic *mantra*s when they were embodied in the narratives of the *Purāṇa*s. A few striking examples will be given here. The references are to the Ānandāśrama edition of the *Brahma Purāna*.

I. Passages where Vedic *mantras* and texts are quoted *verbatim*:

(a) *Brahma*, 140.22-23 state that Ātreya praised Indra with the hymn beginning with *yo jāta eva prathamo* (the whole verse being set out). This is *Ṛgveda*, II.12.1.

(b) *Brahma*, 174.14-17 are the same as *Ṛgveda*, IX.114.3, 4.2 and IX.112.3.

(c) While narrating the story of Soma carrying away the wife of Bṛhaspati, *Brahma*, 152.34 repeats *Ṛgveda*, X. 109.6.

(d) *Brahma*, 233.62 states that there is a text of the *Atharvans* '*dve vidye veditavye*'. This is *Muṇḍakopanisad*, I.1.4.

(e) In several places the *Brahma* quotes brief *śruti* texts such as *ardho jāyā* (compare, *Brahma*, 129.62 and 161.35 with *TaitS*, VI.1.8.5. *ŚatBrā*, V.2.1.10 *ardho ha va eṣa ātmano yaj jāyā*), *iṣe tvā* (in *Brahma*, 170.64 with *TaitS*, I.1.1.1); *yajño vai viṣṇuḥ* (*Brahma*, 161.15).

II. In Some passages the *Brahma Purāṇa*, though not actually quoting the very words of the *Veda*, gives a very close paraphrase of Vedic texts:

(f) *Brahma*, 151.4 and 12 in the story of Purūravas and Urvaśī are couched almost in the same words as *Ṛgveda*, X.95.16 and 15. *Vide ŚatBrā*, XI.5.1 for the story.

(g) *Brahma*, 158.27 says 'Śambhu is one alone without a second, wise men speak of him under different names such as those of Indra, Mitra and Agni for the benefit of those who are ignorant (deluded).' This is close to *Ṛgveda*, I.164.46 (*indraṁ mitraṁ varuṇam agnimāhur . . . ekam sad viprā bahudhā vadanti*).

(h) *Brahma*, 161.35-37 and 44-48 are almost in the same words as some verses of the *Puruṣasūkta* (*Ṛgveda*, X. 90.6-7 and 12-15).

(i) In describing the wretched condition of a gambler and his wife, *Brahma*, 171.32-33 employs almost the very words of *Ṛgveda*, X.34.10-11.

III. In some cases the *Brahma Purāṇa* presses into service famous Vedic legends for the glorification of certain *tīrthas*.

(j) In praising the *tīrthas* named Hariścandra, Śunaḥsepa, Viśvāmitra and Rohita on the southern bank of the river Gautamī (Godāvarī), the *Brahma Purāṇa* (ch. 104) narrates at length the story of Śunaḥsepa and closely follows the story given in the *Aitareya Braḥmaṇa* (ch. 33) sometimes employing the very words of the *Brāhmaṇa* text.[2]

(k) In glorifying Indratīrtha on the Gautamī, *Brahma Purāṇa* (ch. 96) narrates the story how the sin of brāhmaṇa-murder in killing Vṛtra pursued Indra, like a *kṛtyā* (a goblin). The *Taittirīya Saṁhitā* (II.5.1) narrates how Indra incurred the sin of *brahmahatyā* by killing Viśvarūpa, and how he distributed it among the three viz. the earth, plants and women; and elsewhere (V.3.12.1) it states how Indra became free from that sin by performing *Aśvamedha*.

(l) *Brahmapurāṇa* (ch. 102) in eulogizing a *tīrtha* called *Mṛgavyādha* narrates how Brahmā (or Prajāpati) cast a libidinous eye on his own daughter who became a female deer, how Brahmā became a male deer and was pursued by Śambhu, as a hunter. The *Aitareya Brāhmaṇa* (13.9) and *ŚatBrā*, (I.7.4) narrate this story and both state that 'the daughter' intended is 'heaven', according to some, and 'dawn' according to others.

(m) *Brahma Purāṇa* (ch. 105) glorifies Soma-*tīrtha* by narrating how *vāk* (goddess of speech) went to the *Gandharvas* who were fond of women in order to purchase *soma* for the gods from the *Gandharvas*. This story is narrated in the *TaitS*, VI.1.6 and *AitBrā* (5.1.).[3]

(n) In eulogizing the Pippaleśvaratīrtha, the *Brahma Purāṇa* (ch. 110) narrates the story of Pippalāda, son of Vaḍavā Prātitheyī and the sage Dadhīca from whose bones the gods manufactured their weapons. This legend is as old as the *Ṛgveda*, I.84.13.[4]

(o) *Brahma Purāṇa*, 119-20 refers to the story that plants (*oṣadhis*) obtained King Soma as their husband. Some of the verses therein are very similar to *Rgveda*, X.97.[5]

(p) In speaking about Putratīrtha, the *Brahma Purāna* (124. 33-36) refers to the story of Namuci whom Indra killed with the foam of waters. *Ṛgveda*, VI.20.6 and VIII.14.13 state that Indra shattered the head of Namuci with foam and the *TaitBrā*, I.7.1, 6-8 also narrates the legend at some length.[6]

(q) In chapter 131 the *Brahma Purāna* narrates how Saramā, bitch of the gods, who was to guard the cows, was won over by the *rākṣasas* and, when the cows were carried away by the *rākṣasas*, she reported the event to Indra, who, suspecting her treachery, struck her with his foot with the result that she vomited the milk which she had shared with the *Asuras*. In *Ṛgveda*, X.108 we have the dialogue of Saramā and the Paṇis. In that hymn (verse 9) the Paṇis try to win her over offering to adopt her as their sister, but she spurns the offer (verse 10).

(r) In chapter 144 the *Brahma Purāṇa* derives the name 'Aṅgiras', applied to an ancient sage, from *aṅgāra* (red-hot charcoal). The same derivation is given in the *AitBrā* (13.10).[7]

References

[This paper is first published in *Raja Commemoration Volume*, pp. 5-14, Madras, 1946.] ***S.G. Moghe***

1. *Vide* भागवत, I.4.25:
स्त्रीशुद्रद्विजबन्धूनां त्रयी न श्रुतिगोचरा।
इति भारतमाख्यानं कृपया मुनिना कृतम्।।
2. For example, compare :
नापुत्रस्य परो लोको विद्यते नृपसत्तम। — ब्रह्म, 104.7.
with ऐ० ब्रा० — 'नापुत्रस्य लोकोऽस्तीति तत्सर्वे पशवो विदुः'
'किं तु मूलं किमु जलं किं तु श्मश्रूणि किं तपः।' — ब्रह्म. 104.10. [The printed text is corrupt]
with ऐ० ब्रा० (33.) — 'किं नु मलं किमु जलं किमु श्मश्रूणि किं तपः'
3. ब्रह्मपुराण 105.4. says — 'तत्र वाग्विबुधानाह गन्धर्वाः स्त्रीषु कामुकाः'
the ऐ० ब्रा० (5-1) says :
सोमो वै राज्ञा गन्धर्वेष्वासीत्तं देवाश्च ऋषयश्चाभ्यध्यायन् कथय यस्मान् सोमो राजागच्छेदिति। सा वागब्रवीत् स्त्रीकामा वै गन्धर्वा मयैव स्त्रिया भूतया पणध्वमिति।
4. इन्द्रो दधीचो अस्थभिर्वृत्राण्यप्रतिष्कुतः।
जघान नवतीर्नव।। — ऋ०, 1.84.13.
5. Compare *Brahma*, 120.6. ओषध्यः सोमराजन्याः सोमश्चाप्योषधीपतिः with *Ṛgveda*, X. 97.18 या ओषधीः सोमराज्ञीर्बह्वीः शतविचक्षणाः।
ब्रह्म०, 120.9:
ओषधयः संवदन्ते सोमेन सह राज्ञा।
योऽस्मान् कृणोति विप्रेभ्यस्तं राजन् पारयामसि।।
with *Ṛgveda*, X. 97.22:
ओषधयः सं वदन्ते सोमेन सह राज्ञा।
यस्मै कृणोति ब्राह्मणस्तं राजन् पारयामसि।।
6. अपां फेनेन नमुचेः शिर इन्द्रोदवर्तयः।
विश्वा यदजयः स्पृधः।। — *Ṛgveda*, VIII.14.13
स वज्रपाणिस्तरसा फनेनैवाहनद्रिपुम्।
नमुचिर्नाशमगमत् तस्य भ्राता मयोऽनुजः।। — *Brahma*, 124-36.
7. अग्नेरङ्गिरसो जातो ह्यङ्गारैरङ्गिरा यतः। — *Brahma*, 144.5.
येऽङ्गारा आसन् तेऽङ्गिरसोऽभवन्। — *AitBrā*, 13.10.

10

The Predecessors of Vijñāneśvara

THE *Mitākṣarā* of Vijñāneśvara occupies a peculiar position in the legal literature of India. Under the decisions of British Courts in India, the *Mitāksarā* is of paramount authority in matters of Hindu law in the whole of India, except in Bengal where the *Dāyabhāga* is supreme. The *Mitākṣarā* holds a position similar to that of the *Mahābhāṣya* of Patañjali in Grammar or the *Kāvyaprakāśa* of Mammaṭa in Poetics. It embodies in itself the results of centuries of legal speculation that preceded it and becomes in its turn a source of further exegesis and improvements. It is therefore interesting to see who the predecessors of Vijñāneśvara were to find out, what views were either originated or elaborated by them and to estimate the debt of Vijñāneśvara to his predecessors. In the following paper, no account is taken of the *Smṛti* writers that preceded Vijñāneśvara. Attention is centred only upon six writers who are named by the *Mitākṣarā* and who wrote either commentaries or *nibandhas* on the *Dharmaśāstra*. Those six writers are Asahāya, Viśvarūpa, Bhāruci, Medhātithi, Śrīkara, and Dhāreśvara. In the following M. and V. respectively stand for the Mitāksarā and Vijñāneśvara.

Asahāya[1]

The M., in explaining the verse of Yājñavalkya (II.124) that unmarried sisters are entiled to have their marriages celebrated by their brothers who are to give a fourth share to them, says that the explanation of Asahāya and Medhātithi of the words 'fourth share' stands to reason (viz., that the sister gets a fourth of what her brother of the same class as herself gets) and not that of Bhāruci. The only work so far known as Asayāya's is his commentary on the *Nāradasmṛti* which was revised by Kalyāṇabhatta. Dr. Jolly's edition of the *Nāradasmrti* (B.I. Series) contains a portion (viz. up to the middle of the 5th chapter) of the revised version of Asahāya's *bhāṣya*. What liberties Kalyānabhatta took with the *bhāṣya* of Asahāya on Nārada cannot be ascertained definitely. But he seems to have taken great liberties. On p. 9, verse 15 (of Nārada) *rājā satpurusah*, &c. the comment is *Manu — Nārada — Viśvarūpātmakam*. If the Viśvarūpa mentioned here be identical with the commentator of Yājñavalkya (as is very probable), Asahāya could not have regarded him as of almost the same authority as Manu. Therefore the reference to Visvarūpa must be due to Kalyāṇabhaṭṭa. The name of Kalyānabhaṭṭa is frequently cited in the commentary itself (*vide* pp. 81, 86, 89). The M. does not most likely refer to the *bhāṣya* of Asahāya on Nārada, but rather to Asahāya's *tīkā* on Manu, since the M. quotes Manu., IX. 118 which contains a rule similar to that of Yājñavalkya. From a passage of the Sarasvatīvilāsa[2] (para. 33 of Foulke's edition) it follows that Asahāya wrote a commentary on the *Manusmrti*. This conclusion receives support from the fact that the *Vivādaratnākara* quotes the explanation of Asahāya on Manu., IX.182 (*bhrātṛṇām ekajātānām*).[3] The *Hāralatā* of Aniruddha (who was the *guru* of Ballāla Sena of Bengal about AD 1168 tells us that Asahāya composed a *bhāṣya* on the *Dharmasūtra* of Gautama.[4]

Thus it is almost certain that Asahāya wrote *bhāṣyas* on the *Gautamadharmasūtra*, the *Manusmṛti* and the *Nāradasmrti*. His commentaries on the first two have not yet been traced. It is an irony of fate that the very name of such an important and ancient commentator should have been forgotten by late writers. The Bālambhattī in explaining the passage from the M. about Asahāya explains 'Asahāya' as an adjective of Medhātithi meaning independent'.

Dr. Jolly (*Tagore Law Lectures*, p. 5) thought that Asahāya was earlier than Medhātithi mainly on the ground that both V. and the *Sarasvatīvilāsa* place him before Medhātithi whenever authorities on topics of *Vyavahāra* are cited. It had escaped the notice of Dr. Jolly that Medhātithi in his comment on Manu, 8.135 (the verse *adarśayitvā tatraiva*) mentions Asahāya by name. The *Sarasvatīvilāsa* in one place mentions Asahāya after V. (para. 195), though before Medhātithi. It will be seen that Medhātithi flourished about AD 900 or a little later. Medhātithi does not name Viśvarūpa, though he cites Asahāya by name. Hence Asahāya is older than even Viśvarūpa and is certainly not later than about AD 800.

The views of Asahāya are not so freely quoted by any writer as by the *Sarasvatīvilāsa*. This shows that in the sixteenth century Asahāya's works were available. We saw above that V. agreed with Asahāya's view about the fourth share to be given to the unmarried sister. Some of the other views attributed to Asahāya may be collected here. The *Sarasvatīvilāsa*[5] tells us that the definition of *dāya* given by V. was identical with Asahāya's. Asahāya explained the *dictum* of Uśanas that fields were impartible by taking it to refer to the son of a brāhmaṇa from a kṣatriya wife;[6] such a son does not participate in land gifted to a brāhmana. V. on Yāj., II.119) follows this explanation. Asahāya seems to have held that as regards succession to the *śulka* of a woman even step-brothers should be given something, though the major portion would go to the full brothers.[7] According to Asahāya the wealth of a childless brāhmana went to the teacher, then to the teacher's son, and then to the teacher's widow and then to the pupil, to the pupil's son, to the pupil's widow and then to the fellow-student.[8] The *Vivādaratnākara* (p. 578) quotes the Prakāśa as referring to the views of Asahāya and Medhātithi on the verse of Manu (IX.198) that the special rule of Manu applies to all the *strīdhana* belonging to a kṣatriya woman who has a brāhmana co-wife.[9] The M. (on *Yāj*., II.145) gives a similar rule.

[After the foregoing was written, the portion of Visvarūpa's commentary on the *prāyaścitta* section (recently published) was received. On *Yāj.*, III. 263-64 Viśvarūpa mentions Asahāya by name and cites the latter's explanation of a *sūtra* of Gautama (22.13). This shows that Asahāya commented on the *Gautamadharmasūtra* and flourished before Viśvarūpa, i.e., before AD 800].

Viśvarūpa

The commentary of Viśvarūpa called *Bālakrīḍā* on Yājñavalkya has been published at Trivandrum by Pandit Gaṇapatiśāstrī. M. states in the introductory verse that the work of Yājñavalkya was expanded by the voluminous (or ample, *vikaṭa*) words of Viśvarūpa. In commenting on *Yāj.*, I.81 M. tells us that Viśvarūpa understood the words *tasmin yugmāsu saṁviśet* (in *Yāj.*, I.79) as laying down a *niyama*, while M. takes it to be a *parisaṁkhyā*. In Viśvarūpa's commentary this discussion occurs on verse 80 (*evaṁ gacchan*), where Viśvarūpa[10] quotes *Manu.* (III.45) and *Gautama*, 5.1 (*ṛtāv upeyāt*), cites the views of some (*kecit*) that Gautama's dictum is a *parisaṁkhyā* and then gives his own emphatic opinion that Gautama's words must be explained as containing a *niyama*. M. on *Yāj.* (III.24) informs us that Viśvarūpa, Medhātithi and Dhāreśvara looked upon certain texts of Ṛṣyaśṛṅga and others on *āśauca* as in conflict with approved *Smṛtis* and discarded them.

The printed commentary of Viśvarūpa on the *vyavahāra* section is very meagre and hardly merits the epithet 'voluminous' applied to it by M., which is several times larger than Viśvarūpa's discourse on the same section. But the comment of Viśvarūpa on the *ācāra* portion is truly voluminous as compared with M. on the same section. The style of Viśvarūpa is simple and forcible and resembles that of Śaṅkara. He quotes profusely from the Vedic *Saṁhitās*, mentions the Carakas and Vājasaneyins on *Yāj.*, I.32 and often supports his position by quotations from the *Ṛgveda* (e.g., on *Yāj.*, II.121, and II.206), from the *Brāhmaṇas* (e.g. *Śatapatha*, I.8.3.6 on *Yāj.*, I.53) and from the *Upaniṣads* (e.g., on II.117 he quotes the well-known *Chāndogya* passage about the ordeal for theft and on I.50 the *Chāndogya* passage II.23.10 about the three branches of *Dharma*). He very frequently quotes the *Gṛhyasūtra* of Pāraskara and less frequently that of Bhāradvāja and of Āśvalāyana. He cites a host of writers on *Dharmaśāstra*.[11] It is noteworthy that though he quotes scores of *Sūtra*s from the *Dharmasūtra*s of Āpastamba, Baudhāyana, Guatama, Vasiṣṭha, Śaṅkha, and Hārīta, he does not quote Viṣṇu anywhere in the sections on *ācāra* and *vyavahāra*. As Viśvarūpa's is perhaps the earliest extant commentary on a *Dharmaśāstra* work, it is of capital importance in checking the text of the ancient *Dharmasūtras*. Most of the quotations attributed to Svayambhū are found in the extant *Manusmṛti*, but the quotations ascribed to Bhṛgu are not so found. It is remarkable that most of the quotations from Bṛhaspati (even on such topics as repayment of debts, sureties, the right of śūdra-*putra*) are in prose, only a few being in verse (e.g., a verse about ordeals on *Yāj*., II.117, a verse about the method of partition on *Yāj*., II.153). It appears that Viśvarūpa had before him not only the prose work of the *Bārhaspatya Arthaśāstra* but also the versified *Smṛti* of Bṛhaspati and that he looked upon both as the compositions of the same author and made no distinction betweenm them. He quotes (on *Yāj*., I.328) a verse from Viśālākṣa, well-known writer on politics frequently quoted even by Kauṭilya. On *Yāj*., I.307 Viśvarūpa refers to the *Arthaśāstra* of Uśanas along with that of Bṛhaspati. Kauṭilya, the famous author of the *Arthaśāstra*, is nowhere quoted by name. The learned editor of Viśvarūpa's work (in the Trivandrum Series) thinks (Intro., p. v) that Viśvarūpa took Bṛhaspati and Viśālākṣa as *ārṣa* writers long anterior and therefore well-known to Yājñavalkya and used their *dicta* to supplement and support Yājñavalkya, while he omits Kauṭilya's name because he thought Kauṭilya to be posterior to Yājñavalkya. This argument is most fallacious from several points of view. In the first place this argument is wrong because Viśvarūpa quotes verses from Nārada and Kātyāyana to supplement Yājñavalkya. No one can in these days regard the *Smṛti*s of

Nārada and Kātyāyana as anterior to that of Yājñavalkya, nor is there anything to show that Viśvarūpa regarded them as anterior. Further it is possible that Kauṭilya's work was not available to Viśvarūpa. Moreover as Kauṭilya himself looked upon Bṛhaspati and Viśālākṣa as ancient authorities, Viśvarūpa might have naturally quoted from them rather than from Kauṭilya. That Kauṭilya flourished several centuries before Viśvarūpa follows from the express references contained in the works of Kāmandaka, Daṇḍin and Bāṇa. Therefore even granting that Kauṭilya was later than Yājñavalkya it is extremely doubtful whether Viśvarūpa was in possession of the exact chronological position of the two writers. Chronology has never been a strong point with any Indian commentator. Besides the very foundation of the whole argument is shaky as it is based upon premises that are not accepted by many Sanskrit scholars, who place Kauṭilya long before Yājñavalkya. It appears, however, that Vīśvarūpa impliedly refers to Kauṭilya's work in several places. For example, on *Yāj.*, I.307 he speaks of ministers tested by the four allurements (*upadhā*) of *dharma, artha, kāma* and *bhaya*. This is an echo of Kauṭilya (I. chap. 10). On *Yāj.*, I.344 Viśvarūpa refers to the views of some about marching in case of calamities of neighbouring chiefs, which agree with those of Kauṭilya.[12] In the comment of *Yāj.*, I.341 Viśvarūpa speaks of the manifold aspects of the work of a minister, some words of which agree very closely with Kauṭilya.[13]

Viśvarūpa is thoroughly saturated with the lore of the *Pūrvamīmāṁsā*. On *Yāj.*, I.225 he quotes Jaimini by name (*Pūrvam.* VI.8.15 is quoted). It is curious to note that he applies the term *Nyāya* to *Mīmāṁsā*. In explaining *Yāj.*, I.3 (about the fourteen *vidyā*s) he says *nyāya-mīmāṁsā* is one *vidyā*, while others explain *nyāya* as the system of logic propounded by Akṣapāda. He quotes the *sūtra*s of Jaimini as those of *Yājñika*s who know *nyāya*[14] (e.g., on *Yāj.*, I.53 he quotes *Jaimini*, I.3.16 and on I.87 he quotes *Jaimini*, VI.8.17). He applies the epithet *naiyāyika* to a *mīmāṁsaka* like Śabara[15] on *Yāj.*, I.58. He quotes the *Slokavārtika* (I.12) of Kumārila in his introductory remarks

(p. 2, the verse *sarvasyaiva hi* etc.). In his comment on *Yāj*., I.7 he quotes over fifty verses (in the nature of *Kārikās*) dealing with the relation of *Śruti* and *Smṛtis* and kindred topics. These verses are his own composition, as in one of them he assures us that a certain point will be dealt with by him in detail in the section of *Śrāddha.*[16] In numerous cases he relies upon or discusses the maxims of *Mīmāṁsā*. On *Yāj*., I.4-5 he discusses the rule of *Mīmāṁsa*, II.4.8.32 (about *sarvaśākhāpratyam ekaṁ karma*) in its application to *Smṛtis*. On I.225 he relies upon the position that words like *yava, varāha* are to be taken as used in the *Vedas* in the same sense in which *śiṣṭas* use them (*Pūrvam*., I.3.9). On II.144 he speaks of *dravya* (wealth) being *puruṣārtha*. He here alludes to the well-known distinction between *puruṣārtha* and *kratvārtha* (*Pūrvam*., chap. IV).

There is a slight discrepancy in the number of verses commented upon by Viśvarūpa and V. For example, on I.194 Viśvarūpa remarks that some read the verse *rathyākardamatoyāni* after it, but that it is redundant. M. comments on this verse. Viśvarūpa comments on a verse *āgamena viśuddhena bhogo yāti pramāṇatām* after *Yāj*., II.28, which is passed over by the *Mitākṣarā*. This verse is found in the *Nāradasmṛti* and is ascribed to him by the *Vyavahāramayūkha* and other digests. There are many various readings sown broadcast over the whole work (*vide* com. on *Yāj*., I.1, 2, 51, 63, 155; II.119, 179, etc.) Some of these various readings are important. Viśvarūpa reads *pitā mātāmaho bhrātā* (in *Yāj*., I. 63), while he notices the reading *pitāmpitā aho*, that is adopted by M. He reads *asvattaṁ lokavidviṣṭam* (in *Yāj*., I. 155) and notices a reading *asvantam*, while M. reads *asvargyaṁ loka°*. In several places Viśvarūpa suggests several meanings of the same verses and phrases (e.g., I.265; II.41, 47, 160, 173). In numerous places Viśvarūpa cites the explanations of his predecessors about the text of Yājñavalkya (e.g., I.3, 25, 155, 169, 252; II.21, 119, 121, 193). All these circumstances lead unmistakably to the conclusion that there is a gap of several centuries between Yājñavalkya and Viśvarūpa.

In the works of Jīmūtavāhana (viz. the *Vyavahāramātṛkā*

edited by Sir Asutosh Mukerji and the *Dāyabhāga*), in the *Smṛticandrikā*, in the *Sarasvatīvilāsa* and other works, the views of Viśvarūpa are frequently cited. Some of these quotations may be examined here.

(1) The *Dāyabhāga* (p. 145 of the edition of 1829) says[17] that the verse of *Yāj*. (II.149 *aprajastrīdhanam*) refers, according to Viśva. to *strīdhana* acquired at the time of marriage. The words of Viśva. on the verse (*brāhmādivivāhacatuṣṭaye yat strīdhanam*) appear to convey the same view, though not quite clearly.

(2) The *Dāyabhāga* says (p. 188) that Viśva. regarded as exclusive property what was acquired by a man without employing paternal wealth just like dowry at a marriage.[18] Viśva. gives the same rule on *Yāj*., II.122; but it is to be noted that the last few words in the *Dāyabhāga* which are meant to be a direct quotation from Viśva. are not found in the printed text.

(3) The *Dāyabhāga* says (p. 148) that Viśvarūpa's view that the *strīdhana* of a childless woman given to her by her parents married in any of the eight forms from *Brāhma* to *Paiśāca* goes to the brother should be accepted.[19] Viśvarūpa (on *Yāj*., II.148) says that *strīdhana* given by a woman's father and other relations, *Śulka* and *Anvādheya* are taken by her brothers if she dies childless and makes no reference to any particular form of marriage. It is for this that the *Vīramitrodaya* (p. 704) says that Viśvarūpa and Jīmūtavāhana held the view that what a woman obtained from her parents when a maiden goes to her brother.

(4) The *Dāyabhāga* (p. 284) says that Viśvarūpa, Jītendriya, Bhojadeva and Govindarāja assigned a place as an heir to the daughter's son after the daughter. Viśvarūpa is commenting upon *Yāj*., II.138 that the illegitimate son of a śūdra takes the whole estate in the absence of a legitimate son and daughter's and son uses this verse as

indicating that among the three higher castes the daughter's son inherits.[20]

(5) The *Dāyabhāga* informs us (p. 296) that Viśvarūpa and Śrīkara placed the half-brother after the full brother and before the brother's son.[21]

(6) The *Vyavahāramātṛkā* of Jīmūtavāhana (p. 319) says that Viśvarūpa's explanation that even one person approved of by both sides is a proper witness should be accepted. Viśvarūpa propounds this view on *Yāj*., II.74.

(7) The *Vyavahāramātṛkā* (p. 334) says that according to Viśvarūpa if the witnesses of a party depose to more or less than what the party asserts in his plaint, then, as the sages declare, it amounts to no proof. Viśvarūpa[22] holds this view and cites an ancient text to that effect on *Yāj*., II.81. The *Vyavahāratattva* of Raghunandana says that Viśvarūpa does not require that the single witness must be *dharmavid*. As a matter of fact that word, though occurring in *Yāj*., II.74, is passed over by Viśva.

(8) The *Vyavahāramatṛkā* (p. 346) says that the purport of *Yāj*., II.24 (*paśyato'bruvato*) according to Viśva. is simply to censure a man's acquiescence in or indifference to (trespass on his own land) and that the period of twenty years is mentioned in the verse for precluding the possibility of challenging a document (of sale, etc.) after twenty years. The first of these positions is contained in the printed Viśvarūpa[23] but not the second. It is noteworthy that M. on the same verse introduces the same two positions with the words *atha matam* and disapproves of them, just as Jīmūtavāhana does.

(9) The *Smṛticandrikā* (Gharpure's edition, II, p. 294) says that according to the *Saṅgrahakāra* a widow could succeed to her husband's wealth if she submitted to *niyoga*, that the same was the opinion of Dhāreśvara and that Viśvarūpa has well refuted the view of Dhāreśvara. In the printed Viśvarūpa there is no discussion on this

point. But from the fact that Viśvarūpa takes the word *patnī* in *Yāj.*, II.139 to mean a widow pregnant at the time of her husband's death and that Viśvarūpa forbids *niyoga* to brāhmaṇa women, it may be said that he disapproved of the views similar to those of Dhāreśvara.

(10) The *Smṛticandrikā* (II, p. 300) says that the *Saṅgrahakāra* placed the father's mother as an heir after the mother and before the father, that the views of *Saṅgrahakāra* proceeded on the same arguments as those advanced by Dhāreśvara and that Viśvarūpa and others have refuted those arguments. Viśvarūpa places the father after the mother. But there is hardly any argument in the printed text, which does mention the verse of *Manu.*, IX.217 about the *pitāmahī* and which is rather corrupt.

(11) The *Smṛticandrikā* (II, p. 266) says that according to Viśvarūpa a special share to the eldest son on partition is not given, now as it is opposed to the usage of *śiṣṭa*s, just as nobody offers a big bull or a goat to a learned guest in spite of the ancient texts[24] laying down the offering of a big bull, etc. The opinion here ascribed to Viśvarūpa cannot be found in one place in the printed text, but the following points may be considered. Viśvarūpa on *Yāj.*, II.121 distinctly states that *uddhāra* (as laid down in *Manu.*, IX.112) can only take place with the consent of all the brothers. On *Yāj.*, I.155 he cites the views of some that the word *loka-vidviṣṭa* in *Yāj.* implies cow-killing, which is abhorred by all people. He does not approve of this as he says on that interpretation the *vidhi* about *govadha* would be purposeless. On pp. 25-26 on the printed text he discusses the question of *govadha* prescribed by the Vedic and *Smṛti* texts (such as *Manu.*, III.3) in relation to *śiṣṭācāra*. But his opinion seems to be the opposite of what is ascribed to him by the *Samṛti-candrikā*. It is not unlikely that the latter work misunderstands him.

(12) The *Hāralatā* (p. 123) says that Viśvarūpa explained the word *atrivarṣasya* in *Manu.*, V.70 as meaning a child that has not completed its third year and that that explanation is in conflict with the word *jātadantasya*. On *Yāj.*, III.1. Viśvarūpa does quote *Manu.*, V.70 and explains *atri-varṣasya* in the way the *Hāralatā* points out. The same work (p. 174) declares on the authority of Viśvarūpa, Govindarāja and the Kāmadhenu a certain verse as apocryphal.

(13) The *Vyavahāramātṛkā*[25] (p. 308) says that Viśvarūpa explained the verse of *Yāj.* (II.17) as applying to a gift and the like. But the printed Viśvarūpa contains no reference to 'gift' in the comment on this verse and seems to take the word *pūrvavādin* as meaning the plaintiff.

(14) The *Smṛticandrikā* says (II, p. 122) that a certain verse prescribing gradually rising fines for the first, second and subsequent stages of a lawsuit is established by Viśvarūpa to be unauthoritative.[26] This topic cannot be traced in the printed text.

(15) The *Dāyabhāga*[27] tells us (p. 350) that Viśvarūpa declared that if a co-parcener concealed some joint property and it was afterwards discovered, he was not guilty as a thief. A corresponding remark could not be traced in the printed Viśvarūpa. It is to be noted that M. on *Yāj.*, II.126 (*anyonyāpahṛtam*) holds a contrary view.

Later writers frequently quote the views of Viśvarūpa. For example, Kullūka on *Manu.*, II.189, V.68 and other places does so. But considerations of space forbid any further treatment of this matter.

The foregoing examination of quotations from comparatively early works ascribing certain views to Viśvarūpa establishes that in the main the printed text of the latter is authoritative, though in a few cases there are grounds to hold that it is corrupt or deficient.

In certain cases later commentators were misled into ascribing certain views to Viśvarūpa. For example, the Bālambhaṭṭī often regards the words of M. 'the *ācārya* does not approve of this' as referring to Viśvarūpa, when really the word *ācārya* refers to Yājñavalkya. On *Yāj*., I.68-69 M. cites the views of the *ācārya*s that the verses refer to a girl who is only betrothed and not married. The Bālambhaṭṭī says that Viśva. is referred to. But in the printed Viśvarūpa, this view of the matter is ascribed to others. Similarly on *Yāj*., II.80, the Bālambhaṭṭī ascribes the words *tad apy ācāryo nānumanyate* to Viśvarūpa. But there is not a word of explanation in Viśvarūpa on this verse. On the verse *patnī duhitarś caiva*, M. cites the view of some that if the wealth left by the deceased be equal to or less than what is required for maintenance, then the widow takes it in preference to the brothers and if it be more than what is necessary for maintenance, then the brothers take the rest. Then M. says this view also the revered (*bhagavān*) *ācārya* cannot tolerate. Both the Subodhinī and Bālambhaṭṭī say that *ācārya* here means Viśvarūpa. Viśvarūpa does not say a word about this view on this verse. The word *ācārya* is applied to Yājñavalkya by Viśvarūpa also (as in his comment on I.2, 9.22, II.136.288).

Viśvarūpa quotes Śabara and the *Ślokavārtika* of Kumārila and therefore he is later than the first half of the eighth century AD. He is referred to as an authority by M. (about the end of the eleventh century), so viśvarūpa must have flourished between AD 700 and AD 1050. According to the *Smṛticandrikā* (***vide*** Nos. 9 and 10) Viśvarūpa refuted certain views held by Dhāreśvara. Relying on this Rai Bahadur M.M. Chakravarti (*JASB*, for 1912, p. 345 and *JASB*, for 1915, p. 322) holds that Viśvarūpa is later than Bhojadeva. But this does not seem to be right. It has been shown above that the printed Viśvarūpa contains no express mention of Dhāreśvara and contains hardly any refutation. It is likely that Dhāreśvara adopted certain views that were long current before his time and that later writers knowing only the two works and not their predecessors regarded Viśvarūpa as having criticised Dhāreśvara and not his predecessors. The *Smṛticandrikā* was composed after AD 1200 and it is too much to suppose that it correctly knew the chronological position of the two writers. Later writers often invert the chronological positions of early predecessors. For example, the *Sarasvatīvilāsa* often cites the views of M. and then says that Bhāruci and others do not approve of (or tolerate) those views. Similarly in para. 392 it says that on a certain point Dhāreśvara and Devasvāmin follow the views of V. But we know from M. itself that Bhāruci and Dhāreśvara preceded the *Mitākṣarā*. Hence the *Smṛticandrikā* cannot be relied upon as an unimpeachable authority. A greater approximation as to the date of Viśvarūpa can be arrived at by holding Sūreśvara and Viśvarūpa as identical. That they are identical may be regarded as tolerably certain. Eminent writers often connect the well-known works of Sūreśvara, a pupil of the great Śaṅkarācārya, with Viśvarūpācārya. For example, in the *Parāśaramādhava* (Bombay Sanskrit Series, vol. I, part 1, p. 57), a verse from the *Bṛhadāraṇyakopaniṣad-bhāṣya-vārtika* of Sūreśvara (I.1.97) is ascribed to Viśvarūpa.[28] In the *Puruṣārthaprabodha* of Brahmānanda Bhāratī (Ms. in the Bhau Daji collection, Bombay Asiatic Society) composed in 1476 (probably *Śaka*) the *Naiṣkarmyasiddhi*, a work of Sūreśvara, is ascribed to Viśvarūpa.[29] Maṇḍanamiśra is said to have been a pupil of Śaṅkara. Śaṅkara's traditional date is AD 788-820. Therefore Viśvarūpa *alias* Sūreśvara flourished at the latest about the close of the eighth century AD. It is rather far-fetched though not impossible to suppose that nearly about the same time there were two Viśvarūpas, one the author of *Naiṣkarmyasiddhi* and the other the author of the *Bālakrīḍā*. The profound knowledge of the *Mīmāṁsā* displayed in the *Bālakrīḍā* points to the identity of the two authors, but the whole question is further complicated by another circumstance. The learned editor of *Viśvarūpa* (in the Trivandrum Series), while speaking of the three commentaries on the *Bālakrīḍā*, quotes a verse from one of them which identifies Bhavabhūti (the dramatist), Sureśa and Viśvarūpa.[30] The editor does not take Bhavabhūti as a proper name, but only as an adjective of Sureśa. But this seems far-fetched. We know that in a Ms. of the *Mālatīmādhava*, the drama is ascribed to Umbeka, a pupil of Kumārila (*vide* Intro. to *Gauḍavaho*, p. 206). So Bhavabhūti was regarded as a pupil of Kumārila and he was also called Umbeka. Umbeka wrote a commentary on the *Ślokavārtika* of Kumārila (*vide* the *Yuktisnehaprapūraṇī* on the *Śāstradīpikā* (first verse), where Umbeka's explanation on the first verse of the *Ślokavārtika* is cited). The *Citsukhī* (p. 265 of the Nirnayasagara edn.) seems to identify both Bhavabhūti and Umbeka and the commentator expressly says so. So the result of this whole tangle would be to hold that the same individual bore five names, Bhavabhūti, Umbeka, Maṇḍanamiśra, Sūreśvara and Viśvarūpa. This is surely more than one can easily believe. It looks probable that there is some mistake here. Both Bhavabhūti and Maṇḍanamiśra were probably the pupils of Kumārila. The first also was called Umbeka and the latter Sūreśvara or Viśvarūpa. Through lapse of time and through their relation to Kumārila confusion was caused.

The M. holds an elaborate discussion on the question whether ownership arises on partition or whether there is partition of what is owned (jointly with others). Viśvarūpa does not contain an elaborate discourse on this topic, but in his introduction to *Yāj.*, II.124 he refers to these views and finally gives as his own opinion that there is partition of what is already (jointly) owned.[31]

There are great divergences of views between M. and Viśvarūpa. They are too numerous to be set forth here in detail. A few interesting points of difference are briefly discussed below. It has already been seen that they differ as to the interpretation of *Yāj.*, I.78-80.

(1) Viśvarūpa allows the father unrestricted freedom of distribution of ancestral property among his sons during his life-time (on *Yāj.*, II.118 *vibhāgam*, etc., etc.), while M. allows unrestricted freedom only as to self-acquired property.

(2) Viśvarūpa allows a share to the widows of deceased

sons and grandsons of a man where a partition takes place in his life-time, while M. restricts the word *patnyaḥ* to the father's own wives when he effects a partition in his life-time. In this one respect Viśvarūpa is more liberal to women than M. In other cases he is not so liberal as V. towards the rights of women.

(3) Viśvarūpa connects the words 'without detriment to paternal estate' with the words 'whatever else is acquired by himself' and not with *maitra* (gifts from a friend) and *audvāhika* (gifts on marriage), while M. connects the half verse 'whatever else is acquired by a man himself without detriment to the paternal estate' with *maitra, audvāhika* and two more kinds mentioned in the verse *kramād abhyāgatam.*

(4) Viśvarūpa places the verse *kramād abhyāgatam* after the verse *vibhakte'pi savarṇāyāḥ* and takes it to mean that if one member of a family recovers with his own exertions after partition ancestral property lost to the family, he has not to give a share of it to the member (his own brother) who is born after partition, when the partition is reopened on account of his birth after partition. M. takes the verse immediately after *pitṛdravyāvirodhena* and as laying down two varieties of self-acquired property. The arrangement of the M. appears better.

(5) Viśvarūpa allows *Niyoga* only to śūdras as a general rule and to kṣatriyas in case of danger of extinction of the line (on *Yāj.*, I.69 and II.131), while M. forbids *Niyoga* in general and takes the texts speaking of it as applicable to a girl who is only betrothed and not married.

(6) Viśvarūpa allows one share out of ten to the son of a śūdra from a brāhmaṇa without restriction of any kind while M. restricts the share to estate other than land acquired by gift.

(7) Viśvarūpa interprets the expression 'half share' with reference to the illegitimate son of a śūdra as meaning

'some portion, not necessarily exact half', while M. interprets it literally.

(8) Viśvarūpa allows a widow to succeed to her deceased husband only if she is pregnant, i.e., he restricts the meaning of the word *patnī*, while M. allows a widow to succeed without any restriction.

(9) Viśvarūpa takes the word *duhitaraḥ* to mean *putrikā* and so does not allow all daughters to succeed, while M. introduces no such qualification.

(10) Viśvarūpa reads *anyodaryasya saṁsṛṣṭī* for *anyodaryas tu* and *sodaro* for *saṁsṛṣṭo* and his interpretation of *Yāj.*, II.139 is quite different from that of M.

(11) Viśvarūpa reads *ādhivedanikaṁ caiva* for *ādhivedanikādyaṁ ca* of M. and holds that Bandhudatta, *Śulka* and *Anvādheyaka strīdhana* of a childless woman goes on her death to her full brother; while M. connects the three with the preceding verse as kinds of *strīdhana* and takes the half verse *atītāyām aprajasi* as laying down a general rule of succession to *strīdhana* of all kinds, and interprets *bāndhavāḥ* as meaning 'husband and the rest'.

(12) Both differ in the interpretation of the term *anvādheyaka.*

(13) Viśvarūpa takes the verse *adhivinnastriyai* as applicable to a wife superseded without any prescribed ground for supercession; while M. does not introduce any such qualification.[32]

Bhāruci

V. on *Yāj.* (I.81) says that Bhāruci, like Viśvarūpa held that the rule *ṛtau gacchet* was a *niyama* and not a *parisaṁkhyā*. On *Yāj.*, II.124 M. says that the explanation of the 'fourth share' to be given to unmarried sisters offered by Asahāya and Medhātithi was the proper one and not that of Bhāruci. The *Parāśaramādhavīya* (vol. III, part 2, p. 510) and the *Sarasvatīvilāsa* (para. 133) inform us that Bhāruci was of opinion that unmarried sisters were only entitled to a provision for their marriage and that they were not entitled to a fourth share.

Bhāruci being mentioned by the M. is certainly older than AD 1050. Rāmānuja in his *Vedārthasaṅgraha* (reprint from the *Pandit*, edition of 1924, p. 154) mention six *ācārya*s that preceded him as upholders of the *Viśiṣṭādvaita* system, viz. Bodhāyana, Ṭaka, Dramiḍa, Guhadeva, Kapardi and Bhāruci. Similarly the *Yatīndramatadīpikā* of Śrīnivāsadāsa (Ānandāśrama edn.) enumerates (p. 2) the following teachers as the predecessors of Rāmānuja in propounding the *Viśiṣṭādvaita* system, viz, Vyāsa, Bodhāyana, Guhadeva, Bhāruci, Brahmānandin, Draviḍārya, Śrīparāṅkuśa, Nāthamuni and Yāmunamuni. Vyāsa is the reputed author of the *Vedāntasūtra*s, Bodhāyana is said to have composed a *vṛtti* on the *Vedāntasūtra*s, Dramiḍa (or Draviḍa) is credited with a *bhāṣya* on the *Vedāntasūtra*s (which is quoted by Rāmānuja on II.2.3). Nāthamuni preceded Yāmuna. Yāmunācārya was born about AD 916. Rāmānuja refers to him with great reverence as *paramaguru* (*vide Vedārthasaṁgraha*, p. 149) and is said to have been young when Yāmuna died (*vide JRAS* for 1915, p. 147, and *Ind. Ant.* for 1909, p. 129). It is therefore obvious that the series of writers on the *Viśiṣṭādvaita* is arranged in chronological order by the *Yatīndramatadīpikā*. Hence Bhāruci must have been a comparatively ancient author on the *Viśiṣṭādvaita*, being earlier than even Dramiḍa, Nāthamuni and Yāmuna. He could not have flourished later than the first half of the ninth century. How much earlier he flourished it is impossible to say. It is difficult to believe that there were two different writers of the same name nearly about the same time. Hence Bhāruci the writer on *Dharma* and Bhāruci the *Viśiṣṭādvaita* philosopher must be held to have been identical. If the identity of the two be accepted, then Bhāruci the writer on *Dharmaśāstra* becomes comparatively an early writer, being at least as old as (if not older than) Viśvarūpa. It will be seen that he and Viśvarūpa agree on several points (as above on the question of *Niyama* and below Nos. 5, 7, 9) and therefore it is not too much to suppose that he flourished at or about the time when the views found in Viśvarūpa's work were in vogue.

There is one interesting point to be noted about Bhāruci. From numerous notices contained in the *Sarasvatīvilāsa* it appears that Bhāruci either commented upon the *Viṣṇudharma-sūtra* or took great pains to incorporate explanations of several *sūtras* of Viṣṇu in his work. For example, para. 637 of the *Sarasvatīvilāsa* tells us that Bhāruci explained the word *bīja* occurring in a *sūtra* of Viṣṇu as *piṇḍa*.[33] In para. 674 we are told that Bhāruci explained the word *niṣkāraṇa* in a *sūtra* of Viṣṇu and that he held that a daughter's son has not to perform the *śrāddhas* of his maternal grandfather if the latter has a son. Sudarśanācārya in his comment on *Āpastamba Gṛhya*, 8.21.2 ascribes the same view to Bhāruci.[34] In para. 681 the *Sarasvatī-vilāsa* honours Bhāruci by calling him *bhagavat* and gives his explanation of a *sūtra* of Viṣṇu that whoever is authorised to perform the *śrāddhas* of a person and recieves the estate of that person is alone to perform the *śrāddhas* for that person. In para. 711 Bhāruci's explanation of Viṣṇu's *sūtra* (*saṁsṛṣṭadhanaṁna patnyabhigāmi*) is given. In para. 719 Bhāruci's remarks on Viṣṇu's *sūtra* (*pitṛvyapitṛbhrātṛbhir eva saṁsargo nānyaiḥ*) are cited. In para. 724 Bhāruci in commenting upon a *sūtra* of Viṣṇu (*saṁsṛṣṭināṁ piṇḍakṛt aṁśahārī*) is said to have remarked that the capacity to offer *piṇḍas* is the guiding principle in taking the inheritance. In para. 736 Bhāruci is said to have explained the word *bhinnodarāṇām* in a *sūtra* of Viṣṇu (*bhinnodarāṇām saṁsṛṣṭino gṛhṇīyuḥ*).[35] Para. 848 gives Bhāruci's explanation of a long *sūtra* of Viṣṇu about property not liable to partition.[36] There is nothing unnatural in Bhāruci having written a commentary on Viṣṇu. The extant *Viṣṇudharmasūtra* contains doctrines peculiar to the *Viśiṣṭādvaita* system, such as the worship of Nārāyaṇa or Vāsudeva, the four *vyūhas* of Vāsudeva, etc. If Bhāruci was a *Viśiṣṭādvaitin* he would naturally turn to the *Viṣṇudharmasūtra* as having the greatest claim on his attention. One remarkable thing is that none of the eight *sūtras* of Viṣṇu cited above occurs in the printed *Viṣṇudharmasūtra*. This leads to the presumption that the printed work is either a mutilated or abridged version of the original *Dharmasūtra*.

There are numerous points on which there is divergence between Bhāruci and V. A few of the more interesting ones are set out below from the *Sarasvatīvilāsa*.

(1) Bhāruci defined *dāya* as 'that paternal wealth that is liable to partition' and he spoke of *Dravyavibhāga* and *Dharmavibhāga* also. Bhāruci did not approve of the definition of *dāya* given by Asahāya and adopted by the M. as *svāmi-sambandha* is a source of ownership and cannot be the *lakṣaṇa* of ownership (***vide*** para. 8.19-20).

(2) Bhāruci defined *vibhāga* as separation in connection with one out of the two, viz., *dravya* and *dharma* (religious rites), while the definition of M. would exclude mere *dharmavibhāga* (para. 22-25).

(3) V. explains *Yāj*., II.117 (*mātur duhitaraḥ*, etc.) as laying down that the mother's *strīdhana* is first taken by the daughters and in the absence of daughters by the sons of the woman, while Bhāruci explains that in the absence of sons, a woman's *strīdhana* is taken by her daughters and in the absence of daughters by the woman's paternal uncle and others. It is to be noted that the M. follows Viśvarūpa, who refers to the view of some that is the same as Bhāruci's.[37]

(4) V. explained the text of Gautama (28.22) as conferring the *strīdhana* of a woman first on her unmarried daughters, then on married daughters, among whom indigent ones were to be preferred to those who were well off. Bhāruci distributed the *strīdhana* among unmarried daughters and married but indigent daughters equally.[38]

(5) Bhāruci allowed *Niyoga* in the case of a childless widow, while the M. condemned *Niyoga* in the case of every widow and held that the texts on this matter (such as

Manu., IX.59) applied only to a girl betrothed.[39] Thus Bhāruci is nearer to those *Smṛtis* that allowed *Niyoga* to widows than Viśvarūpa who restricts it to śūdra and kṣatriya widows.

(6) Bhāruci explains *Manu*, IX.163 (*eka evaurasaḥ putraḥ pitryasya vasunaḥ prabhuḥ*) as applying to a case where a man having an only son adopts another and as providing for the maintenance of only the *dattaka* and not of others, while M. (on *Yāj.*, II.132) says that the verse of Manu applies only where the *dattaka* and other kinds of sons are inimical to the *aurasa* and where they are devoid of good qualities.[40]

(7) According to M. the word *riktha* should mean *apratibandhadāya* and *saṁvibhāga* should mean *sapratibandhadāya*, although in such passages as *Yāj.*, II.51 (*rikthagrāha ṛṇam dāpyaḥ*) the word *riktha* seems to have been used in the sense of *sapratibandhadāya.* Bhāruci did not make this distinction. It will be noticed that Viśvarūpa also is silent about *sapratibandha* and *apartibandha dāya.*[41]

(8) According to Bhāruci, a fellow student (*sabrahmacārin*) was like a brother and hence if a man dies leaving no fellow student even, then the sons of the fellow student, the widows of the fellow student and the widows of the sons of the fellow student succeeded one after another and in the absence of even all these a *śrotriya* brāhmaṇa took the wealth of the deceased. According to M. in the absence of the fellow student, a *śrotriya* succeeded at once.[42] This shows that Bhāruci was in one respect at least more liberal to women than the M.

(9) On account of the verse of *Yāj.*, II.126 (*anyonyāpahartam*, etc.) Bhāruci thought that if coparceners conceal some joint property there was no offence (of theft), while M. held that there was theft in such a case. It is to be noted that the same view is attributed to Viśvarūpa by the

Dāyabhāga, though nor traced in the printed next. The M. controverts this view without naming any particular writer.

In many other places the *Sarasvatīvilāsa* refers to the views of Bhāruci (e.g. in paragraphs 13, 69, 276, 316, 501, 752, 761).

Śrīkara

The M. on *Yāj.*, II.135 alludes to the view of Śrīkara and.others that the widows succeeded as heir to her deceased husband's estate if it was small.[43] M. gives Śrīkarācārya's explanation of *Yāj.*, II.169 and disapproves of it. It is to be noted that Viśvarūpa also gives two explanations of this verse.

The works of Jīmūtavāhana, the *Smṛticandrikā*, the *Sarasvatīvilāsa* and the *Vīramitrodaya* contain several notices of Śrīkara's views.

(1) Śrīkara, according to the *Sarasvatīvilāsa* (para. 555) held that *duhitaraḥ* in *Yāj.*, II.135 means *putrikā* and that this view of his agrees with that of Dhāreśvara, Devasvāmin and Devarāta. It has been seen that Viśvarūpa held the same view.

(2) According to the *Smṛticandrikā* (II, p. 297), the *Sarasvatī-vilāsa* (para. 573) and the *Vīramitrodaya* (p. 664) Śrīkara gave the wealth of a deceased person to his father and mother equally at the same time.

(3) According to the *Dāyabhāga* (p. 220) Śrīkara preferred the full brother to the half brother on the ground of the superior spiritual benefit conferred by the full brother. Viśvarūpa also did the same as seen above, but it is not clear from his comment whether he did it on the theory of spiritual benefits.

(4) The *Dāyabhāga* (p. 299) very severely criticizes the arguments and explanations of Śrīkara on the verse of

Yāj. (*saṁsṛṣṭinas tu*, etc.). Śrīkara explained that the general rule was that a re-united coparcener took the estate left by a deceased re-united member and that the words *sodarasya tu sodaraḥ* were an exception to that rule (laying down that an un-reunited full brother was preferred to a re-united half-brother). M. gives a different explanation.

(5) The *Dāyabhāga* (p. 314) says that Śrīkara understood the words of *Yāj. anyodaryas tu* as elucidating the words *saṁsṛṣṭinas tu*, etc. It is somewhat remarkable that Viśvarūpa observes that some read the verse *anyodaryasya saṁsṛṣṭī* as an elucidation of the previous verse and explains it in the same way as Śrīkara is said to have done. Viśvarūpa therefore was inclined not to regard the verse as properly authenticated. Our knowledge of the several commentaries on *Yāj.* is so meagre that one is loath to hazard a conjecture. But it looks as if Śrīkara preceded even Viśvarūpa. It is of course possible that Viśvarūpa may refer to some predecessor whose views were later adopted by Śrīkara. In many of the views above set forth Śrīkara either agrees with Viśvarūpa or holds views more antiquated than those of Viśvarūpa.

(6) According to the *Dāyabhāga* Śrīkara explained a verse of Kātyāyana to mean that among re-united coparceners if one acquired some property by employing common funds then the acquirer got two shares and the rest one share each.[44]

(7) The *Dāyabhāga* states that whatever is acquired as a reward for any *vidyā* becomes the self-acquired property of the acquirer and that Kātyāyana entered into detailed illustrations of gains of learning for dispelling the errors of Śrīkara and others. The *Dāyabhāga* does not mean that Kātyāyana wrote after Śrīkara. The meaning is that Kātyāyana wanted to the display such errors as Śrīkara and others committed later on.[45] The *Dāyabhāga* quotes Śrīkara's explanation of Kātyāyana above. Śrīkara

seems to have thought that all property acquired in a state of union by any member was liable to partition and that 'acquisition without detriment to paternal estate' was not a proper criterion for judging self-acquisition.

(8). Śrīkara looked upon wealth obtained by gifts as *vidyādhana* and thus brought about a confusion between wealth obtained by officiating at a sacrifice, teaching and gift. This is very stupid, according to the *Dāyabhāga* (p. 197).

(9) The *Vyavahāramātṛkā* (p. 202) says that in a suit for money (such as 'you owe me a hundred') hundred is said by Śrīkara to be the *dharmī* and 'being liable to pay another the *sādhya* (in the language of the *Nyāya* system) and finds faith with Śrīkara (in the true schoolman style) by saying that the *dharmī* (gold and corn, etc.) is liable to destruction by use and so there will result the fault of *āśrayāsiddha*.

(10) The *Vyavahāramātṛkā* (p. 302) thinks that Yogaloka took an example of *kāraṇottara* from Śrīkara.

(11) Śrīkara refers to the verse of Nārada (*ṛṇādāna* 237) and says that if the witnesses of a party depose to more or less than what the party asserts, then they are no witnesses and the party is defeated (*Vyavahāramātṛkā*, p. 334). A similar view was held by Viśvarūpa.

(12) The *Vyavahāramātṛkā* (p. 342) gives the explanation of Śrīkaramiśra on *Yāj.*, II.24 which comes to this that enjoyment of land for twenty years by one even without title before the very eyes of the owner and without protest from the latter results in the loss of the ownership of the original owner and constitutes a title in itself and that such verses as 'whoever enjoys even for many hundred years without title should be punished as a thief (Nārada) refer to cases where the owner is absent.[46] M. appears to refer to this view in its comment on *Yāj.*, II.24.

(13) The *Smṛticandrikā* (II, p. 266) mentions that Śrīkara said that nobody offers a big bull to a learned guest as there is no such *śiṣṭācāra* now, while Viśvarūpa said that offering of a bull is negatived by *śiṣṭācāra*, which way of stating the matter is improper.

Whether Śrīkara wrote a commentary on some *Smṛti* or a digest (*nibandha*) it is difficult to say. From the numerous explanations of Yājñavalkya's text cited above it appears that he commented on the *Yājñavalkya-Smṛti*. But the *Smṛticandrikā*[47] (II, p. 266) says that Śambhu, Śrīkara and Devasvāmin compiled together several *Smṛti*s into digests (and are hence styled *Smṛti-samuccayakāra*). The *Smṛtisāra* of Harinātha refers to a *Śrīkaranibandha* (India Office Catalogue, p. 448, No. 1489). The *Smṛtyarthasāra* of Śrīdhara (Ānandāśrama edition) says that *Smṛti*s being scattered, Śrīkaṇṭha and Śrīkarācārya made them into one consistent whole (lit. they filled the gaps in the *Smṛti*s). Therefore it looks as if even though Śrīkara wrote a commentary it was of the nature of a comprehensive digest.

As Śrīkara is cited by M. he is certainly earlier than AD 1050. As his views agree in the main with those of Viśvarūpa he is not much later than the latter and if Viśvarūpa be held to be referring to Śrīkara in his reamrks on *Yāj.* (*vide* No. 5 above), then Śrīkara would be earlier than even the first half of the ninth century. At all events he must be placed somewhere between AD 750 and 1050.

Medhātithi

M. (on *Yāj.*, II.124) refers to the views of Asahāya and Medhātithi about the fourth share to be given to an unmarried sister and follows it in preference to Bhārucī's.

On *Yāj.*, II.24 M. refers to the fact that Dhāreśvara, Viśvarūpa and Medhātithi did not accept certain texts of Ṛṣyaśṛṅga.

Medhātithi wrote a *bhāṣya* on the *Manusmṛti*. It was first published about forty years ago by Rao Saheb V. N. Mandlik and recently by Mr. Gharpure and it is in course of translation by Mahāmahopādhyāya Dr. Ganganath Jha. Here Mr. Gharpure's edition has been used. The *bhāṣya* as printed is corrupt in many places, particularly in the 8th, 9th and 12th *adhyāya*s. In Mr. Gharpure's edition there is no comment on verses 182-202 of the 9th chapter. In several Mss. of the *bhāṣya* at the end of several chapters there is a verse which says that a king named Madana son of Sahāraṇa brought from other countries copies of Medhātithi's commentary and brought about a restoration (*jirṇoddhāra*).[48] This refers, as Bühler says, not to the restoration of the text of the commentary, but to that of the library of the King, who was Madanapāla, of Kāṣṭhā, son of Sādhāraṇa and flourished in the latter half of the fourteenth century.

Bühler in his learned and exhaustive introduction to the *Manusmṛti* (*SBE*, Vol. 25) brings together a good deal of information about Medhātithi (pp. cxviii-cxxvi). No useful purpose will be served by repeating what he has already seated. In the following lines a concise statement of the results of his study will be given and some details will be added which were not noticed by that learned scholar.

Bühler is not quite accurate when he states (p. cxx. footnote 1) "though the opinions of 'others' are mentioned very frequently and though sometimes those of three or four predecessors are contrasted, Medhātithi gives only once the name of an early commentator." Medhātithi does mention by name several predecessors. On *Manu.*, VIII.3 Medhātithi refers to other interpretations offered by Bhartṛyajña and asks his readers to refer to the work of that author.[49] On VIII.151 he quotes the differing explanation of Yajvan and on VIII.156 he again mentions Yajvan by name. Yajvan is probably only the later half of some time (like Devarājayajvan). On VIII.156 he mentions by name Asahāya. In his somewhat lengthy comment on VIII.152 Medhātithi twice quotes the explanations of a writer by name Ṛju.[50] Bühler is unable to make out anything of the corrupt word preceding Viṣṇusvāmin in Medhāthithi's comment on *Manu.*,

IX.253. Some Mss. read it as *kāvara*, others as *kovara*. If a conjecture may be hazarded that word is probably *kāvera* (i.e., residing on the Kāverī river). From the quotation[51] it appears that Viṣṇusvāmin is not a commentator on Manu but rather a writer on the *Pūrvamīmāṁsā*. Medhātithi quotes an Upādhyāya (on IX.141 and 147 as Bühler points out and also on II.109, IV.162 and V.43) and Bühler holds that Medhātithi means his own teacher. It seems more likely that Upādhyāya is the name (or rather part of a name) of some previous commentator and does not mean his teacher.

Bühler rightly holds (against the views of Dr. Jolly) that Medhātithi was a man from the North, probably from Kashmir, as he introduces the country of Kashmir in explaining *svarāṣṭre*, *janapadaḥ* (in *Manu.*, VII.32 and VIII.41), in giving the monopoly of the sale of saffron as a privilege of the king of Kashmir in repeatedly referring to the Kāṭhaka Śākhā and in saying that the rainbow is called *vijñāna-cchāyā* in Kashmir (on *Manu.*, IV.59). He very often refers to the northerners, e.g., he says, on *Manu.*, III.234, that *kutapa* is the name of what is well-known as *kambala* among the northern people and on III.238 he says 'northern people wrap their head with *śāṭaka*s (garments). He also says on *Manu.*, II.24 that in the Himālayas in Kashmir it is not possible to perform the daily *sandhyā* in the open nor a bath in the river in *hemanta* and *śiśira*. On III.18 he says 'In other countries, some say, people marry one's maternal uncle's daughter and hence the words of Manu in III.18, but Medhātithi declares it to be opposed to Gautama (4.3 and 5) and proceeds 'even in that country taking food in the same plate with (or in company of) one whose thread ceremony is not performed is not at all regarded as *dharma*.[52] This is clearly a reference in the *Sūtra* of Baudhāyana (I.1.19) according to whom taking food in the same plate with those whose *upanayana* is not performed and marrying *mātulasutā* are two of the five usages peculiar to the South. It is to be noted, however, that later writers like Kamalākara (in his *Nirṇayasindhi*, 3rd *Pariccheda* on *Sāpiṇḍya*) regard Medhātithi as a southerner.

He refers to his own work called *Smṛtiviveka* (on II.6 and X.5), which seems to have been a work in verse or contained numerous verses. In the *Parāśaramādhavīya* (vol. I, part 2, pp. 183-86) there is a long quotation in verse from a work called *Smṛtiviveka* and there are several verses attributed to Medhātithi in the work (***vide*** Vol. I, part 1, p. 276 and part 2, p. 172). A certain writer called Lollaṭa (on *śrāddha*) frequently quotes verses of Medhātithi.

He seems to have been a profound student of the *Pūrva-mīmāṁsā*. His comment is full of the terms *vidhi* and *arthavāda*. He quotes Jaimini's *sūtra*s frequently and applies them to the interpretation of *Smṛti* texts at every step. To take only a few examples at random, on *Manu.*, VIII.100 he construes the *sūtra* of Jaimini (VI.7.3.) forbidding the gift of land in the Viśvajīt as referring to the whole of the earth. On *Manu.*, II.107 he refers to the *sūtra* of Jaimini (IV.3.5) and to the *rātrisattra-nyāya* (IV.3.17-19). On *Manu.*, I.84 he says that *saṁvatsara* means 'a day' in a long *sattra* (for which ***vide*** Jaimini, VI.7.31-40). On II.23 he refers to the *vidhivannigadādhikaraṇa* (I.2.19-20). On II.29 he speaks of the *sarvaśākhāpratyaya-nyāya* (Jaimini, II.4.8-32) and applies it to *Smṛti*s. On the same verse he refers to the *grahikatva-nyāya* (Jaimini, III.1.13-15).

He quotes on *Manu.*, I.19 a verse from *Sāṅkhyakārikā* (*prakṛter mahān*, etc.) He refers to Vindhyavāsa (on *Manu,* I.55). as a *Sāṅkhya*, says that he does not admit a subtle interim body (*antarābhavadeha*) and explains the latter term.[53] This is probably takes from Kumārila's words.[54] He repeatedly refers to the *Purāṇa*s and on III.232 tells us that they were composed by Vyāsa and contained accounts of creation, etc. He refers to Bṛhaspati as a writer on *Vārtā* (on *Manu.*, VII.43 and IX.326) and on VIII.285 refers to the works of Bṛhaspati and Uśanas on politics and government. Uśanas is also mentioned in the comment on *Manu.*, VIII.50. On *Manu.*, VII.43 he refers to Cāṇakya as a writer on *Daṇḍanīti*. In numerous places he seems to have drawn upon Kauṭilya's work. For example, on *Manu.*, VII.54 he mentions the testing of ministers by Upadhās. On

Manu., VII.155 in interpreting *pañcavarga* as *kāpaṭika, udāsthita, gṛhapatika, vaidehika* and *tāpasavyañjana* he explains these terms almost in the words of Kauṭilya (I, chap. 2). ***Vide*** also the quotations on *Manu.*, VII.61, 81, 78 and 148.

Bühler at first took the remark (on *Manu.*, XII.19) about *Śārīraka* as referring to Śaṅkara's *bhāṣya* on the *Vedāntasūtra*, but later on changed his opinion (*SBE*, Vol. 25, p. cxxii) and held that it probably implies a reference to the *Śārīraka sūtras*. Bühler does not seem to be right. The words *yatheha-rājā . . . apaiti* are a summary of Śaṅkara's *bhāṣya* on *Vedāntasūtra*, II.1.34 and II.3.43. In another place (on *Manu.*, II.83) Medhātithi refers to the *Upaniṣadbhāṣya* on *Chāndogya*, II.23.4 and tells us that the *Upaniṣad* passage has been differently explained in the *bhāṣya*. Śaṅkara does explain that passage differently. But this is not all. In various other places Medhātithi appears to be referring to the *bhāṣya* of Śaṅkara on the *Vedāntasūtras*. In his comment on *Manu.*, I.7 he gives several theories and places the *Advaitadarśana* as the last and refers to the *vivartavāda* and the well-known example of the sea and its waves. On I.80 he appears to refer to Śaṅkara's *bhāṣya* on the *sūtra* — *lokavat tu līlākaivalyam* (*Vedāntasūtra*, II.1.33).[55] He, however, seems to have favoured the position that the attainment of the highest *brahma* called *mokṣa* is due not to mere correct knowledge, but to the combination (*samuccaya*) of knowledge and *karma*[56] (***vide*** his remarks on *Manu.*, XII.87, 90 and VI.32, 74-75).

He gives at least three interpretations of the verse of *Yāj.* about twenty years possession (II.24) none of which agree exactly with that of Viśvarūpa. His work is a mine of information on all sorts of topics, but considerations of space forbid any further pursuit of this matter.

As Medhātithi quotes Kumārila and also refers to Śaṅkara and as M. looks upon him as a writer of established reputation Medhātithi is later than AD 825 and earlier than AD 1000 and probably flourished between AD 825 and 900. This conclusion is somewhat strengthened by the fact that though he names

Asahāya, he does not refer to Viśvarūpa or Bhāruci or Śrīkara and therefore could not have flourished much later than Viśvarūpa. If by Miśra in his comment[57] on *Manu.*, XII.118 he refers to Vācaspatimiśra, author of the *Bhāmati* and other works, then his date will be somewhere after AD 850.

Dhāreśvara

M. says (on *Yāj.*, II.135) that Dhāreśvara tries to reconcile the conflicting texts about the right of the widow to succeed to the estate of her deceased husband by saying that she succeeds if her sonless husband was separate and if she is willing to submit to *Niyoga*. M. on the same verse says that Dhāreśvara relying on *Manu.*, 9.217 placed the paternal grandmother immediately after the mother and before the father. On *Yāj.* III.24 M. says that certain texts of Ṛṣyaśṛṅga and others about impurity on death were not accepted as authoritative by Dhāreśvara, Viśvarūpa and Medhātithi. The *Smṛticandrikā*[58] (II, p. 294) quotes a verse from the Saṅgrahakāra which asserts the same views about the widow's rights as those of Dhāreśvara and says that the position of Dhāreśvara was controverted by Viśvarūpa. The *Sarasvatīvilāsa* (para. 576 and 593) says just as M. does, that Dhāreśvara preferred the paternal grandmother to the father. The *Hāralatā* (p. 117) makes the remark (similar to that of M. on *Yāj.*, II.24) that Bhojadeva, Viśvarūpa, Govindarāja and the Kāmadhenu did not cite certain texts as Jātūkarṇa's and that therefore the latter were not authoritative.

That Dhāreśvara is to be identified with Bhojadeva of Dhārā, perhaps the most famous Indian prince as a patron of learned men, follows from several considerations. The *Dāyabhāga* cites Bhojadeva and Dhāreśvara without making any distinction between the two. Some views that are ascribed in one work to Dhāreśvara are ascribed to Bhojadeva by another. The *Vivāda-tāṇḍava* of Kamalākara ascribes to Bhojadeva the same views as to the widow's rights that are ascribed to Dhāreśvara by M. Besides, works on numerous branches of knowledge were composed by (or in the name of) Bhoja, king of Dhārā. Mss. of the *Rājamārtaṇḍa* (commentary on the *Yogasūtra*) have colophons saying that the work was composed by Dhāreśvara Bhojarāja. The introductory fourth verse of that work says that Bhoja composed (beside that work) a work on grammar and on Vaidyaka. He wrote an astronomical work (called *Rājamṛgāṅka*) and two works on poetics, the *Sarasvatīkaṇṭhābharaṇa* and the *Sṛṅgāraprakāśa*.

Dhāreśvara is styled Ācārya by the M. (on *Yāj.*, III.24) and Sūri by the *Smṛticandrikā* (II, p. 257).

Bhoja of Dhārā reigned according to the *Bhojaprabandha* for 55 years. There are two certain dates of his. One is his grant dated *Saṁvat* 1078 (AD 1021-22). ***See*** *Ind. Ant.*, Vol. 6, p. 53. His astronomical work takes *Śaka* 964 (AD 1042-43) as its initial date. His uncle Muñja was slain by Tailapa between 994-997 and Muñja was succeeded by Sindhurāja or Sindhula also styled Navasāhasāṅka. An inscription of Jayasiṁha the successor of Bhoja is dated *Saṁvat* 1112 (AD 1055-56). ***See*** *EI*, vol. 3, pp. 46-50. Therefore Bhoja must have reigned between AD 1005 and 1055.

There are some points (besides those mentioned above about the widow's right of inheritance and about the grandmother succeeding before the father) on which M. differs from Dhāreśvara.

(1) The *Vīramitrodaya* tells us (pp. 528 and 536 of Jīvānanda's edn.) that Dhāreśvara regarded ownership as known only from *Śāstra*, while M. holds it to be *laukika*. It is probably due to Dhāreśvara's position that M. enters into an elaborate discussion on this point.

(2) The *Smṛticandrikā*[59] (II, p. 295-96), the *Sarasvatīvilāsa* (para. 555) and the *Vīramitrodaya* (p. 658) say that Dhāreśvara held, like Viśvarūpa, that the word *duhitaraḥ* in *Yāj.* stands for *putrikā* in the order of succession; M. introduces no such distinction.

On some points Dhāreśvara and M. agree.

The *Sarasvatīvilāsa* (para. 392) tells us that Dhāreśvara and Devasvāmin[60] held the same view as that of V. on the verse of Manu (9.182 *bhrāṭṝṇām ekajātānām*). viz, that the verse forbids the adoption by the other brothers of strangers when they have a nephew. M. expresses this view on *Yāj.*, II.132.

The *Smṛticandrikā* (II. p. 266) says that Dhāreśvara remarked about the verse of Manu (IX.112 *jyeṣṭhasya viṁśa uddhāraḥ*) that he does not discuss such texts as people have come to absolutely ignore them. M. says the same thing on *Yāj.*, II.117.[61]

The *Dāyabhāga* (p. 284) says that Viśvarūpa, Jitendriya. Bhojadeva and Gonvindarāja held that the daughter's son succeeds after the daughter and this decision must be accepted.[62] The order in which the authors are arranged and their known chronological position leads one to presume that Viśvarūpa was probably the first jurist to expressly recognize the daughter's son as an heir after the daugher. M. holds the same view.

The *Dāyabhāga* says that Dhāreśvara explains *Yāj.*, II.121 (*bhūryā pitāmahopāttā*) as meaning that when the father effects a partition at his will during his lifetime, he has no power to give a larger or smaller share to anyone as he can do with regard to self-acquired property. M. construes it similarly.

Some of the other views ascribed to Dhāreśvara may be noticed here.

The *Vyavahāramātṛkā* (p. 284) gives Bhojadeva's explanation of a verse of Nārada (*sottaro' nuttaraś caiva*).

The *Smṛticandrikā* notes (II, p. 254) that Dhāreśvara understands *dāya* to mean wealth that comes to a man through the father and the mother. The *Smṛtisaṁgraha* defines *dāya* in the same way.

The *Smṛticandrikā*[63] says that Dhāreśvara discussed in detail the point that there is nothing that one can use just as one pleases (and that therefore ownership cannot be defined as the power to dispose of the subject of ownership at one's sweet will). The *Smṛtisaṁgraha* gives a verse of similar import.

The *Smṛticandrikā* (II, p. 301) observes that Dhāreśvara reads the verse of Manu (p. 187) as *yo yo hy anantaraḥ piṇḍāt* and explained *piṇḍāt* as meaning *sapiṇḍāt*.

Kullūka on *Manu.*, VIII.184 says that four verses of Manu (VIII.181-84) were arranged by Medhātithi and Bhojadeva in one way and by Govindarāja in another.

The foregoing resumé of the several views ascribed to Dhāreśvara by comparatively early writers makes it clear that Dhāreśvara composed some work on the several branches of *dharma* (such as *vyavahāra, dāya, śrāddha, āśauca*, etc.). Whether his work was a commentary like that of Viśvarūpa or M. or whether it was an independent work or whether he wrote two works (as on Poetics) it is difficult to say. In one place the *Smṛticandrikā* (II, p. 302) says that *Smṛtisaṁgraha* follows Dhāreśvara's views. Probably nothing more is meant than this that they held identical views. It appears that Bhoja's work on *Dharmaśāstra* was called *Rājamārtaṇḍa*. In the *Śuddhi-Kaumudī* (B.I. edn.) of Govindānanda (wherein intercalary months from *Śaka* 1400 to 1457 are examined thereby showing the period when the author lived) a verse is cited as occurring in the *Rājamārtaṇḍa* of Bhojarāja about *Śrāddha*.[64]

References

[For Dhāveśvara Bhojadeva read Kane's *History of Dharmaśāstra*, Vol. I/I, pp. 585-91. ***Also see*** Dr. Kane's paper on Bhoja' published elsewhere in this Volume.]

S.G. Moghe

1. [***Also see***, Kane's *History of Dharmaśāstra*, Vol. I/I, pp. 548-49 for Asahāya and also a paper on Asahāya published elsewhere in this Volume.]

   S.G.Moghe

2. धर्मविभागो मनुयाज्ञवल्क्यादिस्मृतिकाराणां तत्स्मृतिव्याख्यातॄणामसहायमेधातिथि-विज्ञानेश्वरापरार्काणां निबन्द्धृणां चन्द्रिकाकाराणां च संमत एव।

3. अत्रासहायेनोक्तं पुंसां सति भ्रातृजे स्त्रीणां सपत्नीपुत्रे क्षेत्रजादयः प्रतिनिधयो न कर्तव्या इति।

4. हारलता (B.I. edn.), p. 35 : गौतमः — बालदेशान्तरितप्रव्रजितानां सपिण्डानां सद्यः शौचम् (गौ० ध० स० १४.४१)। यत्र मृतोऽशौचारभ्यन्तरे न श्रूयते तद्देशान्तरं तत्र मृतो देशान्तरित इति गौतमभाष्यकृताऽसहायेन व्याख्यातम्। — *Vide* p. 97 also.

5. Para 19 : असहायविज्ञानयोगिप्रभृतीनां तु यत्स्वामिसंबन्धादेव निमित्रादन्यस्य स्वं भवति तद्दायशब्देनोच्यत इति।

6. Para 195 of *Sarasvatīvlāsa*.

7. अतश्च कन्याशुल्कविषये सोदरासोदरविभागेऽसोदराणामपि किंचिद्देयमित्यसहाय-व्याख्यानमसहायम्। (Para. 314) — There is a play on the word *asahāya* (which means 'unsupported, baseless).

8. सरस्वतीविलास, para. 608.

9. पित्रा दत्तमिति स्त्रीधनमात्रोपलक्षणामत्यसहायमेधातिथिरिति(?थी इति) प्रकाशकारः(।)

10. गौतमीयं त्वनृतुपरिसंख्यार्थमृतावुपेयादिति केचित्। . . . तस्मात्तदपि नियमार्थमेव व्याख्येयम्।

11. The writers on *Dharmaśāstra* named are: अङ्गिरस्, आत्रेय, आपस्तम्ब, उशनस्, कात्यायन, गार्ग्य, वृद्धगार्ग्य, गौतम, जातूकर्ण (or °र्णि), दक्ष, नारद, पितामह, पुलस्त्य, बृहस्पति, बौधायन, भृगु, मनु, वृद्धमनु, यम, वृद्धयाज्ञवल्क्य, वसिष्ठ, व्यास, शङ्ख, शातातप, शौनक, संवर्त, स्वयम्भू, हारीत.

12. तथा चाहुः सामन्तयोर्व्यसनसाम्ये न यातव्यं तममित्रमेव यायादिति। विश्वरूप. Cf. तुल्यसामन्तव्यसने यातव्यममित्रं वा इत्यमित्रमभियायात्। कौटिल्य (VII.5.1).

13. किं पुनस्तन्मन्त्रणीयम्। उक्तं च दिक्प्रचारदूतसंप्रेषणकापटिकोदास्थितगृहपतिकवैदेहकता-पसव्यञ्जनावस्थितचारप्रपञ्चपरिनिरूपणपरप्रयुक्तकापटिकाद्युच्छेददुर्गादिकरणकन्यासंप्रदानकुमारचि-न्तान्तःपुरप्रचाराद्यनेकविधं च। विश्वरूप. words कापटिको . . . व्यञ्जन occur in कौटिल्य (I.11.1), कौटिल्य has chapters on राजपुत्ररक्षण (i.e. कुमारचिन्ता), अवरुद्धवृज (i.e. अन्तःपुरप्रचार)? दुर्गविधान, दूतप्रणिधि।

14. न्यायविदश्च याज्ञिकाः 'अपि वा सर्वधर्मः स्यात्' etc.; न्यायविदश्च याज्ञिकाः सर्वार्थत्वात् पुत्रार्थे न प्रयोजयेदित्याहुः।

15. तथा च नैयायिका नहि वचनस्यातिभारोस्तीत्याहुः। These words occur in शबरभाष्य on III.2.3.

16. p. 16 : सर्व चैतत्प्रपञ्चेन वक्ष्यामः श्राद्धसंग्रहे।

17. अतो विवाहकाललब्धस्त्रीधनविषयं ब्राह्मादिवचनमिति विश्वरूपोक्तमादरणीयम्।

18. अत एवोक्तं विश्वरूपेण पितृद्रव्यं दत्त्वा यदि नोपार्जितं धनं तदा तस्यैवासाधारणं वैवाहिकवदेवोक्तं न तु भक्षणाद्युपभोगमात्रेण तस्य स्तनपानादितुल्यत्वादित्यन्तेन। दायभाग; पितृधनानुपधातेन यदन्यदर्जितं तथा मैत्रमौद्वाहिकं च तदाजेयितुरेव। . . . पितृद्रव्योपघातेनापिमैत्राद्यविभाज्यमेवारम्भसामर्थ्यात्। अन्ये तु मैत्रादिकमेव पितृ-धनानुपघातार्जितमविभाज्यमिच्छन्ति। . . . तत्तु सामान्यद्रव्यसाध्यत्वाद्विवाहस्या-युक्तमेव। विश्वरूप.

19. सर्वदापेन (in the text of वृद्ध कात्यायन 'पितृभ्यां चैव यद्दत्तं दुहितुः स्थावरं धनम्। अपजायामतीतायां भ्रातुगामि तु सर्वदा') ब्राह्मादिपैशाचान्तविवाहिताया अप्रजसो धनं भ्रातृगाम्येव भवतीति विश्वरूपोक्तमादरणीयम्।

20. अस्मादेव च दौहित्राभाववचनाद् द्विजातीनामपि पुत्राभावे दौहित्रा धनभाज इति। — विश्वरूप.

21. भ्रातरस्तथेति तथाशब्दः प्रकारार्थः सापत्न्यादिसर्वभ्रातृसंग्राहकः। — विश्वरूप on याज्ञ. II.139.

22. विश्वरूपस्य मते ऊनाधिकारभिधाने तद्युक्त (?तदप्यनुक्त) मिति मुनिभिरभिहितत्वात् etc. व्यवहारमातृका; बह्वर्थप्रतिज्ञायां च न्यूनमभ्यादिकं चार्थं प्रब्रूयुर्यत्र साक्षिणः। तदप्यनुक्तं विज्ञेयमेवसाक्ष्यविधिः स्मृतः — इतिः अतः कृत्स्नप्रतिज्ञातार्थसत्यत्वे एव ध्रुवो जयः।

23. उपेक्षानिषेधमात्रं चैतत्। हानिवचनं तु निन्दामात्रत्वेनोपेक्षकस्य व्यवहारप्रवृत्त्ययोग्यता-मात्रज्ञप्तिफलम्।

24. यत्पुनर्विश्वरूपेणोक्तं तथा महोक्षं वा महाजं वा श्रोत्रियायोपकल्पयेत् इत्यस्य शिष्टाचारेण बाधितत्वादकरणमेवमुद्धारस्यापीति।

25. विश्वरूपेणापि साक्षिणः पूर्ववादिन इत्यादि प्रतिग्रहादिविषयं व्याख्यातं तत्रैव पूर्वबल-वत्त्वात्।

26. यत्तु स्मृत्यन्तरं। आद्ये तु दण्डपादस्य द्वितीयेर्धं तृतीयके। पादन्यूनं चतुर्थे च पादे संपूर्णदण्डभाक्।। तद्विगीतत्वादप्रमाणमिति प्रपञ्चितं विश्वरूपाचार्येण।

27. तदुक्तं विश्वरूपेणापि तस्करदोषो नास्तीति वचनारम्भसामर्थ्यात् स्तेयधात्वर्धानिष्पत्ते रित्यभिप्रायः।

28. इदं च वाक्यं नित्यकर्मविषयत्वेन वार्तिके विश्वरूपाचार्य उदाजहार। आम्रे फलार्थे इत्यादि ह्यापस्तम्बस्मृतेर्वचः। फलवत्वं समाचष्टे नित्यानामपि कर्मणाम्। — पराशरमाधवीय. The *sūtra* आम्रे फलार्थे is आपस्तम्बधर्म. I.7.20.3.

29. इत्येवं नैष्कर्म्यसिद्धौ ब्रह्मां शैर्ब्रह्मवित्तमैः। श्रीमद्भिर्विश्वरूपाख्यैराचार्यैः करुणार्णवैः।। — पुरुषार्थप्रबोध (folio 6).

30. यत्प्रसादादयं लोको धर्ममार्गस्थित्सुखी। भवभूतिसुरेशाख्यं विश्वरूपं प्रणस्य तम्।।

31. अथ किं विभागास्वत्वमुत। स्वत्वे सति विभाग इति। विभागात्स्वत्वमित्याहुः। . . . अतः स्वत्वे सति विभाग इति सिद्धम्।

32. [For Viśvarūpa, ***Also see*** Kane's *History of Dharmaśāstra*, Vol. I/I, pp. 553-565] *S.G. Moghe*

33. Para 637: यथाह भारुचिरेतद्विष्णुवचनव्याख्यानावसरे बीजशब्दः पिण्डवाचीति.-The *sūtra* of विष्णु is बीजग्रहणानुविधायमंशं गृह्णीयात् (para 636).

34. Para 674 : अत्र भारुचिः। निष्कारणमिति वदता विष्णुना समनन्तरकर्तृणां पुत्रादीनां विद्यमानत्वे दौहित्रस्य न कर्तृत्वसंक्रान्तिरिति। The *sūtra* of विष्णु is दौहित्रस्य मातामहश्राद्धं निष्कारणम्. The words of सुदर्शन are इममेवार्थं भारुचिरप्याह यस्मिन्पक्षे अपुत्रो मातामहः पुत्रिकासुतश्चाखिलद्रव्यहारी तस्मिन्पक्षे तस्य पिण्डदाननियमः इत्यादिना ग्रन्थेन।

35. अत्र भारुचिः। भिन्नोदराणामिति निर्धारणे षष्ठी। भिन्नोदराणां मध्ये संसृष्टिन एव धनं गृह्णीयुः।

36. The *sūtra* is अपित्र्यं गार्भं धार्मं मैत्रं वैद्यमाकस्मिकमादशाब्दं प्रविभाज्यमत ऊर्ध्वं सर्वमविभाज्यम्।

37. एतच्च मातुर्दुहितरःशेषमितिवचनमन्यथा व्याकुर्वन्ति भारुचिप्रभृतयः। पुत्राभावे मातुर्धनं दुहितरो विभजेरन् तदभावे स्वान्वयः पितृत्र्यादिर्गृह्णीयात्। (para 142); अन्ये तु ताभ्यो दुहितृभ्य ऋते तदीय एवान्वय इति वर्णयन्ति तत्त्वयुक्तम्। — विश्वरूप.

38. Para. 302.

39. Para 350-51 : पुत्रवत्याः शय्यापालनं दुहितृमत्या वा तदभावे नियोगादप्यपत्योत्पादन-मावश्यकम्। . . . शय्यापालनात्संताननिर्वाह एव श्रेयामिति भारुच्यपरार्कसोमेश्वरा-दीनां मतम्।

40. Para. 383.

41. Para 464-65.

42. Para. 607.
[*Also see* for Bhāruci, Kane's *History of Dharmaśāstra*, Vol. I/I, pp. 565-71.]
S.G. Moghe

43. एतेनाल्पश्नविषयत्वं श्रीकरादिभिरुक्तं निरस्तं वेदितव्यम्।

44. किं च कात्यायनवचनं विभक्ताः पितृवित्ताच्चेदकत्र प्रतिवासिनः। विभजेयुः पुनर्द्व्यशं सलभेतोदयो यतः। इदं संसृष्टस्य साधारणधनोपधातेनार्जकस्य भागद्वयमितरेषामेकैको भाग इति श्रीकरेण व्याख्यातम्। — दायभाग (p. 174).

45. तदयमर्थो यथा कयाचिद् विद्यया यल्लब्धमर्जकस्यैव तन्नेतरेषां प्रदर्शनार्थं तु कात्यायनेन विस्तरेणोक्तं श्रीकरादिभ्रमनिरासार्थम्। — दायभाग (p. 196).

46. श्रीकरमिश्राणां समाधानं पश्यतः प्रतिवादिनो विवादमकुर्वत भूमेर्विंशतिवर्षभोगः प्रमाणान्तरनिरपेक्षः प्रमाणं तावता च प्रतिवादिनस्तद्भूमिस्वत्वहानिः। . . . आगमरहितायाश्च भुक्तेः प्रामाण्यबोधकवचनानि अनागमं तु यो भुङ्क्ते इत्यादीनि प्रतिवादिपरोक्षविषयाणि। — व्यवहारमातृका।

47. ये पुनः स्मृतिसमुच्चयकाराः शम्भुश्रीकरदेवस्वाम्यादयः संप्रत्युद्धारविषमविभागयोः शिष्टाचारं मन्यमाना उद्धारादिविषयाणि स्मृतिवाक्यानि विचारयितु ग्रन्थविस्तारं चाक्रिरे।
[*Also see* Kane's *History of Dharmaśāstra*, Vol. I/I, pp. 571-73.]
S.G. Moghe

48. मान्या कापि मनुस्मृतिस्तदुचिता व्याख्या हि मेधातिथेः सा लुप्तैव विधेर्वशात् कुचिदपि प्राप्यं न यत्पुस्तकाम्। क्षोणीन्द्रो मदनः महापरणसुतो देशान्तरादाहृतैर्जीर्णोद्धारमचीकरस्त इतस्तत्पुस्तकैर्लेखितैः।।

49. व्याख्यानान्तराणि भर्तुयज्ञेनैव सम्यक्कृतानीति तत एतावगन्तव्यानि सर्वथा प्रमाणमूलानि etc.

50. एतत्तु ऋतुना पुरुषान्तरमसंक्रान्तमिति व्याख्यातम्। . . . ऋजुस्तु तस्मादेवाधर्मणा-दनवीकृते प्रयोगे द्विगुणाधिकां वृद्धिं नेच्छति।

51. अतो यावती काचित्फलश्रुतिः सा सर्वार्थवाद इति कोवरविष्णुस्वामी।

52. अस्मिन्नपि देशेऽनुपनीतेन सह भोजनादिराचारो नैव धर्मत्वेनेष्यते।

53. सांख्या अपि केचिन्नान्तराभवमिच्छन्ति विन्ध्यवासप्रभृतयः।

54. अन्तराभवदेहस्तु नेष्यते विन्ध्यवासिना।

55. लीलयापि कौतुकेनापि लोके राजादीनां प्रवृत्तिर्दृश्यते इति ब्रह्मविदः। मेधातिथि; यथालोके कस्यचिदाप्तैषणस्य राज्ञो . . . लीलारूपाः प्रवृत्तयो भवन्ति etc. — शाङ्करभाष्य.

56. अतश्च ब्रह्मनिष्ठारेणापि वेदाभ्यासदीन्यनुष्ठेयानि। यस्य यस्य कर्मन्यासः श्रूयते स षष्ठे व्याख्यातः — मेधातिथि on *Manu.*, XII.87; इदं तु ज्ञानकर्मणोः समुच्चयान्मोक्ष इति श्लोकद्वय ज्ञापकम्। — मेधातिथि on *Mann.* VI.74-75.

[For Medhātithi, ***also see*** Kane's *History of Dharmaśāstra*, Vol. I/I, pp. 573-83. ***Also see*** a Ph.D. Thesis on "Mimāṁsā in Medhātithi" by Dr. A.R. Joshi, in the Library of Bombay University, 1983.] *S.G. Moghe*

57. प्रमाणान्तराणामपि एकत्वप्रतिपादनपरत्वादेव ग्राहिणः प्रत्यक्षस्य मिश्रैः कृत एव क्लेशः।

58. तथा संग्रहकारः। भ्रातृषु प्रविभक्तेषु संसृष्टेष्वसत्सु च। गुर्वादेशान्नियोगस्था पत्नी धनमवाप्नुयात्।

59. एवं सोपपत्तिकीं पत्न्यभावे दुहितृगामितां ब्रुवता बृहस्पतिनैव यद्दुहितृगामि धनमिति विधायकं वचनजातं तत्पुत्रिकाविषयमेव न पुनरपुत्रिकादुहितृविषयमिति धारेश्वरदेव-स्वामिदेवरातमतं स्मृतितन्त्राभिज्ञत्वाभिमानोन्मादकल्पितं निरस्तं वेदितव्यम्।

60. धारेश्वरदेवस्वामिनौ तु विज्ञानयोगिमतानुवर्तिनावेव।

61. अयं विषमो विभागः शास्त्रदृष्टस्तथापि लोकविद्विष्टत्वान्नानुष्ठेयः।

62. तस्माद्विश्वरूपजितेन्द्रियभोजदेवगोविन्दराजैर्दुहित्रभावे दौहित्रास्याधिकारो निरूपित आदरणीयः।

63. यथेष्टविनियोज्यं किपपि नास्ति। प्रपाञ्चितं चैतद्धारेश्वरसूरिणा।

64. अत एव राजमार्तण्डे भोजराजः। श्राद्धविघ्ने समुत्पन्ने मृतस्याविदिते दिने। अमावास्यां प्रकुर्वीत वदन्त्येके मनीषिणः।।

11

Kalivarjya*

(Actions Forbidden in the Kali Age)

AMONG ancient peoples the Golden Age has been in the past. India is no exception. Even in the *Ṛgveda* we come across a verse betraying the feeling that as time passes there will be progressively greater deterioration, both moral and physical. In the famous dialogue of Yama and Yamī, Yama is represented as saying "those later ages are yet to come when sisters would do what is not sister-like". (*Ṛgveda,* X.10.10) But the *Ṛgveda* does not give any indication that the theory of four *yuga*s had been evolved at that time. The word *yuga* occurs at least thirty-eight times in the *Ṛgveda*, but the meaning is rather doubtful. In a few places *yuga* means yoke (*ṚV*, X.60.8 and X.101.3 and 4). In many places it appears to refer to a very brief period, e.g., in *vaiśvā-naraḥ kuśikebhir — yuge yuge*' (*ṚV*, IIII.26.3), where Sāyaṇa renders *yuge yuge* by *pratidinam*. Generally *yuga* appears to mean in the *Ṛgveda* 'generation', e.g., *praminatī manuṣyā yugāni* (lessening the life of human generations, *ṚV*, I.92.11 and I.124.2). *Vide also* *ṚV*, I.103.4, II.2.2, III.33.8, V.52.4. In other places *yuga* must be given the sense of a 'long period of time', *e.g.*, *tvām dūtam-agne amṛtaṁ yuge yuge dadhire* (*ṚV*, VI.15.8 'they made you, O Agni, an immortal messenger, carrying oblations in each period'),

---

*This paper which was accepted by the Eighth All-India Oriental Conference is now published with the permission of the Conference.

devānām pūrvye yuge asataḥ sadajāyata (*ṚV*, X.72.2 'in the primeval period of the gods developed matter come out from the undeveloped one); ***vide also*** *ṚV*, VI.8.5, X.94.12, X.97.1. In *ṚV*, I.158.6 *dīrghatamā māmateyo jujurvān daśame yuge* (Dīrghatamas, the son of Mamatā, had grown old in the tenth *yuga*), *yuga* probably means a period of four years. Whatever be the meaning attached to the word *yuga*, the *Ṛgveda* does not contain the names of the four well-known ages. The word *kṛta* seems to have been used in the sense of the best throw of dice or of the seeds of the *vibhātaka* tree in gambling in *ṚV*, X.34.6 'the seeds of *vibhātaka* bestowing the *kṛta* throws on the rival gambler that (increase) the gambler's desire (appetite) for gambling'. Kali is the name of the author of *ṚV*, VIII.66 and in verse 15 of the hymn the composer says 'O descendants of Kali do not be afraid' (*kalayo mā bibhītana*). In *ṚV*, X.39.8 the Aśvins are said to have rejuvenated Kali who had become old. But there is no reference in the *Ṛgveda* to Kali as a throw in gambling or to Kali as the name of an age. The words *kṛta, tretā, dvāpara* and *āskanda* (for Kali) occur in the *Taittirīya-Saṁhitā* (4.3.3). In the *Vājasaneya Saṁhitā* (30.18) also these very words occur.[1] In the *Śatapatha Brāhmaṇa* (*SBE*, Vol. 44, p. 416) also the same words are used 'to the *kṛta* one who takes advantage of mistakes in the game; to the *tretā* one who plays on a regular plan; to the *dvāpara* one who plans to over-reach (his fellow-player); to the *āskanda* a post of the gaming room' (Eggeling's tr.). In the *TaiBrā*[2] we read 'to the *kṛta* the master of the gaming hall, to the *tretā* one who takes advantage of mistakes, to the *dvāpara* one who sits outside, to the *Kali* (one who is like) a post of the gaming house (*i.e.*, never leaves it).' Here Kali is substituted for the word *āskanda*. It is clear that in all these places *kṛta* and the other three words are throws in gambling. *Kṛta* is the most lucky throw and *kali* is the most unlucky. The *TaiBrā* (I.5.11) says 'the four *sṭomas* (*viz.*, *trivṛt, pañcadaśa, saptadaśa, ekaviṁśa*) are *kṛta* and the five are *kali*, therefore the *catus-ṣṭoma* (should be performed).'[3]

This shows that *kṛta* meant either four or any multiple of four and *kali* a throw which when divided by four left one as remainder. When we come to the *Aitareya Brāhmaṇa*[4] in the well-known story of Śunaḥśepa ('one lying down becomes *kali*, when about to leave the bed he becomes *dvāpara*, when rising he becomes *tretā* and he becomes *kṛta* when moving about') we find that the words *kṛta, tretā, dvāpara* and *kali* have come to be used in a figurative sense as representing either the *yuga*s (periods of varying standards of morality) or at least progressively higher and higher stages of human activity. The *Śatapatha Brāhmaṇa*, V.4.4.6 identifies *kali* with *abhibhū* and appears to suggest that *kali* is a throw of five dice that vanquishes all other throws (*aya*).[5] In the *Chāndogya Upaniṣad*[6] also (IV.I.4) we read 'as (in a game of dice) all the lower castes belong to him who has conquered with the *kṛta* cast' and in the *Muṇḍaka Upaniṣad*[7] (I.2.1) we are told 'this is the truth; the sacrificial works which they (the poets) saw in the hymns have been performed in many ways in the *tretā*.' Here the word *tretā* is explained even by Śaṅkarācārya first as referring to the threefold priestly duties (*hautra, ādhvaryava* and *audgātra*) based on the three *Veda*s and alternatively as referring to the *tretā* age. There are thus grave doubts whether the theory of four ages called *kṛta, tretā, dvāpara* and *kali* was known to the ancient Vedic Literature.

The *Nirukta* (I.20) makes a distinction between sages of ancient times and those of later times 'the (ancient) sages had an intuitive perception of *dharma* and they imparted by instruction the (Vedic) *mantra*s to later (sages) who had no intuitive perception of *dharma*.[8] Āpastamba[9] declares that 'among sages of old are observed transgressions of the precepts of *śāstra* and also violent actions, but that on account of their distinguished spiritual greatness they incurred no sin and that if a person of these latter days were to look upon them as worthy of imitation and were to do those acts he would sink into sin'. The *Gautama-dharmasūtra*[10] (I.3-4) expresses a similar view almost in the same words. Āpastamba[11] further says that sages are not born among men of latter days on account of the transgressions of religious ordinances (rampant in later ages). But the ancient *dharmasūtra*s do not exhibit the full-fledged theory of four *yuga*s with their peculiar characteristics.

It is only in the *Viṣṇudharmasūtra*, the *Mahābhārata* (e.g. *Vanaparva*, 149 and 183), *Manusmṛti* (I.81-86), the *Purāṇa*s (e.g. *Brahma*, chs. 122-23, *Matsya* chs. 142-43, *Nāradīya*, *pūrvārdha*, ch. 41) that we have a complete theory of the four *yuga*s, their characteristics and of the progressive religious, moral and physical decadence in them. It would be impossible to fix the period when this theory was first proclaimed. But it may be conjectured that it was perfected during the five or six centuries preceding Christ when the great schism due to the genius of Buddha spread over India. The evidence of inscriptions does not carry the antiquity of this theory far enough. Among the earliest is the Pīkira grant[12] of Pallava Siṁhavarman where we have the words. 'Who was ever ready to extricate *dharma* that had become sunk owing to the evil effects of *kaliyuga*'.

This theory of four *yuga*s provided a formidable weapon to writers on *dharma* when inconvenient texts had to be explained away. Many of our authorities[13] have one verse in common viz. 'the religious ordinances are different in the *kṛta* age and in *tretā* and *dvāpara* also; in the *kali* age different ordinances apply to men in order to suit the decadence (of *dharma*) in each age.' Any practices that shocked the feelings of later writers were declared to be forbidden in the present age and were consigned to remote ages. Very amusing results follow from this. Parāśara (I.24) claims that his *smṛti* contains the ordinances peculiar to the *kali* age.[14] Parāśara lessened the periods of impurity due to death or birth according as a man was learned in the *Veda*s or otherwise;[15] he allowed a woman to remarry in case of five calamities viz. when the husband was missing or dead or had become an ascetic, was impotent or guilty of a *mahāpātaka*;[16] he allows even brāhmaṇas to take cooked food from *dāsa*s, cowherds, barbers &c.[17] But it will be noticed from the extracts given later on that all these practices are condemned by later writers as forbidden in the *kali* age.

In many digests like the *Smṛticandrikā*, the works of Hemādri; the *Parāśaramādhavīya*, the *Udvāhatattva* of Raghunandana, the *Samayamayūkha* of Nīlakaṇṭha long extracts are given from a few *Purāṇa*s and from Śaunaka which condemn certain practices as forbidden in the *kali* age (*kalivarjya*). It is an interesting question to find out when these verses about *kalivarjya* came to be composed.

Even Āpastamba (II.6, 14.6-10) condemns the practice[18] of giving all property to the eldest son as opposed to *śāstra*, but he does not use the word *kalivarjya*. Among the earliest references to practices once current but forbidden in the *kali* age is a passage of Bṛhaspati[19] quoted by Aparārka (p. 97 Ānandāśrama edn.) where *niyoga* is said to be impossible owing to decadence (of *dharma*) in the several ages and where the several kinds of sons are declared as impossible in the present age. The *Prajāpatismṛti* refers to the ancient practice of offering flesh in *śrāddha* and prescribes that wine and all flesh are to be eschewed in *śrāddha* in the *kali* age.[20] The *Laghu-Āśvalāyana-smṛti* (21.14-15) says that the two kinds of sons called Kuṇḍa and Golaka were permitted in other ages but are condemned in *kali*. It deserves to be noted that Viśvarūpa and Medhātithi do not quote a single verse about *Kalivarjya*. Even Vijñāneśvara quotes a single verse about *kjalivarjya*[21] in which *niyoga*, the giving of a special share to the ,eldest son and the killing of a cow in sacrifice are condemned as not allowable in the present age. Even when almost all the *Purāṇa*s wax very eloquent over moral and physical decline in the *kali* age, most of them do not contain any verses about *kalivarjya*. The *Nāradīya Mahāpurāṇa* contains four verses about *kalivarjya*.[22] Aparārka quotes one verse and a half from the *Brahma Purāṇa* on practices forbidden in the *kali* age, viz. perpetual *brahmacarya* (student-hood), the taking of a *kamaṇḍalu*, marriage with a *sagotra* or *sapiṇḍa* girl, killing a cow, human sacrifice and *aśvamedha* (horse sacrifice).[23] I was not able to trace these in the *Brahma Purāṇa* published by the Venkateshwar Press. The *Prāyaścittatattva* of Raghunandana (p. 520, Jivananda's edn.) says that these passages of the

Brahma Purāṇa were quoted as from that *Purāṇa* by Halāyudha, Śūlapāṇi and Gṛhastha-ratnākara. Aparārka (p. 98) quotes one verse and a half more from the *Brahma Purāṇa* forbidding remarriage of women, procreation of a son from the husband's brother and independence of women in the *kali* age.[24] The *Smṛticandrikā*[25] quotes from the *Āditya Purāṇa* a verse saying that five actions should not be practised in *kali*, viz, the remarriage of a woman once married, the special share given to the eldest (on a partition), the killing of a cow, (intercourse) with the wife of one's brother and taking up of a *kamaṇḍalu*. Aparārka (p. 233) quotes a verse from the *Mārkaṇḍeya Purāṇa* in which the view of Bhrgu that in the *kali* age no animal is to be offered in Madhuparka is mentioned. Aparārka[26] (p. 233) quotes two verses from a *Smṛti* without naming the author, one of which forbids in the *kali* age the killing of a cow in a sacrifice, the procreation of a son from the husband's brother (by *niyoga*), sacrificial sessions called *sattras*, the carrying of a *kamaṇḍalu*, the employment of wine (in the *sautrāmaṇi* sacrifice), and being a *saṁnyāsin* (of the Paramahaṁsa type), while the other forbids (the remarriage of) a girl whose marriage has not been consummated, human sacrifice, sacrifice of a cow, taking a *kamaṇḍalu* and *niyoga*. The *Smṛticandrikā*, the *Caturvargacintāmaṇi* of Hemādri, the *Parāśaramādhavīya*, the *Nīrṇayasindhu*, the *Samayamayūkha* and other digests quote a very long passage from a *Purāṇa* (which most of them cite as *Āditya Purāṇa*) which enumerates the practices that were forbidden by the great sages at the beginning of the *kali* age after considering the reasons for and against them. That passage is set out in the appendix and a translation is given here with brief notes wherever necessary. The foregoing discussion shows that definite rules on *kalivarjya* began to be prescribed about the fourth century AD with Bṛhaspati and other older *smṛtikāras*, that the work called *Saṁgraha* (which is certainly earlier than the tenth century) contained such a list, that Viśvarūpa and Medhātithi (both of whom flourished between 800-925) do not quote verses on *kalivarjya* and that from the twelfth century onwards (as the

Smṛticandrikā and Hemādri show) long lists of *kalivarjya*s come to be quoted in the digests on *dharma*. Therefore the period during which *kalivarjya* practices figure in the *Purāṇa*s and other works must be taken to be from about the fourth century AD to the eighth or ninth century AD, when Buddhism was vanquished and the Indian social fabric was being reconstructed.

The several *kalivarjya*s as mentioned in the passage of the *Āditya Purāṇa* will now be set out.

1. To appoint the husband's brother for procreating a son on a widow.

This refers to the practice of *niyoga*, which was allowed by Gautama (18.9-14), Nārada (*strīpuṁsa*, verse 58), Yājñavalkya (I.68-69), though it was condemned by Manu (9.64-68), and Bṛhaspati.

2. The re-marriage of a (married) girl (whose marriage is not consummated) and of one (whose marriage was consummated) to another husband (after the death of the first). This refers to re-marriage of widows. Nārada (*strīpuṁsa*, verses 98-100) allowed re-marriage of even brāhmaṇa widows in certain calamities and Parāśara did the same (***vide*** note 16), while Vasiṣṭha (17.74) and *Baudhāyana-dharmasūtra* (IV.1.18) allow the re-marriage of a girl whose first marriage was not consummated.

The passage is read *bālikākṣatayonyāśca* also; in that case it will mean only 'a married girl whose marriage has not been consummated' while the other reading refers to two kinds of widows (whose marriage is consummated and whose marriage is not so).

3. The marriage with girls of different *varṇa* among persons of the three twice-born classes.

Most ancient *smṛtis* allowed *anuloma* marriages e.g. *Baudhāyana-dharmasūtra*, I.8.2-5, *Vasiṣṭha*, I.24-27, *Manu*, III.14-19. *Yājñavalkya*, I.56-57.

4. The killing even in a straight fight of brāhmaṇas that have become desperadoes.

This is a subject which very much exercised the minds of writers on *dharma*; *Manu* (8.350-51), *Viṣṇu*, V.180-90, *Vasiṣṭha* (III.15-18) permit the killing of an *ātatāyī*-brāhmaṇa, while Sumantu says 'there is no sin in killing an *ātatāyin*, except a brāhmaṇa and a cow', and so forbids the killing even of an *ātatāyī*-brāhmaṇa. ***Vide*** *Mitākṣarā* on *Yāj*. II.21 for a discussion on this.

5. The acceptance (for all ordinary intercourse such as eating with him) of a twice-born person who is in the habit of voyaging over the sea in a ship, even after he has undergone a *prāyaścitta*.

Baudhāyana-dharmaśutra, I.1.20 mentions sea voyage as a practice peculiar to brāhmaṇas of northern India and condemns it, by placing it first among *patanīyas* (II.1.41). Some writers say that the prohibition applies to one who often crosses the sea as the compound *nau-yātuḥ* shows. Auśanasa says that *samudraga* is *patita* (p. 525, of Jivananda).

6. The initiation for a *sattra*.

7. The taking a *kamaṇḍalu* (a jar for water).

Baudhāyana-dharmasūtra (I.3.4) prescribes among the observances of *snātakas* (those who have finished their study and have married or are about to marry) that they should carry a (earthen or wooden) pot filled with water; *Vasiṣṭha*, 12.14 and *Manu*, 4.36 and *Yāj*., I.132 also do the same. The *Madanapārijāta* (pp. 15-16) while quoting some of these verses says that *kamaṇḍalu-vidhāraṇa* refers to perpetual studenthood, but that is not correct, since in the *Nāradīya Purāṇa* quoted above (note 5, p. 6) the two are separately mentioned as forbidden.

8. Starting on the Great Journey.

This refers to the practice of starting towards the north-east in the case of those who had become forest-dwellers (***vide*** *Manu*,

VI.31 and *Yāj.*, III.55) and the practice of old men killing themselves by starting on the great journey till the body falls, by falling from a precipice or by entering the Ganges at a holy place like Prayāga or by entering fire. ***Vide*** Aparārka, p. 536 where the *smṛti* passages allowing this are quoted. Note that Śūdraka, the reputed author of the *Mṛcchakaṭika*, is said to have entered fire and ***vide*** *Raghuvaṁśa*, 8.94; Atri, verses 218-19 which are quoted even by Medhātithi on *Manu*, V.88; *EI*, Vol. I, p. 140 and *EI*, XIII.205 for instances of kings throwing themselves into the Ganges at Prayāga.

9. The killing of a cow in the sacrifice called *gomedha*; ***vide*** *Sāṅkhāyana-śrauta*, 14.15.1, *Kātyāyana-śrauta*, XXII.11.3-4 and *Manu*, XI.74.

10. The partaking of wine even in the *sautrāmaṇi* sacrifice.

This is a sacrifice principally to Sutrāman (i.e. Indra) in which three cups of wine were offered to the Aśvins, Sarasvatī and Indra and a brāhmaṇa had to be hired for drinking the remnants of wine offered. ***Vide*** *Taittirīya Brāhmaṇa*, I.8.6.2, *Sāṅkhāyana-śrauta*, 15.15.I-14 and Śabara on *Pūrva-mīmāṁsa-sūtra*, III.5.14-15.

11-12. Licking the ladle (*surc*) after the *agnihotra homa* in order to take off the remains of the offerings and using the ladle in the *agnihotra* afterwards when it has been so licked. ***Vide*** *TaiBrā*, II.1.4 and *Satyāṣādhaśrauta* for this.

13. Entering into the stage of forest hermit as laid down in *śāstras* about it. *ĀpDhS*, II.9.21.18-II.9.23.2, *Manu*, VI.1-32, *Vasiṣtha*, IX.1-11 contain elaborate rules about this stage.

14. Lessening the periods of impurity (due to death and birth) in accordance with the conduct the *Veda* learning of a man.

Vide Parāśara (note 3, p. 5) quoted above saying that a brāhmaṇa who is endowed with both Vedic learning and *agnihotra* has to observe *āśauca* (mourning) only for one day and he who is only learned has to observe it for three days. ***Vide also*** Bṛhaspati quoted by Haradatta on *Gautama*, 14.1. In *kali* a flat rule of ten days for all came to be prescribed. Viśvarūpa on *Yāj.*, III.30 has an elaborate discussion on this text and ultimately gets rid of it by saying that it is only an *arthavāda* meant to praise the absence of greed and presence of excellent conduct. It is not quite unreasonable to infer that if Viśvarūpa had attached any value to or known these verses on *kalivarjya* he would not have failed to make use of them for explaining away Parāśara.

15. Prescribing death as the penance (*prāyaścitta*) for brāhmaṇas.

Manu (II.89 and 146) says that for wilfully killing a brāhmaṇa and drinking wine the *prāyaścitta* is death. *Gautama*, 21.7 says the same, following Manu.

16. Expiation (by secretly performed *prāyaścitta*s) of the mortal sins other than theft (of gold) and the sin of contact (with those guilty of *mahāpātaka*s).

Manu, XI.54 enumerates contact with those guilty of the four *mahāpātaka*s as a fifth *mahāpātaka*. *Gautama*, 24 and *Vasiṣṭha*, 25 prescribe secret *prāyaścitta*s even for *mahāpātaka*s like *brahma-hatyā*. This rule says that there are no secret *prāyaścitta*s in *kali* for *brahmahatyā*, or drinking wine and for incest. ***Vide*** Aparārka, p. 1212 for rules as to who was entitled to secret *prāyaścitta*s.

17. The act of offering with *mantra*s animal flesh to the bridegroom, the guest, and the *pitṛ*s.

Madhuparka was offered to honoured guests among whom the bridegroom was included. ***Vide*** *Gautama*, V.25-35, *Yāj.*, I.109. The offering of flesh of various animals in *śrāddha* was supposed to conduce to the enjoyment of *pitṛ*s. ***Vide*** *Yāj.*, I. 258-260, *Manu*, III.123. According to *Āśvalāyana Gṛhyasūtra*, I.24.26 *Madhuparka* could not be offered without flesh. ***Vide*** *Vasiṣṭha*, IV.5-6.

18. The acceptance as sons of those other than the *aurasa* (natural) and adopted sons.

Manu, 9.165-80, *Yāj.*, II.128-32 and others speak of twelve kinds of sons.

19. Ordinary intercourse with those who incurred the sin of (having intercourse with) women of higher castes, even after they had undergone the *prāyaścitta* for such sin.

Gautama (IV.20 and 22-23) severely condemns the intercourse of men of lower castes with women of higher castes and holds that their progeny is *dharmahīna*.

20. The abandonment of the wife of an elderly person (or of one who is entitled to respect) when she has had intercourse with one with whom it is severely condemned.

Vasiṣṭha, 21.10 says 'four kinds of women viz., one who has intercourse with a pupil or with the husband's teacher, or one who kills her husband or commits adultery with a man of degraded caste, should be abandoned'.

Yāj. (III.296-97) is against and says that even such women should be kept near the house and given starving maintenance. ***Vide*** Atri, V.1-5.

21. Killing oneself for the sake of another.

The *smṛtis* say that a man should run the risk of life for cows and brāhmaṇas; ***vide*** *Manu*, XI.79 and *Viṣṇu*, III.45.

22. Giving up food left after one has partaken of it.

Vasiṣṭha, 14.20-21 says that food left after one has partaken of it from what was taken out for oneself or food touched by such leavings should not be eaten. Or this may mean 'given to another the leavings of food'; some *smṛtis* permit giving *ucchiṣṭa* to śūdras and the like, which is forbidden here. ***Vide*** *Gautama*, X.61 and *Manu*, X.125.

23. Resolve to worship a particular idol for life (in return for payment). *Manu*, III.152 makes a brāhmaṇa performing worship for money unfit for invitation in *śrāddha* and *devakṛtya*.

24. Touching the bodies of persons who are in impurity due to death after the charred bones are collected.

Collection of charred bones took place on the fourth day after cremation. *Viṣṇu*, 19.10-12; *Vaikhānasa Smārtasūtra* V.7.; *Saṁvarta*, verses 38-39.

25. The actual slaughter by brāhmaṇas of the sacrificial animal.

26. Sale of the *soma* plant by brāhmaṇas. *Kātyāyana-Śrauta* (VII.6.2-4) says that *soma* should be purchased from a brāhmaṇa of the Kautsa *gotra* or a śūdra; but *Manu*, X.88 forbids a brāhmaṇa the sale of *soma* along with many other things even though living by agriculture and the avocations of a vaiśya and *Manu* (III.158 and 170) condemns a brāhmaṇa who sells *soma* as unfit for being invited at a *śrāddha*.

27. Securing food even from a śūdra when a brāhmaṇa has had no food for six times of meals (i.e., for three days).

Manu, XI.16 allows a brāhmaṇa who has had no food for three days to take food for one day from one whose actions are low and so does *Yāj*., III.43. If we read *hīnakarmaṇā* it would mean 'even by doing what is low' (i.e., by begging or theft or by such actions as are described in Nārada, *abhyupetyāśuśrūṣā*, verses 5-7).

28. Permission to (a brāhmaṇa) householder to take cooked food from śūdras if they are his *dāsa*s, cowherds, hereditary friends, persons cultivating his land on an agreement to pay part of the produce.

Many *smṛti*s allow a brāhmaṇa to have cooked food from śūdras if they are that brāhmaṇa's *dāsa*s, barber, cowherd or cultivator of his land, hereditary friend. *Vide Gautama*, 17.6, *Manu*, IV.253, *Yāj*., I.166 (where the first half is the same as here), *Aṅgiras*, 120, *Parāśara*, XI (note 17).

29. Going on a very distant pilgrimage.

30. Behaviour of a pupil towards his teacher's wife as towards a teacher that is declared (in *smṛtis*).

Manu, II.210 prescribes that the wives of one's teacher, if they are of the same *varṇa* as the teacher, are to be honoured like the teacher and if they are not of the same *varṇa* then by rising to receive them and by saluting them.

31. The maintenance by brāhmaṇas in adversity (by following unworthy avocations) and the mode of livelihood in which a brāhmaṇa does not care to accumulate for to-morrow.

Gautama, VII.1-7, *ĀpDhS*, I.7.20.11-I.7.21.4, *Yāj.*, III.35-44 and others allow a brāhmaṇa to live by the occupations of a kṣatriya or vaiśya in adversity. *Manu*, IV.7 places before a brāhmaṇa the ideal that he should not accumulate more corn than what is required for three days or for the current day. Both these extremes are forbidden here.

32. The acceptance of *araṇis* (two wooden blocks for producing fire) by brāhmaṇas (in the *homa* at the time of *jātakarma)* in order that all the ceremonies for the child from *jātakarma* to his marriage may be performed therein. The *Saṁskāra-kaustubha* quotes a *gṛhyapariśiṣṭa* for this.[27]

33. Constant journeys by brāhmaṇas.

34. Blowing of fire with the mouth (i.e., without employing a bamboo *dhamanī*).

In *Manu*, IV.53 also the same prohibition occurs. In Vedic passages blowing at the fire with breath from the mouth direct was allowed. *Vide* Haradatta on *ĀpDhS*, I.5.15.20.

35. Allowing women who have become polluted by rape, &c. to freely mix in the caste (when they have performed *prāyaścitta*) as declared in the śāstric texts.

Even so late a *smṛti* as Devala's (verse 47) allows a woman raped even by *mlecchas* to become pure after *prāyaścitta* for three days. The *Āditya Purāṇa* appears to be most harsh on innocent and unfortunate women.

36. Begging of food by a *saṁnyāsin* from persons of all *varṇas* (including śūdra).

Baudhāyana-dharmasūtra, II.10 allows a *saṁnyāsiṇ* to beg food from all *varṇas*, while *Manu* (VI.43) and *Yāj.*, III.59 prescribe that he should beg in a village in the evening and Vasiṣṭha also (X.7) requires him to beg at seven houses not selected beforehand. But Vasiṣṭha says a little later on (X.24) that he should subsist on what he would get at the houses of brāhmaṇas.

37. To wait (i.e., not to use) for ten days water that has recently been dug in the ground.

38. Giving fee to the teacher as demanded by him (at the end of study) according to the rules laid down in the śāstra.

Yāj., I.51 prescribes that a student after finishing Vedic study and performing *vratas* should give fees to the teacher as the latter desires and should perform the ceremonial bath.

39. The employment of śūdras as cooks for brāhmaṇas and the rest.

The *Āpastamba-dharmasūtra*, II.2.3.4 allowed śūdras to be cooks for the three higher *varṇas* under the supervision of *āryas*.

40. Suicide of old people by falling from a precipice or into fire.

Vide item no. 8 above.

41. Performing *ācamana* by respectable people in water that would remain even after a cow has drunk it to its heart's content.

Vasiṣṭha, III.35 says that water accumulated in a hole on the ground would be fit for *ācamana* if it is as much as would quench the thirst of a cow. ***Vide** Manu*, V.128 and *Yāj.*, I.192.

42. Fining witnesses who depose to a dispute between father and son.

Yāj., II.239 prescribes a fine of three *paṇa*s for witnesses in disputes between father and son.

43. *Saṁnyāsin* should stay where he happens to be in the evening.

This may also mean 'a *saṁnyāsin* should beg at the houses in the evening'.

Manu, VI.55-56 and *Yāj.*, I.59 prescribe for *yati* begging in the evening.

These are the *kalivarjya*s set out in the *Āditya Purāṇa.*

Besides these, the passages quoted above also mention the following as *kalivarjya.*

Govadha — A cow was killed in *madhuparka* (*Mānavagṛhya*, I.9.19), in the *aṣṭakā śrāddha* (*Hiraṇyakeśi-gṛhya*, II.15.1) and a barren cow was sacrificed for Mitra and Varuṇa *SBE*, Vol. 26, pp. 387-91).

Uddhāravibhāga — giving a larger share to the eldest brother on a partition. ***Vide** Manu*, 9.112 and 117.

Puruṣamedha — ***Vide** ŚataBrā*, 13th *kāṇḍa, adhyāya* 6; *Śāṅkhāyana-Śrauta-sūtra*, 16.10-14.

Aśvamedha — ***Vide** ŚataBrā*, 13th *kāṇḍa, adhyāya*s 1-4 for it.

Brahmacarya for a very long time or perpetual studenthood.

Parāśara, II.5, *Bhāradvājagṛhya*, 1.9, *Baudhāyana-dharmasūtra*, I.2.1 prescribed *brahmacarya* for 48 years. ***Vide*** Śabara on Jaimini, I.3.3 who shows how Baudhāyana is opposed to Vedic injunctions (quoted in *History of Dharmaśāstra*, p. 26, n. 73).

Madya — Wine was forbidden to brāhmaṇas at all times and

in all stages (*Gautama*, II.25). There was divergence about kṣatriyas and vaiśyas. Many authorities agreed that wine from flour was forbidden to kṣatriya and vaiśya householders, but not that which was prepared from raw sugar and honey. ***Vide*** *Mitākṣarā* on *Yāj*., III.253.

Appendix

Verses on *kalivarjya* collected from the *Smṛticandrikā*, Hemādri (*Pariśeṣakhaṇḍa*), *Parāśara-mādhavīya*, Vol. I, part 1, pp. 134-37), *Nirṇaya-sindhu, Samaya-mayūkha, Udvāhatattva.*

विधवायां प्रजोत्पत्तौ देवरस्य नियोजनम्।
बालिकाक्षतयोन्योस्तु वरेणान्येन संस्कृतिः।।

कन्यानामसवर्णानां विवाहश्च द्विजातिभिः।
आततायिद्विजाग्र्याणां धर्मयुद्धेन हिंसनम्।।

द्विजस्याब्धौ तु नौयातुः शोधितस्यापि संग्रहः।
सत्रदीक्षा च सर्वेषां कमण्डलुविधारणम्।।

महाप्रस्थानगमनं गोसंज्ञप्तिश्च गोसवे।
सौत्रामण्यामपि सुराग्रहणस्य च संग्रहः।।

अग्निहोत्रहवण्याश्च लेहो लीढापरिग्रहः।
वानप्रस्थाश्रमस्यापि प्रवेशो विधिचोदितः।।

वृत्तस्वाध्यायसापेक्षमघसंकोचनं तथा।
प्रायश्चित्तविधानं तु विप्राणां मरणान्तिकम्।।

संसर्गदोषः स्तेनाद्यैर्महापातकनिष्कृतिः।
वरातिथिपितृभ्यश्च पशूपाकरणक्रिया।।

दत्तौरसेतरेषां तु पुत्रत्वेन परिग्रहः।
सवर्णान्याङ्गनादुष्टौ संसर्गः शोधितैरपि।।

अयोनौः संग्रहे वृते परित्यागो गुरुस्त्रियाः।

*परोद्देशात्मसंत्याग उच्छिष्टस्यापि वर्जनम्।
*प्रतिमाभ्यर्चनार्थाय संकल्पश्च सधर्मकः।

अस्थिसंचयनादूर्ध्वमङ्गस्पर्शनमेव च।
शामित्रं चैव विप्राणां सोमविक्रयणं तथा।

षड्भक्तानशनेनान्नहरणं हीनकर्मणः।
शूद्रेषु दासगोपालकुलमित्रार्धसीरिणाम्।

भोज्यान्नता गृहस्थस्य तीर्थसेवातिदूरतः।
शिष्यस्य गुरुदारेषु गुरुवद्वृत्तिरीरिता।

अपाद्वृत्तिर्द्विजाग्र्याणामश्वस्तनिकता तथा।
प्रजार्थं तु द्विजाग्र्याणां प्रजारणिपरिग्रहः।

ब्राह्मणानां प्रवासित्वं मुखाग्निधमनक्रिया।
बलात्कारादिदुष्टस्त्रीसंग्रहो विधिचोदितः।

यतेस्तु सर्ववर्णेषु भिक्षाचर्या विधानतः।
नवोदके दशाहं च दक्षिणा गुरुचोदिता।

ब्राह्मणादिषु शूद्रस्यं पचनादिक्रियापि च।
भृग्वग्निपतनाद्यैश्च वृद्धादिमरणं तथा।

गोतृप्तिशिष्टे पयसि शिष्टैराचमनक्रिया।
पितापुत्रविरोधेषु साक्षिणां दण्डकल्पनम्।

यतेः सायंगृहत्वं च सूरिभिस्तत्त्वतत्परैः।
एतानि लोकगुप्त्यर्थं कलेरादौ महात्मभिः।

निवर्तितानि कर्माणि व्यवस्थापूर्वकं बुधैः।
समयश्चापि साधूनां प्रमाणं वेदवद्भवेत्।।

---

* These two half lines do not occur in some of the older digests like the *Smṛticandrikā*.

References

[This paper is first published in *JBBRAS* (New Series) Vol. XII, pp. 1-18, 1936. For a more detailed discussion on *Kalivarjyam* ***Vide*** Dr. P.V. Kane's *History of Dharmaśāstra*, Vol. III, pp. 885 to 968. The stanzas quoted here, however, have no place, in the above volume.] *S.G. Moghe*

1. अक्षराजाय कितवं कृतायादिनवदर्शं त्रेताय कल्पिनं द्वापरायाधिकल्पिनमास्कन्दाय सभास्थणुम्। — वाज० सं० 30.18.
2. कृताय संभाविनं त्रेताया आदिनवदर्शं द्वापराय बहिःसदं कलये सभास्थणुम्। — तै० ब्रा०, III.4.16. The interpretations of आदिनवदर्श given by महीधर and सायण differ.
3. ये वै चत्वारः स्तोमाः कृतं तत्। अथ ये पञ्च कलिः सः। तस्माच्चतुष्टोमः। — तै० ब्रा०, I.5.11.
4. कलिः शयानो भवति सञ्जिहानस्तु द्वापरः। उत्तिष्ठंस्त्रेता भवति कृतं संपद्यते चरन्।। — ऐ० ब्रा०, ch. 33, *khaṇḍa*, 3. The *Śāṅkhāyana-śrauta-sūtra* reads (15.9) 'शयानः पुरुषः' and 'उत्थितस्त्रेता।'
5. अथास्मै पञ्चाक्षान् पाणावावपति। अभिभूरस्येतास्ते पञ्च दिशः क पन्नामित्येष वा अयानभिभूर्यत्कलिरेव हि सर्वानयानभिभवति तस्मादाहाभिभूरसीति। — शतपथ ब्रा०, V.4.4.6.
6. यथा कृताय विजितायाधरेयाः संयन्त्येवमेनं सर्वं तदभिसमेति। — छा० उ०, IV.1.4.
7. तदेतत्सत्यं मन्त्रेषु कर्माणि कवयो यान्यपश्यंस्तानि त्रेतायां बहुधा सन्ततानि। — मुण्डकोपनिषद्, I.2.1.
8. साक्षात्कृतधर्माण ऋषयो बभूवुस्तेऽवरेभ्योऽसाक्षात्कृतधर्मभ्य उपदेशेन मन्त्रान्संप्रादुः। — निरुक्त, I.20. Almost the same words occur in the *Mahāhbhārata, Vanaparva*, 183.67 (Bom. edn.).
9. दृष्टो धर्मव्यतिक्रमः साहसं च पूर्वेषाम्। तेषां तेजोविशेषेण प्रत्यवायो न विद्यते। तदन्वीक्ष्य प्रयुञ्जानः सीदत्यवरः। — आप० ध० सू०, II.6.13.7-9; the भागवतपुराण, X (पूर्वार्ध, ch. 33.30) has 'धर्मव्यतिक्रमो दृष्ट ईश्वराणां च साहसम्। तेजीयसां न दोषाय वह्ने सर्वभुजो यथा।।'
10. दृष्टो धर्मव्यतिक्रमः साहसं च महताम्। अवरदौर्बल्यात्। — गौ०, I.3-4.
11. तस्मादृषयोऽवरेषु न जायन्ते नियमातिक्रमात्। — आप० ध० सू०, I.2.5.4.
12. *EI*, Vol. VIII, p. 162 — 'कलियुगदोषावसन्नधर्मोद्धरणनित्यसंनद्धस्य।'
13. अन्ये कृतयुगे धर्मास्त्रेतायां द्वापरेऽपरे। अन्ये कलियुगे नृणां युगह्रासानुरूपतः। — मनुस्मृति, I.85; पराशर, I.22.

14. कृते तु मानवो धर्मस्त्रेतायां गौतमः स्मृतः। द्वापरे शाङ्खलिखितः कलौ पाराशरः स्मृतः।। — पराशरस्मृति, I.24.

15. एकाहाच्छुध्यते विप्रो योऽग्निवेदसमन्वितः। त्र्यहात्केवलवेदस्तु द्विहीनो दशभिर्दिनैः।। — पराशरस्मृति, III.5.

16. नष्टे मृते प्रव्रजिते क्लीबे च पतिते पतौ। पञ्चस्वापत्सु नारीणां पतिरन्यो विधीयते।। — पराशर, IV.

17. दासनापितगोपालकुलमित्रार्धसीरिणः। एते शूद्रेषु भोज्यान्ना यश्चात्मानं निवेदयेत्।। — पराशर, XI.

18. ज्येष्ठो दायाद इत्येके। . . . तच्छास्त्रैर्विप्रतिषिद्धम्। — आप० ध० सू०, II.6.14.6 and 10.

19. उक्तो नियोगो मनुना निषिद्धः स्वयमेव तु। युगह्रासादशक्योयं कर्तुं सर्वैर्विधानतः।। . . . द्वापरे च कलौ नृणां शक्तिहानिर्विनिर्मिता।। अनेकधा कृताः पुत्रा ऋषिभिर्ये पुरातनैः। न शक्यास्तेऽधुना कर्तुं शक्तिहीनतया नरैः।। — बृहस्पति quoted by अपरार्क, p. 97.

20. 'मद्यमप्यमृतं श्राद्धे कलौ तत्तु विवर्जयेत्। मांसान्यपि हि सवाणि युगधर्मक्रमाद्भवेत्' — प्रजापति, verse 151 (Ānandāśrama edn.).

21. उक्तं च। यथा नियोगधर्मो नो नानुवन्ध्यावधोपि वा। तथोद्धारविभागोपि नैव संप्रति वर्तते। — मिताक्षरा (on याज्ञ०, II.117.) The स्मृतिचंद्रिका (व्यवहार काण्ड, edn. Gharpure) says that this verse is taken from the संग्रह (i.e., स्मृतिसंग्रह).

22. समुद्रयात्रास्वीकारः कमण्डलुविधारणम्। द्विजानामसवर्णासु कन्यासूपयमस्तथा।। देवराच्च सुतोत्पत्तिर्मधुपर्के पशोर्वधः। मांसादनं तथा श्राद्धे वानप्रस्थाश्रमस्तथा।। दत्ताक्षतायाः कन्यायाः पुनर्दानं वराय च। नैष्ठिकं ब्रह्मचर्यं च नरमेधाश्वमेधकौ।। महाप्रस्थानगमनं गोमेधश्च तथा मखः। एतान् धर्मान् कलियुगे वर्ज्यानाहुर्मनीषिणः।। — नारदीयपुराण, पूर्वार्ध, ch. 24, vv. 13-16 (Venkateshwar Press edn.). These verses are quoted as from the बृहन्नारदीय in the उद्वाहतत्त्व of रघुनन्दन (p. 112, Jivananda's edn.), the निर्णयसिन्धु (p. 367 Nirṇayasagar edn.).

23. दीर्घकालं ब्रह्मचर्यं धारणं च कमण्डलोः। सगोत्राद्वा सपिण्डाद्वा विवाहः गोवधस्तथा।। नराश्वमेधौ मद्यं च कलौ वर्ज्यं द्विजातिभिः। — ब्रह्मपुराण quoted by अपरार्क pp. 15 and 63; स्मृतिचंद्रिका, आह्निककाण्ड, p. 12 (ed. by Gharpure), पराशरमाधवीय, Vol. 1, part 1, p. 133. The last two lines are quoted in the निर्णयसिन्धु, (p. 367), but following the स्मृतिचन्द्रिका it reads 'गोत्रान्मातुः सपिण्डाच्च विवाहः' & c. This last will mean 'marriage with a *sagotra* girl or with a girl who is a *sapiṇḍa* of one's mother' (or who is the maternal uncle's daughter, as some explain).

24. स्त्रीणां पुनर्विवाहस्तु देवरात्पुत्रसन्ततिः। स्वातन्त्र्यं च कलियुगे कर्तव्यं न कदाचन।। यतः पातकिनो लोके नराः सन्ति कलौ युगे। — ब्रह्मपुराण quoted in अपरार्क, p. 98.

25. ऊढायाः पुनरुद्वाहं ज्येष्ठांशं गोवधं तथा। कलौ पञ्च न कुर्वीत भ्रातृजायां कमण्डलुम्।। — आदित्यपुराण quoted in स्मृतिचन्द्रिका, आह्निक, p. 83; *vide also*, p. 12 of the same and p. 266 of स्मृतिचंद्रिका, व्यवहारकाण्ड; हेमाद्रि, परिशेषखण्ड, p. 666.

26. अत एव स्मरन्ति। गोपशुं देवरात् पुत्रं सत्रयागं कमण्डलुम्। सुराप्रयोगं भिक्षुं च न कुर्वीत कलौ युगे।। तथा। अक्षता नरमेधश्च गोयज्ञश्च कमण्डलुः। देवराच्च सुतोत्पत्तिः कलौ पञ्च विवर्जयेत्।। — अपरार्क, p. 233.

27. परिशिष्टान्तरे तस्मिन् कुमारस्य तु जातस्य अरणीं षोडशाङ्गुलिम्। आहृत्य चोत्तरामणीं ताभ्यामग्निं तु मन्थयेत्। कुमारकर्माणि विवाहान्तानि कारयेत्।

12

Tilaka Mark

IN modern times Hindu women whose husbands are living have generally three ever-present distinguishing signs, viz. they wear a neck ornament called *maṅgalasūtra* (or *māṅgalyasūtra*), they apply to the forehead a *tilaka* (mark made with saffron, red powder or some other substance) or put vermilion in the parting of the hair, and they wear bangles (of gold, glass, etc.). In my *History of Dharmaśāstra* (Vol. II, p. 537) I showed that the practice of wearing the *maṅgalasūtra* is not very old, is not known to any *sūtra* or ancient *smṛti* and that it is provided for by such late *smṛtis* as those of Śaunaka and Laghu-Āśvalāyana. The practice of applying *tilaka* was not dealt with in that work. A few facts about that practice are brought together here.

First, a few literary references may be set out. The *Nāṭyaśāstra* of Bharata refers to the *tilaka* mark in several connections. For example, after defining the *tripatākā* posture of the hand (in 9.26, Nir. edn.) it provides that the wiping of tears and the application of *tilaka* should be represented by that posture. In chapter 21, while speaking of the four kinds of ornaments, it refers to the *tilaka* on the forehead (in verse 24) and further states (verse 27) that the cheek may be ornamented by means of *tilaka* and *patrarekhā*. The *Rāmāyaṇa*[1] (*Ayodhyā*, 95.17) states that Rāma rubbed his finger on a head of *manaḥśilā* (red arsenic) and made a beautiful mark (*tilaka*) therewith on the forehead of Sītā and that when Sītā embraced him that *tilaka* mark was seen impressed on the chest of Rāma. In the *Araṇyakāṇḍa*[2] it is said that when the Sun (in his apparent motion) came to be associated with the southern part (of the celestial hemisphere) the northern quarter (of the skies) like a woman devoid of a *tilaka* mark did not appear beautiful (or to advantage). In the *Saundarānanda*[3] of Aśvaghoṣa (IV.13) the heroine puts a mirror in the hands of the hero with the words "hold this mirror in front of me while I apply the *viśeṣaka* mark". The *Amarakośa* says that *tamālapatra* (a mark made with musk on the forehead which resembles the dark leaf of *tamāla* tree), a *tilaka* (mark resembling sesame grain), *citraka* and *viśeṣaka* are synonymous and the commentator Kṣīrasvāmī adds that these are all different *tilaka* marks. In the *Raghuvaṁśa*[4] (IX.41) Kālidāsa displays a fine play on the two meanings of *tilaka* (a tree, a mark on the forehead): "Not that the *tilaka* (tree) did not lend a charm (i.e., it did lend a charm) to the sylvan spot when it (the tree) was marked with lovely collyrium-like bees that fell upon its beautiful flowers, just as a *tilaka* (mark) set near bee-like stretches of collyrium in the midst of floral wreaths (put on by her on the head) does enhance the charms of a young damsel." In the *Kumārasambhava*[5] also Kālidāsa reverts to the same imagery of *tilaka* (tree, mark) and the blue bees. In the *Mālvikāgnimitra*[6] (III.5) the poet harps on the same idea when he states that vernal beauty treats with contempt the efforts of women to enhance the charms of their faces, viz. the colour of *alaktaka* dye applied to their lips by women is surpassed by the brilliance of the red Aśoka flower; the *kurabaka* flower, dark-white and reddish, throws into the shade the *viśeṣaka* and the (beauty due to the) application of *tilaka* (mark) is eclipsed by the *tilaka* (trees or flowers) to which collyrium-like bees cling. In another place in the same drama,[7] Kālidāsa speaks of the face of the heroine turned away from the hero as one the *tilaka* mark (on which) was split up into segments by the knitting of her eyebrows. It should be noted here that Mālavikā who was only a maiden (and not a married woman) had a *tilaka* of dark-red hue on her forehead between the eyebrows. In the *Mṛcchakaṭika*[8] (I) the *sūtradhāra* asserts that the ground which is rendered dark and variegated by dragging about an iron pan appears more attractive like a young woman who has decked herself with a *viśeṣaka*. The *Śiśupālavadha*[9] (III.63) speaks of divine Vāsudeva, the (*tilaka*) ornament of the three worlds, adding to the charm of the capital as a *viśeṣaka* does in the case of a young married woman (*vadhū*). There are double-meaning epithets applicable both to Vāsudeva and *viśeṣaka* which show that the *tilaka* on the forehead was round in shape and glossy dark in hue. The *Matsya Purāṇa*[10] in the tale of Satyavān and Sāvitrī makes the former say to his beloved "this sylvan spot possessing beautiful *tilaka* trees appears lovely like you who wear a beautiful *tilaka* mark".

In the *Kādambarī* of Bāṇa there are frequent references to the *tilaka* on the forehead of women. Tārāpīḍa asks his weeping queen,[11] "why does your forehead not bear a *tilaka* mark made with the paste of *gorocanā* (yellow orpiment)?" This shows that *gorocanā* was used for making the *tilaka* mark, while a little above the same passage shows that the cheeks were painted by ladies with figures made with saffron. On the birth of a prince to Tārāpīḍa the women in the harem gave themselves up to dancing and singing[12] to such an extent that their clothes were rent asunder by the sharp tips of their arm ornaments when they violently collided with each other, but that they took care to have at least some portion of their *tilaka*s remaining (and did not allow the *tilaka* to be entirely rubbed off). In the gorgeous description of Patralekhā[13] who was presented to Candrāpīḍa in the early morning on a certain day the poet states that her broad forehead was adorned by a *tilaka* of sandal paste that looked pale because it was stale (made the previous day).

These literary references are enough to show that from at least the beginning of the Christian era married women as well as maidens applied a *tilaka* (mark) on their forehead made with musk, saffron or even sandalwood paste. But these passages do not clearly indicate that the making of a *tilaka* mark on the forehead was an absolute necessity, a *sine qua non* in the case of all married women whose husbands were living. They rather lead one to infer that the *tilaka* mark was intended only to set off the charms of young ladies.

In the *Vṛddha-Hārītasmṛti*[14] (ch. XI) the author expatiates at length upon the daily duties of wives. In verses 86-87 it is prescribed that a wife should get up before her husband in the last watch of the night, should perform *śauca* and brush her teeth, that she should have an auspicious bath and wear a white *sārī*, should sip water and apply white *ūrddhvapuṇḍra* with (holy) clay or with sandalwood paste or musk or with saffron, if (one or the other be) not available. The Śūdrakamalākara quotes from the *Madanaratna* a passage of the *Skanda Purāṇa* in which occur the following verses: a woman who desires long life for her husband should never be without turmeric powder, *kuṅkuma* (either saffron or red paste for applying to the forehead), red lead, collyrium, bodice, *tāmbūla*, auspicious ornaments (such as *maṅgalasūtra*, nosering, etc.), applying perfumes to the hair, braiding the hair, ornaments on the wrist and in the ear. These verses show that the *Saknda Purāṇa*[15] required married women to apply saffron paste (to their forehead). It must, however, be said that there is hardly any *smṛti* passage that expressly makes the applying of a *tilāka* obligatory.

The same result is arrived at in another but an indirect way. In the *Vṛddha-Hārītasmṛti* (XI.205-7) certain rules of conduct are laid down for widows that do not become *satī*s on the death of their husbands. A widow should always give up the perfuming of her hair, *tāmbūla*, using unguents and flowers, ornaments, coloured clothes, taking food from plates of bell-metal, taking two meals a day, applying collyrium to the eyes. In this long list no reference is made to the giving up of *tilaka*. So it appears to follow that *tilaka* was not an absolute necessity for women whose husbands were living; similarly in the *Skanda Purāṇa*[16] (*Kāśīkhaṇḍa*, ch. 4, verses 75ff.) there are many verses forbidding a widow to braid her hair, to sleep on a cot, to apply unguents to her body, to wear a bodice, to wear coloured clothes, etc. But a direction not to apply *tilaka* is altogether wanting in that passage.

The *Matsya Purāṇa*,[17] ch. 260, gives a picturesque description of the image of Śiva in the *ardhanārīśvara* form. It says, "the half representing Śiva should have matted hair and the digit of the moon, while in the other representing Umā, *sīmanta* (parting of hair) and *tilaka* should be shown". The same chapter also describes the Umāmaheśvara image and states that the goddess should be seated on the left thigh of Śiva and that she should be shown as resplendent with the *tilaka* on the forehead.[18] It is not unlikely that the necessity for a *tilaka* on the forehead of women arose by analogy from the practice of males applying a *puṇḍra* mark to the forehead with ashes or sandal-paste. This last practice of applying ashes to the forehead, the head, shoulders, etc., with *mantras* is certainly old (***vide*** *History of Dharmaśāstra*, Vol. II, pp. 672-75).

The evidence of ancient paintings would have been very valuable in this connection. But extant paintings do not go as far back as the literary evidence carries the matter. Even the Ajantā paintings do not disclose that women had *tilaka*s on their foreheads. It is not unlikely that in the course of centuries the *tilaka* on the forehead in some of the paintings even if it existed in the beginning might have become faint or become altogether obliterated.

References

[This paper was first published in *JBBRAS* (new series), Vol. XXI (pp. 33-37), 1945. This paper is again published in the English section of the Volume *Ṛṣikalpanyāsa* presented to Pundita Rajeshwarashāstrī Dravid, pp. 287-92 in the year 1970.]

S.G. Moghe

1. स निघृष्याङ्गुलिं रामो धौते मनःशिलोच्चये।
चकार *तिलकं* तस्या ललाटे रुचिरं तदा।।
मनः*शिलायास्तिलकः* सीतायाः सोऽथ वक्षसि।
समदृश्यत संक्रान्तो रामस्य विपुलौजसः।।

— रामायण, अयोध्या, 95.17
(ed. with com. of गोविन्दराज)

2. सेवमाने दृढं सूर्ये दिशमन्तकसेविताम्।
विहीनतिलकेव स्त्री नोत्तरा दिक्प्रकाशते।।

— अरण्यकाण्ड, 6.8

3. दत्त्वाथ सा दर्पणमस्य हस्ते ममाग्रतो धारय तावदेनम्।
विशेषकं यावदहं करोमीत्युवाच कान्तं स च तं बभार।।

— सौन्दरानन्द, IV.13

4. अलिभिरञ्जनबिन्दुमनोहरैः कुसुमपङ्क्तिनिपातिभिरङ्कितः।
न खलु शोभयति स्म वनस्थलीं न तिलकस्तिलकः प्रमदामिव।।

— रघुवंश, IX.41

5. लग्नद्विरेफाञ्जनभक्तिचित्रं मुखे मधुश्रीस्तिलकं प्रकाश्य।

— कुमारसम्भव, III.30

6. रक्ताशोकरुचा विशेषितगुणो बिम्बाधरालक्तकः
प्रत्याख्यातविशेषकं कुरबकं श्यामावदातारुणम्।
आक्रान्ता तिलकक्रियापि तिलकैर्लीनद्विरेफाञ्जनैः
सावज्ञेव मुखप्रसाधनविधौ श्रीर्माधवी योषिताम्।।

— मालविका, III.5

7. पश्य ते सख्या मुखम्।
भ्रूभङ्गभिन्नतिलकं स्फुरिताधरोष्ठं
सासूयमाननमितः परिवर्तयन्त्या।

— मालविका, IV.9

8. लोहकटाहपरिवर्तनकृष्णसारा कृतविशेषका इव युवतिरधिकतरं शोभते भूमिः।

— मृच्छकटिक, I

9. स्निग्धाञ्जनश्यामरुचिः सुवृत्तौ वध्वा इवाध्वंसितवर्णकान्तेः।
विशेषको वा विशिशेष यस्याः श्रियं त्रिलोकीतिलकः स एव।।

— शिशुपाल, III.63

10. विभाति चारुतिलका त्वमिवैषा वनस्थली।

— मत्स्य, 209.8

11. इमां च केन हेतुना मानिनि धारयस्यनुपरचितगोरोचनाबिन्दुतिलकामसंयमितालकिनीं ललाटरेखाम्।

— कादम्बरी, पूर्वभाग, para 53

12. किञ्चिदवशिष्टतमालपत्रेण . . . नृत्तक्रीडाप्रसक्तेनान्तःपुरिकाजनेन।

— कादम्बरी, पूर्वभाग, para 67

13. पर्युषितधूसरचन्दनरसतिकालङ्कृतललाटपट्टया . . . अनुगम्यमानं कन्यया etc.

— कादम्बरी, पूर्वार्ध, para 99

14. उत्थाय पश्चिमे यामे भर्तुः पूर्वमतन्द्रिता।
कृत्वा शौचं विधानेन दन्तधावनमाचरेत्।।
कृत्वाथ मङ्गलस्नानं धृत्वा शुक्लाम्बरं तथा।

आचम्य धारयेदूर्ध्वपुण्ड्रं शुभ्रं मृदैव तु।।
चन्दनेनापि कस्तूर्या कुङ्कुमेनापि वाऽसति।
— वृद्धहारीत, XI.85-87

15. मदनरत्ने स्कान्दे —
हरिद्रां कुङ्कुमं चैव सिन्दूरं कज्जलं तथा।
कूर्पासकं च ताम्बूलं माङ्गल्याभरणं शुभम्।।
केशसंस्कारकबरीकरकर्णविभूषणम्।
भर्तुरायुष्यमिच्छन्ती दूरयेन्न क्वचित्सती।।
— शूद्रकमलाकर 4th प्रकरण (स्त्रीधर्म)
The verse occurs in स्कन्दपुराण, (ब्रह्मखण्ड, धर्मारण्य section, ch. 7.28-29).

16. *Vide History of Dharmaśāstra*, Vol. II, p. 585 n. 1370 for the passage from स्कन्दपुराण.

17. ईशार्धे तु जटाभागो बालेन्दुकलया युतः।
उमार्धे चापि दातव्यौ सीमन्ततिलकावुभौ।।
— मत्स्यपुराण, 260.2

18. वामे तु संस्थिता देवी तस्यौरौ बाहुगूहिता। . . .
सबालिका कर्णवती ललाटतिलकोज्ज्वला।।
— मत्स्य, 260.14-15

13

The Pārijāta and the Madana-Pārijāta

IN the *History of Dharmaśāstra* (Vol. I, p. 309) the *Pārijāta*, often quoted by the *Kalpataru* and the *Ratnākaras* of Caṇḍeśvara, was assigned to a period between AD 1000 and 1125 and it was pointed out that the *Pārijāta* quoted by the *Kalpataru* was altogether a different work from the *Madana-Pārijāta*. The *Madana-Pārijāta* was assigned to a period between AD 1360 and 1390 in the *History of Dharmaśāstra*, Vol. I, p. 389. In a recent case before the Patna High Court[1] a passage of the *Madana-Pārijāta* assumed importance and incidentally the date of the *Madana-Pārijāta* came in for discussion. Mr. Justice Dhavle, himself a Sanskrit scholar, after quoting the views of Ghose, Sarvadhikari and myself about the date of the *Madana-Pārijāta* ultimately left the question of date undecided (p. 579) but remarked, 'we have had lawyers on both sides in this case who are familiar with Sanskrit and none of them, though invited to do so, has referred us to any quotation in the *Ratnākara* or the *Cintāmaṇi* from the *Pārijāta*, which is not to be found in the *Madana-Pārijāta*'. Among the lawyers engaged in the case was the eminent Sanskrit scholar and antiquarian, the late Mr. K.P. Jayaswal. It becomes necessary to examine this question very carefully in view of the failure of eminent scholars and lawyers to shed light on it by setting forth some passages or opinions attributed to the *Pārijāta* in early works like the *Ratnākaras* of Caṇḍeśvara and to search for them in the *Madana-Pārijāta* and to show from this investigation that the *Pārijāta* quoted by the *Kalpataru* and

Caṇḍeśvara is different from the *Madana-Pārijāta*. A detailed or extensive examination of all passages cited from the *Pārijāta* (which are several hundred in number) cannot be attempted here within the space allowed, nor is it necessary to do so. The passages may be divided into three classes: (1) Those in which certain views are attributed to the *Pārijāta* which are not found in the *Madana-Pārijāta*; (2) those in which the *Madana-Pārijāta* holds views or gives explanations which are opposed to or different from the views or explanations attributed to the *Pārijāta*; (3) those in which certain views or texts are stated to have been not mentioned in the *Pārijāta* which are yet found in the *Madana-Pārijāta*.

In this paper *VR*, *KṛR* and *GṛR* respectively stand for the *Vivādaratnākara*, the *Kṛtyaratnākara* and *Gṛhastharatnākara*; *MPā* stands for *Madana-Pārijāta*.

I. Passages in which certain remarks are attributed to the *Pārijāta* which are not found in the *Madana-Pārijāta*.

(a) The *VR* quotes (on p. 465) a *sūtra* of Śaṅkha-Likhita *sa yadyekaputraḥ syād dvau bhāgāvatmanaḥ kuryāt* and notes (on p. 466) that the *Pārijāta* explained *ekaputra* as *jyeṣṭhaputra*. But this explanation is not found in the *MPā*.

(b) The *VR* on p. 476 refers to *Manu*, IX.125 (that among sons born to a man from wives of the same caste there is no seniority due to the seniority of wives in accordance with the dates of marriage but there is seniority among sons according to the date of birth) and states that Lakṣmīdhara holds that the special share given on partition to the eldest son is to be given to that son, who though younger in age (than other sons) is the son of the eldest among wives and that the *Pārijāta* also accepted the same view.[2] There is nothing in the *MPā* corresponding to this.

(c) The *VR* (p. 505) quotes several verses of Kātyāyana on

property impartible by its very nature, one of which is 'pastures, ways and clothes on the body, *prayojya* and the materials used by craftsmen (such as cotton) are not divisible according to Bṛhaspati' and then states that according to Halāyudha *prayojya* means 'money lent to a debt', while *prayojya* means 'a book and the like' according to the *Pārijāta*.[3] In *MPā* (on p. 685) the first quarter about a debt consigned to a document is quoted, but nothing is said by way of explaining *prayojya*.

(d) The *VR* (p. 589) quotes *Manu*, IX.190 (the widow of a sonless deceased person should secure a son through a *sagotra* and should hand over to that son whatever wealth may have been that of the deceased) and adds the view of the *Pārijāta*[4] that the widow should not herself take the wealth. The *MPā* does not say anything about *Manu*, IX.190.

(e) The *GṛR* (p. 147) says that certain texts of Devala (on *śauca*) were explained by the *Pārijāta*[5] as applicable only to women, śūdras and persons whose *Upanayana* had not yet been performed. In the *MPā* (pp. 44-50) there is a section on *śauca* in which, though many of the verses on *śauca* quoted from the *Smṛti*s in *GṛR* are also cited, this explanation about the passages of Devala is not found.

(f) On *snāna* the *GṛR* (p. 195) quotes *Yāj.*, I.159 that one should not bathe in the reservoir of another without taking out five lumps of clay (or vessels of water) and observes that this applies only when the reservoir has been dedicated to the public and that this is the view of the Prakāśakāra, of the *Pārijāta*[6] and of Śrīdatta. In the *MPā* (p. 243) *Yāj.*, I.159 is quoted but there is no such explanation of that verse as is ascribed to the *Pārijāta*.

(g) The *GṛR* (p. 205) quotes a verse which reads *srotaso vai naraḥ snātvā sarvapāpaiḥ pramucyate* and remarks that the *Pārijāta* reads *srotasi* for *srotasaḥ* in that verse. That verse and the reading noted is not found in the *MPā*.

(h) The *GṛR* (p. 249) quotes a verse of Vasiṣṭha on *Japa* (26.13) and then sets out the explanation of the *Pārijāta* that one who has mastered the whole *Veda* should repeat texts from his *Veda*, one who has learnt only a portion of the *Veda* of his school should mutter the *Puruṣasūkta* and the like, and one who knows only the *Gāyatrī* should repeat verses from some *Purāṇa*.[7] This is wanting in the *Japa* section of the *MPā*.

II. Passages where the explanation of the *Pārijāta* differs from that of the *MPā*:

(a) After quoting Nār., (*Dāyabhāga*, verse 7) that the husband of the girl is the father of the Kānīna, Sahoḍha and Gūḍhaja sons and declaring them to be entitled to a share in his wealth, the *VR*, (p. 565) mentions the explanation of the *Pārijāta* that if the girl's father (i.e., maternal grandfather of the Kānīna and Sahoḍha) be sonless, then the Kānīna and Sahoḍha become his (i.e., maternal grandfather's) sons, but if the maternal grandfather has a son, then the Kānīna and Sahoḍha belong to the husband of their mother and that if both the maternal grandfather and the husband are sonless, then they become the sons of both. The *MPā* (p. 652) on the other hand says that the Kānīna becomes the son of the husband when the girl is married, but if she is not, then the Kānīna belongs to the maternal grandfather.[8]

(b) In the *Vyavahāraprakāśa* of Mitramiśra (p. 524) it is stated that the view of several digests such as the *Smṛticandrikā*, the *Madanaratna, Kalpataru, Ratnākara* (of Caṇḍeśvara) and the *Pārijāta* was that the mother succeeded as an heir after the father. But the *MPā* (p. 672) on the other hand holds the view that the mother succeeds as heir before the father.[9]

(c) The *GṛR* (p. 140) after quoting Manu, IV.46-47 forbidding the answering of the calls of nature on *parvata* and *parvata-mastaka* says that according to the *Pārijāta* both *parvata* and its top are mentioned for the purpose of conveying that where it is impossible to avoid answering such calls of nature on a mountain, at least the top of the mountain should be avoided. On the other hand the *MPā* (p. 43) does not first read *parvata-mastaka* (but *na bhasmani, na gomaye*) in *Manu*, IV.47; then notices the reading *parvata-mastaka* and remarks that *parvata-mastaka* is employed to indicate that more blame attaches to answering calls of nature on a mountain summit than on a mountain.[10]

(d) After quoting Dakṣa, II.9 that the morning bath is commended because it yields seen and unseen rewards the *GṛR*, 180 cites the explanation of seen and unseen rewards from the *Pārijāta* which do not agree with the explanation given by the *MPā* (p. 62) of the same.[11]

(c) The *Śuddhitattva* (ed. by Jīvānanda, 1895, p. 398) says that *sāpiṇḍya* of brothers and the like based on the offering of *piṇḍa*s in *śrāddha* was propounded by the *Matsya Purāṇa* and by Baudhāyana and was so explained by the *Kāmadhenu*, *Hāralatā*, *Kalpataru*, *Pārijātakāra* and others. But the *MPā* (pp. 129-31) explains at great length that *sāpiṇḍya* is based on connection or continuance of particles of the same body, that this theory is simple and easy of application, while the theory of *sāpiṇḍya* based upon the offering of *piṇḍa*s is vitiated by cumbrousness (*Kalpanā-gaurava*).[12]

III. An interesting passage in which a text is stated not to have been mentioned in the *Pārijāta* which as a matter of fact is found in the *MPā* is as follows:

> The *VR* (p. 499) states that in a certain *saṁhitā* verse ascribed to Hārīta is quoted (viz., that

> when one member of a joint family recovers by his own labour land that once belonged to the family but was lost to it, the other members get a share therein after giving one-fourth to the acquirer) but that this is improper, since that verse is not contained in the *Smṛtimahārṇava*, the *Kāmadhenu*, the *Kalpataru*, the *Pārijāta* and other works. The *Dāyatattva* after quoting the words of the *VR* argues that *VR* is not correct since the same verse (ascribed to Śaṅkha) is found in the *Dāyabhāga*, the *Mitākṣarā* and other works. That verse is quoted in the *MPā* (p. 684) as from Śaṅkha and is also explained.[13]

In the *Kṛtyaratnākara* the views of the *Pārijāta* are quoted several times on matters which are not dealt with in the *MPā* at all; e.g., *KṛR*, p. 31 (that even *Pancarātra* and *Pāśupata Śāstra*s are authoritative when they do not contradict the *Veda*), p. 54 (about general rules on *vrata*), p. 59 (about the *devatā* of a *mantra* when it is not expressly stated), p. 61 (explanation of a passage from the *Brahma Purāṇa* about a *samidh* of Aśvattha), p. 66 (about the requirements of proper *kuśa*s), p. 92 (about *Homa-dravya*).

The above discussion will, it is hoped, convince scholars that the *Pārijāta* is entirely different from the *Madana-Pārijāta*. It is further to be noted that the chronological position of the two referred to above makes their identity impossible.

References

[This paper is first published in the proceedings *AIOC*, XII-ii, pp. 267-72, 1943-44.] **S.G. Moghe**

1. *Vide* Kamla Prasad *vs.* Murli Manohar, 13 Patna, 550 at pp. 578-80.
2. लक्ष्मीधरेण ज्येष्ठापुत्रस्य कनीयस एव ज्येष्ठत्वप्रर्युक्तोद्धारव्यवस्थापनाच्च। पारिजातस्याप्येवं परिग्रहाच्च।। – वि० र०, p. 477.

3. धनं पत्रनिविष्टं तु धर्मार्थं यन्निरूपितम्। · · · · · गोप्रचारश्च रथ्या च बार यच्चांगयोजितम्। प्रयोज्यं न विभज्येत शिल्पार्थं च बृहस्पतिः। प्रयोज्यं प्रयुक्तमृर्णाः हलायुधः। प्रयोज्यं प्रयोगार्हं पुस्तकादि तन्न विभज्येत मूर्खादिभिरिति पारिजातः। — वि० र०, p. 505.

4. तत्र मनुः। संस्थितस्यानपत्यस्य · · · · · प्रतिपादयेत्।। अनपत्यस्य मृतस्य पत्नी सगोत्राद्देवरसपिण्डयोरन्यतरस्मात् अपत्यमुत्पाद्य अस्मै मृतस्वामिस्वत्वोपलक्षितं रिक्थजातं दद्यान्न स्वयमाददीतेति पारिजातः। — वि० र०, p. 589.

5. पारिजाते तु देवलवचनानां चतुराश्रयेषु स्त्रीशूद्रानुपनीतविषयत्वाद् व्याख्यातम्। तत्र संख्योदरश्रुतेः। उदकविषयं वा। — गृह० र०, p. 147.

6. अत्र च परनिपानं प्रतिष्ठितं विवक्षितं, अप्रतिष्ठिते चौर्यापत्तेः। परकीयनिपानेषु अपेयं सलिलं भवेत्। इति वाक्याच्चेति प्रकाशकारादयः। एवमेव पारिजाते श्रीदमाह्निके च। — गृह० र०, p. 195.

7. अत्र समस्तवेदाध्ययनवतां आदावरभ्य वेदपाठेन स्याध्यायः करणीयः। एकदेशाध्यायिना पुरुषसूक्तादिपाठेन सावित्रीमात्राध्यायिना पुराणपाठेनेति व्यवस्थेति पारिजातः। — गृह० र०, p. 249.

8. नारदः। कानीनश्च सहोढश्च गूढायां यश्च जायते। तेषां वोढा पिता ज्ञेयस्ते च भागहराः स्मृताः। सहोढो गर्भजातः। अत्रापुत्रो यदि मातामहस्तदा तस्य पुत्रः कानीनः सहोढश्च। सपुत्रश्चेतदा वोढुः। उभयोरपुत्रत्वे चोभयोरिति पारिजातः। — वि० र०, p. 565. तत्र वोढुरिति उपादानात् विवाहिता चेत्तदा वोढुर्नो चेत् मातामहस्येत्येतदवगम्यते। — मद० पा०, p. 952 वोढुः refers to मनु, IX.172.

9. तस्मात् स्मृतिचन्द्रिकामदनरत्नाकरकल्पतरुरत्नाकरपारिजातकारप्रभृतीनां बहूनां पितुरभावे मातुः पुत्रधनाधिकार इत्येव सिद्धान्तः। — व्य० म०, p. 524, ततश्च प्रथमं माता गृह्णाति तदभावे पिता। — मद० पा०, p. 672.

10. यत्र पर्वतेष्वशक्यो परीहारस्तत्रापि मस्तकवर्जनार्थमिति पारिजातः। गृह० र०, p. 140, न च पर्वतमस्तके इति पाठे पूर्वकृतपर्वतग्रहणेनैव तन्मस्तकसिद्धावपि पुनर्ग्रहणाद् दोषाधिक्यं द्योत्यते। तद्भाष्ये तु अत्यन्तार्तस्य पर्वते दोषाभावप्रतिपादनार्थयित्युक्तम्। — मद० पा०, p. 63.

11. प्रातःस्नानं प्रशंसन्ति दृष्टादृष्टकरं हि तत्। नित्यत्वाज्जपादिद्वारा परलोकशुद्धिरिति पारिजातः। — गृह० र०, p. 180, दृष्टं मलापनयनादङ्गशुद्धिः। अदृष्टं नित्यत्वेन पापक्षयः। — मद० पा०, p. 62.

12. लेपभाज इत्यादिवाचनिकेर्थे सापिण्डये एकशरीरावयवान्यवरूपस्वकपोलरचिता-थाँनवकाशात् निर्वाप्यपिण्डसम्बन्धेन भ्रात्रादीनां सापिण्ड्यस्य मत्स्यपुराणबौधायनाभ्यां पूर्वमुक्तवात् कामधेनुहारलत॰कल्पतरुपारिजातकारादिभिस्तथैव व्याख्यानत्वाच्च। — शुद्धितत्त्व, p. 394, अथैवं मन्यसे एकपिण्डदानक्रियान्वयित्वमेकपिण्डदान-क्रियान्वयान्वयित्वं चेति निमित्तद्वयमिति न कल्पनागौरवमिति। तर्हि अस्मत्पक्षेपि एकमेव निमित्तमिति ततोपि लाघवम्। तच्चैकशरीरारावयवायन्वायित्वमेव। — मद० पा०, p. 130.

13. यच्च संहितायां हारीतः-पूर्वनष्टां तु यो भूमिमेक एवोद्धरेच्छमात्। यथाभाग लभन्तेऽन्ये दत्त्वांशं तु तुरीयकम् – इति वाक्यं लिखति स्म। तच्च स्मृतिमहार्णव-कामधेनु-कल्पतरु- पारिजातप्रभृत्यलिखनादयुक्तमेव। – वि० र०, p. 499. भूमौ तु विशेषयति शङ्खः। पूर्वनष्टां ··· तुरीयकम्-एतद्वचनं स्मृति ······ लिखनादयुक्तमेवेति रत्नाकरः। तन्न। दायभागमिताक्षराप्रभृतिधृतत्वात्। – दायतत्त्व, p. 177.

14

Paurāṇa-Dharma

PURĀṆA as a class of literature appears to have existed in very ancient times. The *Śatapatha Brāhmaṇa*, XI.5.6.8 refers[1] to *Itihāsa-Purāṇa*. In *Śatapatha*, XIII.4.3.13 it is stated that on the 9th day of the *Pāriplava* some part of *purāṇa* called *Veda* should be recited. In the *Chāndogyopaniṣad*, III.4.1 it is said that the hymns of the Atharvaṅgiras are the bees and *Itihāsa-Purāṇa* is the flower and in enumerating the sacred literature known at that time the same *Upaniṣad* (VII.1-2 and 4) designates *Itihāsa-Purāṇa* as the fifth *Veda*. The *Bṛhadāraṇyakopaniṣad* (II.4.10 and IV.1-2) contains a long list of sacred literary works in which after the four *Veda*s occur *Itihāsa, Purāṇa, Vidyā*s and *Upaniṣad*s. The *TaiĀ* (II.10) speaks of *Brāhmaṇa*s, *Itihāsa*s, *Purāṇa*s, *Kalpa*s and *Nārāśaṁsī-gāthā*s. In the *Atharvaveda*, XI.7.24 it is said that from *ucchiṣṭa* were produced *ṛk*s, *sāman*s, *chanda*s, *Purāṇa* together with *Yajus*.[2] The *Sāṅkhāyana Śrautasūtra* (16.2.27) mentions *Purāṇa-Veda* and states that on the 9th day of *Pāriplava* one should recite the *Purāṇa* (in the singular) while the *Āśvalāyana-śrauta* (X.7) provides that *Purāṇa-vidyā* (which is *Veda*) should be recited on the 8th day of *Pāriplava*. The *GautamaDhS* (8.6 and 11.19) states that a well-read brāhmaṇa is one who is clever in *vākovākya* (riddles, questions and answers) *Itihāsa* and *Purāṇa*. The *ĀpDhS* quotes the view of a *Purāṇa*, twice quotes two somewhat archaic verses from a *purāṇa* and the view of *Bhaviṣyat Purāṇa* (*vide*, I.10.29.7, I.6.19.13, II.9.23.3 and II.9.24.6). These references are sufficient to establish that centuries before the Christian era there was either one work called *Itihāsa-Purāṇa* or there were two works, one called *Itihāsa* and the other called *Purāṇa* which contained also verses. That work or those two are now lost. It is not possible to hold that the extant *Purāṇa*s are the works referred to in the *Śatapatha*, the *Upaniṣad*s and the *Śrauta* and *Dharmasūtra*s. The *Matsya Purāṇa* probably echoes a well-known tradition of its day when it asserts (53.3-4) that Brahmā remembered *Purāṇa* first among all *Śāstra*s, that then the four *Veda*s issued from the mouths of Brahmā and that originally there was one *Purāṇa* alone, its extent being one hundred crores of verses. The first portion of these words occurs in *Vāyu*, 1.60-61, *Brahmāṇḍa*, I.1.40-41 and *Padma*, V.1.45, while *Nāradīya*, I.92.22 has the verse *purāṇam-eka-mevāsīt sarvakalpeṣu mānava.* The extant *Purāṇa*s may probably be recasts of the ancient *Itihāsa-Purāṇa* or *Purāṇa* made in the first centuries of the Christian era. The extant *Purāṇas* were composed at a time when there was a re-statement of the Brāhmaṇical religion, philosophy and practices after Buddhism and Jainism had begun to show signs of waning. They effected a silent revolution in the religious ideas and practices of the people, without saying directly that the ideals of Vedic society were to be given up. They follow a procedure which has been a special characteristic of Hindu society and its leading works from the most ancient times. Flesh-eating and offerings of flesh to gods were common in the Vedic age. But even in the *Ṛgveda* there is apparently an undercurrent in certain verses that offerings of fuel sticks and oblations of *ghī* are as efficacious in securing favours from gods as flesh offerings. For example, *Ṛgveda*, VIII.19. 5-6 assert 'whoever offers (worships) to Agni with a fuel stick or with an oblation of *ghī* or by means of *Veda* (study) or who performs a good sacrifice by bowing (to Agni), for him alone run fleet horses and his alone is the most brilliant fame'. Compare *ṚV*, VI.16.47 also. A similar attitude is found in some of the *Upaniṣads*. The *Muṇḍakopaniṣad* says[3] (I.1.4-5) 'one should know two *vidyā*s *parā* (the higher) and *aparā* (the lower); the latter is constituted by the four *Veda*s and the six subsidiary lores, while the higher *vidyā* is the one whereby that Imperishable (Reality) is known.' Here the four *Veda*s are said to be inferior lore and the *Upaniṣad*s are said to be superior lore. The same *Upaniṣad* (I.2.7) condemns *aparā-vidyā* when it states that sacrifices are infirm or leaky boats and that those foolish people who look upon these (sacrifices) as the highest good become subject to a cycle of births and deaths. The *Kaṭhopaniṣad* (I.2.4) says in the same strain that what are known as *avidyā* and *vidyā* are very contradictory on all sides. In the dialogue between Sanatkumāra and Nārada (*Chāndogyopaniṣad*, VII.1.) the former replies that all the four *Veda*s, *Itihāsa-Purāṇa* and the other lores that Nārada studied are mere names and that he will tell him (Nārada) what is beyond. Though there are some *Upaniṣad* passages which treat the *Veda*s as inferior, the *Upaniṣad*s generally treat the *Veda* as authoritative for certain purposes and actually quote several Vedic verses in support of their statements. For example the *AitUp*, II.5 quotes *ṚV*, IV.27.1 (*garbhe nu*), *Praśnopaniṣad*, I.10-11 quote *ṚV*, I.164.12 (*pañcapādam*), *BṛUp*, II.5.16-17 and 19 quote *ṚV*, I.116.12, I.117.22, VI.47.18 respectively. The *Muṇḍakopaniṣad*,[4] III.2.10 emphasizes that *brahmavidyā* is to be imparted only to those who are *śrotriya*s (who have studied the *Veda*), who engage in their duties, and who have properly performed *śirovrata*. Similarly, it is said, in the *BṛUp*[5] (IV.4.22) that brāhmaṇas desire to know this (great Self) by means of the study of the *Veda*, by sacrifices, by gifts, by *tapa*s (penance) and by fasting. Thus it is clear that the *Upaniṣad*s accept the *Veda*s and the religious rites enjoined therein as preparatory means to a knowledge of the higher truths about the supreme spirit and do not altogether give up the *Veda*s and sacrifices as quite useless.

The extant *Purāṇa*s adopt a similar attitude. They speak highly of the *Veda*s, prescribe many Vedic *mantras* for different religious rites and ceremonies; but at the same time they introduce such revolutionary changes in the conceptions, rites, duties, usages and practices of the people that the whole aspect of Hindu society dominated by the *Purāṇa*s becomes a great deal different from the Vedic society or the society at the time of the *Śrauta* and *Gṛhyasūtras*. This will be illustrated below:

The *Mahābhārata* and some of the *Purāṇas* exhibit a famous verse which says[6] "one should strengthen the *Veda* by (the study and application of) *Itihāsa* and *Purāṇa*. The *Veda* is afraid of the man of meagre learning (with the thought) that he (the man of little learning) may injure it." The *Vāyu Purāṇa* (1.200) emphasizes[7] in this connection that *dvija* who knows the four *Vedas* together with the *aṅgas* (subsidiary lores of grammar, etc.) but who does not know *Purāṇa* would not be a conspicuous (or clever) man. Similarly, the *Kūrma* observes[8] (II.46.129): if all the *Purāṇas* together with *Itihāsa* are placed on one side and the highest *Veda* on another, it is the *Purāṇas* that will surpass (the *Veda*).

Many of the *Purāṇas* describe how the several *Vedas* and their *śākhās* came into existence. For example *Vāyu* chapters 60, 61 and 65 (verses 24-27), *Agni*, 150.23-31 and 271.1-10, *Varāha*, 2.76-80 (*Ṛgveda, Yajurveda,* and *Sāmaveda* are respectively Nārāyaṇa, Brahmā and Rudra), *Viṣṇu Purāṇa*, II.11.13 (*Ṛgveda, Yajurveda* and *Sāmaveda* are respectively Brahmā, Viṣṇu and Rudra), *Brahmāṇḍa*, II ch. 34-35.

A few striking examples to show how the *Purāṇas* utilize Vedic *mantras* and legends may now be cited. As the *Brahma Purāṇa* is said to be the first of the 18 *Purāṇas* (e.g. by *Viṣṇu Purāṇa*, III.6.20, by *Brahma*, 245.4, by the *Mitākṣarā* on *Yājñavalkya*, I.3 and by Hemādri on *Śrāddha*, p. 1551), it will be dwelt upon first. *Brahma*, 129.62 (*ardho jāyā iti śruteḥ*) refers to *Taittirīya-Saṁhitā*, VI.1.8.5 (*ardho vā eṣa ātmano yat patnī*) and *Śatapatha Brāhmaṇa*, V.2.1.10 (*ardho ha vā eṣa ātmano yaj-jāyā*); *Brahma*, 140.22 quotes *ṚV*, II.12.1 (*yo jāta eva*); *Brahma*, 174.14-16 are *ṚV*, IX.114.2-4 (in a different order) and 174.17 is *ṚV*, IX.112.3; *Brahma* ch. 151 contains the story of Purūravas and Urvaśī, verses 4 and 12 of which echo the very words of *ṚV*, X.95.16 and 15; *Brahma*, 152.34 is the same as *ṚV*, X.109.6; *Brahma*, 120.9 is almost the same as *ṚV*, X.97.22; *Brahma*,[9] 233.62 refers to *Muṇḍakopaniṣad; Brahma*,[10] 158.27 is a close paraphrase of *ṚV*, I.164.46; *Brahma*,

161.41 expressly mentions *Puruṣasūkta* and verses 44-49 echo the words of *ṚV*, X.90.7-8, 12-14; *Brahma*, 171.28-38 are a condemnation of gambling, verse 32 of which is based on *ṚV*, X.34.10-11.

A few passages from some other *Purāṇa*s on the same topic may now be set out. The *Viṣṇu Purāṇa*, IV.6.64 (in the story of Urvaśī and Purūravas) states that the king uttered a Vedic hymn (*ṚV*, X.95).[11] The *Matsya Purāṇa*, ch. 93 (dealing with *homa* to the nine *graha*s, planets) employs nine Vedic *mantra*s five of which are different from those employed by Yājñavalkya (I.300-1). The same *Purāṇa* (237.13) prescribes that when evil portents indicated by animals or birds occur the five verses of the hymn (*ṚV*, X.165, beginning with *devāḥ kapota*) should be recited; *Matsya*, 265.9 prescribes for bringing about the purification of an image or *liṅga* four *mantra*s, viz. *ṚV*, VII.49.1-3 and X.9.1. *Agni*, 41.6-8 prescribes numerous Vedic *mantra*s at the time of laying down stones or bricks when building a temple. The *Kāśī-khaṇḍa* (of the *Skanda Purāṇa*) in 9.60-61 quotes *Vājasaneya-saṁhitā*, 32.4 (*eṣo ha devāḥ*).

It is very interesting to note that the *Purāṇa*s not only prescribe Vedic *mantra*s in several rites, but also insist on the inclusion of Pauraṇic *mantra*s in many rites. For example, *Yāj.*, I.229 prescribes only *ṚV*, II.41.13 as the *mantra* for invoking Viśve-Devas in *śrāddha*, but the *Mitākṣarā* adds that a *smārta mantra* — *āgacchantu mahābhāga*[12] should also be recited. This is *Garuḍa Purāṇa*, I.218.7. It is ascribed to both Bṛhaspati and *Brahma Purāṇa* by the Kalpataru on *śrāddha* and by Aparārka (pp. 478, 481). The *Vāyu Purāṇa* (74.15-16) prescribes that the *mantra* 'Perpetual adoration to the gods, the *pitṛ*s and to the great *yogins*, to *svadhā* and to *svāhā*' should be repeated thrice at the beginning and end of a *śrāddha* and at the time of offering *piṇḍa*s'. This *mantra* is prescribed for this purpose by seven *Purāṇa*s and is called *saptārcis*[13] (one having seven flames).

The peculiar features introduced by the *Purāṇa*s in religious rites and practices may now be alluded to. The most characteristic thought and the key-note of *Purāṇas* is how great results could be secured with little effort. Vyāsa states in *Brahma Purāṇa* (229.61-65[14]) 'in the blessed *kali* age great rewards arise in return for a little trouble.' The same note is struck by *Matsya* (69.3 and 78), *Viṣṇu Purāṇa,* VI.2.34, *Padma*, VI.53.5-6. As a consequence of the above dominant principle, the *Purāṇa*s lay great emphasis on *dāna*s (gifts, particularly of food), on pilgrimages and baths in sacred waters at certain times, *vratas*, performance of *śrāddha*, *ahiṁsā* and *bhakti*. These will be briefly illustrated by quotations.

Gifts have been highly eulogised from the *Ṛgveda* downwards. The subject of *dāna* has been dealt with in the *History of Dharmaśāstra*, Vol. II, pp. 837-88. Here I shall refer only to two points viz. gifts of food and gifts to brāhmaṇas. Several *Purāṇa*s wax eloquent over gifts of various kinds such as *Agni*, 208-213, *Matsya,* 82-92 and 274-289, *Varāha*, 99-111. The *Ṛgveda* (X.117.6 condemns[15]as purely sinful the man who did not offer food to the gods or men (such as friends and guests) and used food cooked by him for himself alone. The *Bhagavadgītā* contains the same dictum. The gift of food, particularly to brāhmaṇas, is highly praised in some *Purāṇa*s such as *Brahma*, 218.10.32, *Padma*, V.19.289-307, *Agni*, 211.44-46. The Brahmā says that the gift of food is superior to all other gifts, since food is very life of men and that on feeding ten thousand brāhmaṇas a man even if always addicted to sins becomes free from *adharma.*[16] It is said in the *Agni Purāṇa* (211.44-46) that there is nothing higher than gifts of food, that gifts of elephants, horses, chariots, slaves (male and female) and houses do not come up even to a 16th part of *annadāna* (in merit) and that a man having committed very great sins and then making gifts of food becomes free from all sins and secures inexhaustible worlds. Almost up to the present days all Hindu house-holders regard it as a duty to give food to the needy and particularly to poor and deserving brāhmaṇas and students, but during the last few years the shortage of food, high prices and rationing have gradually lessened the age-long sentiments on *annadāna*.

Some of the *Purāṇa*s set at naught the rule of Manu (III.149) that in rites for ancestors the family and character of brāhmaṇas to be invited should be carefully investigated. Both *Padma* (V.29.212) and the *Skanda* (*Kāśī-khaṇḍa*, 6.56-57) recommend that at *tīrtha*s one should not engage in the investigation of the worth of brāhmaṇas but should give them food if they ask for it. The *Vāyu Purāṇa* (82.26-28) provides[17] that the brāhmaṇas established at Gayā by Brahmā are supermen, that one should not embark on examining their family, character, learning or *tapas*, that when those Gayā brāhmaṇas are gratified the Gods together with *pitṛ*s become gratified and the pilgrim secures *mokṣa*. The *Varāha Purāṇa* goes so far as to say that at Mathurā a pilgrim should prefer to honour a brāhmaṇa born and living in Mathurā rather than a brāhmaṇa who has studied the four *Veda*s (but is a stranger to Mathurā), since those men that dwell in Mathurā are like Viṣṇu.[18] Hindu society had come to believe in the great merit of feeding brāhmaṇas and the *Purāṇa*s only echo the general sentiments of people. If the people in general had not believed in this, I think no amount of interpolations or insistence by crafty brāhmaṇas would have been effective.

The *BaudDhS*, II.8.30, *Manu*,[19] III.126, *Vasiṣṭha*, XI.28 contain the same verse which emphatically asserts that a large company destroys five *desiderata* viz. the respectful treatment (of those invited), the securing of a proper place and time, purity and (the choice of) meritorious brāhmaṇas and that therefore one should not desire a large company (of brāhmaṇas at a *śrāddha*), yet several *Smṛti*s and *Purāṇa*s lay emphasis on profuse expenditure for *śrāddha*s at *tīrtha*s. The *Vāyu Purāṇa*, the *Viṣṇu* and *Varāha* expressly provide that no stinginess lit. cheating in money matters) in spending wealth should be shown at Gayā.[20]

Some of the *Purāṇa*s draw a comparison between sacrifices and pilgrimages to and bathing in sacred places and recommend the latter in preference to the former. The *Matsya Purāṇa* says that sacrifices require numerous implements, collection of various materials, the cooperation of priests and therefore can be performed only by kings or rich people; but going on a pilgrimage is possible even for the poor and yields results equal to sacrifices and is therefore superior to sacrifices.[21] These very verses and ideas occur in the *Padma Purāṇa* and the *Viṣṇudharmottara Purāṇa*.

In pursuance of the dominant idea of inculcating matters that are easy but yield great rewards, the *Purāṇa*s speak highly of *vrata*s. Thousands of verses in the *Purāṇa*s deal with *vrata*s (e.g. *Agni*, chs. 175-200, *Garuḍa*, 116-137, *Nāradīya*, I.17-23 and 110-124, *Matsya*, 54-80, 94-100, *Varāha*, 39-65). They were put far above *yajña*s as in *Padma*,[22] III.21.29 and VI.96.25. Hemādri, himself a great minister of the Yādava King of Devagiri, wrote the *Vratakhaṇḍa* (of *Caturvargacintāmaṇi*) which contains descriptions of about 100 *vratas* to which over 2500 printed pages are devoted by him. It makes one very sad to think how even responsible Ministers of States, instead of devoting deep and constructive thought to the question of the driving out of ruthless foreign invaders of Bhāratavarṣa, spent time and energy in such matters as *vrata*s, *śrāddha*s and *dāna*s in the thirteenth century and thereafter.

Another great characteristic of the *Purāṇa*s is that they lay great emphasis on *bhakti* and *nāmasmaraṇa* (taking or remembering the name of God). The *Padma Purāṇa* says[23] 'even Pulkasas, Śvapacas and Mleccha tribes if they are solely devoted to Hari, should be honoured'. The germs of the doctrine of *bhakti* may be traced even to the *Ṛgveda* (in the hymns to Varuṇa particularly).[24] The word *bhakti* occurs in the *Śvetāśvataropaniṣad*.[25] But it is the *Purāṇa*s that devote great space to *bhakti* (religion of faith in and love of God). Many *Purāṇa*s particularly the *Bhāgavata* are replete with the eulogy, the theory and practice of *bhakti*. For reasons of space it is not possible to quote many verses from the *Purāṇa*s on this subject. Because the *Purāṇa*s often speak of the *bhakti* of Śiva or Viṣṇu or Kṛṣṇa or Devī and because they are full of stories of fights even among gods themselves, one should not run away with the notion that the real teaching of the *Purāṇa*s is one of pure polytheism. The *Purāṇa*s never tire of saying that there is only one God and Brahmā, Viṣṇu, Śiva are only suppositions imposed by men.[26]

The *Purāṇa*s lay great emphasis on remembering or taking the name of God. The *Vāmana Purāṇa* asks: "What has that man to do with many *mantra*s who has *bhakti* for Janārdana?[27] The *mantra* — *namo nārāyaṇāya* is able to accomplish all objects. Success is for those who have faith in Viṣṇu. How can there be failure for them in whose heart dwells Janārdana dark like a blue lotus?" Stories such as that of the sinful Ajāmila,[28] who is said to have secured *mokṣa* (final liberation from birth and death) when on his death-bed he whole-heartedly called upon Nārāyaṇa (his son), were meant to emphasize the doctrine that a single heart-felt invocation of the name of God, a single act of faith and complete surrender to God cancels the results of a whole life of sin and iniquity. This is also the teaching of the *Gītā* in IX.30 'if even a very sinful man worships me with a single-minded devotion, he should be regarded as a saintly person, since he has resolved to pursue the right course." The *Vāmana Purāṇa*[29] (94.63) and *Padma*, VI.245.85 say that a man secures the same results by repeating the name of Viṣṇu that one would secure by visiting all the *tīrtha*s and holy shrines in the world. Many persons often say that the doctrine of *ahiṁsā* arose in India owing to the spread of Buddhist and Jain teachings. This is not correct. That doctrine is inculcated by the *Upaniṣads* (***vide*** *Chāndogya*, III.17.4 and VIII.15 *ahiṁsan sarvabhūtānyanyatra tīrthebhyaḥ*) and in the *Dharmasūtra*s (***vide*** *Gautama*, II.19, 23 and VIII.24 *dayā sarvabhūteṣu*, frequently in the *Mahābhārata, Ādi*, 11.13, *Droṇa*, 192.38, *Śānti*, 263.30, 266.6, 330.18, *Anuśāsana*, 115.25, 116.38, *Āśvamedhika*, 28.16-18, 43.21) and the *Yogasūtra*, II.30 (*ahiṁsā* is the first of five *Yama*s). The *Purāṇa*s very frequently eulogise *ahiṁsā*. The *Padma Purāṇa* again and again reverts to the doctrine of *ahiṁsā*. In one place it says[30] 'men who kill animals do not reach Heaven even with all the *Veda*s (they study), nor with gifts, nor with *tapas* nor with sacrifices. Sages always say that *ahiṁsā* is the highest *dharma*, the highest *tapas* and the highest gift. Those men, that are compassionate, look upon flies, snakes, lice, stinging insects and man as the self (comparing all with himself); *vide Mārkaṇḍeya*, 25.32, *Brahmāṇḍa*, II.30.35, *Padma*, V.18.440, *Matsya*, 52.8 and 143.31-32. *Vāyu*, 59.43 (for compassion for all beings). The *Brahmāṇḍa Purāṇa* states: non-enmity, freedom from avarice, *tapas*, compassion for all beings, restraint of senses, celibacy, truthfulness, sympathy forbearance, patience — these are said to be the root of the ancient *dharma*.[31]

Though *ahiṁsā* was very much emphasized, some of the *Purāṇas* were bold enough to say that if by killing one person many would live in happiness then there is no sin either great or small, in killing that person.[32]

Manu (IV.226-27) divides *dharma* into *iṣṭa* and *pūrta*. The former is constituted by *Agnihotra, tapas,* truthfulness, preservation of the *Veda*s, hospitality and Vaiśvadeva (*Agni*, 209.3), while the latter comprehends construction of wells with steps, deep wells, tanks, *annasatra* (where food is distributed gratis) and the laying out of parks (*Agni*, 209.2). Some of the *Purāṇas* assert that by the *dharma* called *iṣṭa* a person secures heaven, but by performing works of charity (*pūrta*) he secures *mokṣa*.[33]

Sometimes the *Purāṇas* give expression to ideas that strike us as very modern, because they raise social service and removal of distress and suffering as the highest *dharma*. The *Brahma Purāṇa* says[34] 'that man's life is blessed who always strives for the good of others; fire, water, the sun, the earth and various kinds of crops exist for the sake of others and particularly the good'. The *Skanda* (*Kāśī-khaṇḍa*) avers:[35] adversities vanish in the case of those good men in whose hearts doing good to others is always active and prosperity comes to them at every step. That purity is not secured by baths at sacred places, that reward is not obtained by numerous gifts, that reward is not obtained by very severe austerities, which are all obtained by doing good to others. After churning out all dicta this is the conclusion viz., 'There is no *dharma* higher than doing good to others and there is no greater sin that harming others'. In the *Mārkaṇḍeya Purāṇa* a king gives expression to a fine thought[36] 'I think that men would not obtain that happiness in heaven or in the world of Brahmā, which arises by bringing about the deliverance of distressed beings'.

The last item that I would mention here is a surprising conception well in advance of modern socialistic doctrines: 'men should have ownership over only so much as would fill their belly; he who thinks as his own what is more than that, is a thief and deserves to be punished.'[37]

References

[This paper is originally published in *P.K. Gode Commemoration Volume* (pp. 70-82), Poona, 1960. In fact, this paper may be treated as improvement on his work *History of Dharmaśāstra*, Vol. I/I, pp. 1-19 on account of the review on his work by Shri G.M. Joshi in the Marathi Journal *Samāja-Jīvana*.]

S.G. Moghe

1. मध्वाहुतयो ह वा एता देवानां यदनुशासनानि विद्या वाकोवाक्यमितिहासपुराणं गाथा नाराशंस्यः। – शतपथ, XI.5.6.8.

   अथ नवमेऽहन्। . . . तानुपदिशति पुराणं वेदः कोऽयमिति किंचित्पुराणमाचक्षीत।
   – शतपथ, XIII.4.3.13.

2. ऋचः सामानि छन्दांसि पुराणं यजुषा सह।।
   उच्छिष्ठाज्जज्ञिरे सर्वे दिवि देवा दिविश्रितः।। – अथर्व, XI.7.24.

3. द्वे विद्ये वेदितव्ये परा चैवापरा च। तत्रापरा ऋग्वेदो यजुर्वेदः सामवेदोऽथर्ववेदः शिक्षा कल्पो व्याकरणं निरुक्तं छन्दो ज्योतिषमिति। अथ परा यया तदक्षरमधिगम्यते।
   – मुण्डक, 14.1-3.

4. तदेतदृचाभ्युक्तम्। क्रियावन्तः श्रोत्रियाः ब्रह्मनिष्ठा स्वयं जुह्वत एकर्षिं श्रद्वयन्तः। तेषामेवैतां ब्रह्मविद्यां वदेत शिरोव्रतं विधिवद्यैस्तु चीर्णम्।।
   – मुण्डक, III.2.10.

5. तमेतं *वेदानुवचनेन* ब्राह्मणा विविदिषन्ति यज्ञेन दानेन तपसाऽनाशकेन।
   – बृह. उप., IV.4.22.

6. इतिहासपुराणाभ्यां वेदं समुपबृंहयेत्।
   बिभेत्यल्पश्रुताद्वेदो मामयं प्रहरिष्यति।।

— आदिपर्व, I.267-68. वायुपुराण, 1.201, वसिष्ठधर्मसूत्र, 27.6, पद्मपुराण, V.2.51-52, वृद्धात्रि, ch. 3, p. 50 in Jivananda's edition (which reads प्रतरिष्यति); in the स्मृतिचन्द्रिका, p. 3 (Gharpure's edn.) this verse is ascribed to बृहस्पति।

7. यो विद्याच्चतुरो वेदान्साङ्गोपनिषदो द्विजः।
न चेत्पुराणं संविद्यान्नैव स स्याद्विचक्षणः।। — वायु, I.200; पद्म (V.2, 50-51) reads last half as पुराणं च विजानाति यः स तस्माद्विचक्षणः।

8. एकतस्तु पुराणानि सेतिहासानि कृत्स्नशः।
एकत्र परमं वेदमेतदेवातिरिच्यते।। — कूर्म, II.46.129.

9. द्वे विद्ये वेदितव्ये इति चाथर्वणी श्रुतिः।। — ब्रह्म, 233,62; *vide* मुण्डक, I.1.4. quoted above in note 3 on p. 259.

10. एक एवाद्वयः शम्भुरिन्द्रमित्राग्निनामभिः। — ब्रह्म, 158.27.
वदन्ति बहुधा विप्रा भ्रान्तोपकृतिहेतवे।।

Compare *ṚV*, I.164.46:
इंद्रं मित्रं वरुणमग्निमाहुरथो दिव्यः स सुपर्णो गरुत्मान्।
एकं सद्विप्रा बहुधा वदन्त्यग्निं यमं मातरिश्वानमाहुः।।

11. जाये हे तिष्ठ मनसि घोरे तिष्ठ वचसि कपटिके तिष्ठेत्येवमनेकप्रकारं सूक्तमवोचत्।।
— विष्णु, IV.6.64. Compare ऋग्वेद, X.95.1:
हये जाये मनसा तिष्ठ घोरे वचांसि मिश्रा कृणवावहै नु।

12. *vide History of Dharmaśāstra*, Vol. IV, p. 440, not 984, for this verse.

13. *Vide History of Dharmaśāstra*, Vol. IV note 1077, p. 479 for details about this *mantra*.

14. धन्ये कलौ भवेद्विप्रास्त्वल्पक्लेशैर्महत्फलम्।।
. . . धर्मोत्कर्षमतीवात्र प्राप्नोति पुरुषः कलौ।।
स्वल्पायासेन धर्मज्ञास्तेन तुष्टोऽस्म्यहं कलौ।। — ब्रह्म, 229.61.65.
अल्पेनैव प्रयत्नेन धर्मः सिध्यति वै कलौ।। मत्स्य, 69.78 and विष्णुपुराण, VI.2.34.
सुखोपायमल्पधनमल्पक्लेशं महाफलम्।।
पुराणानां च सर्वेषां सारभूतं महामते।।
एकादश्यां न भुंजीत पक्षयोरुभयोरपि।। — पद्म, VI.53.5-6.

15. मोघमन्नं विन्दते अप्रचेताः सत्यं ब्रवीमि वध इत्स तस्य।
नार्यमणं पुष्यति नो सखायं केवलाघो भवति केवलादी।।

— ऋ०, X.117.6, तै० ब्रा०, II.8.8.3. The भगवद्गीता echoes the last quarter, 'भुंजते ते त्वघं पापा ये पचन्त्यात्मकारणात्। 3.13 and Manu, III.113 also does the same (अयं स केवलं भुंक्ते यः पचत्यात्मकारणात्) and विष्णुधर्मसूत्र, 67.43 is to the same effect.

16. सर्वेषामेव दानानामन्नं श्रेष्ठमुदाहृतम्।
. . . . . प्राणा ह्यन्नं मनुष्याणां तस्माज्जंतुः प्रजायते।।
अन्ने प्रतिष्ठिता लोकास्तस्मादन्नं प्रशस्यते।।

— ब्रह्म, 218.10-12. The ऐतरेयब्राह्मण, 33.1 asserts 'अन्नं प्राणः'; the बोधायनधर्म-सूत्र, II.3.68 says:

अन्ने श्रितानि भूतानि अन्नं प्राणमिति श्रुतिः।।
तस्मादन्नं प्रदातव्यमन्नं हि परमं हविः।। The तैत्तिरीयब्राह्मणं, II.8.8.3 has 'अन्नं प्राणमन्नमपानमाहुः'

17. अमानुपतया विप्रा (अमानुषागयाविप्रा?) ब्राह्मणा (ब्रह्मणा?) ये प्रकीर्तिताः। तेषु तुष्टेषु संतुष्टाः पितृभिः सह देवताः।। न विचार्यं कुलं शीलं विद्यां च तप एव च।। पूजितैस्तैस्तु राजेन्द्र मुक्तिं प्राप्नोति मानवः।। — वायु, 82.26-28.

18. चतुर्वेदं परित्यज्य माथुरं पूजयेत्सदा।।
मथुरायां ये वसंति विष्णुरूपा हि ते नराः।। — वराह, 165.57.

19. सत्क्रियां देशकालौ च शौचं ब्राह्मणसंपदः।।
पंचैतान् विस्तरो हंति तस्मान्नेहेत विस्तरम्।। — मनु, III.126.

20. वित्तशाठ्यं न कुर्वीत गयाश्राद्धे सदा नरः।।
वित्तशठ्यं तु कुर्वाणो न तीर्थफलभाग्भवेत्।। — वायु, 82.19.

अपि धन्यः कुले जायादस्माकं मतिमान् नरः।।
अकुर्वन् वित्तशाठ्यं यः पिंडान्नो निर्वपिष्यति।।
रत्नं वस्त्रं मही यानं सर्वभोगादिकं वसु।।
विभवे सति विप्रेभ्यो योस्मानुद्दिश्य दास्यति।।

— विष्णुपुराण, III.14.22-23, वराहपुराण, 13.5-51 (reads महायानं सर्वं तोयादिकं वसु)

21. ऋषिभिः क्रतवः प्रोक्ता देवैश्चापि यथाक्रमम्।
न हि शक्या दरिद्रेण यज्ञाः प्राप्तुं महामते।।
बहूपकरणा यज्ञा नानासम्भारविस्तराः।।
प्राप्यन्ते पार्थिवैरेतैः समृद्धैर्वा नरैः क्वचित्।।
यो दरिद्रैरपि विधिः शक्यः प्राप्तुं नरेश्वर।
तुल्यो यज्ञफलैः पुण्यैस्तन्निबोध युधिष्ठिर।।
ऋषीणां परमं गुह्यमिदं भरतसत्तम।।
तीर्थानुगमनं पुण्यं यज्ञेभ्योपि विशिष्यते।।

— मत्स्य, 112.12-15. Almost the same verses occur in वनपर्व, 82.13-17, अनुशासनपर्व, 107.2-4, पद्मपुराण (आदिखण्ड, 11.13-17 and 49.12-15.), विष्णुधर्मोत्तर, III.273.4-5.

22. श्रेष्ठं विष्णुव्रतं विप्र तत्तुल्या न शतं मखाः।। — पद्म, III.21.29,
वरं विष्णुव्रतं ह्येतज्ज्ञेयं यज्ञशताधिकं।। यज्ञकृत्प्राप्नुयात्स्वर्गं वैकुंठं कार्तिकव्रती।। —पद्म, VI.96.25.

23. पुल्कसः श्वपचो वापि ये चान्ये म्लेच्छजातयः।।
तेपि वन्द्या महाभागा हरिपादैकसेवकाः।। — पद्म, I.50.10.

24. [This is the view of many Western scholars shared by Dr. R.N. Dandekar. Prof. H.D. Vekankar in his *Path of Devotion in the Ṛgveda* (in Marathi, pp. 1-90) takes the view that the real *bhakti* is to be traced in the Indra *Sūktas*.]
S.G. Moghe

25. यस्य देवे परा भक्तिर्यथा देवे तथा गुरौ।।
तस्यैते कथिता ह्यर्थाः प्रकाशन्ते महात्मनः।। — श्वेताश्वतर, VI.23;

26. A few verses of this type may be set out here:
प्रसीद सर्व सर्वात्मन् क्षराक्षरमयेश्वर।
ब्रह्मविष्णुशिवाख्याभिः कल्पनाभिरुदीरितः।।
— विष्णुपुराण, V.18.51, ब्रह्म, 192.51.
स्वमूर्तिभेदैः स्थित एक ईशः।। — नारदीय (पूर्वार्ध, 2.32.);
योहं स भगवान्विष्णुर्यश्चासौ सोहमव्ययः।।
नाऽवाभ्यां वै विशेषोस्ति एका मूर्तिर्द्विधा स्थिता।। — वामन, 67.27-28.
यो भेदं कुरुतेस्माकं त्रयाणां द्विजसत्तम।।
स पापकारी दुष्टात्मा दुर्गतिं समवाप्नुयात्।। — वराह, 70.27.

27. किं तस्य बहुभिर्मन्त्रैर्भक्तिर्यस्य जनार्दने।।
नमो नारायणायेति मन्त्रः सर्वार्थसाधकः।।
विष्णुर्येषां जयस्तेषां कुतस्तेषां पराजयः।।
येषामिन्दीवरश्यामो हृदयस्थो जनार्दनः।। — वामन, 94.58-59.

28. विक्रुश्य पुत्रमघवान्यदजाभिलोपि नारायणेति म्रियमाण इयाय मुक्तिम्।।
— पद्म, I.31.109, ***vide also*** पद्म, IV.87.7. The भागवतपुराण (IV.1.20 ff and IV.2) sets out the story of Ajāmila at some length.
सर्वेषामप्यघवतामिदमेव सुनिष्कृतम्।।
नामव्याहरणं विष्णोर्यतस्तद्विषया मतिः।। — भागवत, VI.2.10.

29. पृथिव्यां यानि तीर्थानि पुण्यान्यायतनानि च।।
तानि सर्वाण्यवाप्नोति विष्णोर्नामानुकीर्तनात्।।
— वामन, 94.63, पद्म, VI.245.85.

30. न वेदैर्न च दानैश्च न तपोभिर्न चाध्वरैः।।
कथंचित् स्वर्गतिं यान्ति पुरुषाः प्राणिहिंसकाः।।
अंहिसा परमो धर्मो अहिंसैव परं तपः।।
अहिंसा परमं दानमित्याहुर्मुनयः सदा।।
मशकान्सरीसृपान्दंशान् यूकाद्यान्मानवांस्तथा।।
आत्मौपम्येन पश्यन्ति मानवा ये दयालवः।।
— पद्म, आदि 31.26-28. Compare पद्म, VI.243.71 for the last verse.

31. अद्रोहश्चाप्यलोभश्च तपो भूतदया दमः।।
ब्रह्मचर्यं तथा सत्यमनुक्रोशः क्षमा धृतिः।।
सनातनस्य धर्मस्य मूलमेतद्दुरासदम्।।
— ब्रह्माण्ड, II.30.37-38, मत्स्य, 143.31-32 (with slight variations). In

आश्वमेधिकपर्व, 91.33, we have the words 'सनातनस्य धर्मस्य मूलमेतत्सनातनम्' One of the earliest epigraphic references to सनातनधर्म occurs in the Kharmapur plates of Mādhavavarman in *EI*, Vol. 27, p. 312.

32. यस्मिंस्तु निहते भद्रे जीवन्ते बहवः सुखम्।।
तस्मिन्हते नास्ति शुभे पातकं चोपपातकम्।। — ब्रह्माण्ड, II.36.188.
Compare ब्रह्म, 141.22.
यस्मिन् निपातिते सौख्यं बहूनामुपजायते।।
मुनयस्तद्वधं प्राहुरश्वमेधशताधिकम्।।

33. इष्टेन लभते स्वर्गं पूर्ते मोक्षं च विन्दति।।
— वराह, 172.83. *vide also* Agni, 209.2-3.

34. जीवितं सफलं तस्य यः परार्थोद्यतः सदा।।
अग्निरापो रविः पृथ्वी धान्यानि विविधानि च।।
परार्थं वर्तनं तेषां सतां चापि विशेषतः।। — ब्रह्मपुराण, 125.36-37.

35. परोपकरणं येषां जागर्ति हृदये सताम्।।
नश्यन्ति विपदस्तस्य सम्पदः स्युः पदे पदे।।
तीर्थस्नानैर्न सा शुद्धिर्बहुदानैर्न तत्फलम्।।
तपोभिरुग्रैस्तन्नाप्यमुपकृत्य यदाप्यते।।
परिनिर्मथ्य वाग्जालं निर्णीतमिदमेव हि।।
नोपकारात्परो धर्मो नापकारात्परमघम्।। — काशीखण्ड, 6.4.5-7.

36. न स्वर्गे ब्रह्मलोके वा तत्सुखं प्राप्यते नरैः।।
यदार्तजन्तुनिर्वाणदानोत्थमिति मे मतिः।। — मार्कण्डेय, 15.57.

37. यावद्भ्रियेत जठरं तावत्स्वत्वं हि देहिनाम्।।
अधिकं योभिमन्येत स स्तेनो दण्डमर्हति।। — भागवत, VII.14.8.

15

The Arthaśāstra of Kauṭilya

THIS epoch-making work was first published by Dr. Shama Sastri in 1909 in the Mysore Sanskrit Series and was also translated by him. Pandit T. Gaṇapati Śāstrī of Trivandrum has published two parts with his own commentary called *Śrīmūla* (up to end of the 7th *adhikaraṇa*). Recently (1923) Dr. Jolly and Dr. Schmidt have edited the text with a valuable Introduction in the Panjab Sanskrit Series at Lahore. For this paper the edition of 1919 by Dr. Shama Sastri has been used. This work has given rise to frequent and fierce controversies about its authorship, its authenticity and its age, and it cannot be said that we have heard the last of this din of controversy. Moreover this work has inspired several monographs with somewhat high-sounding titles, such as Narendranath Law's *Studies in Ancient Indian Polity*, Dr. P. Banerji's *Public Administration in Ancient India*, Ghosal's *History of Hindu Political Theories*, Majumdar's *Corporate Life in Ancient India*, Benoy Kumar Sarkar's *Political Institutions and Theories of the Hindus*; Jayasval's *Hindu Polity*, Prof. S.V. Visvanatha's *International Law in Ancient India* (1925). It is not possible to discuss at great length all the problems about Kauṭilya here. Only a brief statement can be attempted. For further study reference may be made to the following works and papers: Hillebrandt's *Uber das Kauṭilīyaśāstra and Verwandtes* (Breslau 1908); *ZDMG*, Vol. 67, pp. 49-96 (Dr. Jolly), *ZDMG*, Vol. 63, pp. 345-59, Vol. 69, p. 369ff; *JRAS*, 1916, pp. 130-37 (Prof. Keith); *IA* for 1918, pp. 157-61 and pp. 187-95 (Dr. Jacobi translated by Dr. Sukthankar); Dr. Kalidas Nag's *Les Théories Diplomatiques de l'Inde ancienne et l'Arthaśāstra* (Paris 1923), Dr. Otto Stein's *Megasthenes und Kauṭilya* (Vienna 1922), K.V. Rangasvami Ayyangar's *Lectures on Ancient Indian Polity* (Madras, 1916), Dr. Winternitz in *Calcutta Review* (1924) and in his *History of Sanskrit Literature* (Vol. III, pp. 509-24); *IA* for 1924, pp. 128-36 and 141-46 (Jacobi, translated by Utgikar).

The *Kauṭilīya* is the oldest extant work on *Arthaśāstra*. Though *Arthaśāstra* and *Dharmaśāstra* are often contradistinguished, on account of the difference of the two *śāstra*s in ideals and in the methods adopted to reach them, *Arthaśāstra* is really a branch of *Dharmaśāstra* as the former deals with the responsibilities of kings for whom rules are laid down in many treatises on *dharma*.[1] According to the *Caraṇavyūha* of Śaunaka, *Arthaśāstra* is an *Upaveda* of *Atharvaveda*. The purpose of this *Śāstra* as stated in the *Kauṭilīya* itself is to prescribe means for securing and preserving (power over) the earth.[2] Yājñavalkya distinctly states (II.21) that in case of conflict between *Dharmaśāstra* and *Arthaśāstra*, the rule is that the former prevails.[3] Nārada also (I.39) says the same thing.[4] From comparatively ancient times Cāṇakya *alias* Kauṭilya or Viṣṇugupta has been credited with the composition of a work on *Arthaśāstra*. The *Kāmandakīyanītisāra* pays a glowing tribute of praise to Viṣṇugupta, who, single-handed, brought about the downfall of Nanda, bestowed the earth on Candragupta and distilled from the ocean of *Arthaśāstra* the quintessence, his work on politics[5] Kāmandaka further tells us that he looked upon Viṣṇugupta as his *guru*.[6] The *Tantrākhyāyikā* (*HOS*, Vol. 14) which is certainly not later than AD 300 pays homage to Cāṇakya the Great as one of the authors of treatises on Politics.[7] Daṇḍin in his *Daśakumāracarita* (section VIII, p. 131 2nd edn. B.S. Series) says that the teacher Viṣṇugupta compressed *Daṇḍanīti* for the sake of the Maurya King into six thousand *śloka*s and quotes passages from Cāṇakya.[8] Bāṇa associates the work of Kauṭilya with harsh and cruel expedients.[9] The *Pañcatantra* identifies Cāṇakya and Viṣṇugupta and speaks of Cāṇakya as the author of *Arthaśāstra* (*vide* part I, p. 2 ed. by Kielhorn, part II, p. 65 and part III, p. 50 ed. by Buhler). Kauṭilya figures very largely in the *Purāṇas* (*vide* Pargiter's *Dynasties of Kali age*, pp. 69-70 and *Viṣṇu Purāṇa*, 4.24.26-28). He had a prominent place in the *Bṛhatkathā* of Guṇādhya, as appears from the works of Kṣemendra and Somadeva. The *Mudrārākṣasa* identifies Cāṇakya and Kauṭilya and suggests the derivation of the latter name from *kuṭila* (crooked).[10] Some of the above items of information are supported by the personal references contained in the *Arthaśāstra* itself. At the end of the first chapter of the first *adhikaraṇa*, Kauṭilya is said to be the author of the *Śāstra* and at the end of the 10th chapter of the second *adhikaraṇa* Kauṭilya is said to have laid down the rules for royal edicts for the sake of king.[11] The last verse tells us that he who impatiently wrested the earth from the Nanda king composed the work and after the colophon a verse tells us that seeing the differing interpretations of *bhāṣyakāra*s on the *Arthaśāstra*, Viṣṇugupta himself composed the *sūtra* and the *bhāṣya*.[12]

The first question that arises for consideration is the authenticity of the work, that is, the question whether it can be the work of the famous minister of Candragupta Maurya, who was a contemporary of Alexander and who must therefore have flourished about 320 BC. This question very largely depends upon the age of the work. But other considerations, more or less of a subjective character and depending upon the absence of certain things from the *Kauṭilīya* must be dealt with first. Jolly, Keith and Winternitz hold that the extant *Kauṭilīya* is not the work of the Maurya minister. One argument viz. that a person like Cāṇakya who had to build a vast empire such as that of Candragupta and who was bent down with the cares of the empire, could not have found time to write such a work, may be brushed aside as entirely futile, being a purely subjective argument. Some persons may say that he could have found time to write such a work in the midst of all cares, while others may deny the possibility of such a thing. Similarly most of the arguments from the silence of the *Kauṭilīya* are also quite unconvincing and lead to no certain and universally acceptable conclusion. The non-mention of Pāṭaliputra, or the empire of Candragupta is of very little use in deciding the question of the authenticity of the work. The argument of Stein and Winternitz that in Megasthenes' account of India no great person named Cāṇakya or Kauṭilya appears and that the former's account of the condition of India does not tally with that presented by Kauṭilya is of very little weight. We have no means for finding out what proficiency Megasthenes had acquired in the languages of India so as to be able to hold conversation with all sorts and conditions of men. Besides, it is well-known that Megasthenes' writings have been handed down in a fragmentary state and that he often spins his own yarns. Megasthenes declares the Indians to be unacquainted with writing. But no Western scholar would now subscribe to the view that writing was unknown in India about 320 BC. Dr. Jolly himself has to remark that the idealising tendency in Megasthenes greatly impairs the trustworthiness of his statements (p. 40 Introduction of *Kauṭilīya*). This question of the authenticity of the work is bound up with the question whether it can be the work of an individual author or whether it is the product of a school. Hillebrandt vehemently argues that it is the product of a school and Jacobi as vehemently repudiates that hypothesis. The great stumbling block in the way of regarding Kauṭilya as the author of the work is the fact that the views of Kauṭilya are cited by name about 80 times in the work itself almost always in opposition to the views of other teachers. But there is nothing specially to be wondered at in this. In order to avoid looking too egoistic ancient authors generally put their own views in the third person, as said by so early a writer as Medhātithi or Viśvarūpa.[13] It has to be admitted that the first person singular also is used by ancient writers, though rarely,[14] Jacobi (*IA*, for 1918, p. 188) and Keith are both wrong in thinking that the view of Kauṭilya is criticized by Bharadvāja in V.6. Kauṭilya states his position first and then mentions the view of his predecessor.[15] Dr. Jolly (Intro. to *Kauṭilīya*, p. 44) is wrong in his explanation of *apadeśa* (in XV.1). That word is applied to passages which mean 'this or that author says so and so', and the *Kauṭilīya* cites a case of the statement of various views on a certain point. These words do not at all indicate that according to the *Arthaśāstra* Kauṭilya was a stranger.[16] Keith thinks (*JRAS*, 1916, p. 135) that as Kauṭilya is derived from *kuṭila*, an author will not cite his own views under such an epithet. It is not unlikely that Cāṇakya acquired the epithet Kauṭilya on account of his methods in dealing with the Nandas and that as he did so from no purely selfish motives but for ridding the country of such tyrants as the Nandas are represented to have been, he might have rather come to relish the name given to him by the people. It has to be noted in this connection that many of the writers quoted in the Kauṭilya bear nicknames (such as Piśuna, Vātavyādhi, Kauṇapadanta). This leads to the question as to whether the name is Kauṭilya or Kauṭalya. Hillebrandt seems to imply that all Mss. employ the first form, while Pandit T. Gaṇapatiśāstri says his Mss. support the latter form. Mss. of the *Kādambarī*, The *Pañcatantra* and other works support the form Kauṭilya and the *Mudrārākṣasa* does the same by pointedly hinting at the etymology. A commentary on the *Kāmandakīyanīti-sāra* styles the *Kauṭilīya* as *Kuṭalabhāṣya* and Kuṭala is said to be a *gotra*. It is very difficult to decide between the rival claims of the two forms, but it appears that the form of the name, Kauṭalya, is due to a later attempt to solve the difficulty of an author parading his views as those of a man nicknamed 'crooked'. We have to remember that so early a writer as Kāmandaka (who was well-knwon to Bhavabhūti and Vāmana's *Kāvyālaṅkāra-sūtravṛtti*) who is assigned to the third century AD by Jacobi and other scholars and the *Tantrākhyāyikā* distinctly assign a work on politics to the minister of Candragupta. No weighty arguments have been advanced so far why this tradition vouched for so early should be disregarded. Keith finds it impossible that in the words 'six thousand *śloka*s' used by Daṇḍin the word *śloka* could mean a unit (in prose) of 32 letters. But Daṇḍin is evidently repeating the words that occur in the *Arthaśāstra* itself at the end of the first chapter.[17]

Before proceeding to discuss the age of the *Kauṭilīya*, it is advisable to say a few words on the form, style and contents of the work. The work is divided into 15 *adhikaraṇa*s, 150 chapters, 180 topics and contains 6000 *śloka*s (i.e., units of 32 letters). The work is in prose interspersed with a few verses. Each chapter has at the end at least one verse and sometimes more. A few verses occur also in the midst of some chapters as in I.8, I.15, II.10, II.24, V.6, VII.5, VII.6, VII.9, VII.13, X.3, XIII.4. There are about 340 verses excluding *mantra*s. Almost all these verses are in the *anuṣṭubh* metre, only eight verses being in the classical *indravajrā* or *upajāti* metres (in II.9, II.10 and X.3). In our utter ignorance about the literature on *Arthaśāstra* prior to Kauṭilya it is impossible to say how many of these verses are borrowed and how many are his own compositions. There can be no doubt that some of these verses were composed by him (e.g. the two verses in I.10. where the views of *ācāryāḥ* are given and the words *etat kauṭilya-darśanam* occur). It appears that some verses are clearly quotations. For example, the verse *nāsya guhyam* at the end of I.15, and the verse *saṁvatsareṇa patati* at the end of IV.7 are Manu, 7.105 and 2.180 respectively. The last occurs in *BaudhDhS*, II.1.62 and also *Vasiṣṭha*, I.22. The two verses in the *upajāti* metre in X.3 *yān yajñasaṅghais* and *navam śarāvam* occur respectively in the *Parāśaradharmaśāstra* (ch. III, p. 12 of Jīvānanda part II) and in the *Pratijñā* (IV.3).[18] It is noteworthy that they are introduced with the words *apīha ślokau bhavataḥ* and follow a quotation from or summary of a Vedic passage. Twelve verses in VII.9 are introduced with the words *tatraitad bhavati* and may be quotations. A few of the verses bear a close resemblance to verses of other works; e.g. the verse *pṛṣṭaḥ priyahitam brūyāt* (in V.4) which is very simlar to *Manu*, 4.138. In some cases he connects verses with his own words e.g. the words *kurvataśca* with *nāsya guhyam* (at end of I.15) and the last verse of II.25. The style of the *Kauṭilīya* is simple and direct. It is not concise like that of the *Vedānta* or *Vyākarana-sūtra*s. It resembles the *Dharma-sūtra*s of Gautama, Hārīta and Śaṅkha-Likhita, but is not as archaic as that of Āpastamba. It abounds in numerous technical and rare terms. It is generally in accordance with Pāṇini's grammar, though such un-Pāṇinean words as *pāpiṣṭhatama* (in VII.11) rarely occur. He employs the word *avyaya* in the masculine (II.10) while Pāṇini (I.1.37) emplys *avyayam*. The whole work on account of its careful arrangement of topics and unity of design impresses one as the product of a single brilliant mind.

It would be interesting to say a few words separately on the chapter about judicial administration. Dr. Jolly has collected together the passages of the *Kauṭilīya* on judicial administration that bear a very close resemblance to the several works on ancient Indian Law (***vide*** *ZDMG*, Vol. 67, pp. 51-90). It will be seen therefrom that there is the greatest correspondence between the *Kauṭilīya* and Yajñavalkya. It is no doubt true that many passages of Manu and Nārada agree closely with those of the *Kauṭilīya* but not to the same extent as those of Yājñavalkya. A few striking examples are quoted below.[19] The question then arises whether there is borrowing and if so who the borrower is. The agreement in phraseology is so close that it must be regarded as a case of borrowing and in my opinion it is the *Yājñavalkyasmṛti* that borrows. The reasons are many. Yājña-valkya represents on numerous points of law a very great advance upon the doctrines of Kauṭilya. Kauṭilya does not contain distinct directions upon the four stages of a law-suit (plaint, reply, proof and judgement), nor upon the threefold aspects of proof (documents, witnesses, possession). Yājñavalkya goes into all these matters. The *Kauṭilīya* does not recognise the widow, or mother as heir to a sonless man; Yājñavalkya does so. Kauṭilya does not mention the *bandhus* as heirs; he hardly says anything about re-union.[20] The *Kauṭilīya* divides the *strīdhana* of a woman dying during her husband's life-time among her sons and daughters, while *Yāj.* prefers the daughters to the sons.[21] It is not necessary to multiply examples. It goes without saying that Yājñavalkya represents a far too advanced stage of juristic principles than the *Kauṭilīya* and so must be later than the latter by several centuries. The *Kauṭilīya* agrees very closely with

Manu also, but considerations of space prevent me from going into the points of agreement. There are, however, numerous fundamental points on which Manu and Kauṭilya disagree. Kauṭilya allows *niyoga* even in the case of brāhmaṇas (last verse of III.6 and at the end of I.17 about kings). Manu first speaks of *niyoga* and then condemns it (*vide* 9.57-63 and 9.64-68). As Bṛhaspati refers to this fact in Manu's work, it appears that the passages condemning *niyoga* were put in probably earlier than the first centuries of the Christian era.[22] Though the *Kauṭilīya* speaks of almost the same 18 titles as those in Manu (8.4-7) almost under the same names, there is a slight difference. Manu has no such title as *prakīrṇaka*. Kauṭilya speaks of *upanidhi* and extends the same rules to *nikṣepa*, while Manu speaks of the title as *nikṣepa*. Manu positively says (9.155) that the son of any member of the first three *varṇa*s from a śūdra woman does not inherit his father's wealth (though the preceding verses, 151-54 seem to lay down different rules), while Kauṭilya allows such a son a tenth share when there are sons born to a brāhmaṇa from wives of the higher castes or one-third when he has no other son (III.6). Manu expressly mentions the mother and the paternal grandmother as heirs (9.217), while Kauṭilya appears to ignore them. Manu prohibits the remarriage of widows (V.161-165), while Kauṭilya allows not only widows to remarry, but also wives whose husbands have not been heard of for a year or more according to circumstances (III.4). Kauṭilya allows a wife to desert her husband, if the latter is of bad character, has become a traitor to the king, endanger her life or has become an outcaste or impotent (last verse of III.2).[23] Kauṭilya further seems to have allowed divorce which is unknown to any other known law-giver, but he bases it only on the ground of mutual hatred and says that a marriage in the approved forms cannot be dissolved (III.3).[24] Manu is very harsh upon gamblers and asks the king to suppress gambling and punish gamblers (9.221-224), while Kauṭilya only brings gambling under the control of the king for the purpose of detecting thieves &c. (III.20). Manu first allows a brāhmaṇa to marry even a śūdra woman and then condemns such a thing (III.13-19), while Kauṭilya does not condemn such unions. These divergences and others lead us to conclude that the *Kauṭilīya* is much older than the extant *Manusmṛti*, which is in many matters carried away by puritanic zeal, while in its older portion is more in harmony with the spirit of the *Kauṭilīya*.

Therefore the *Kauṭilīya* is long anterior to the time when the extant *Manusmṛti* took its present form. The *Kauṭilīya* refers to the opinion of *mānavas* in five places. Two of the views ascribed to the *mānavas* by Kauṭilya are the same as those which Kāmandaka (II.3 and XI.67) ascribes to Manu. According to the *mānavas*, the *vidyās* to be studied by a prince were three, viz. *trayī, vārtā* and *daṇḍanīti*, what is called *ānvīkśikī* being but a branch of *trayī*; and the council of ministers was to consist of twelve. *Manusmṛti* (7.43) appears to regard the *vidyās* as four and lays down (7.54) that the council should consist of seven or eight *sacivas*. Bühler and others, on account of this difference in the views of the *mānavas* and the *Manusmṛti*, thought that Kauṭilya was referring to the *Mānava-dharmasūtra*. In my humble opinion the evidence for the existence of a *Mānavadharmasūtra* is practically nil. From the references to Svāyambhuva Manu and Prācetasa Manu contained in the *Mahābhārata*, particularly in the *Śānti* and *Anuśāsana parvans* it appears that there were two works in verse on *dharma*, and politics attributed to these two, or there was one work containing both. These works were subsequently recast as the *Manusmṛti*. It is therefore that some difference is noticed between the views ascribed to the *mānavas* and the extant *Manusmṛti*. Besides there is no real conflict in the matter of the *vidyās*. The *Manusmṛti* does not positively say that the *vidyās* are four and not three; it simply says from whom *trayī* and the other three are to be learnt. The *Manusmṛti* (in 7.60) allows more ministers than seven or eight. It is possible that in recasting several changes were made. The third opinion is about the fine to be imposed on officers of the State occasioning loss of revenue (II.7). The other two views of the *mānavas* quoted are concerned with the fine to be imposed on false witnesses and for forcible seizure of jewels,[25] etc. It must be admitted that in the extant *Manusmṛti* there is nothing exactly corresponding with these views. But from this fact no one conclusion alone can be drawn. There may be a mistake in quoting, or there may be interpolations; it is also possible that some of the verses in the original *Manusmṛti* have dropped out, or that Kauṭilya is quoting not the *Manusmṛti* itself, but the views of works based on or explanatory of Manu. It is noteworthy that Bṛhaspati contains a verse very similar to the views on *sāhasa* attributed to the *mānavas*.[26] Bṛhaspati's work was more or less a *bhāṣya* or *vārtika* on Manu. He probably represents older *bhāṣyas* in verse on Manu. The only authors or schools besides the *mānavas* cited by name in the *dharmastīya* section are the Bārhaspatyas and the Auśanasas. It is remarkable that the well-known and ancient *Dharmasūtrakāras* like Gautama, Āpastamba, Baudhāyana, Vasiṣṭha, Hārīta are nowhere quoted by name. It is noteworthy that in the *dharmasthīya* section Kauṭilya several times quotes the views of *ācāryas* and of some others under the word *apare*. Some of these views correspond closely with the discussions in the ancient *dharmasūtras*. One of these is the question as to whom the child belongs, to the begetter or to him on whose wife it is begotten.[27] Kauṭilya first quotes the view of the *ācāryas* that it belongs to the husband of the mother of the child, then says that some hold that it belongs to the begetter, while Kauṭilya holds that it belongs to both. It is to be noted here that both Baudhāyana and Āpastamba say that according to the brāhmaṇas the son belongs to the begetter, while Vasiṣṭha says there is a dispute on the point, both views being supported by ancient authorities. Gautama speaks of both views and at last (18.13 *dvayorvā*) seems to come to the same conclusion as Kauṭilya. It is not unlikely that Kauṭilya has in mind this discussion in the *dharamasūtras* and also in Manu (9.48-54 where the view is that the child belongs to the husband of the woman). Some of the other views attributed to *ācāryas* are that a woman could visit the houses of her husband's relations, of prosperous men, of village headmen, of female ascetics &c. (III.4); that very poor men could divide even water-pots at a partition (III.5); that the master who did not employ a servant ready to work according to agreement had to pay the wages agreed upon as if the work had been finished (compare *Viṣṇu*, V.157); he who forcily confined a man or woman or who by force released from imprisonment was to be fined between 500 and 1000 (III.17); that disputes of a remote date shall not be complained of and that he who is the first to complain wins, since one runs (to court) as one cannot bear the pain (III.19); that in a complaint by one gambler against another, the successful party has to pay the fine called *pūrvasāhasa* and the defeated party the fine called *madhyasāhasa* (III.20).

The ancient *dharmasūtra*s do not give technical names of the eighteen titles, though some of them do occur in them. The terms *vākpāruṣya* and *daṇḍapāruṣya* occur in Gautama (*DhS*, 12.1) and Vasiṣṭha (*DhS*, 17.61). Baudhāyana seems to have known the term *strīsaṁgrahaṇa* (*DhS*, II.2.54). *Steya* is known to all. Gautama (*DhS*, 12, 39) speaks of *nidhi*.

The foregoing discussion about the *dharmasthīya* section shows that in the sphere of the administration of justice, Kauṭilya is far in advance of the *dharmasūtra*s of Gautama, Āpastamba and Baudhāyana and so is much later than these (though in certain matters such as the rights of women to succeed to males he closely agrees with Gautama and Āpastamba), while he is earlier than the extant *Manusmṛti* (though not earlier than the oldest kernel of the *Manusmṛti*) and very much earlier than Yājñavalkya.

The question of the date of Kauṭilya can be settled only approximately and for that we have to rely on the internal evidence. The external evidence does not carry us far; we can only say that the *Kauṭilīya* is certainly not later than the second century AD, as writers from the fourth century onwards (e.g., Kāmandaka, the Tantrākhyāyika and Bāṇa) speak of it with admiration. No one claims it to be earlier than 300 BC. Even Keith who assigns it a late date and cannot place it earlier than 100 BC; at the most he has to admit (*JRAS*, 1916 p. 135) that for a precise date we have no real ground.

The *Kauṭilīya* quotes five schools by name, *mānavāḥ* (5 times), *bārhaspatyāḥ* (6 times), *auśanasāḥ* (7 times), *pārāśarāh* (4 times), *āmbhīyas* (once) and the following individual authors: Kātyāyana (1), Kiñjalka (1), Kauṇapadanta (4), Ghoṭamukha (1), (Dīrgha) Cārāyaṇa (1), Parāśara (2), Piśūna (6), Piśūnaputra (1), Bāhudantiputra (1), Bhāradvāja (7, once as Kaniṅka Bhāradvāja), Vātavyādhi (5), Viśālākṣa (6). He either differs from all these authors or they differ from each other in all the places where they are cited. All the individual authors that are cited only once occur on the same page (except Bāhudantiputra). He quotes the views of *ācāryas* over fifty times and in each case differs from them. *Ācāryas* means the ancient authors on a *śāstra* collectively. Kauṭilya is cited about 80 times. The *Kāmasūtra* of Vātsyāyana mentions a Ghoṭakamukha and a Cārāyaṇa. Whether they are identical with the authors cited by Kauṭilya is extremely doubtful. The *Mahābhārata* mentions among writers on *Daṇḍanīti* the following who occur in the *Kauṭilīya* also: Bṛhaspati, Manu, Bhāradvāja, Viśālākṣa, Śukra (the same as Uśanas) and Indra (probably Kauṭilya's Bāhudantiputra) whose abridgement of Brahmā's work is called Bāhudantaka in the *Śāntiparva* (ch. 59). The *Mahābhārata* mentions other writers on politics viz. Gauraśiras, Kāśyapa, Utathya, Vāmadeva, Vasuhoma, Kāmandaka (*Śāntiparva*, 123.11) and a few others which are not found in the *Kauṭilīya*.

The *Kauṭilīya* knows the four *Vedas*, the charms and incantations of the *Atharvan*, the six *aṅgas*, includes under *itihāsa Purāṇas*, *Dharmaśāstra* and *Arthaśāstra*; it knows the *Sāṁkhya*, *Yoga* and *Lokāyata* schools of thought.[28] It mentions Mauhūrtikas, Kārtāntikas (astrologers), Jupiter and Venus. It refers to *dhātuśāstra* (metallurgy). Sanskrit was the official language and in the *śāsanādhikāra* it mentions such *guṇas* of composition as *mādhurya*, *audārya*, *spaṣṭatva*, which show the beginnings of the *Alaṅkāraśāstra*. There is nothing to wonder at in this. In the second century AD we have the inscription of Rudradāman, which enumerates the *guṇas* of *kāvya*. It does not mention edicts on stone or copper. It refers to *Vaiśika-kalājñāna* (II.27). The *Kauṭilīya* closely agrees with the *Kāmasūtra* in several respects and the two works contain several identical passages (such as the lists of kings that fell victims to intrigues and about *trivarga*). Keith argues from this that the *Kauṭilīya* and the *Kāmasūtra* are not separated by a long interval and that it is a late work. Dr. Jolly also is of the same opinion (p. 24 Intro. to A.). If the *Kāmasūtra* held up *Kauṭilīya* as its model, then the two works would certainly look very much alike. There are points of difference between the two works, e.g. they differ in their attitude towards flesh-eating and the *Kāmasūtra* speaks of planetary influence *lagna*, while Kauṭilya is silent on these points, and condemns in general terms the consulting of stars. It is noteworthy that Kauṭilya (IX.4) speaks of consulting *nakṣatra*s which were known from the earliest Vedic period and some of which were looked upon as auspicious for sacrificial purposes, even in the *Śatapatha Brahmaṇa* (*SBE*, Vol. 44, pp. 1-2) and the *śrauta* and *gṛhya sūtra*s. Keith argues that the *śloka*s in the *Kauṭilīya* are more classical than even those of the *Rāmāyaṇa* and that it contains correct *triṣṭubh* stanzas which are wanting in the *Bṛhaddevatā* (a work of the fourth century BC). But this argument can produce no impression on those scholars who ascribe the *Rāmāyaṇa* to the fifth century BC or earlier. Nor is the date of the *Bṛhaddevatā* beyond the pale of discussion. There is no consensus of opinion among scholars as to the exact time when classical *śloka*s and correct *triṣṭubh*s first came into vogue. It is to be noted that *Kauṭilīya* defines *pada* as *Varṇasaṅghāta* and not as in Pāṇini (*sup-tiṅantam padam*).

Among the countries and peoples frequently mentioned by Kauṭilya, several are interesting. He speaks of silks from the land of the Cīnas[20] and blankets from Nepal. Keith says that the name 'Cīna', derived from the Thsin dynasty in China (which began its rule in 247 BC), would show that the *Kauṭilīya* could not have been composed about 300 BC. No one however knows how the word Cīna was derived and besides as Keith admits the passage may be an interpolation. He speaks of the *saṅgha* of the *Vṛṣṇi*s (I.6), the *śreṇī*s (corporations) of kṣatriyas in the countries of Kāmboja and Surāṣṭra that lived by *vārtā* (agriculture and trade) and by the profession of fighting and the Corporations of the Licchivika, Vṛjika, Mallaka, Madraka, Kukura, and the Kurupāñcālas that live on the title *rāja*. Some of these tribes such as the Licchavis, Vṛjis (Vajjis in Pāli) and Nallas are well-known from ancient Buddhist works. What is meant by *rājaśabdopajīvinaḥ* is not quite clear. It probably means that the organisation of the Licchavis and others was on democratic lines and that there was very keen competition for the honour of being elected the chief or President of those Corporations, the latter being designated *rāja*.[30] We are told that the bread of horses from Kāmboja, Sindu, Āraṭṭa and Vanāyu was the best and that Bāhlika, Pāpeya, Sauvīra and Taitila breeds were of middle quality. The *Kauṭilīya* speaks of Mleccha tribes and tells us that among them one's own children could be sold or pledged without incurring punishment (III.13). The country of Kāmboja was known to Yāska and Pāṇini.

There is hardly any distinctive reference to things Buddhist, except one passage (III.20) where a fine of one hundred (*paṇa*s) is prescribed for him who invites to dinners in honour of gods or Manes a Buddhist (Śākya), an Ājīvika, a śūdra[31] &c. There is a reference to *stūpa* in the last *sūtra* of XIII.2. This shows that the work was written at a time when Buddhism was yet not a wide-spread religion and had not secured an honourable place among the people. Ājīvika was a well-known sect in ancient India said to have been founded by Makkhali Gosāla (*vide* V.A. Smith's *Aśoka*, pp. 134, 198 of edition of 1909: *IA*, 1912, p. 286, *Dialogues of Buddha*, I., p. 71, n. 1). Aśoka bestowed some caves on them. It is worth noting that Kauṭilya says that weights should be made of iron or of stones from Magadha and Mekala (country near the sources of the Narmadā).[32]

It is extremely doubtful whether the *Kauṭilīya* knew the extant text of the *Mahābhārata*. Most of the stories used as illustrations in the *Kauṭilīya* occur in the *Mahābhārata* (e.g. Aila, Duryodhana, Haihaya Arjuna, Vātāpi, Agastya, Ambarīṣa). But in some cases there is a slight divergence between the two works, e.g. Janamejaya is said to have perished through having attacked brāhmaṇas in anger, while the *Mahābhārata* (XII.150) gives a different version; Kauṭilya[33] says (IV.8) that Māṇḍavya, though not a theif, declared himself to be a theif while the *Mahābhārata* (I.107.9) says that he spoke nothing; Kauṭilya mentions Jayatsena as the opponent of Nala (VIII.3). in gambling, while the *Mahābhārata* gives his name as Puṣkara; the *Mahābhārata* and the *Rāmāyaṇa* do not know that a Jāmadagnya ruled long as a king.[34] Kauṭilya seems to have known the *Purāṇas*. He says (III.7) that Sūta and Māgadha of the *Purāṇas* are quite different from members of the mixed castes called Sūta and Māgadha[35] and includes *Purāṇa* (I.5) among the subject of royal study grouped under the head of *itihāsa*.

Kauṭilya exhibits a wonderful knowledge of herbs and drugs and Dr. Jolly thinks that his materia medica is more extensive than even Suśruta's. But the dates of Caraka and Suśruta are far from being settled and no approximately certain conclusion can be drawn from the drugs mentioned in the *Kauṭilīya*. Kauṭilya speaks of *rasada* (one who administers mercurial poison) and prescribes banishment for those who trade in or administer *rasa* for money in order to do away with a person secretly (IV.4). In II.13 he speaks of gold that is *rasa-viddha* (amalgamated with mercury) and in II.12 of liquids containing gold (*rasāḥ kāñcanikāḥ*) and of *hiṅgulūka*. Dr. Jolly thinks that this knowledge of metallurgy alchemy is of Graco-syriac origin and so the *Kauṭilīya* is a work of the third century AD. When mercury began to be used medicinally in India it is difficult to say, and some of these passages about drugs may be later additions.

It is of great importance to note that Kauṭilya lays down that in the midst of the fort were to be constructed the temples of Śiva, Vaiśravaṇa, the Aśvins, Lakṣmī and Madirā (wine?) and niches were to be set apart for Aparājita, Apratihata, Jayanta and Vaijayanta and that the tutelary deities of the gates were to be Brahmā, Indra, Yama and Senāpati (i.e., Skanda). We know from the *Mahābhāṣya* (Kielhorn vol. II, p. 429 on Pāṇini, V.3.99

jīvikārthe cāpaṇye) that the Mauryas set up images out of greed for money and that in its day images of Śiva, Skanda Viśākha were worshipped.

The foregoing clearly shows that the *Kauṭilīya* has certainly an ancient atmosphere about it, that all that has so far been gathered from it agrees with its traditional date of 300 BC and no evidence has been yet brought forward that would compel us to assign it a later date.

References

[This paper is first published in *ABORI*, Vol. 7, pp. 85-100, 1926.] *S.G. Moghe*

1. *Vide* the मिता० on याज्ञ०, II.21 'धर्मशास्त्रान्तर्गतमेव राजनीतिलक्षणमर्थशास्त्रमिह विवक्षितम्।'
2. 'तस्याः पृथिव्या लाभपालनोपायः शास्त्रमर्थशास्त्रमिति' कौटि०, 15.1. The very first sentence of the कौटिलीय is पृथिव्या लाभे पालने च यावन्त्यर्थशास्त्राणि पूर्वाचार्यैः प्रस्थापितानि प्रायशस्तानि संहृत्यैकमिदमर्थशास्त्रं कृतम्।
3. अर्थशास्त्रात्तु बलवद्धर्मशास्त्रमिति स्थितिः।
4. यत्र विप्रतिपत्तिः स्याद्धर्मशास्त्रार्थशास्त्रयोः। अर्थशास्त्रोक्तमुत्सृज्य धर्मशास्त्रोक्तमाचरेत्।।
5. यस्याभिचारवज्रेण वज्रज्वलनतेजसः। पपात मूलतः श्रीमान् सुपर्वा नन्दपर्वतः।। एकाकी मन्त्रशक्त्या यः शक्त्या शक्तिधरोपमः। आजहार नृचन्द्राय चन्द्रगुप्ताय मेदिनीम्।। नीतिशास्त्रामृतं धीमानर्थशास्त्रमहोदधेः। समुद्दध्रे नमस्तस्मै विष्णुगुप्ताय वेधसे।। — काम्०, I.4-6.
6. विद्याश्चतस्र एवैता इति नो गुरुदर्शनम्। — काम०, II.6. Compare चतस्र एव विद्या इति कौटिल्यः। — कौटिलीय, I.2.
7. मनवे वाचस्पतये शुक्राय पराशराय ससुताय। चाणक्याय च महते नमोस्तु नृपशास्त्रकर्तृभ्यः।। (verse 2).
8. इयमिदानीमाचार्यविष्णुगुप्तेन मौर्यार्थे षड्भिः श्लोकसहस्रैः संक्षिप्ता। — दश., VIII; सत्यमाह चाणक्यः 'चित्तज्ञानानुवर्तिनोऽनर्था अपि प्रियाः स्युः। दक्षिणा अपि तद्भावबहिष्कृता द्वेष्य भवेयुः।' — दश०, VIII. Compare कौटिलीय, V.4 (verses at the end).
9. येषामतिनृशंसप्रायोपदेशनिर्घृणं कौटिल्यशास्त्रं प्रमाणम्। — कादम्बरी, p. 109 (Peterson's edn.).

10. कौटिल्यः कुटिलमतिः स एष येन क्रोधाग्नौ प्रसभमदाहि नन्दवंशः। — मुद्राराक्षस, I.

11. सुखग्रहणविज्ञेयं तत्त्वार्थपदनिश्चितम्। कौटिल्येन कृतं शास्त्रं विमुक्तग्रन्थविस्तरम्।। — कौटिलीय, I.1; 'सर्वशास्त्राण्यनुक्रम्य प्रयोगमुपलभ्य च। कौटिल्येन नरेन्द्रार्थे शासनस्य विधिः कृतः।। — कौटिलीय, II.10.

12. येन शास्त्रं च शस्त्रं च नन्दराजगता च भूः। अमर्षेणोद्धृतान्याशु तेन शास्त्रमिदं कृतम्।। दृष्ट्वा विप्रतिपत्तिं बहुधा शास्त्रेषु भाष्यकाराणाम्। स्वयमेव विष्णुगुप्तश्चकार सूत्रं च भाष्यं च।। कौटिलीय अर्थशास्त्र, 15.1.73 and last verse (Prof. Kane's edition).

13. 'प्रायेण ग्रन्थकाराः स्वमतं परापदेशेन ब्रुवते। — मेधातिथि; 'किंतु भगवतैव परोक्षीकृत्यात्मा निर्दिश्यते स्वप्रशंसानिषेधात्' — विश्वरूप on याज्ञ०, I.2.

14. तान्यप्येके समामनन्ति . . . . . . तत्समामने। — निरुक्त, VII.13; 'न तन्मम मतं यस्मात्तत्रायं जायते स्वयम्। — याज्ञ०, I.56; सजातीयेष्वयं प्रोक्तस्तनयेषु मया विधिः। — याज्ञ०, II.133.

15. एवमेकैश्चर्यममात्यः कारयेदिति कौटिल्यः। नैवमिति भारद्वाजः।

16. एवमसावाहेत्यपदेशः 'मन्त्रिपरिषदं द्वादशामात्यान् कुर्वीतेति मानवाः, षोडशेति बार्हस्पत्याः, विंशतिमित्यौशनसाः, यथासामर्थ्यमिति कौटिल्यः' इति।

17. शास्त्रसमुद्देशः पञ्चदशाधिकरणानि सपञ्चाशदध्यायशतं साशीतिप्रकरणशतं षट्श्लोकसहस्राणीति। These words in the *Kauṭilīya*, I.1.18 (p.3), must mean 6000 units of 32 letters and nothing else.

18. The manner in which the गात्रसेवक brings in this verse does not show that it is the author's own. The verse is preceded by the words शृण्वन्तु भवन्तः and is probably put in as a weighty utterance from some ancient source.

19. अभियुक्तो न प्रत्यभियुञ्जीत अन्यत्र कलहसाहससार्थसमवायेभ्यः। न चाभियुक्तेभियोगोस्ति। — K.A., III.1.25.26; अभियोगमनिस्तीर्य नैनं प्रत्यभियोजयेत्। अभियुक्तं च नान्येन नोक्तं विप्रकृतिं नयेत्।। कुर्यात्। प्रत्यभियोगं च कलहे साहसेषु च। — याज्ञ०, II.9-10; प्रतिरोधकव्याधिदुर्भिक्षभयप्रतीकारे धर्मकार्ये च पत्युः। — कौ०, III.2.16. दुर्भिक्षे ध र्मकार्ये च व्याधौ संप्रतिरोधके। गृहीतं स्त्रीधनं भर्ता न स्त्रिये दातुमर्हति।। — याज्ञ०, II.147; सोदर्याणामनेकपितृकाणां तु पितृतो दायविभागः। — कौ०, III.5.15. अनेकपितृकाणां तु पितृतो भागकल्पना। — याज्ञ०, II.120; नष्टापहृतमासाद्य स्वामी धर्मस्थेन ग्राहयेत्। देशकालातिपत्तौ वा स्वयं गृहीत्वोपहरेत्। — कौ०, III.16; नष्टापहृतमासाद्य हर्तारं ग्राहयेन्नरम्। देशकालातिपत्तौ च गृहीत्वा स्वयमर्पयेत्। — याज्ञ०, II.169; वानप्रस्थयतिब्रह्मचारिणामाचार्यशिष्यधर्मभ्रातृसमानतीर्थ्या रिक्थभाजः। — कौ०, III.16.37; वानप्रस्थयतिब्रह्मचारिणा रिक्थभागिनः। क्रमेणाचार्यसच्छिष्यध र्मभ्रात्रैकतीर्थिनः। — याज्ञ०, II.137.

20. (अपितृद्रव्या विभक्तपितृद्रव्या सहज़ीवन्तः पुनर्विभजेरन्) contains a reference to re-union. This is K.A. III.5.7.

21. जीवति भर्तरि मृतायाः पुत्रा दुहितरश्च स्त्रीधनं विभजेरन्। अपुत्राया दुहितरः। तदभावे भर्ता।। — कौ० III.2.36; अप्रजः स्त्रीधनं भर्तुर्ब्राह्मादिषु चतुर्ष्वपि। दुहितॄणां प्रसूता चेच्छेषेषु पितृगामि तत्।। — याज्ञ०, II.145.

22. बृहस्पति's words are 'उक्ते नियागो मनुना निषिद्धः स्वयमेव तु'; *vide* कुल्लूक on मनु०, 9.68 for the whole quotation.

23. नीचत्वं परदेशं वा प्रस्थितो राजकिल्बिषी। प्राणाभिहन्ता पतितस्त्याज्यः क्लीबोपि वा पतिः।।

24. अमोक्ष्या भर्तुरकामस्य द्विषती भार्या। भार्यायाश्च भर्ता। परस्परं द्वेषान्मोक्षः। ...... अमोक्षोधर्मविवाहानामिति।

25. कूटसाक्षिणो यमर्थमभूतं वा नाशयेयुस्तद्दशगुण दद्युरिति मानवाः – कौ०, III.11.45; रत्नसारफल्गुकुप्यानां साहसे मूल्यसमो दण्ड इति मानवाः।

26. स्त्रीपुंगोहेपरत्नानि देवविप्रधनं तथा। यौषेयं चोत्तमद्रव्यमेषां मूल्यसमो दमः।। – बृहस्पति quoted in the व्यवहारमयूख on साहस।

27. परपरिग्रहे बीजमुत्सृष्टं क्षेत्रिण इत्याचार्याः। माता भस्त्रा यस्य रेतस्तस्यापत्यमित्यपरे। विद्यामानमुभयमिति कौटिल्यः। – कौ०, III.7.1-3. Compare गौ० ध० सू०, 18.9-13; बौ० ध० सू०, II.2.34-36; आप० ध० सू०, II.6.13.5-6 (where the same three verses in Baudhāyana occur and वसिष्ठधर्मसूत्र, 17.6-9).

28. लोकायत occurs in the महाभाष्य on वर्णकातान्तवे (पा०, VIII.3.45). *Vide* Kielhorn's edn. Vol. III, pp. 325-26.

29. तथा कौशेयं चीनपट्टाश्च चीनभूमिजा व्याख्याताः। – कौ०, II.11. The position of this sentence suggests that it may have been tacked on by a later redactor, when copying the work.

30. In the *Jātakas* (ed. by Fausboll, Vol. I, p. 504 and Vol. III, p. 1) reference is made to the 7707 *rājas* of Licchavis in the Veśālī.

31. शाक्याजीवकादीन् वृषलप्रव्रजितान् देवपितृकार्येषु भोजयतः शत्यो दण्डः।

32. प्रतिमानान्ययोमयानि मागधमेकलशैलमयानि। – कौटिल्य, II.19.

33. यथाहि माण्डव्यः कर्मक्लेशभयादचोरः चोरोस्मीति ब्रुवाणः।

34. शत्रुषड्वर्गमुत्सृज्य जामदग्न्यो जितेन्द्रियः। अम्बरीषश्च नाभागो बुभुजाते चिरं महीम्।। – कौ०, I.6.

35. पौराणिकस्त्वन्यः सूतो मागधश्च ब्रह्मक्षत्राद्विशेषतः।

16

King Bhoja and His Works on Dharmaśāstra and Astrology

NUMEROUS works[1] on different branches of Sanskrit literature are ascribed to Bhojadeva such as on Poetics (viz., *Sarasvatīkaṇṭhābharaṇa* and *Śṛṅgāraprakāśa*), on Grammar (*Sarasvatīkaṇṭhābharaṇa*), on *śilpa*, painting and architecture (*Samarāṅgaṇasūtradhāra* edited by Ganapati Sastri in the *GOS*), a commentary on *Yogasūtra* (*Rājamārtaṇḍa*),[2] *Tattvaprakāśa* (on Śaivāgama published in the *TSS*), a work on Astronomy called *Rājamṛgāṅka* composed about AD 1042-43, and *Yuktikalpataru* on *Rājanīti* edited by Dr. N.N. Law (Calcutta, 1917). That he composed some extensive work on Law and Administration of justice follows from the numerous references to him in the *Mitākṣarā*, *Smṛticandrikā* and other works (***vide*** *History of Dharmaśāstra*, Vol. I, pp. 276-78). Recently in the critical edition of the *Śāntiparvan* published by the Bhandarkar Oriental Institute (ch. 121.14-15), the commentary *Durghaṭārthaprakāśikā*[3] cites the lengthy explanation of the one and a half verses beginning with *yatra śyāmo lohitākṣaḥ* given by the *Vyavāharamañjarī* of Bhojadeva. From this we come to know that at least one work called *Vyavahāramañjarī* composed or compiled by Dhāreśvara Bhojadeva existed long ago.[4]

In the present paper I propose to deal with several works of Bhojadeva concerned with astrological matters in relation to topics of *Dharmaśāstra*. The earliest work of this type ascribed to Bhoja is the one called *Bhīmaparākrama*.[5] This work is thrice mentioned by name and quoted by the *Bhujabalanibandha* to be described a little later on. I have not been able to secure any Ms. of the *Bhīmaparākrama.* Aufrecht in his Catalogue does not refer to any Ms. of this work, but only mentions digests where the *Bhīmaparākrama* is quoted. The three groups of verses quoted by *Bhujabalanibandha*[6] as from the *Bhīmaparākrama* are cited in the note below.[7] The first group of two verses, that in fn. 7-a declare that Monday, Wednesday, Thursday and Friday always lead to fulfilment of actions undertaken and the other three week days are to be employed only when expressly stated, that the Sun is recommended for dyes made from Kusumbha, lac and *mañjiṣṭhā*, Mars for ornaments of gold and Saturn for work in which iron enters. The next group of two verses deal with the terrifying effects of the *karaṇa* called *viṣṭi.* A very curious state of things is that the two lengthy verses about *viṣṭi* are found in the Ms. of *Rājamārtaṇḍa* (verses 1021-22). Not only so, many verses quoted as those of the *Bhīmaparākrama* and the *Bhujabalibandha* are found in the *Rājamārtaṇḍa* or *vice versa* as the sequel will show. The probable explanation of this will be offered later on.

The *Ekādaśītattva* of Raghunandana (p. 6, Jivananda's edn.) quotes a verse of *Bhīmaparākrama* on *Saṅkrānti.* That verse is quoted in the *Varṣakriyākaumudī* (p. 215) as from the *Bhaviṣya Purāṇa.*[9] It will later on be shown that the *Bhujabalanibandha* and the *Rājamārtaṇḍa* borrow without acknowledgement numerous verses from Varāhamihira's works, from Manu, *Purāṇa*s and others. It is therefore quite possible that the *Bhīmaparākrama* took over a verse from the *Bhaviṣya Purāṇa.* About twelve verses are quoted from the *Bhīmaparākarma* by the *Śuddhikaumudī* and in most of these the quotation is preceded or followed by a verse or verses from the *Rājamārtaṇḍa.* The verse *vivāha-cūḍā* apparently quoted from *Bhīmaparākrama* in *Śuddhikaumudī,* p. 223, is *Rājamārtaṇḍa* folio 67, verse 1057. A verse quoted from the *Bhīmaparākrama* by the *Śuddhikaumudī,* p. 229, is almost the same as a verse in *Bhujabala.*[9] The *Tithitattva*[10] (Vol. I, p. 150) quotes a verse from the *Bhīmaparākrama* on *Sankrānti.* The *Malamāsa-tattva*[11] (Vol. I, p. 828) quotes two verses from the *Bhīma-*

parākrama on Jupiter being in Leo, and the same *Tattva* appears to quote (p. 778) a prose passage from it.[12] The commentary of Mahādeva on the *Ratnamālā* of Śrīpati quotes a verse from the *Bhīmaparākrama* about the lords of the *ṛtus* (seasons).[13] In the commentary called *Mārtaṇḍavallabhā* (composed in AD 1573) on the *Muhūrtamārtaṇḍa* in the *BBRAS* collection of Mss. a half verse is quoted from the *Bhīmaparākrama*[14] to the effect that when a bridegroom is taking his recently married bride (to his own village or place) the usual astrological rule that one should not proceed on a journey when one has to face Venus does not hold good. The *Bhīmaparākrama* is quoted about fifty times in the several *Tattva*s of Raghunandana.[15] Some quotations have already been cited above. The *Jyotiṣatattva* quotes from it on pp. 571, 581, 594 (two verses), 606 (three verses, one of which occurs also on p. 594), 608 (two verses), 614, 621 ten verses), 630 (two), 663 (three verses, introduced with the words *bhīmaparākrame bhojarājaḥ*), 675-676 (a long prose passage which provides for certain rites for the removal of fever if it seized a man on anyone of the *nakṣatra*s from *Kṛttikā* to *Bharaṇī*), 679 (1 verses on the *nakṣatra*s and astrological aspects favourable for taking medicine), 685 (two, both of which occur in *Bhujabala*, pp. 245-46, verses 1199, 1202, on how to yoke bulls in ploughing), 702 (three verses), 717 (6 verses, the first of which occurs in *Bhujabala* p. 285, v. 1284), 722 (4 verses). The *Tithitattva* quotes verses from the *Bhīmaparākrama* on pp. 55 (one verse on *Goṣṭhāṣṭamī*), 146 (on *Agastyārghyadāna*), the *Māsatattva* quotes from it on pp. 775 (when marriage should not be performed), 761 (on intercalary month) and the *Saṁskāratattva*, pp. 884-85 (what should not be done in an intercalary month). It was not possible owing to the labour involved to find out whether all these verses could be identified with verses from *Bhujabala* and *Rājamārtaṇḍa*. A few identifications have been noted below.

The *Bhujabalanibandha* is an extensive work containing about 1740 verses in different metres, though the *anuṣṭubh* metre preponderates. It is divided into 18 chapters, but express mention of the number of the chapter in the colophons is made only up to the 6th chapter. The opening verse contains an obeisance to Hari and states that the work undertaken is a *Jyotiḥ-śāstra*. The second verse asserts that (an army of) a thousand elephants and four thousand horses cannot secure what a single astrologer well-versed in *deśa* (country) and *kāla* (time) can do. The colophon[16] at the end of the several chapters and at the end of the work tell us that it is the composition of Bhojarāja called Bhujabala and is a *Jyotiḥ-śāstra*. The contents may be briefly stated as follows: The astrological effects of the moon when occupying the several houses in the horoscope, the relative powers of *tithi*, *nakṣatra*, week-day, *karaṇa*, *yoga*, of the Sun and the Moon, time when the Moon is powerful or not, the periods for which each planet occupies a division of *nakṣatra*s into groups; (pp. 1-5); what effects the several planet produce by themselves or when occupying the several houses in a horoscope (pp. 5-10); week-days (pp. 10-13); the activities that are successful when undertaken on each of the groups; what actions should be done on the several *tithi*s and the presiding deities of the fifteen *tithi*s; the names of the twelve *rāśi*s, the twelve houses and the nine planets (including Rāhu and Ketu), friendship, enmity or indifference among planets (pp. 14-19); the figures of the several *nakṣatra*s and the number of individual stars in each *nakṣatra*; classification of *nakṣatra*s as *ūrdhvamukha, adhomukha, sthira, cara, tīkṣṇa, ugra, mṛdu, pumnāma* (pp. 21-27); definitions of *Yoga*s like *dagdha, siddha, mṛtyu, amṛta* (pp. 28-34); usages of countries as to some of the astrological conjunctions (pp. 34-36); *karaṇa*s and effects of *karaṇa*s like *viṣṭi* (pp. 36-39); classification of *māsa*s (months) and the acts that should be done in each kind of *māsa; tithi*s called *yugādi* (pp. 40-42); meaning of *vargottama*, the effects thereof, *dvipada* and *catuṣpada rāśi*s (pp. 42-44); meaning of *paṇaphera, apoclima, trikoṇa, caturasra, upacaya*; division of *nakṣatra*s into *deva, nara* and *rākṣasa* (pp. 44-46); *gaṇḍadoṣa* and its *śānti* (pp. 49-51); *grahāriṣṭa*s and their *śānti* (pp. 54-64); special features of persons born on the twelve *rāśi*s and on each of the twelve *rāśi*s as the *lagna* (pp. 65-69); on *dṛṣṭi*s of planets and the results of the *dṛṣṭi*s of each planet of the other planets (pp. 70-74); results of a planet being in its own house or being *paramocca* or *paramanīca* (pp. 75-76); on *Horā* and *Drekkāṇa* and the limbs of the *Kālapuruṣa* (pp. 76-79); results of the yogas called *anaphā, sunaphā, durudhura* and *kemadruma* (pp. 80-81); the results of the several planets being in one of the twelve *bhāva*s in the horoscope for men and women (pp. 82-88); results of the several arrangements or order of planets in a horoscope such as *Dhvaja, Ekāvalī, Rājahaṁsa, Kemadruma, Lalāṭī* (pp. 89-98); *daśā*s and *antardaśā*s of the several planets, the maximum life of a person being held to be 108 years (verse 451, p. 99) *aṣṭottaraśatam bhadre paramāyuḥ prakīrtitam*, (pp. 100-116); years for each planet in case of the *viṁśottarīdaśā* (pp. 118-19); rites to be performed on the birth of a child, worship of Ṣaṣṭhīdevī (on the 6th day after birth); the astrological aspects on which the child is to be named or which are to be avoided for *nāmakaraṇa* and *niṣkramaṇa* (taking out of the house); the charateristics of the name to be given to a child (pp. 119-23); *tāmbūlabhakṣaṇa* and *annaprāśana* (pp. 123-27); astrological requirements for *cūḍākaraṇa* and *karṇavedha* and for the usual shaving of grown up persons (pp. 127-34); proper aspects and proper year for *upanayana* and the proper characteristics of a student's staff, *samāvartana* (pp. 135-47); *vivāha* and favourable positions of the Sun and Jupiter for it, proper age for a girl's marriage from eight to ten, if a girl remains unmarried up to a late age, no astrological requirements to be seen except the Moon's position and the rising sign at the time of marriage, desirable qualities in a bridegroom and in a bride, undesirable qualities in both, undesirable astrological aspects between the horoscopes of the bride and bridegroom such as *ṣaḍaṣṭaka* and *dvirdvādaśa; varṇa* and *vaśya*; astrology based on *nakṣatra*s only such as the *nakṣatra* of birth, 10th, 16th, 18th, 23rd, 25th therefrom; results of the positions of the planets in relation to the sign of birth and the 7th house (*jāmitra*); *godhūli-yoga* as an auspicious time for marriage and in the case of married women; all actions are to be done on astrological aspects derived from the husband's horoscope except in the case of marriage and *garbhādhāna* (pp. 147-72); results of the week-day, *tithi, nakṣatra, lagna* on which a woman has monthly illness for the first time and rites for preventing evil effects (pp. 180-91); *tithi*s and days on which sexual intercourse is to be had or is to be avoided (pp. 192-98); auspicious times for *puṁsavana*, for parting of the pregnant woman's hair, for putting on new clothes, for education in crafts and in *nāṭya*, for the construction of a lotus pool or a well (pp. 192-213); examination of a building site, astrological aspects for the beginning of the construction of a house and the auspicious trees on a site (pp. 213-28); inauspicious happenings when land is being measured for a house, position and number of doors in a house (pp. 228-36); auspicious times for entering the capital for coronation, for an audience of the king, for seeking service and auspicious times for putting the plough in the field, for sowing corn, for gathering in crops, for planting trees and creepers (pp. 237-53); recovery of lost or stolen property and times for taking medicines and examination of the times of rainfall (pp. 256-69); on seeing the *khañjana* bird (p. 270); the auspicious and inauspicious times for marching on an invasion, good and bad dreams, results of several planets being in the same *rāśi* (pp. 271-329); discussion about *tithi*s (pp. 329-31); conclusions about *ekādaśī*, the *tithi*s on which several gods go to sleep and become awake (pp. 330-34); rules about *saṅkrānti, vāhana*s of *saṅkrānti*, bath on *saṅkrānti*; the appropriate *dāna*s on each of the twelve *saṅkrānti*s in a year (pp. 334-47); on eclipses (pp. 347-48); intercalary month (*adhimāsa* or *malamāsa* or *malimluc*); the religious acts allowed and forbidden in an intercalary month (pp. 348-50); the religious rites in the twelve months of the year; Indradhvaja festival, offering *arghya* to Agastya, *śrāddha* when the Sun is in the sign of Virgo; honouring horses in Āśvina bright half and *śānti* connected therewith, *Durgāṣṭamī* and *Mahānavamī*; propitiating Yama, *Goṣṭhāṣṭamī, Bhīṣmāṣṭamī, Ardhodayayoga, Govindadvādaśī, Aśokāṣṭamī*, auspicious times for performing *śāntika* and *pauṣṭika* rites (pp. 350-68).

The original Ms. of this large work appears to be rather incorrect. In some cases there are gaps, i.e., some letters or some parts of verses are missing. The author offers only a few explanations of his own, as on pp. (of the transcript) 23, 26, 118, 172-73, 209, 216, 235, 236, 261, 256-57, 359-60. As there are gaps in the Ms. and it is corrupt some names of authorities may be lost. The Ms. of *Bhujabala* names a number of authorities, viz., Aṅgiras (p. 274), Atri (p. 295), Bhāradvāja (pp. 295-96), Bhṛgu (295-96), Bhṛguja (pp. 311 on Yātrā), Cyavana (p. 295), Cūḍāmaṇi (p. 313, a mutilated verse, which looks like a *Prākṛt* verse),[17] Devala (p. 179), Durgāditya (p. 206, p. 13 where Durgādayaḥ appears to be a copyist's mistake for Durgāditya), Garga (241, 246, 250, 261, 272, 274, 295, 296, 312), Gautama (295), Hārīta (273, 274), Hari (44), Indra (as author of *Yāmala* 287), Parāśara (127, 222, 261, 274), *Ratnasārasamuccaya* (39), Satya (127, 145), Śrīnivāsa (99, 317, 322), Varāha (44, 130, 135, 200, 221, 234, 264, 275), Vasiṣṭha (212, 295), Vātsya (168, 261), Vyāsa (124, 125, 168, 206, 211, 271, 273), *Vyavahārasamuccaya*,[18] an astrological work (173), Yavanādhipati[19] (58). It also refers to other works in the word °*granthāntare* (pp. 115, 165). Among the *Purāṇa*s the *Brahma Purāṇa* (365), *Devī Purāṇa* (337), *Nāradīya* (116) and *Vāmana Purāṇa* (343) have been quoted,[20] but I have not been able to locate all these verses. Two works most frequently quoted are the *Dīpikā* (44, 200, 235, 246, 275, 318, 319, 320, 321, 323) and the *Ratnamālā*[21] (pp. 4, 10-12, 209, 252). Several verses from the *Ratnamālā* (*Jyotiṣaratnamālā*) of Śrīpati are borrowed by the *Bhujabalanibandha* expressly or without acknowledgement. On p. 4 *Bhujabala* quotes the verse *na khalu bahulapakṣe* expressly from the *Ratnamālā* (ch. XI.5). The verses *rājābhiṣeka* (*Bhujabala*, pp. 10-12, verses 48-55) on what should be undertaken on the several week-days are expressly taken from the *Ratnamālā* (III.2-9). The verse on *Vidyārambha vidyārambhaḥ suragurusita* (*Bhujabala*, p. 209) is expressly quoted from *Ratnamālā* (III.19). On p. 252 a verse about the prognostications on the fall of *pallī* (house-lizard) or a chameleon on several parts of the body is expressly quoted from the *Ratnamālā*, but I have not been able to trace it. The verse *manvarka-digvāstu* in *Bhujabala* (p. 14) on *Kulikavelā* is the same as *Ratnamālā* (III.21); *Bhujabala* (p. 37) three verses beginning with *pauṣṭikasthira* on the several *karaṇa*s are the same as *Ratnamālā*, V.4-5 and 12; the verse *kṛtakautukamaṅgalacāruvapuḥ* of *Bhujabala* (pp. 178-79) is the same as *Ratnamālā* (XVI.35). From the *Ratnamālā*[22] are borrowed two verses by *Bhujabala* that provide that a learned astrologer should not break the usages of families and countries by sticking to the words of the (astrological) *śāstra* since those usages have their root in the recensions of the *Veda* that are now lost and since if (those usages are not observed), the fault of violating established religious usages might be incurred and then another verse explains how Gauḍas, Dākṣiṇātyas, Lāṭas (country about modern Surat) and people from Avantī (country of which Ujjayinī was capital) differ in their usages about astrologically favourable positions of planets at the time of marriage.

These verses cited in the preceding sentences are borrowed without acknowledgment. The *Dīpikā* cannot be the *Śuddhidīpikā* of Śrīnivāsa if the date of one of his works, the *Gaṇitacintāmaṇi*, given by MM. Haraprasad Sastri in Vol. III of his Catalogue, Preface, p. vi (AD 1158) be correct. The *Śuddhikaumudī* quotes five verses from *Paśupatidīpikā* (pp. 206, 210-12, 229) and distinguishes it from *Śuddhidīpikā* quoted on the same pages. Several dozen verses have been traced by me as borrowed by *Bhujabala* from Varāhmihira's works without acknowledgment. The verse *Sutamadana* (*Bhujabala*, p. 63) is *Bṛhajjātaka*, VI.11 and the whole chapter XVII of the same work (verses 1-13) is bodily taken over by *Bhujabala* (pp. 64-67) on the characteristics of persons having *Meṣa* and the other *rāśis*; *Bṛhat-saṁhitā*, 103-13 on *Godhūli-muhūrta* is same as *BB*., pp. 177-841. The verse *jyotiṣam āgama-śāstram* (*Bṛhat-saṁhitā* 9.7) is quoted in a somewhat mutilated form on p., 178 of the *Bhujabala*. Seven verses from the *Bṛhat-saṁhitā* (906.12) on the classification of *nakṣatras* into *sthira, cara, tīkṣṇa* are taken up by *Bhujabala* on pp. 26-27. Over twenty verses on dreams are borrowed by *Bhujabala* on pp. 297-304 from *Bṛhad-yogayātrā* of Varāhamihira ch. 16.1-31 (with the omission of some verses). On *Bhujabala*, p. 42 the three verses *Vaiśākha-māsasya* on *Yugādya tithi*s are the same as *Viṣṇu Purāṇa*, III.14.12-14 and on *Bhujabala*, p. 193 the two verses *caturdaśyāṣṭamī* on *parva* days are *Viṣṇu Purāṇa*, III.11.118-19. *Bhujabala*, p. 152 (*kāman āmaraṇāt*) is *Manu*, IX.89 and pp. 153-54 about the auspicious characteristics of a marriageable maiden *avyaṅgāṅgīm* are the same as *Manu*, III.8-10 (but in a different order). *Parāśarasmṛti*, VII.5-8 (*aṣṭavarṣā bhavet, mātā caiva, yastām*) occur in *Bhujabala*, p. 151, and Nārada (*strī-puṁsayoga* verses 36 and 37) are the same as *Bhujabala* (pp. 153-54), *viz.*, *unmattaḥ* and *dīrghaḥ*.

On p. 50 there is a verse which appears to be in Prākrit.[23]

It would involve great labour to identify all the verses that are borrowed from other works. Such a labour would be appropriate only if an edition based on several Mss. is brought out. A few examples where borrowing is probable are mentioned here. On p. 355 the *Bhujabala* sets out four verses on the proper time for *śrāddha* all of which appear to be quotations from earlier *Smṛtis* or *Purāṇas*.[24] The *Śrāddhaviveka* of Rudradhara (Chowkhamba series) quotes[25] a verse from *Bhujabalabhīma* the first half of which is cited from Uśanas by the *Smṛticandrikā* (on *Śrāddha*, p. 492). The *Bhujabala* has taken the verse *kālanarasyāvayavān* (p. 79, verse 368) from the *Sārāvalī* of Kalyāṇavarman (III.6).

From certain verses of the *Bhujabala* it appears that the work was addressed to a queen or a noble lady. ***Vide***, pp. 64, 99 and 100.[26]

Not only does the Ms. of *Bhujabalanibandha* ascribe it to king Bhoja, but medieval digests expressly ascribe the work to Bhojadeva.[27] It has however to be noticed that the work is generally called by these digests *Bhujabalabhīma*. In the *Malamāsatattva* (Jiv. Vol. I, p. 743) it is said *vyaktam bhujabale grahaśuddhim abdaśuddhim . . . kanyakānām*. The *Saṁskāratattva* (p. 912) quotes three verses from *Bhujabala* (and not *Bhujabalabhīma*) which occur in the transcript of *Bhujabala*, pp. 201-22, verses 961, 967, 968 (but in a different order and with some variant readings). On p. 928 of the *Saṁskāratattva* two verses from *Bhujabala* (and not — *balabhīma*) on the topic as to when *upanayana* and other auspicious rites should not be undertaken are cited. I was not able to trace these. It is possible to hold that the *Kālaviveka* of Jīmūtavāhana knew the *Bhujabalanibandha*. It quotes two texts as from Bhojadeva,[28] the first of which is found in *Bhujabala*, p. 346. The *Varṣakriyākaumudī* (p. 104) states that these two verses were quoted by the Kāmadhenu from the *Kūrma Purāṇa*.

In the *Tithitattva*[29] of Raghunandana (Jiv., p. 25) two verses are quoted from Bhojarāja, which are found in *Bhujabalanibandha*. Similarly, on the rites of the sixth day after the birth of a son the *Kṛtyatattva* quotes a passage inclusive of a verse from Bhojarāja, which verse occurs in *Bhujabala*.[30]

We must now turn to the *Rājamārtaṇḍa*. This is a valuable work on astrology in its relation to topics of *Dharmaśāstra*.[31] The *Śuddhikaumudī*, the *Śrāddhakaumudī* and the *Varṣakriyākaumudī* of Govindānanda and some *Tattva*s of Raghunandana quote over two hundred verses from the *Rājamārtaṇḍa*. The first seven verses are introductory. The first verse performs an obeisance to the Sun, who, it is alleged, was the author of an extensive *Jyotiḥśāstra* in three branches and who came down again to the earth in the form of Varāhamihira. The second verse promises that the author would propound what is excellent and clear in the views of former teachers. It is said in the 4th and 6th introductory verses that a family priest, an astronomer, a councillor and an astrologer — these four should always be supported by a king and that long life and prosperity follow where honour is paid to the gods, the astrologer, the family priest, the *guru*s, planets and *nakṣatra*s. In the Ms. I have used there are no chapters, but only the matters dealt with are mentioned in a verse or at the end of the treatment of a topic words like *iti yātrāyām māsaśuddiḥ* are added in reddish yellow pigment. The contents of the work may be briefly stated as follows: the several names of the Sun, Moon, the other planets, Rāhu and Ketu; the several names of the 27 *nakṣatra*s from Aśvinī to Revatī and the lords of the 27 *nakṣatra*s (verses 16-41); names of the twelve *rāśi*s from Meṣa to Mīna and the distribution of the 27 *nakṣatra*s among the twelve *rāśi*s (42-53); lords of the twelve *rāśi*s (54); the horoscope of a married woman's husband alone is to be considered in all actions relating to her except in a few cases such as *garbhādhāna*, when both horoscopes are to be considered, and in the case of a widow her own horoscope is to be considered (55-63); astrological rules about tying up the hair (*bālabandha*) after monthly illness for three days (64-75); astrological rules about proper days for sexual intercourse after monthly illness and the qualities of the child to be born (76-91) and inauspicious *nakṣatra*s and times for the rite of *puṁsavana* (92-124); what is *gaṇḍa* and *gaṇḍānta* and *śānti* rites for obviating evil effects thereof (125-48); about *Ṣaḍvarga* (156-59); *horāphala* (160-72); the physical and mental qualities due to the seven *graha*s from the Sun to Saturn (173-79); when *riṣṭa* (*aśubha*) is averted (180-85); seven kinds of *bala* of the planets and their causing desirable or undesirable results (186-95); *veśi* and its conjunctions (196-201); *vṛddhiśrāddha* to be performed at the time of the several *saṁskāra*s before and after the birth of a son, on *cūḍākaraṇa, upanayana,* marriage, establishment of an image, entering a newly built house (202-13); rules about naming a child (214-20); times and astrological details about *niṣkramaṇa* (carrying of the child out of the house), making it (first taste), a *tāmbūla* and food (221-53); rules and aspects about *cūḍākaraṇa* (254-85); *karṇavedha* (piercing the lobes of the child's ears, verses 286-96); *vidyārambha* (296-303); times, astrological and other rules for *upanayana* and the length and wood of the staff (304-79); astrological rules about the age of the marriage for girls, condemnation of parents and brothers for not getting a girl married before she is 12 years of age; when no astrological matters are to be looked into at the marriage of a girl, usages of countries as to astrology, requirements about favourable position of Jupiter in marriage, auspicious months for marriage, such aspects as *ṣaṭṣaṭkāṣṭaka* and *dvidvādaśa* in the horoscopes of the bride and bridegroom, auspicious *nakṣatra*s and aspects for actual *pāṇigrahaṇa*, rules about *parivedana* (marriage of a younger brother or sister before an elder one), the auspicious *muhūrta* called *godhūlikā*, ten *yogas*, *saptaśalākācakra* consideration of the 7th house (*jāmitra*) in relation to the Moon and other planets, respective strength of the Moon and Tārā, entrance of the newly married girl into the house, the results of journeying when Venus is in front, favourable aspects for putting on new clothes and ornaments (380-652); king's marching out for an invasion, when the time of his birth is known or not known (653-804), classification of *tithi*s into Nandā, Bhadrā, Vijayā, Riktā, Pūrṇā and the *tithi*s that are commended for all actions and the effects of marching on the several *tithi*s, the several *karaṇa*s, the several week-days, *nakṣatra*s, zodiacal signs rising, the planets in the several directions, the *navāṁśa* of the *lagna*, effects of the planets being in the several houses of the king's horoscope, and the eight guardians of the quarters from the east in order, *viz*., Sun, Venus, Mars, Rāhu, Saturn, Moon, Mercury and Jupiter, what is *Lolātiyoga*, consideration of the question in what direction a king should march, results of marching on *Vyatīpātayoga*, or in rains out of season, proper month for marching, procedure of *prasthāna* (654-779); the six *nakṣatra*s, viz., of birth, of 10th, 16th, 20th, 23rd and 25th from birth are respectively called *ādya, karma, sāṅghātika, samudāya, vaināśika* and *mānasa*; in the case of the king there are three more to be considered, viz., *jāti* (caste), *deśa* and the *nakṣatra* on which he was crowned and appropriate rites of *śānti* when these are affected by evil aspects and for-removing the effects of solar and lunar eclipses (780-804); building of a house (*vāstu*), sixteen kinds of houses due to their shape, viz., square, rectangular, round, triangular, etc., effects of planting trees in the several directions round the house, trees and flowering plants that should be or should not be near the house, position of a house on a house site, houses facing certain directions to be avoided, at what times, what positions of a house should be used for what purposes (805-84); removal of inauspicious signs when measuring the site or digging foundations (885-99); astrological aspects at entering a newly built house (900-8); construction and dedication of wells, tanks, temples, monasteries, swimming baths and *caitya*s and auspicious and inauspicious astrological details about them (909-43); times for digging a well, for beginning agricultural operations, for planting trees (944-52); about *ūrdhvamukha* and other *nakṣatras*, when to begin eating new crops recently harvested, on what astrological conjunctions one may begin taking medicine, when to ride a horse or elephant for the first time, about *dhaniṣṭhāpañcaka* (953-1000); the effects of the Moon being eighth from the *lagna* or an evil planet being in the 8th house, evil effects of doing a thing on *viṣṭi* (1001-22); Yogas, unfavourable *lagna*, Nandā and other *tithis* in relation to planets (1023-45); *Amṛtasiddhi, Dagdhayoga, Mṛtyuyoga* and Jupiter in the sign Leo, effects of Jupiter and Venus being in the stage of *bāla, vṛddha* and *sandhyāgata* (1046-77); about the intercalary month and what actions are allowed or forbidden therein (1078-1115); effects of the *pūjā* of the Sun on 7th *tithi* after a fast on 6th and of Śiva on the 8th or 14th, and of Devī on 9th and 13th, rules about the *vedha* of a *tithi* by another (1116-31); three kinds of *tithis*, viz., *kharva, darpa* and *hiṁsra*, rules about the appropriate *tithi* on which a *vrata* is to be performed when on the same day two *tithis* are mixed up (1136-47); rules about *Ekādaśīvrata* (1148-71); *saptamyarkavrata*, the *śayana* (lying down) and *utthāna* of various gods, particularly of Viṣṇu (1173-90); *upākarma, yugādi tithis* (1200-5); procedure of offering *arghya* to Agastya (1206-28); *Śrāvaṇadvādaśī* and *Jayantīvrata* (1229-55); *Haritālikā* (1256-59); on the raising of *Indradhvaja* (1260-92); *Upākarma* of followers of *Sāmaveda* (1293-94) on *śrāddhas* (1295-1326); *Durgotsava* and *nīrājana* (1327-34); *Kaumudī*, Viṣṇu's rising from sleep (1335-38); *Pretacaturdaśī* (1339-45); *Sukharātrī, Bhrātṛdvitīyā, Ākāśadīpa* (1346-57); *Kārtikasnāna* and *Māghasnāna* (1358-68); *Māghasaptamī, Bhīṣmāṣṭamī, Puṣyadvādaśī, Aśokāṣṭamī* (1369-80); *Caitrāvalī, Mahājyaiṣṭhī, Mahāmāghī* and other Full Moon days with the attribute *mahā* and the holy places where each of them has special sanctity (1381-92); *Sāvitrīvrata, Pāṣāṇacaturthī, Araṇyaṣaṣṭhī, Daśaharā* (1394-1405); on *Saṅkrānti* (1406-29); day called *Trahaspṛk* explained, *dinakṣaya*, the four kinds of *māsas* and the actions for which they are appropriate (1430-35); *prāṇa, vikalā, kalā, aṁśa, rāśi, yugas* and similar measures of time (1436-42); *Vakrāticāra* of planets (1443-47);

prognostications from clothes eaten by rats, burnt or torn; signs on the different parts of the body of a male prognosticating his qualities and achievements; the effects when *Meṣa* or one of the other eleven *rāśis* is the *lagna* of a person (1456-62).

The *Rājamārtaṇḍa* does not mention by name any *nibandha* but only ancient writers. The verses therein are numbered from one to one hundred and sometimes the total number is given in hundreds and sometimes not (the figures for 600, 900, 1000, 1100, 1300 and 1400 are wanting).[32] The following are mentioned by name, most of them being writers on astronomy and astrology: Aṅgiras (1448), Atri (775), Bhāguri (134), Bhāradvāja (769), Bhārgava (317), Bhṛgu (691, 769, 878), Bhṛguja (probably the same as Bhārgava, 556), Bṛhaspati (134), Cyavana (775), Garga (59, 362, 370, 560, 1059), Gārgya (769, 1040, 1443), Gautama (59, 61, 775, 1064), Hārīta[33] (59, 106ff, 376, 1057), Maṇittha (729), Māṇḍavya (376, 479, 482, 1443), Manu (56), Parāśara (307, 319, 376, 479, 1443), Raibhya (479), Satya (307, 319, 745), Śaunaka (1064), Vālmīki (370, 1064), Varāhamihira (1, 137), Vasiṣṭha (729, 769), Vātsya (479), Viśālākṣa (129), Viśvāmitra (133), Viṣṇu (130), Vyāsa (370), Yavana (387), Yavanāḥ (255, 275, 457, 1055), Yavanācārya (128), Yavanādhipati (134, 197). It is very probable that the last four names stand for only one another. It appears probable that some Greek of high standing settled in India, learnt Sanskrit and composed a large Sanskrit work on astrology from which Varāhamihra, Utpala and others draw several hundred verses.[34] There is the Besnagar column (Garuḍadhvaja) inscription (of 2nd century BC) which recites that Heliodora, son of Diya (Dion), the Yona (Yavana) ambassador of king Antalikita (Antialkidas) to king Bhāgabhadra in India who had become a Bhāgavata raised that coloumn in honour of Vāsudeva (*JRAS*, 1909, p. 1033, 1087, and *JBBRAS*, vol. 23, 1910, p. 104, *JOR*, XV (1945-46, 135-37).

The *Rājamārtaṇḍa* quotes numerous verses without acknowledgment from several sources. A few examples may be given. *Manu*, III.235 (*trīṇi śrāddhe pavitrāṇi*) is the same as *RM*, 1301 and the two verses *Manu*, III.171-72 occur in *Rājamārtaṇḍa*,

544-45 (on *parivedana*), the verse *punarbhojanam adhvānam RM*, 1323 is *Kūrma Purāṇa*, II.22.6, *RM*, 86 (*caturdaśyāṣṭamī caiva*) is the same as *Viṣṇu Purāṇa*, III.11.118, the two verses of *RM*, 1229-30 are among 4 verses cited by the *Varṣakriyākaumudī*) (p. 320) from the *RM* (but taken from the *Bhaviṣya Purāṇa*). A large number of verses is taken from the *Bṛhat-saṁhitā*, e.g., *Bṛhat-saṁhitā* 98.14 (*nṛpājñayā brāhmaṇa-sammatena*) is the same as *RM* folio 18a verse 279; *RM*, 780-81 (about the names of the *nakṣatra* of birth and the 10th, 16th, 18th, 23rd and 25th from the *janma-nakṣatra*) are taken from Varāhamihira's *Yogayātrā*, IX.1-2. The *Rājamārtaṇḍa* borrows several verses from the *Ratnamālā*. For instance, the verse of *Ratnamālā*, XV.37 (on *prasthāna*) occur in *Rājamārtaṇḍa* (folio 49b verse 776) and also in *Bhujabala*, p. 295 verse 1336. It is somewhat remarkable that the 2nd introductory verse of the *Rājamārtaṇḍa* is the same as the second introductory verse of Utpala's commentary on the *Bṛhajjātaka*.[35] As Utpala wrote his commentary in *śaka* 888 (AD 966) and as he is mentioned by Al-beruni in his work on India composed in AD 1030, it follows that the *Rājamārtaṇḍa* borrows this verse from Utpala, ***vide*** my paper on 'Varāhamihira and Utpala' in *JBBRAS*, Vol. 24-25 New Series, 1948-49, pp. 22-23 and 30-31 for the date of Utpala.

Hundreds of verses are the same in both *Bhujabala* and *Rājamārtaṇḍa*. Considerations of space forbid a detailed examination. A few examples alone are cited here. *RM*, 56 and 48 (*strīṇām sarvakriyārambhe* and *vivāhakāryam*) are *Bhujabala*, p. 180 verses 851-52; four verses in *RM*, 77, 86-88 are *BB*, pp. 192-93 verses 913-16; *RM*, 96, 103-5 are *BB*, 955, 957-59; *RM*, 106-11 (dialogue of Vyāsa and Hārīta) are *BB*, pp. 198-99 verses 943-48; *RM*, 123-25 are *BB*, p. 201 verses 960-62; *RM*, 360-63 are the same as *BB*, 649, 652-53, 684;[36] *RM*, 540, 541, 552, 555, 559 are *BB*, verses 845-46, 842, 840, 143; the five verses and the *mantra* at the end in *gaṇḍa-doṣaśānti* in *RM*, 144-48 are the same as *BB*, p. 57 verses 226-30. Verses quoted as from *Rājamārtaṇḍa* in the medieval digests are found in it and also in *Bhujabala*. For example, the verse *yātrām vivāham* which is cited in the

Śuddhikaumudī (p. 222) from the *Rājamārtaṇḍa* is found in the latter (folio 67a, verse 1058) and also in *Bhujabala* (p. 274 verse 236). The verse *vāpīkūpataḍāga-yāgagamanam* cited in the *Śuddhikaumudī* (p. 223) from the *Bhīmaparākrama* occurs in the *Bhujabala*, p. 271 (verse 222) except that the last quarter is slightly different. Verses 143-44, 150 of *Bhujabala* are interesting. They[37] inculcate that the astrologer should not be a hide-bound pedant, but must observe the customs and usages of various countries and families even though they may be opposed to the dicta of *śāstra*. The *Rājamārtaṇḍa* also contains these verses. Both works refer to usages of several countries about the astrological requirements in the case of marriages.

So late a work as the *Kālatattvavivecana* of Raghunātha (AD 1620) refers to the *tithi*s on which several deities lie down for sleep according to Bhojadeva. Both the *Rājamārtaṇḍa* (folio 72a verse 1175) and the *Bhujabala* (p. 333 verse 1532) present the same verse on this matter.[38] It is remarkable that two verses on the *karaṇa* called *viṣṭi*[39] which are quoted by the *Bhujabala* from the *Bhīmaparākrama* occur in *Rājamārtaṇḍa* (verses 1021-22).

In a few cases exactly opposite views appear to have been taken by *Bhujabala* and the Ms. of *Rājamārtaṇḍa*. The latter states in verse 307, 'Satya,[40] Parāśara and other sages lay down that proper of auspicious years to be calculated in the case of *upanayana* and marriage are to be calculated from conception, while others say that they are to be calculated from birth, but *Bhujabala* attributes to Satya, Parāśara and *guru*s the view that the years are to be calculated from birth and to others from conception. Various explanations are possible to account for this conflict, viz., the copyists are at fault or the author changed his mind or that the compilers of the two works commissioned by king Bhoja were different. To me the third alternative appears more probable.

Sometimes there is contradiction between the quotation from *Rājamārtaṇḍa* in a digest and the Ms. of the *Rājamārtaṇḍa*. For example, *Varṣakriyākaumudī*, p. 116 quotes from *Rājamārtaṇḍa* the prescription that for obviating the effects of undesirable *nāḍī*s one should give to a young brāhmaṇa in order cow's milk, a cake of flour with jaggery, *ghī*, curds, honey or *pāyasa* (rice grains cooked in milk), while the Ms. of *Rājamārtaṇḍa* provides that the things mentioned above should be given to an **old** brāhmaṇa.[41]

Though both in the *Bhujabala* and in the *Rājamārtaṇḍa* many of the topics dealt with are common yet there is some difference of treatment in the two works. The *Bhujabala* is a little larger than the *Rājamārtaṇḍa* and is almost exclusively concerned with purely astrological matter. The *Bhujabala* devotes verses 450-529 to *daśā*s and *antardaśā*s but in the *Rājamārtaṇḍa* there is nothing corresponding to this topic. On the other hand the *Bhujabala* devotes only nine verses (1521-29) to the subject of intercalary month, while the *Rājamārtaṇḍa* devotes 38 verses to it (four verses being the same in both); the *Bhujabala* devotes verses 1502-14 to a dissertation on *tithi*s in general, while *Rājamārtaṇḍa* has 32 verses on that topic (1116-47); the subject of offering *arghya* to Agastya takes up 23 verses in the *Rājamārtaṇḍa* (1206-28), while *Bhujabala* devotes only one verse to that subject; the treatment of *gaṇḍadoṣa*s is more elaborate in *Rājamārtaṇḍa* (verses 92-148) as compared with that in the *Bhujabala* (215-51).

It is somewhat remarkable that in some cases the verses quotes from the *Rājamārtaṇḍa* in such digests as the *Varṣakriyākaumudī* and *Śuddhikaumudī* are not all found in the Ms. of *Rājamārtaṇḍa*. For example, the *Varṣakriyākaumudī* quotes (on p. 320) 4 verses from the *Rājamārtaṇḍa* and adds that they were taken from the *Bhaviṣya Purāṇa*, but in the Ms. of *Rājamārtaṇḍa* only two of them occur (1229-30). On pp. 341-42 the *Varṣakriyākaumudī* quotes 14 verses on the procedure of offering *arghya* to Agastya from *Rājamārtaṇḍa*. Only eight are common to both. Out of five verses quoted by the *Śuddhikaumudī* (p. 198) from the *Rājamārtaṇḍa* only three occur in my Ms. of the latter (viz, verses 617, 618, 607). Similarly, out of three verses cited by the *Śuddhikaumudī*[42] (p. 204) from the *Rājamārtaṇḍa* only one (verse 401) occurs in the Ms. of the latter work and the other two are found in *Bhujabala*.

This state of things leads one to infer that either the Ms. used by me is defective and the digests referred to above had better Mss. before them or that the *Rājamārtaṇḍa* was revised and enlarged after it was first composed. In this connection it is pertinent to note that some *Tattva*s of Raghunandana several times mention or quote from a work called *Bṛhad-rājamārtaṇḍa* and in some of these the quotation from the *Bṛhad-rājamārtaṇḍa* is immediately followed by a quotation from the *Rājamārtaṇḍa*. A few examples may be cited. On p. 25 of the *Tithitattva* (Jiv. Vol. 1) there is mention of the view of the *Bṛhad-rājamārtaṇḍa* and a little lower down two verses of Bhojarāja (which occur in *Bhujabala*, p. 129 verse 600 and p. 132 verse 615) are quoted and immediately afterwards two verses (63 and 277) of *Rājamārtaṇḍa* are cited. The *Jyotiṣtattva*[43] (Jiv. I, p. 605), after quoting from the *Bhujabalabhīma* a verse that in the case of maidens the sages declare that the proper (or auspicious) character of planets, the year, *ayana*, season, month and day are to be considered (only) till they become ten years old, and a verse from *Kṛtyacintāmaṇi*, quotes a verse from the *Bṛhad-rājamārtaṇḍa* to the effect that all auspicious acts except marriage, *upanayana* and *yātrā* (king's starting on an invasion) may be done even when Venus is invisible. On p. 655 of the *Jyotiṣtattva* some verses on *karṇavedha* are quoted from *Māṇḍavya, Bṛhad-rājamārtaṇḍa* and *Kṛtyacinitāmaṇi* and then immediately afterwards a verse on the subject of the inausipicious times for *karṇavedha* is cited from *Rājamārtaṇḍa*.[44] The *Malamāsatattva* (Jiv. I, p. 745) cites a verse from the *Bṛhad-rājamārtaṇḍa* to the effect that if a woman undergoes no ceremony of *sīmantonnayana* and gives birth to a son, then after placing the child on her lap that ceremony should be performed on her. In *Saṁskāratattva* (913) the verse quoted from the *Bṛhad-rājamārtaṇḍa* in the *Malamāsatattva*, p. 745 and two more are cited from the latter work on *sīmantonnayana*. These verses cannot be traced in the *Rājamārtaṇḍa* nor in the *Bhujabala*. On p. 826 (Jiv., Vol. 1) the *Malamāsatattva* quotes a verse from *Bṛhad-rājamārtaṇḍa* about the retrograde motion of Mars and other planets.[45] The *Bṛhad-rājamārtaṇḍa* is also quoted in *Tithitattva*, p. 166, in *Malamāsatattva*, p. 824 (two verses), 845 (same as in *Tithitattva*, p. 166) and *Saṁskāratattva*, p. 913 (3 verses, one of which is the same as the one quoted by *Malamāsatattva* on p. 745).

It appears to me from the preceding discussion that the *Rājamārtaṇḍa* and the *Bṛhad-rājamārtaṇḍa* are distinct works, but the former has been far more popular than the latter.

A few words must be said about the *Vyavahārasamuccaya*. There is a Ms. in the Bombay University's Mss. collection called *Vyavahārasamuccaya* described in Prof. Devasthali's Cat. of Sanskrit and Prākrit Mss. in the Bombay University Library (p. 190 No. 457). The verse cited above (in note 18) as quoted from the *Vyavahārasamuccaya* was found by me in that Ms. on folio 18b (verse 192). The work contains only 677 verses, i.e., it is less than half of the extent of the *Bhujabala* or *Rājamārtaṇḍa*. In the colophon at the end the work is styled *Jyotiḥśāstra* and is said to have been composed by Upādhyāya Musthara. This colophon creates a problem. Musthara is a strange name and seems to be corrupt. We have the evidence of the *Malamāsatattva* (p. 831) which quotes a verse[46] from *Bhojadeva-Vyavahārasamuccaya* that Bhoja wrote a *Vyavahārasamuccaya*.[47] A few quotations from the *Vyavahārasamuccaya* are noted later on. Even on a cursory examination it turned out that dozens of verses therein are identical with verses from *Bhujabala* and *Rājamārtaṇḍa*.[48] On folio 8a there is verse 84 (*gauryāḥ putro . . . ṣaṣṭhike namaḥ*) which is the same as *Bhujabala*, p. 121 verse 557. Four verses of *Rājamārtaṇḍa* (1389-92) about the special merit accruing to bathers at different tīrthas on Mahāmāghī and other Paurṇimās occur in the *Vyavahārasamuccaya* on folio 49b. A characteristic verse on *yātrā* occurs in both *Vyavahārasamuccaya* folio 60b and *Bhujabala*. A verse (*vāpīkūpataḍāgayāgagamanam. . . astam gate bhārgave*) of the *Vyavahārasamuccaya* (folio 4a, verse 37) is quoted with a slight variation in the 4th *pada* by the *Śuddhikaumudī* (p. 223) from the *Bhīmaparākrama*. The *Nirṇaya-sindhu* (I, p. 23) quotes two verses from *Vyavahārasamuccaya*[49] on the *karaṇa* called *viṣṭi* or *bhadrā*. The same work quotes a verse which sets out the ten *doṣas* of a *muhūrta* enumerated in *Vyavahārōccaya*.[50]

We know from the *Mitākṣarā* (on *Yāj*., III.17) that Dhāreśvara was styled *ācārya* and was spoken of as *sūri* by the *Smṛticandrikā* (on *śrāddha*, p. 257, Gharpure's edn.). If the *Vyavahārasamuccaya* was compiled by some scholar at the bidding of Bhoja the work could have been ascribed to him. It is possible that Musthara is a corruption of *Camūsthira* formed on the analogy of Yudhiṣṭhira as an epithet of Bhoja and that some scribe called him Upādhyāya. I am of the opinion that there is weighty evidence for holding that the *Vyavahārasamuccaya* quoted in the *Bhujabala* is a work of Bhoja (or one compiled under his patronage). The following is a list of striking verses from the Ms. of *Vyavahārasamuccaya*, that occur in the *Bhujabala* or *Rājamārtaṇḍa* or both. Some abbreviations are used here in this list, viz., *BP* for *Bhīmaparākrama*, *BB* for *Bhujabala*, *RM* for *Rājamārtaṇḍa*, *VS* for *Vyavahārasamuccaya* and v. for verse or verses.

1. *VS* folio 1, v. 2 and 3, *śaśāṇkatārayoḥ* and *janmatriṣaṣṭha* are same in *BB*, p. 1, v. 3 and 6.
2. *VS*, v. 52, folio 5b *kṛtvāticāram* is *BB*, p. 273 v. 1234, while the *Śuddhikaumudī*, p. 229 quotes it from *BP*.
3. *VS* folio 5b, v. 58 *svaśuddhyā yoṣitām karma* is *RM* folio 4b, v. 59.
4. *VS* folio 8a, v. 85 *tṛtīye śaśinaḥ pakṣe'* is *BB*, p. 121, v. 559.
5. *VS* folio 8b, v. 93-95 *sārdhamāsadvaye, dinakaracandra*, and *duścikya-lābhāri* are *BB*, p. 124 v. 574-76 and *RM* folio 14b, v. 230, 234.
6. *VS* folio 11b, v. 122 *na janmamāse* is *BB*, p. 135, v. 623.
7. *VS* folio 12b, v. 132 *abde viśuddhe* is *RM* folio 24a, v. 376.
8. *VS* folio 13a, v. 137 *saptamī cāṣṭamīviddhā* is *BB*, p. 139, v

652 and *RM* folio 23a, v. 363. Both read *aṣṭamī saptamīviddhā*.

9. *VS* folio 13b, v. 144 *grahe ravīndvoḥ* is *BB*, p. 145, v. 680.
10. *VS* folio 14a, v. 147, *pauṣādi caturo* is *RM* folio, 23b, v. 368.
11. *VS* folio 21a, v. 226, *godhūlīm trividhām* is *BB*, p. 176, v. 840 and *RM* folio 35a, v. 555.
12. *VS* folio, 43b *yugmāgnikṛta* and *pratipadyapy-amāvāsya'* are same as *RM* folio 69b verses 1123-24 and *BB*, p. 329, v. 1502-3.
13. *VS* folio 43b, *ekādaśyāṣṭamī* and *kharvo darpastathā* are *BB*, p. 330, v. 1504 and 1510 and *RM*, folio 69b and 70a, v. 1121 and 1132.
14. *VS* folio 44a *suklapakṣe tithir* is *RM* folio 70b, v. 1136 and *BB*, p. 331, v. 1511.
15. *VS* folio 45b *mandā mandākinī* is *BB*, folio 335, v. 1544.
16. *VS* folio 51a *simhaḥ prasenam avadhīt* (This is to be recited as a *mantra* if one happens to see the Moon on Bhādrapada-śukla 4 to avoid a false charge of theft). *BB*, p. 353 prescribes the same verse. It occurs in the story of the fight of Kṛṣṇa with Jāmbavān. *Vide Brahma Purāṇa*, 16.36, *Vāyu* 96.42.[51]
17. *VS* folio 51b-53b has 30 verses on *Agastyārghyadāna* out of which several occur in *RM* such as *aprāpte bhāskare*, *dvijo yathālābham* (folio 73a v. 1213, 1221-22, 1226).
18. *VS* volio 50b and 51a *ehyehi sarvāmara*, *vajrahasta* are the same as *RM* folio 77a, v. 1289-90 (*mantras* at the end of Indradhvaja festival).

The state of affairs described at length in the preceding pages is somewhat bewildering. It is clear, however, that the *Bhīmaparākrama* and the *Vyavahārasamuccaya* were both composed before the *Bhujabala*, since both are quoted in the *Bhujabala*. It appears to me that the *Rājamārtaṇḍa* was composed after *Bhujabala*, since the former deals far more elaborately with certain subjects than the latter. Similarly, the *Bṛhad-rājamārtaṇḍa* is later than the *Rājamārtaṇḍa*. The important question is why five distinct works (*Bhīmaparākrama, Vyavahārasamuccaya, Bhujabala, Rājamārtaṇḍa* and *Bṛhad-rājamārtaṇḍa*), very often covering the same topics were given to the world, if the author was king Bhoja himself. It is difficult to give a categorical reply to this question. One has to remember that distinguished authors often write two sets of books on the same subject. The name of Varāhamihira who preceded Bhoja by at least five centuries at once leaps up to one's mind. Varāhamihira[52] composed his famous major work, the *Bṛhat-saṁhitā* and also a shorter work called *Samāsa-saṁhitā* or *Svalpa-saṁhitā, Vivāhapaṭala* and *Bṛhad-vivāhapaṭala, Yogayātrā* and *Bṛhad-yogayātrā*. In these double sets of works, the same ideas, rules and principles are couched in different words though here and there the same verses occur in the different works. But here we have at least five works ascribed to Bhoja in which many topics are the same and hundreds of verses are common. It appears to me probable that Bhoja held discussions with his *paṇḍit*s on matters of astrology and its bearing on *Dharmaśāstra*, commissioned several of them to compose in their own way several works, the *paṇḍit*s took their own time to write the works and they were made public at different times, but as the inspiration to write them came from Bhoja, their great patron, they were ascribed to him. This hypothesis would explain all the known facts, particularly the large number of works composed on the same subjects by apparently the same author, the occurrence of hundreds of common verses in *Bhujabala* and *Rājamārtaṇḍa* and the circumstance that *Bhujabala* quotes the *Bhīmaparākrama* and *Vyavahārasamuccaya*.

A word may be said about the titles *Bhujabala* (or *Bhujabalabhīma*) and *Bhīmaparākrama*. They were *biruda*s applied to or assumed by Bhoja, the first meaning 'whose strength is in his arms' or 'who was a veritab'e Bhīma in the prowess of his arms' and the second meaning 'whose valour was terrific' or 'whose valour was like that of Bhīma, the Pāṇḍava hero'. Further, it is not surprising if some later copyist wrote *upādhyāya camūsthira*'. It should be noted that the *Mitākṣarā* on *Yājñavalkya*, III.24 speaks of Dhāreśvarācārya. For high-sounding names of royal or high placed authors, ***vide*** *History of Dharmaśāstra*, Vol. I, p. 407 note 993 (for Dalapati), p. 411 note 1004 (Pratāparudra), p. 445 note 1114 for Vīrasiṁha, patron of Mitramiśra.

But we have not yet done with Bhoja and his works on *Dharmaśāstra* and astrology. It appears from quotations in the *Kṛtyaratnākara* and other works that he composed a work variously called *Bhūpālasamuccaya* or *Bhūpālakṛtyasamuccaya* or briefly *Kṛtyasamuccaya* on *vrata*s, *dāna*s, etc. On p. 313 the *Kṛtyaratnākara* tells us that a certain *vrata* was called *Navamīvrata* by *Bhūpālakṛtyasamuccaya* and on p. 496 the same work states that what *Bhūpālakṛtyasamuccaya* called *Tiladvādaśī* was described by the *Kalpataru* and *Pārijāta* not under *vrata*s but under *Naiyatakālika* (i.e., matters which it was one's duty to perform at certain fixed times). After quoting two verses about the importance of *upavāsa* and *nakta* the *Kṛtyaratnākara* (p. 58)[53] states that the *Pārijāta* held the view that the verse enjoins the observance of *nakta* and the first three *pāda*s of it are in the nature of an *anuvāda* and explains away the view of Bhojabhūpāla. On p. 205 the *Kṛtyaratnākara* says that the *Bhūpālasamuccaya* states that Viṣṇu is to be raised from his couch on *Kārtika-śukla-ekādaśī*, which leads on to the proper conclusion that Viṣṇu goes to sleep on *Āṣāḍha-śukla-ekādaśī*. In several other places the *Kṛtyaratnākara* speaks of *Kṛtyasamuccaya* only (on pp. 289, 449, 512, 515, 536). But it is clear from the way in which the *Kṛtyaratnākara* deals with the names *Bhūpālasamuccaya* and *Kṛtyasamuccaya* that reference is to a *Bhūpālakṛtyasamuccaya*. The *Kṛtyaratnākara* (p. 171) refers to the view of Bhūpāla on the procedure of the gift of a black antelope skin from *Matsya Purāṇa* (ch. 206). On p. 175 the *Kṛtyaratnākara* mentions Bhūpāla in the same breath with

Kalpataru. The *Kṛtyaratnākara* (p. 635)[54] quotes an interesting verse and remarks on the view of Bhūpāla thereon. In the *Samayapradīpa* of Śrīdatta which is a work earlier than the *Kṛtya-ratnākara* the views of Bhoja-bhūpāla are mentioned. For example, on folio 8b it first refers[55] to the interpretation of texts relied upon by Gauḍas as regards decision when *tithi*s are mixed up (*viddhā*), it refers to the views of Bhūpāla. On the materials so far available the reference must be held to be to the *Bhūpāla-kṛtyasamuccaya*. Even a somewhat late work like the *Nirṇayasindhu* (composed in AD 1612) mentions the view of *Bhūpāla*[56] on the question of the avoidance of certain vegetables, fruits, corn, salt, oil, shaving and sexual intercourse on certain *tithi*s from the first to the 15th.

There is another work called *Vidvajjanavallabha*[57] ascribed to king Bhoja dealing with astrological matters; ***vide*** *Descriptive Catalogue of Mss.*, Tanjore, Vol. XVI, No. 11604 (for two Mss. of it in 18 chapters such as *lābha, śatrusamāgama, yātrāphala*, etc.); there is also a fragment of it in the Bikaner Library (***vide*** Mitra's Catalogue No. 753) and another fragment in Florence. I have not been able to secure the Mss. of this work or a transcript. This paper has already become rather long. The *Vidvajjanavallabha* may be dealt with in a separate paper later on.

In conclusion I express the hope that critical editions of the *Ratnamālā* (about first half of 11th century AD) and of the *Rājamārtaṇḍa* so profusely quoted in medieval *Dharmaśāstra* works would be undertaken by some young scholars in the near future. There are two good Mss. of the *Ratnamālā* in the *BBRAS* and one Ms. with the commentary of Mahādeva composed in *śaka* 1185 (i.e., AD 1263) in Bombay University Library and several Mss. in the Bhandarkar Oriental Institute, Poona. Of the *Rājamārtaṇḍa* also there are many Mss. These two are amongst the earliest extant *nibandhas* on such topics of *Dharmaśāstra* as *saṁskāra*s, intercalary month, *tithi*s, *vrata*s and *utsava*s of various kinds.

References

[This paper was first published in *JOR*, XXIII (pp. 94-127), Madras, 1953-54. Dr. Kane in his *History of Dharmaśāstra*, Vol. I/II, p. 588 makes a passing reference to the present paper. This paper is a welcome addition to our fund of knowledge and has not received its proper place in other volumes of *History of Dharmaśāstra*.] **S.G. Moghe**

1. ***Vide*** Intoruction (pp. xv-xvii) to the *Saraśvatīkaṇṭhābharaṇa* by Dr. T.R. Chintamani (Madras University Sanskrit Series No. 11, 1937) and Dr. V. Raghavan, Bhoja's *Śṛṅgāraprakāśa*, Vol. I., p. 5, fn. 2, for a long list of works ascribed to Bhoja.
2. In the Commentary on *Yogasūtra* he mentions (4th verse in Introduction) that he composed a work on Grammar, a commentary on Patañjali's *Yogasūtra* and a work on medicine called *Rājamṛgāṅka*.
3. The Ms. of the commentary is D.C. No. 84 of 1869-70 and I have gone over the whole of it carefully. The important remark is on folio 63b 'अयं च सार्धश्लोको भोजदेवेन व्यवहारमञ्जर्यामन्यथा व्याख्यातः' and on the very next page (folio 64a) the com. says: 'अयं च पक्षो बहुभिधरिश्वरादिभिरपि निबन्ध-कैरनुमत इति यथेष्टं व्यवहर्तव्यमिति।' The verse यत्र श्यामो लोहिताक्षः occurs in several works such as *Manu*, VII.25, *Matsya Purāṇa*, 225.8, and *Viṣṇu Dharmasūtra*, V.95.
4. ***Vide*** Dr. Derret's remarks on this passage in the *Bulletin of the School of Oriental and African Studies*, Vol. 15, pp. 598-602.
5. Dr. Raghavan has drawn attention to the fact that, according to Ājada, commentator on Bhoja's *Sarasvatīkaṇṭhābharaṇa*, each of the 84 works of Bhoja was called after one of the titles or *birudas* of Bhoja, ***Vide*** Bhoja's *Śṛṅgāraprakāśa*, I. p. 5, fn. 2.
6. There is only a single Ms. of the *Bhujabalanibandha* so far known, viz., the one described in the Triennial Catalogue of Madras Government Mss. Library, 1919-22, p. 4562, No. 3079. As the original Ms. could not be secured for study a transcript of it was made for the Bhandarkar Oriental Institute, which I have used in this paper. The references are to the pages of the transcript in the B.O.R.I. The original Ms. does not count the verses, which I have counted and it is possible that I may have committed a mistake here and there in counting.
7. भुजबल०, p. 10.

   (a) भीमराक्रमः—

   भृगुजीवेन्दुजेन्दूनां वाराः सर्वत्र सिद्धिदाः।
   सूर्यसौरवारास्तु शस्ताः स्वोक्तेषु कर्मसु।।

तथा—

कुसुम्भलाक्षारसरागक्लृप्तो मञ्जिष्ठरागेषु रविः प्रशस्तः।
भौमस्तु चामीकरभूषेणेषु सौरिस्तु कालायसकर्मणीषु (? कर्मसु स्यात्)।।
आर means Mars and सौरि is Saturn.

(b) भुजबल०, p. 38. भीमपराक्रमे —
पूर्वस्यां दिशि शूलिनी समुदिता विष्टिश्चतुर्थ्यां तथा-
प्यष्टम्यां विकटा युता शनिदिशि (? हुताशनदिशि) स्यादर्थनाशंकरौ।

याम्यायामथ भानवी समुदिता नूनं तथैकादशी
नैर्ऋत्यां च करालघोरवदना सा भुज्यते (? भूतेश्वरी) पौर्णिमा।।

वारुण्यां च सुदारुणा प्रकथिता कृष्णे तृतीया पुनः
सप्तम्यां वरखड्गपाणिविभवा वायव्यतो दृश्यते।

कौबेर्यां दिशि सुघोरवदना (? कौबेर्यां दशमीषु घोरवदना) यातोदये सर्वदा
चैशान्यां यमदूतिका प्रकथिता प्राप्ता तिथिं भूतिजाम्।।

(c) भुजबल०, p. 194. भीमपराक्रमे —
पित्र्यं पौष्णं नैर्ऋतं चापि धिष्ण्यं
त्यक्त्वा नारीं सुप्रसन्नः प्रसन्नाम्।
पृष्ठे या मां (? क्षामां) पुत्रकामो हि गच्छेत्
सल्लक्षण्यं पुत्रमाप्नोति पुण्यम्।।

8. उपोष्यैव च संक्रान्त्यां स्नात्वा योऽभ्यर्चयेद्रविम्।
स्नातः पञ्चोपचारेण स कामफलमाप्नुयात्।। इति

— भीमपराक्रमैकवाक्यतया etc. एकादशीतत्त्व (p. 6). वर्षक्रियाकौमुदी (p. 215) quotes this verse from भविष्यपुराण (with slight variations). It should be noted that the कालविवेक of जीमूतवाहन (pp. 388-89) quotes this verse as occurring in a work called समुच्चय. This appears to be भूपालकृत्यसमुच्चय (for which see towards the end of this paper). The readings in कालविवेक are योऽर्चयते रविम्। प्रातः for स्नातः and काम्यं फलम्।

9. महातिचारे वर्षपर्यन्तं कर्मलोपमाह भीमपराक्रमे —
'कृत्वातिचारं यदि पूर्वगेहं
न याति मन्त्री विबुधाधिपानाम्।
यानं विवाहं व्रतचौडगेहं
वर्षं तदा हन्ति मतं मुनीनाम्।।'

— शुद्धिकौ०, p. 229. This is the same as भुजबल, p. 273 verse 1234. (Reads पूर्वराशिं for पूर्वगेहं and यात्राविवाहं व्रतबन्धतोयं सर्वम्।

10. अर्धरात्रे व्यतीते तु संक्रान्तिर्यदहर्भवेत्।
पूर्वे व्रतादिकं कुर्यात् परेद्युः स्नानदानयोः।।
इति भीमपराक्रमीयम्। — तिथितत्त्व, p. 150.

11. भीमपराक्रमे —
वापीकूपतटाकादि निषिद्धं सिंहगे गुरौ।
मकरस्थे ततः कार्यं न दोषः काललोपतः।।
कार्यं मकरगे जीवे विवाहाद्यखिलं बुधैः।
न तु सिंहगते जीवे कुर्याद्विप्रः कथञ्चन।।

— मलमासतत्त्व, p. 828. These two occur in the भुजबल, p. 274 verses 1237-38 (except that it reads जीवे कुतो मृत्युमवाप्नुयात्।)

12. मलवासतत्त्व, p. 788. अथाधिमासे विवाहादिनिषेधः। भीमपराक्रमे — अधिमासे विवाहयात्रां चूडां तथोपनयनादि कुर्यान्न सावकाशं माङ्गल्यं न तु विशेषेत्याह।

13. एषामृतूनां देवताः भीमपराक्रमात् — मरुतोऽग्निास्त्रिदशपतिर्विश्वेदेवाः प्रजापतिः सौम्यः। इति शिशिरप्रभृतीनां क्रमादृतूनां स्मृताः पतयः।। Folio 7b of Mahādeva's commentary on रत्नमाला (Ms. Bs. 185 in the Bombay University Mss. collection).

14. तथा च भीमपराक्रमे — स्वामिना नीयमानायाः प्रतिशुक्रो न विद्यते। मार्तण्डवल्लभ Folio 137b (In Prof. Velankar's Cat. of BBRAS. Mss. p. 106, No. 321). The *Rajamārtaṇḍa* (Folio 40b verse 635) has the verse एकग्रामे चतुःशाले दुर्भिक्षे राजविप्लवे। स्वामिना नीयमानायाः प्रतिशुक्रो न विद्यते।। and the भुजबल (p. 182 verse 862) reads राष्ट्रविप्लवे and पत्यानीय . . . पुरः शुक्रो न दुष्यति।

15. भीमपराक्रमे —
वापीकूपतटाकादि निषिद्धं सिंहगे गुरौ।
मकरस्थे तु तत्कार्यं न दोषः काललोपतः।।
कार्यं मकरगे जीवे विवाहाद्याखिलं बुधैः।
न तु सिंहगते जीवे कुर्वाणो मृत्युमाप्नुयात्।।

— ज्योतिस्तत्त्व p. 584; these occur in भुजबल, p. 275 verses 1237-38 (the last reads जीवे कुतो मृत्युमवाप्नुयात्); षडष्टकादौ तारानियममाह भीमपराक्रमः — सौहृद्ये ह्युभयोर्द्वयोरपि तयो . . . कार्यो विवाहस्सदा। This is भुजबल, p. 160 verse 766; भीमपराक्रमे भोजराजः — स्वामिहस्तप्रमाणेन धर्मपत्नीकरेण वा। मापयेद्गर्भमात्रं तु गृहकर्माणि कोविदः। ज्योतिस्तत्त्व, p. 663; compare राजमार्तण्ड folio 53b verse 884 स्वामि . . . ज्येष्ठपत्नीकरेण च। गर्भमात्रं भवेद् गेहं नृणां प्रोक्तं पुरातनैः।।

16. The colophon at the end of the first chapter is 'इति श्रीभोजराजकृतौ भुजबलनाम्नि ज्योतिःशास्त्रे रिष्टाध्यायः प्रथमः समाप्तः'; the colophon at the end of the work is इति श्रीभोजराजकृतौ भुजबलनिबन्धे ज्योतिश्शास्त्रे द्वादशमासकृत्यं समाप्तम्। समाप्तोऽयं ग्रन्थः।।

17. A writer called Cūḍāmaṇi is mentioned by the *Sārāvalī* on *āyurdāya* (ch. 39.8).

18. The verse quoted by the *Bhujabala* (p. 173 verse 825) from the *Vyavahārasamuccaya* is :

उदयास्ताधिपदृष्टो लग्ने यो व्यापको भवेदंशः।

तैलस्याम्भसि बिन्दुस्तरङ्गनिवहैर्यथा कीर्णः।।
— व्यवहारसमुच्चय folio 18b, verse 192.

19. क्षीणे शशिनि विलग्ने पापैः केन्द्रेषु मृत्युसंस्थैर्वा।
भवति विपत्तिरवश्यं यवनाधिपतेर्मतं चैतत्।।

— भुजबल, p. 58 verse 271. In a verse quoted from भीमपराक्रम by the शुद्धिकौमुदी, p. 218 the view of the Yavanas appears as follows:

'वक्रातिचारोपगतः सुरेज्यो यद्यन्यराशौ परिवर्जनीयः।
यथाक्रमस्थः स्वगृहस्थितो वा न वर्जनीयो यवना वदन्ति।।'

20. भुजबल (p. 365) ब्रह्मपुराणे —
माघमासे कृष्णपक्षे मकरस्थे दिवाकरे।
अमावास्याव्यपीपाते श्रवणर्क्षेऽर्कवासरे।।
अर्धोदया यामावास्या महापातकनाशिनी।;

भुजबल (p. 337) देवीपुराणे —
पूर्वाह्णे पीड्यते राजा मध्याह्ने च द्विजोत्तमाः।
अपराह्णे तथा वैश्याः शूद्राश्चास्तमिते रवौ।।
पिशाचाश्च प्रदोषे च रात्र्यर्धे राक्षसास्तथा।
अर्धरात्रे व्यतीते तु पीड्यन्ते नटनर्तकाः।।

भुजबल (p. 343) वामनपुराणे —
नन्दासु नाभ्यङ्गमुपाचरेत क्षौरं च रिक्तासु जयासु मांसम्।
पूर्णासु योषित्परिवर्जनीया भद्रासु सर्वाणि समाचरेच्च।। This is *Vāmana Purāṇa*, 14.48-49.; भुजबल (p. 116) नारदीये। (the verse is corrupt)

संक्रान्तेग्रहनक्षत्रं वा . . . न्युभयपार्श्वयोः।
नेष्ठशूलं षष्ठशुभं पर्यायाच्च पुनः पुनः।।

I set out the verses in full here in the hope that some scholars would be able to trace these.

21. The Ms. of the *Ratnamālā* in the Bhau Daji collection of the *BBRAS* 311 has been used in this paper. It has 20 chapters and 490 verses in all. It mentions that the author studied the works of Garga, Varāha and Lalla. There are sometimes slight variations in the readings of the Ms. of *Ratnamālā* and those in the *Bhujabala*. But they are not important and are often due to the mistakes of copyists. The work was composed in the first half of the 11th century, since in the *Dhīkoṭidakaraṇa* he takes *śaka* 961 (AD 1039) as the *ārambha-varṣa*. ***Vide*** S.B. Dikshit's *Bhāratīya Jyotiḥ-śāstra* (2nd edn.) p. 237.

22. The रत्नमाला verses (XVI. 30 and 32) are :
न शास्त्रदृष्ट्या विदुषा कदाचिदुल्लङ्घनीयाः कुलदेशधर्माः।
मूलं हि तेषां च्युतवेदशाखा भूयान्न धर्मस्थितिभङ्गदोषः।।
गौडाः सूर्यागोचरे न प्रमाणं वाञ्छन्त्यार्या दाक्षिणात्या विवाहे।

लाटाः प्रायो स्थानवीर्याश्रिताः स्युरावन्त्यानां गोचरे न प्रमाणम्।।

These are भुजबल, pp. 35-36, verses 147-49 and somewhat corrupt therein; the last quarter of the first has "भृङ्गात् स्थितिधर्मदोषात्" and in the second the variations are गोचरेण प्रशस्तं, तद्वद्वर्ज्यं दाक्षिणात्याः. For the view of authoritativeness of usages of countries and families, *vide History of Dharmaśāstra*, Vol. III, pp. 843-44 and pp. 879-81.

23. यत्र दण्डे गण्ड पावई गण्डवषे(वर्षे?) तासु गुणज्जइ।
गण्डवर्षे दण्डहरिआण अट्ठमासदिनदण्ड जाण।।

— भुजबल, p. 50, verse 223 on गण्डदोष.

24. सूर्ये कन्यागते श्राद्धं यो न कुर्याद् गृहाश्रमी।
धनं पुत्राः कुतस्तस्य पितृनिःश्वासतृष्णया।
कन्यागते सवितरि पितरो यानि सुतालयम् (यान्ति वै सुतान्?)।।

तावत्प्रेतपुरी शून्या यावद् वृश्चिकदर्शनम्।
अन्ते वा यदि वा मध्ये यत्र कन्यां च वर्जयेत् (कन्यां रविर्व्रजेत्?)।।

स पक्षः सकलः प्रोक्तस्तस्य श्राद्धं विधीयते।
आषाढीमवधिं कृत्वा यस्याः (यः स्यात्?) पक्षस्तु पञ्चमः।
सः विज्ञेयः परः पक्षः कन्यां गच्छतु वा न वा।।

— भुजबल, pp. 355-56 verses 1562-65. The first verse सूर्ये is quoted from सुमन्तु by अपरार्क, p. 424 (it reads निःश्वासपीडनात्); the second verse कन्यागते सवितरि is quoted by अपरार्क, p. 424 from कार्ष्णाजिनि and from an unspecified *Purāṇa* by the स्मृतिचन्द्रिका (श्राद्ध, p. 366, ed. by Gharpure); as cited in the भुजबल the second *pāda* of that verse would have nine syllables instead of eight; the वर्षक्रियाकौमुदी, p. 346 cites it from the भविष्यपुराण and reads the second *pāda* as पितृराजानुशासनात्। The Third verse अन्ते वा is quoted by अपरार्क, p. 423 from कार्ष्णाजिनि and from वृद्धमनु by the स्मृतिच० (on श्राद्ध, p. 365); the last verse (आषाढीमवधिं) is quoted by अपरार्क, p. 423 and वर्षक्रियाकौमुदी, p. 345 from जातूकर्ण्य and by the स्मृतिच० (on श्राद्ध, p. 365) from आदिपुराण.

25. भुजबलभीमे —
अपत्नीकः प्रवासी च यस्य भार्या रजस्वला।
आमश्राद्धं द्विजैः कार्यं शूद्रेण तु सदैव हि।।

— श्राद्धविवेक of रुद्रधर, p. 16; this is also राजमार्तण्ड, folio 78a verse 1307.

26. भुजबल, p. 64. मूर्ध्नि राजा महादेवि बालानां जन्मतो भवेत्।
ibid. चरणर्क्षे च यो जातः सोऽल्पायुर्भवति प्रिये।
p. 99 अष्टोत्तरशतं भद्रे परमायुः प्रकीर्तितम्।;
p. 100 बलहीने वित्तनाशं करोति वरवर्णिनि।

27. "गौतमः —
आरभ्य कुतपे श्राद्धं कुर्यादारोहिणं बुधः।

विधिज्ञो विधिमास्थाय रौहिणं तु न लङ्घयेत्।।"
एतद्वचनं भुजबलभीमे भोजदेवेन धृतम्। — तिथितत्त्व, p. 17; *vide* श्राद्धतत्त्व, p. 267 for the words 'एतद्वचनद्वयं भुजबलभीमे भोजदेवेन धृत्तम्'; भुजबलभीमे
ग्रहशुद्धिमब्दशुद्धिं शुद्धिं मासायनर्तुदिवसानाम्।
अर्वाग्दशवर्षेभ्यो मुनयः कथयन्ति कन्यकानाम्।। — उद्वाहतत्त्व, p. 124.

In the transcript of भुजबलनिबन्ध I could not find these verses.

28. यथा भोजदेवपठितं वचनम् —
नाद्यात्सूर्यग्रहात्पूर्वमह्नि सायं शशिग्रहात्।
ग्रहकाले च नाश्नीयात् स्नात्वाश्नीयात्तु मुक्तयोः।
मुक्ते शशिनि भुञ्जीत यदि न स्यान्महानिशा।
स्नात्वा दृष्ट्वा परेऽह्नन्यद्याद् ग्रस्तास्तमितयोस्तयोः।।

— कालविवेक, p. 539; The two verses are कूर्मपुराण उत्तरार्ध, ch. 19.15-16.

29. भोजराजः —
यो जन्ममासे क्षुरकर्म यात्रां कर्णस्य वेधं कुरुते च मोहात्।
नूनं स रोगं धनपुत्रनाशं प्राप्नोति मूढो वधबन्धनानि।
जातं दिनं दूषयते वसिष्ठश्चाष्टौ (त्वष्टा च?) गर्गो यवनो दशाहम्।
जन्माख्य (जन्मर्क्ष?) मासं किल भागुरिश्च चूडा विवाहे क्षुरकर्णवेधे।।

— तिथितत्त्व, pp. 25-26; these two respectively occur in भुजबल, p. 129 (verse 601) and, p. 132 verse 615 (which reads the last *pāda as* (व्रते विवाहेषु च कर्णवेधे). Immediately after quoting these verses the तिथितत्त्व (p. 26) quotes राजमार्तण्डः.

30. षष्ठीं संपूज्य ओम् — गौर्याः पुत्रो यथा स्कन्दः शिशुः संरक्षितस्त्वया।
तथा ममाप्ययं बालो रक्ष्यतां षष्ठिके नमः।

इत्युच्चार्य ओं षष्ठ्यै नम इति त्रिः पूयजेदिति भोजराजः। — कृत्यतत्त्व, p. 473. The verse is भुजबल, p. 121 verse 557. The next verse is षष्ठि देवि नमस्तुभ्यम्।

31. The Ms. of राजमार्तण्ड used for this paper is D.C. No. 342 of 1879-80 (now in the Bhandarkar Oriental Research Institute, Poona). The Ms. has 83 folios with about 10 to 12 lines (rarely 16 lines) on each side with about 35 letters in each line and contains 1462 verses. It was copied in *Saṁvat* 1655, Caitra bright half, 8th *tithi* and Friday (i.e., AD 1598). It is thus rather old and contains *pṛṣṭhamātrās*. The colophon at the end is:

इति श्रीमहाराजाधिराज-श्रीभोजविरचितं राजमार्तण्डाभिधानं ज्योतिःशास्त्रं समाप्तः (प्तम्)। ***Aslo see*** this manuscript partly published in this volume (pp. 107-44).

It is much more correct than the Ms. of *Bhujabala*.

32. I mention the number of the verse as shown in the Ms. I have used. In this paper *RM* is an abbreviation for *Rājamārtaṇḍa* and *BB* for *Bhujabala*.

33. It may be noticed that both the *Bhujabala* (pp. 198-99, verses 943-48) and *Rājamārtaṇḍa* (106-11) contain the same story in identical verses that Hārīta asked Vyāsa what *nakṣatras*, *tithis*, *lagnas* and *yogas* were commended and condemned for *puṁsavana*.

34. ***Vide*** my paper on 'Varāhamihira and Utpala' for further details about Yavana and Yavaneśvara, in *JBBRAS*, Vol. 24-25 for 1948-49, pp. 19-20.It has to be noted that the opinions of Yavana, Yavanas and Yavanādhipati are cited on such matters as *Cūḍākaraṇa*, forbidding marriage when Jupiter is in Leo, on *gaṇḍa* and *veśi*. [Dr. Kane has revised the date of Utpala as AD 966 decided in his earlier paper to AD 850 on the basis of the reference to Utpala by Abu Ma'shar in his later paper contributed to *JBBRAS*, Vol. XXXIII, pp. 147-49.]

35. यच्छास्त्रं सविता चकारं विपुलैः स्कन्धैस्त्रिभिर्ज्योतिषां
    तस्योच्छित्तिभयात् पुनः कलियुगे संस्मृत्य यो भूतलम्।
    भूयः स्वल्पतरं वराहमिहिरव्याजेन सर्वं व्यधा-
    दित्थं यत् प्रवदन्ति योगकुशलास्तस्मै नमो भास्वते।।

    — राजमार्तण्ड second verse; Utapala's Comm. (as printed) reads संसृत्य for संस्मृत्य, सर्वे for सर्वं and मोक्षकुशलाः for योगकुशलाः।

    The same verse occurs as the 2nd introductory verse in his commentary on the *Bṛhat-saṁhitā*.

36. One of these verse is striking:
    अथ यौधिष्ठिरी सेना गाङ्गेयशरपीडिता।
    प्रतिपत्पाठशीलानां विद्येव तनुतां गता।। — राजमार्तण्ड 361,

    — भुजबल, 684 (reads शरताडिता). It is in the *Rāmāyaṇa* that we have the verse:
    सा प्रकृत्यैव तन्वङ्गी तद्वियोगाच्च कर्शिता।
    प्रतिपत्पाठशीलस्य विद्येव तनुतां गता।। — सुन्दरकाण्ड, 59.32.

37. देशाचारस्तावदादौ विचिन्त्यो देशे देशे या स्थितिः सैव कार्या।
    लोकद्विष्टं पण्डिता वर्जयन्ति दैवज्ञोऽतो लोकमार्गेण यायात्।।
    कालस्य वृत्तस्य च चित्तवृत्तिर्न लङ्घनीया विदुषा कदाचित्।
    दोषः प्रतिख्याय कृतोपयाता (कृताऽपि यत्र?) संभाव्यते ज्यौतिषिकस्य तर्कैः।।
    भौमे विशुद्धे यमुनातटोद्भवा हिमालयस्थाः शशिजे शुभर्क्षगे।
    कैलासदेशप्रभवाः शनैश्चरे द्वीपान्तरस्थाश्च भृगौ जगुः शुभे (शुभम्)।।

    — भुजबल (pp. 34-35 verses 143-44 and 150, राजमार्तण्ड folio 25b verses 399, 400 and 402. (reads लोकाचारस्तावदादौ, कुलस्य देशस्य च चित्त, सद्भाव्यते ज्योतिषिकस्य सोऽज्ञः) and देशान्तरस्था भृगुजे जगुः शुभम्).

38. कालतत्त्वविवेचन (Sarasvati Bhavan Series, p. 176) says 'इति भोजदेवलिखित-शयनतिथिक्रमविरोधात्'. The verse in question is:
    वह्निस्कन्दपुरन्दरा गणपतिर्लक्ष्मीयमौ भास्करो
    वायुः पार्वतिका तथा वसुमती तोयाधिपः केशवः।

ब्रह्मा शम्भुजिनादयः प्रतिपदारम्भे तिथौ शेरते
उत्तिष्ठन्त्यमुना क्रमेण वरदाः स्वे स्वे दिने पूजिताः।।

— राजमार्तण्ड 1175. The भुजबल verse is corrupt, but reads the third पाद as कन्दर्पश्च सरस्वती त्रिभुवनस्तम्भः स्वयंभूस्तथा। The वर्षक्रियाकौमुदी, p. 286 mostly follows राजमार्तण्ड, but reads 3rd पाद as ब्रह्मा चैव महेश्वरो धनपतिः सर्वेऽप्यमी शेरते.

39. भीमपराक्रमे — पूर्वस्यां . . . वारुण्यां च सुदारुणा भूतेश्वरी पूर्णिमा। . . . विकथिता प्राप्तातिथिं भूतजाम्।

— राजमार्तण्ड, 1021-22. Vide note 6(b) above for the verses.

40. सत्यपराशरमुनयो गर्भादिमुदीरयन्ति वर्षाणाम्।
परिशुद्धिं परिणयने व्रते च जन्मादितश्चान्ये।।

राजमार्तण्ड verse 307, while भुजबल, (p. 127 verse 591) reads सत्यपरायणरस-गुरवो (?पराशरगुरवो) जन्मादिमुदीरयन्ति वर्षाणाम्। परिशुद्धिं परिणयने व्रते च गर्भादितश्चान्ये। The following verses may be noted for explanation. गर्भाष्टमेऽब्दे कुर्वीत ब्राह्मणस्योपनायनम्। . . . विशः।। — मनु, II.36; अष्टवर्षा भवेद् गौरी नववर्षा च रोहिणी। दशवर्षा भवेत् कन्या त्वत ऊर्ध्वं रजस्वला। — भुजबल, p. 151 verse 714; उपनयनमाहुरिष्टं द्विजस्य गर्भाष्टमेऽष्टमे वापि।। — भुजबल, p. 140 verse 656.

41. तथा राजमार्तण्डे —
गव्यपयो गुडपूपं घृतदधिमधुपायसं क्रमेणैव।
तरुणद्विजाय दद्यादनिष्टनाडीविशुद्ध्यर्थम्।।

— वर्षक्रियाकौमुदी, p. 116. The Ms. of राजमार्तण्ड reads (folio 51a verses 786-97) गव्य पयो गुडधूप (?) सृतघृतपायसं क्रमेणेह। वृद्धद्विजाय दद्यादनिष्टताराविशुद्ध्यर्थम्। The six things, cow's milk, etc., are to be given respectively in the case of the six evil *nāḍīs*.

42. राजमार्तण्डे —
रविशुद्धौ गृहकरणं रविगुरुशुद्धौ व्रतोद्वाहौ।
क्षौरं तारकशुद्ध्या शेषं चन्द्राश्रितं कर्म।।
गौडेऽमरेज्यार्कशशाङ्कशुद्धौ पूज्यस्तथैकस्य च कामरूपे।
कर्णाटनाटङ्ग (लाटाङ्ग ?) कलिङ्गदेशे जीवस्य चाभ्युन्नतिदो विवाहः।।
बृहस्पतौ शोभनगोचरस्थे विवाहमिच्छन्ति हि दाक्षिणात्याः।
रवौ विशुद्धे प्रवदन्ति गौडा न गोचरो मानवके (मालवके?) प्रमाणम्।।

— शुद्धिकौमुदी, p. 204. The last is राजमार्तण्ड verse 401, the first is भुजबल (p. 135, verse 629, reads रविशुद्धौ परिणयनं) and the second is read in भुजबल (p. 36 verse 151) as ओड्रेऽमरेज्यार्कशशाङ्कशुद्धौ बुधस्य चैकस्य च कामरूपे)

43. सार्वकालिक इत्यस्य विषयमाह भुजबलभीमे —
ग्रहशुद्धिमब्दशुद्धि शुद्धिं मासायनर्तुदिवसानाम्।

अर्वाग्दशवर्षेभ्यो मुनयः कथयन्ति कन्यकानाम्।। . . .
कृत्यचिन्तामणौ। . . . बृहद्राजमार्तण्डे –
सर्वाणि शुभकर्माणि कुर्यादस्तंगते सिते।
विवाहं मेखलाबन्धं यात्रां च परिवर्जयेत्।।

— ज्योतिस्तत्त्व (Jiv., Vol. I, p. 605).

44. राजमार्तण्डे –
न जन्मासे न च चैत्रपौषे न युग्मवर्षे न हरौ प्रसुप्ते।
रवौ च दुष्टे न च कृष्णपक्षे न जन्मभे कर्णविधिः प्रशस्तः।।

— ज्योतिस्तत्त्व, p. 655. I could not trace this verse in my Ms. of राजमार्ताण्ड, but a very similar verse occurs in भुजबल, p. 133 v. 623 :
'न जन्म . . . पौषे न भाद्रसंज्ञे न हरौ प्रशस्ते (? प्रसुप्ते)।
तिथौ च रिक्ते न च विष्टिदुष्टे कर्णस्य वेधं मुनयो वदन्ति'।।

45. बृहद्राजमार्तण्डे –
वक्रातिचारोपगताः कुजाद्या यद्यन्यराशौ परिवर्जनीयाः।
यथाक्रमस्थाः स्वगृहस्थिता वा न वर्जनीया यवना वदन्ति।।

— मलमासतत्त्व, p. 826.

46. भोजदेवव्यवहारसमुच्चये –
सर्वं कार्यं न कुर्वीत गुरौ सिंहेऽस्तगेऽपि च।
व्रतदीक्षे न कुर्वीत तमोयुक्ते बृहस्पतौ।।
— मलमासतत्त्व, p. 831. तमोयुक्ते means राहुयुक्ते.

47. व्यवहारसमुच्चये कृत्यचिन्तामणौ च हारीतः –
कृत्वातिचारं यदि पूर्वराशिं नायाति मन्त्री विबुधाधिपानाम्।
यानं विवाहं व्रतबन्धगेहं सर्वं तदा हन्ति मतं मुनीनाम्।।

अतिचारं गते जीवे वृषे वृश्चिककुम्भयोः।
यज्ञोद्वाहादिकं कुर्यात्तत्र कालो न लुप्यते।।

— मलमासतत्त्व, p. 286. The first is भुजबल, p. 273 verse 1234 and occurs on folio 5b verse 52 of the Ms. of व्यवहारसमुच्चय।

48. किं कुर्वन्ति ग्रहाः सर्वे यत्र केन्द्रे बृहस्पतिः।
मत्तवारणसङ्घातः सिंहेनैकेन हन्यते।।

— व्यवहारसमुच्चय folio 60b, भुजबल, p. 280 verse 1262.

49. व्यवहारसमुच्चये –
दशम्यामष्टम्यां प्रथमघटिकापञ्चकपरं
हरिद्युस्सप्तम्यां द्विदशघटिकान्तेभिघटिकम्।
तृतीया राकायां ख-यमघटिकाभ्यः परभवं
शुभं विष्टेः पुच्छं शिवतिथिचतुर्थ्योऽस्तु विरमे।।

तत्रैव –
सर्पिणी तु सिते पक्षे कृष्णे चैव तु वृश्चिकी।

सर्पिण्यास्तु मुखं त्याज्यं वृश्चिक्याः पुच्छमेव च।।

— निर्णयसिन्धु I, p. 23. There is a व्यवहारसमुच्चय by हरिगण.

50. अथ दश दोषाः —

व्यवहारोच्चये —
वेधश्च लत्ता च तथैव पातः खर्जूरवेधो दशयोगचक्रम्।
युतिश्च जामित्रमुपग्रहश्च बाणाख्यवज्रे च दशैव दोषाः।

एषां लक्षणं ज्योतिषे ज्ञेयम्। — निर्णयसिन्धु (III पूर्वार्ध, p. 309). There is a *Vyavahāroccaya* by सुरेश्वर उपाध्याय. This and the quotations in the preceding note do not appear to have been taken from the *Vyavahāra-samuccaya* of Bhoja's reign.

51. The *Samayapradīpa*, folio 37b, says भाद्रपदशुक्लचतुर्थ्यां चन्द्रदर्शनेन मिथ्याभिशापभागी स्यादिति प्रवादसहितश्चन्द्रादर्शनसमाचारः।

52. For the works of Varāhamihira and for the same verses being common to several works of his, ***see*** my paper on 'Varāhamihira and Utpala' in the *JBBRAS*, Vol. 24-25 for 1948-49, pp. 1-4 and pp. 21-22 may be consulted.

53. उपवासात्परं भैक्ष्यं भैक्ष्यात्परमयाचितम्।
अयाचितात्परं नक्तं तस्मान्नक्तेन वर्तयेत्।।
एकभक्तेन नक्तेन तथैवायाचितेन च।
उपवासेन भैक्ष्येण नैवाद्वादशिको भवेत्।।

पारिजातस्तु नक्तमात्रविधिरेवायम्, उपवासात्परं भैक्ष्यमित्यादि खण्डत्रयमनुवादमात्रमित्याह। इदं तु युक्तम्। भोजभूपाललिखितनक्तवाक्यसन्दर्भान्तर्गतत्वेन नक्तविधायकत्वेऽस्य स्थितेऽसङ्गतमपीदं नक्ते प्रवृत्तिमतिशयेनाधातुमुक्तम्। — कृत्यरत्नाकर, pp. 57, 58. The first verse is quoted from भविष्यपुराण by कृत्यरत्नाकर.

54. दशम्येकादशीविद्धा गान्धारी तामुपोषिता।
तस्याः पुत्रशतं नष्टं तस्मात्तां परिवर्जयेत्।।

इति निन्दानुवाद इत्यपि। तदेवं तिथिद्वयमात्रमभिधाय मूकायां स्मृतौ सङ्कल्परूपप्रधानव्रतपदार्थानुरोधादेश्च भूपालानुगतस्याप्यतिप्रसज्जनसभाकुलत्वे महाजनपरिगृहीतवचनमेव व्यवस्थायां शरणम्।। — कृत्यर०, p. 635. The verse दशम्येकादशीविद्धा is राजमार्तण्ड folio 71a v. 1154 and quoted in the समयप्रदीप of श्रीदत्त (folio 6b of D.C. Ms. No. 371 of 1875-76 which is a work on *vrata*s earlier than the *Kṛtyaratnākara* that mentions on p. 66 श्रीदत्त, author of the समयप्रदीप, and the latter itself on p. 233.

55. तदेवं गौडीयवचनानि प्रमाणयतां तदनुसारेण व्यवस्थोक्ता। भूपालादिमते तु सप्तम्येकादश्योर्वाचनिकी व्यवस्था। तिथ्यन्तरेषु तु प्रधानकालानुरोधन्यायादुदयकालव्यापिन्यादर इति प्रागेव दर्शितम्। folio 8b of समयप्रदीप D.C. Ms. No. 371 of 1875-76. In the same Ms. on folio 37a there is a reference to *Bhūpālanibandha* on *Rohiṇī-Aṣṭamī* 'भूपालादिनिबन्धेष्वपि रोहिण्यष्टम्यां शिवपूजोपवासादिकृत्यमुक्तं किं तु न भाद्रोल्लेखेन।।

56. भूपालः —

कूष्माण्डं बृहती क्षारं मूलकं पनसं फलम्।
धात्री शिरःकपालान्त्रं नख-चर्म-तिलानि च।
क्षुरकर्माङ्गनासेवां प्रतिपत्प्रभृति त्यजेत्।।

— निर्णयसिन्धु, I, p. 37; धात्री means आमलक, शिरः means cocoanut, *kapāla* is the white gourd, अन्त्र is snake gourd, *nakha* is beans like *pāvtā* (in Marathi) and *Carma* is the *dal* called *masūrikā*.

57. I owe the references to the Mss. of *Vidvajjanavallabha* to the kindness of Dr. V. Raghavan.

17

Mahābhārata Citations in the Śābara-Bhāṣya

IN a brief but interesting paper on "Mahābhārata citations in the *Śābara bhāṣya*' (*Bulletin of the Deccan College Research Institute*, Vol. V for 1943-44, pp. 221-29). Dr. V.M. Apte and Mr. D.V. Garge discuss what passages Śabara appears to have borrowed from the *Mahābhārata*. Somehow or other they failed to note another verse which Śabara evidently quotes from the *Mahābhārata* without expressly saying so. On Jaimini, VIII.1.2. Śabara remarks "All this has been stated here in a brief manner. The detailed treatment given later on is meant for the benefit of the pupils. They cite also a verse 'The sage first gave (spread) a wide net and again also stated (the matter) in a succinct manner; for, in the world the wise desire both a brief statement and also a detailed one." This verse[1] is taken from the *Ādiparva* of the *Mahābhārata* (ch. I verse 49 of the Poona critical edn.). It is in the *Anukramaṇīparva* and differs from Śabara's quotation only as to the first *pāda*. If it be accepted that Śabara quotes from the *Anukramaṇīparva*, that will have an important bearing on the authenticity and antiquity of the *Anukramaṇīparva*. No scholar would assign Śabara to a date later than the fifth century AD and there are several who would place him some centuries before that date.

While reading recently Jaimini's *Pūrvamīmāṁsā-sūtra*, it occurred to me that some of the *sūtra*s read like verses of *pāda*s of verses. For example, *Jai.*, IV.4.3 *madhyastham yasya tanmadhye* reads like an *anuṣṭubh pāda*. Similarly *Jai.*, IV.4.12 *vaiśvānaraśca nityaḥ syān-nityaiḥ samānasaṅkhyatvāt* is a half verse (*Anuṣṭubh*) *Jai.*, IV.4.25-28 would constitute one *Anuṣṭubh* verse *svaruścāpyeka-deśatvāt, niṣkrayaśca tadaṅgavāt, paśvaṅgaṁ vārthakarmatvāt, bhaktyā niṣkrayavādaḥ syāt. Jai.*, V.1.8 *pravṛtyā tulyakālānām guṇānām tadupakramāt* constitutes a half verse (*Anuṣṭubh*). *Jai.*, VI.2.18 reads like an *Anuṣṭubh* verse *aśāstrā tūpaṣamprāptiḥ śāstram syān — na prakalpakam, tasmādarthena gamyetāprāpte vā śāstramarthavat.* Even *Jai.*, VI.2.19 constitutes three *pāda*s of an *anuṣṭubh*. More examples may be given. But it is not necessary to do so. The important question is whether it is a mere fortuitous circumstance that some *sūtra*s at least read like verses or parts of verses or whether Jaimini indended them to be read as verses. It is difficult to answer this question with certainty.

Reference

[This note is published in *ABORI*, Vol. XXVIII, pp. 135-36, 1948] *S.G. Moghe*

1. तदेतत्संक्षेपेणात्रैव सर्वमुक्तम्। शिष्याहितार्थमुत्तरः प्रपञ्चः। श्लोकमप्युदाहरन्ति – वितीर्य हि महज्जालमृषिः संक्षिप्य चाब्रवीत्।

   इष्टं हि विदुषां लोके समासव्यासधारणम्।। इति

   The verse in आदिपर्व, I.49 is विस्तीर्यैतन्महज्ज्ञानमृषिः संक्षेपमब्रवीत्। इष्टं हि . . . धारणम्।।

18

Utpala and the Arthaśāstra of Kauṭilya

IN the Bhau Daji collection of Sanskrit Mss. there is a good commentary (called *vivṛtti*) of Utpala on the *Yogayātrā* of Varāhamihira. That ms. is of very great use in correcting and supplying the gaps in the edition of the *Yogayātrā* published by Mr. Jagadish Lal at Lahore (1944). Utpala quotes as Cāṇakya's some prose passages from Kauṭilya's *Arthaśāstra*, which are valuable for the authenticity of the text of the *Arthaśāstra*. On *Yogayātrā*, XIII.4 where the word *dharmārtha-śāstrāṇi* occurs (folio 78a) Utpala explains *arthaśāstrāṇi cāṇakyaprabhṛtīni*. On folio 8a the commentary quotes a passage which is somewhat corrupt, but which most probably refers to certain words in the *Arthaśāstra* (on p. 313 of Shama Sastri's edn. of 1919).[1] On the same folio Utpala quotes a prose passage from the *Arthaśāstra* and also a verse (probably of some later work on the *Arthaśāstra* or a versified commentary thereon) which contains the same words.[2] On the same folio, Utapala quotes the definition of *saṁśraya* given by the *Arthaśāstra* followed by a prose passage from some other work.[3] On *Yogayātrā*, IV.5 Utpala quotes (folio 26a) a verse in the *āryā* metre from Cānakya[4] which I cannot trace in the extant *Arthaśāstra*.

References

[This small note is published in *ABORI*, Vol. XXVIII, pp. 136-37, 1948.] *S.G. Moghe*

1. तथा च चाणिक्यः। तथा च। समसन्धिः समाधिश्च व्यवस्थाकारणे तथा। शब्दा इमे समानार्थाः बुद्धिमद्भिरुदाहृताः।। In the अर्थशास्त्र (VII.17) the very first sentence 'शमः सन्धिः समाधिरित्येकोर्थः' — It appears that in the Ms. of Utpala the scribe's eye travelled over the words of Kauṭilya and he only copied the verse which began with the same words as in Kauṭilya.
2. चाणिक्य आह। स्थानमासनमुपेक्षा चेत्यासनपर्यायाः। तथा च। त्रयः शब्दाः समानार्था उपेक्षा स्थानमासनम्। folio 8a of the विवृति. On p. 272 of the अर्थशास्त्र we have the words स्थान . . . पर्यायाः (VII.4).
3. चाणिक्य आह। परार्पणं संश्रयः। तथा च। विद्वेषिणा बलवता गृहीतेन यदर्पणं परस्य क्रियते शक्तिः शालिप्रस्थश्च संश्रय इति। folio 8a of उत्पल's विवृति. *Vide* अर्थशास्त्र, p. 263 for the words 'परार्पणं संश्रयः'
4. तथा च चाणिक्ये। आत्ययिककार्ये घाते (र्यघाते?) दैवेन च पीडिते च यातव्यम्। केवलविलग्नयोगादपि घातासिद्धमाप्नोति।। विवृति (folio 26a).

[For *Kauṭilīya Arthaśāstra*, the edition Shama Shastri of 1919 is used by Dr. Kane. The ms. of *Vivṛtti* of Utpala in Bhau Daji Collection, Bombay is used by Dr. Kane.] *S.G. Moghe*

19

The Kauṭilīya and the Matsya Purāṇa

INTENSIVE study of the *Arthaśāstra* of Kauṭilya has been going on for about thirty-five years. The controversies about its date and authorship cannot be said to have been set at rest. Much work remains to be done as regards the relation of the *Kauṭilīya* to the *Mahābhārata*, the *Purāṇa*s and other branches of Sanskrit Literature. Recently while reading the *Matsya Purāṇa* I noticed a very close correspondence between the *Kauṭilīya*, I.20 and 21 and ch. 219 of the *Matsya Purāṇa*. Some of the most striking passages of the *Matsya Purāṇa* that agrees with the very words of the *Kauṭilīya* are noted below and such words of the *Purāṇa* are in **bold type**.

Arthaśāstra, I.20	*Matsya*, 219
1. मानुषेणाग्निना त्रिरपसव्यं परिगत-अन्तःपुरमग्निरन्यो न दहति।	गृहे **त्रिरपसव्यं** तु क्रियते यत्र पार्थिव। **नान्योग्निर्ज्वलते** तत्र नात्र कार्या विचारणा।। 5.
2. ना चात्रान्योग्निर्ज्वलति वैद्युतेन स्पत्वा मृत्संयुक्तेन करकवारिणावलिप्तं च।	सामुद्रसैन्धवयवा **विद्युद्दग्धा** च **मृत्तिका**। तयानुलिप्तं यद्देश्म नासिता दक्षते नम।। 7.
3. शुकः सारिका भृङ्गराजो वा सर्पविष-शङ्कायां क्रोशति। क्रौञ्चो विद्याभ्यासे	**विरज्यति चकोरस्य दृष्टिः** पार्थिवसत्तम्। विकृतिं च खरो याति कोकिलस्य तथा

माद्यति। ग्लायति जीवंजीवकः। *Arthaśāstra*, I. 20	नृप। गतिः स्खलति हंसस्य **भृङ्गराजञ्च**
म्रियते मत्तकोकिलः। चकोरस्याक्षिणी विरज्येते।	**कूजति। क्रौञ्चो मदमथाभ्येति** कृकवाकुर्विरौति च।। **विक्रोशति शुको** राजन् **सारिका** वमते ततः . . . मेहते वानरो राजन् **ग्लायते जीवजीवक**।
I.21	*Matsya*, 219, 18-19, 20a and 21a
4. विषप्रदस्य तु शुष्कश्याववक्रता वाक्सङ्गः खेदो विजृम्भणं चातिमात्रं वेपथुः प्रस्खलनं वाक्यविप्रेक्षण-मावेगः (वेगः v. 1.) कर्मणि स्वभूमौ चानवस्थानमिति।	स्याच्चासौ **वक्रसन्तप्तः सोद्वेगं** च निरीक्षते। **विषदोथ** विषं दत्तं यच्च तत्र परीक्षते।। स्रस्तोत्तरीयो विमनाः स्तम्भकुड्यादिभिस्तथा। प्रच्छादयति चात्मानं लज्जते त्वरते तथा।। **भुवं विलिखति ग्रीवां** तथा **चालयते** नृप। — *verses* 11-12-13a.
5. अग्नेर्ज्वालाधूमनीलता शब्दस्फोटनं च विषयुक्तस्य।	समीपैर्विक्षिपेवह्नौ तदन्नं त्वरयान्वितः। इन्द्रायुधसवर्णं तु रूक्षं **स्फोटसमन्विम्**।।
6. व्यञ्जनानामाशुशुष्कत्वं क्वाथध्याम-फेनपटलविच्छिन्नभावो गन्धस्पर्शर-सवधश्च।	**व्यञ्जनानां** तु **शुष्कत्वं द्रवाणां बुद्बुदोद्भवः**।
7. कठिनानां मृदुत्वं मृदूनां कठिनत्वं च।	**मृदुता कठिनानां स्यान्मृदूनां च विपर्ययः**
8. लोहमणिमयानां पङ्कलोपदेहता (पङ्कोपलिप्तदेहता?)	**लोहानां च मणीनां** च **मलपङ्कोपदिग्ध**। *Matsya*, 219-15, 24a, 29a & 30b

It is not necessary to multiply examples. It may be argued by some that both works might have borrowed from another work. But there are other considerations from which it follows that the *Matsya Purāṇa* is based on the *Arthaśāstra* of Kauṭilya and on no other work. In the first place it has to be noticed that the *Matsya Purāṇa* adds many details to the meagre statement of the *Arthaśāstra*. In the story of Indra and Diti, where it is narrated the Indra cut Diti's embryo into 49 parts, the *Matsya Purāṇa* (7.63) makes Indra say 'this evil deed was prepetrated by me by relying on (the methods propounded in) the *Arthaśāstra*'.[1] In ch. 272.22 the *Matsya Purāṇa* speaks in a prophetic vein that Kauṭilya will uproot the sons of Mahāpadma and then the earth will come to the Mauryas.[2] Therefore it appears that the *Matsya Purāṇa* knew of the *Arthaśāstra* of Kauṭilya and its last verse.[3]

The date of the *Matsya Purāṇa* is far from being certain. It is clear that the *Matsya Purāṇa* had attained to the position of a very authoritative work on *Dharmaśāstra* before the tenth century AD. The *Mit.* on Yājñavalkya, I.297 quotes all the nine verses of chapter 94 of the *Matsya Purāṇa* as regards the images of the nine *grahas*. The *Rājadharmakāṇḍa* of the *Kalpataru* (about AD 1120) quotes hundreds of verses from the different chapters of the *Matsya Purāṇa* such as chapters 215-19, 253-57, etc. Similarly Aparārka quotes hundreds of verses from the chapters of the *Matsya Purāṇa* on the *Mahādānas*. In my opinion for reasons which cannot be set out here the *Matsya Purāṇa* cannot be later than the sixth century AD.

References

[This paper first published in *B.C. Law Commemoration Volume*, II, 1, pp. 13-15, Poona, 1946.] *S.G. Moghe*

1. अर्थशास्त्रं समास्थाय मयैतद् दुष्कृतं कृतम्। – मत्स्य, 7.63. (Ānandāśrama edn.).
2. उद्धरिष्यति कौटिल्यः समैर्द्वादशभिः सुतान्।
   भक्त्वा महीं वर्षशतं ततो मौर्यान् गमिष्यति।। – मत्स्य, 272.22.
3. येन शास्त्रं च शस्त्रं च नन्दराजगता च भूः।
   अमर्षेणोद्धृतान्याशु तेन शास्त्रमिदं कृतम्।। – अर्थशास्त्र, last verse. i.e., 15.1.73.
   (Prof. Kane's edition, Bombay, 1969).

[For *Matsya Purāṇa*, the Ānandāśrama edition of Poona is used by Dr. Kane. For *Kauṭilīya Arthaśāstra*, I have consulted Prof. R.P. Kane's critical edition; while Dr. Kane has used the edition of Gaṇapatī-Shastri.] *S.G. Moghe*

20

Naming a Child or a Person

VERY elaborate rules are given in the *Gṛhya-sūtra*s about naming a child. In this paper I propose to compare those rules with the practices deducible from the Vedic literature as also to discuss how persons were named in India from very ancient times.

In the *Ṛgveda* (VIII.80.9) we read[1] 'when you give us a fourth name connected with the (the performance of) a sacrifice we long for it, immediately afterwards you, our lord, take us (forward or towards glory)'. Here is a clear reference to the fact that the performer of a *yajña* took a name indicative of that fact and that was his fourth name. Sāyaṇa explains these four names thus: one derived from the *nakṣatra* (at birth), the second a secret name, the third a publicly known one and the fourth an epithet like Somayājī (due to one's having performed a *Soma* sacrifice). Later works like the *Vaikhānasamārta-sūtra*[2] (III.19) prescribe that a man may assume a name after consecration of the sacred fires (such as *Agnicit, Vājapeyakṛt* etc.). In *ṚV*, X. 54.4 also there appears to be a reference to four names (though Sāyaṇa here takes *nāma* as meaning *śarīra* or *karma*) *ṚV*,[3] IX.75.2 has 'The son has a third name which is unknown to the parents and which is in the bright parts of the heaven'. This is a reference to the three names of a person, two being his ordinary name and his *nakṣatra* name and the third (which his parents could not foresee) was given for his performance of a sacrifice.[4] In the *ṚV*, frequent reference is made to the secret name of a person. 'He does know that secret and concealed name given to these cows'[5] (*ṚV*, IX.87.3). Similarly in *ṚV*, X.55.1-2 there is a reference to a secret name (*guhyam nāma*). In the *ŚatBrā*, after recommending the consecration of fires (*agnyādhāna*) on the constellation of Falgunīs it is said that they are the *nakṣatras* presided over by Indra, that Arjuna is the secret name (*guhya-nāma*) of Indra and that the Falgunīs are called Arjunīs in an indirect (or esoteric) way. The *BṛUp.* (VI.4.26) says that the father on the birth of his son bestows on him a name with the words 'thou art *Veda*' and that name becomes the boy's secret name.

In the *TaitS* (VI.3.1). It is said 'therefore a brāhmaṇa who has two names prospers (or is successful).' In another place the *TaitS* (I.5.10.1) has 'O Fire Jātavedas, that first name which my father and mother bestowed on me aforetime, bear it until my return. O fire, I shall bear thy name.'[8] This verse occurs with several variations in other *saṃhitās*[9] and it is quoted in several *sūtras* also. In this way reverence was paid to the *āhavanīya* fire by one who was about to go on a journey.

In the Vedic literature we come across some cases of three names for the same person. In *ṚV*, V.33.8 we find *trasadasyu paurukutsya gairikṣita*, the first being his ordinary name, the second a derivative from Purukutsa (his father's name) and the last derived from Girikṣita (a *gotra*). From *ṚV*, VII.33.10-13 it seems to follow hat Agastya was also called Māna and Maitrāvaruṇa (***vide also***, I.117.11) In the *AitBrā* (40.5) a king named Sutvan Kairiśi Bhārgāyaṇa is mentioned, where the second name is derived from his father's name and the third is a *gotra* name. In the same *Brāhmaṇa* (33.5) Śunaḥeśepa Ājīgarti (son of Ajīgarta) is addressed as Āṅgirasa (a *gotra* name). Hariścandra (a king) is spoken of (in *AitBra*, 33.1) as Vaidhasa (son of Vedhas) and Aikṣvāka (born in Ikṣvāku's family). In the *TāṇḍyaBrā* (XIII.3.12) we hear of a king Tyaruṇa Traidhātva (son of Tridhātu) Aikṣvāka (descendant of Ikṣvāku). In the *ŚataBrā* (XIII.5.4.1). Indrota Daivāpa (son of Devāpi) Śaunaka is said to have been the priest of Janamejaya at the latter's horse sacrifice. In the *Chāndogya Upaniṣad* (V.3.1 and 7) Śvetaketu Āruṇeya (son of Āruṇi and grandson of Aruṇa) is styled Gautama. In the same *Upaniṣad* both Indradyumna Bhāllaveya and Buḍila Āśvatarāśvi are addressed as Vaiyāghrapadya (a *gotra* name) by king Aśvapati Kaikeya (*ChāUp*, V.14.1 and V.16.1). In the *Klaṭhopaniṣad* (1.1.1) Naciketas is said to be Vājaśravasa's son and in I.1.11 his father's name is given as Auddālaki Āruṇi and Naciketas himself is addressed by Yama as Gautama (a *gotra* name) in II.5.6. This practice of giving three names is in accordance with the recommendation of the *ŚataBrā* (VI.1.3.9) 'therefore when a son is born (the father) should bestow on him a name, thereby he (the father) drives away the evil (*pāpman*) that might attach to the boy; (the father gives) even a second, even a third (name)'.[10] The same *Brāhmaṇa* has in another place 'therefore a brāhmaṇa when he does not prosper should give to himself a second name; he who knowing thus bestows upon himself a second name does indeed prosper (or succeed).'[11] In the *Drāhyāyaṇa Śrauta-sūtra* (I.3.19) reference is made to the fact that a *yajamāna* (sacrificer) may have three names and that they were all to be recited at certain rites.[12]

Usually however a person is referred to in Vedic literature by two names. Sometimes a person is mentioned by his own name and a *gotra* name, e.g. we have Medhyātithi Kāṇva (*ṚV*, VIII.2.40), Hiraṇyastūpa Āṅgirasa (*ṚV*, X.149.5), Vatsaprī Bhālandana (*TaitS*, V.2.1.6), Bālāki Gārgya (*BṛUp*, II.1.1), Baka Dālbhya (*ChāUp*, I.2.13), Cyavana Bhārgava (*AitBrā*, 39.7), Kabandhī Kātyāyana (*PraśnaUp*, I.1), Patañcala Kāpya (*BṛUp*, III.7.1). In other cases a person is referred to by his name and another derived from a country or locality e.g. Kaśu Caidya (*ṚV*, VIII.5.37), Bhīma Vaidarbha (*AitBrā*, 35.8), Durmukha Pāñcāla (*AitBrā*, 39.23) Janaka Vaideha (*BṛUp*, III.1.1), Ajātaśatru Kāśya (*BṛUp*, II.1.1), Bhārgava Vaidarbhi (*PraśnaUp*, 1.1), Hiraṇyanābha Kauśalya (*PraśnaUp*, VI.1). In some cases a matronymic is added to a person's name e.g. we have Dīrghatamā Māmateya (son of Mamatā, in *ṚV*, I.158.6), Kutsa Ārjuneya (son of Arjunī, in *ṚV*, IV.26.1, VII.19.2, VII.1.11), Kakṣīvat Auśija (son of Uśik, in *ṚV*, I.18.1 and *VājS*, III.28), Prahlāda Kāyādhava (son of

Kayādhū, in *TaitBrā*, I.5.10.7), Mahidāsa Aitareya (son of Itarā, in *ChāUp*, III.16.7). This practice of mentioning a man by his mother's own name or her *gotra* name (derived from her father's *gotra*) was continued till later times, as will be shown hereafter. In the *vaṁśa* added at the end of the *Bṛhadāraṇyaka Upaniṣad*, we have about forty names of sages that are matronymic.

The most usual method of referring to a person even in the *Ṛgveda* is to give his name along with another epithet derived from his father's name. A few examples may be given. Ambarīṣa, Ṛjrāśva, Sahadeva and Surādhas are all called Vārṣāgira (sons of Vṛṣāgir, *ṚV*, I.100.17). King Sudās is called Paijavana (son of Pijavana) and in the same verse he is said to have been the grandson (*naptṛ*) of Devavat (*ṚV*, VII.18.22). We have in the *Ṛgveda* itself such names as Trita Vaibhūvasa (son of Vibhūvas *ṚV*, X.46.3), Trita Āptya (*ṚV*, VIII.12.16), Dadhyaṅ Ātharvaṇa (*ṚV*, I.116.12), Purumīḷha Vaidadaśvi (*ṚV*, V.61.10), Pṛthuśravas Kānīta (son of Kanīta, *ṚV*, VIII.21.24), Devāpi Ārṣṭiṣeṇa (son of Ṛṣṭiṣeṇa, *ṚV*, X.98.5, 6 and 8), Trasadasyu Paurukutsi or Paurukutsya (son of Purukutsa, *ṚV*, VII.19.3 and VIII.19.36), Ṛjiśvan Vaidathina (son of Vidathin, *ṚV*, IV.16.13), Sṛñjaya Daivavāta (*ṚV*, IV.15.4), Somaka Sāhadevya (*ṚV*, IV.15.9). A few examples from other Vedic works may also be cited; Śaṃyu Bārhaspatya (*TaitS*, II.6.10), Vasiṣṭha Sātyahavya (*TaitS*, VI.6.2.2-3 and *AitBrā*, 40.1), Bhṛgu Vāruṇi (*AitBrā*, 13.10 and *TaitUp*, III.1), Bharata Dauṣṣanti (*ŚataBrā*, XIII.5.4.11, *AitBrā*, 39.9), Kavaṣa Ailūṣa (*AitBṛā*, VIII.1), Nābhānediṣṭha Mānava (*AitBrā*, 22.9), Brahmadatta Caikitāneya (son of Caikitāna and grandson of Cikitāna, *BṛUp*, I.3.24), Satyakāma Śaibya (*PraśnaUp*, I.1).

We find that sometimes the same speaker is referred to by his own name, sometimes by his *gotra* name and sometimes by a name which is patronymic. For example, Naciketas is addressed as Naciketas (in *KaṭhaUp*, I.1.19, 21, 24, I.2.3, etc.) and sometimes as Gautama (II.4.15, II.5.6). Śvetaketu Āruṇeya is throughout addressed as Gautama by Pravāhaṇa Jaivali (*ChāUp*, V.3ff.).

In some of the *Gṛhyasūtras* the ceremony of giving a name to the child is included in the *Jātakarma* rite following apparently the passage of the *Śatapatha-Brāhmaṇa* quoted above (note 10). For example the *ĀśvaGṛS* (I.13 Trivandrum edn.)[13] says 'when a son has been born (the father) should, before other people touch him, give him to eat from a golden vessel clarified butter and honey in which gold has been rubbed . . . And let (them) give the son a name beginning with a sonant, with a semivowel in it, with a *visarga* at its end, consisting of two syllables or four syllables; of two syllables if he is desirous of firm position, of four syllables if he is desirous of spiritual glory; but in every case with an even number of letters for men, an uneven for women. And let (the father) thoughtfully find out (for the son) a name to be used at respectful salutation (at the time of *upanayana*); that (name) his mother and father alone should know till his *upanayana*'. This shows that the boy was to have a public name (*vyāvahārika*) and an *abhivādanīya* name, which was to be kept secret by his parents and to be used at the time of respectfully bowing to his teacher at the *upanayana.* Even now boys at the time of *upanayana* have a name communicated to them which they are to keep secret. The *Āpastamba-gṛhya-sūtra*[11] similarly prescribes that on the birth of a son the father indicates the *nakṣatra* name which is kept secret and that 'on the 10th day after the mother has risen (from the lying-in chamber) and bathed, the father and the mother give a name to the son, which is of two syllables or four syllables; the first part being a noun, the latter part a verb; it should have a long vowel in the middle, or it should contain the *upasarga su*, since such a name has a firm basis; thus it is said in a Brāhmaṇa. A girl's name should have an odd number of syllables.' The *Gobhila-gṛhyasūtra*[15] also prescribes the giving of a secret name at the time of Jātakarma and says that the *nāmakaraṇa* is to be performed after the passing of ten nights, a hundred nights or a year from birth.[16] It then prescribes that the name to be given on that day must be a word ending in a *kṛt* termination and must not be *taddhita*, the other requirements are the same except that the names of girls were to end in the syllable *dā*. The *Gobhilagṛhya*[17] (II.10.22-25) says that in the *upanayana* rite the teacher asks the student what his name is and adds 'the teacher settles for him a name which he is to employ when bowing at the feet of his teacher, (a name) derived from a deity or a *nakṣatra* or also from his *gotra*, according to some teachers'. We know from the story of Satyakāma Jābāla that his teacher asked him what his *gotra* was (*ChāUp*, IV.4.4). It will be noted that in the *ChāUp* (V.14.1, V.16.1, V.17.1, etc.), *BṛUp* (III.7, 2), *KauṣītakiUp* (I.17) when a person approaches another for knowledge, the latter very frequently addresses him by his *gotra* name such as Vaiyaghrapadya, Gautama, etc. The *Śāṅkhāyana gṛhya-sutra*[18] (I.24) first prescribes the giving of a name at the time of *Jātakarma* almost in the same words as the *Gobhilagṛhya* (but adds that the name may be of six syllables also) and proceeds 'that name only his father and his mother should know. On the tenth day a name be given common use which is pleasing to the brāhmaṇas'. The *Khādira gṛhya*[19] (II.2.30-31, II.3.6 and 10-12) prescribes the giving of a secret name immediately on birth, of another name after ten nights, a hundred nights or a year from birth, but adds no further details. The *Khādira gṛhya*[26] (II.4.12) further lays down that in the *upanayana* rites "the student who has been asked by the teacher 'what is the name' should declare a name derived from (the name of) a deity or a *nakṣatra*, which he is to use while bowing to his teacher with the words 'I am so and so' ". This follows the custom which is referred to even in the *BṛUp* (I.4.1), "Therefore even when a person is called he first says 'here am I' and then pronounces his name whatever it may be." The *Hiraṇyakeśigṛhya-sūtra* (II.4.10-15) is silent about giving a name in *Jātakarma* and prescribes that on the twelfth day after the birth of a child a name is to be given to a child (and the details are the same as in *Āpastambagṛhya*) and adds 'let the father and the mother pronounce that name first. For it is understood 'my name first O Jātavedas' (***vide*** note 8). He should give him two names. For it is known 'therefore a brāhmaṇa who has two names has success' (note 7). The second name should be a *nakṣatra* name. The one name should be secret; by the other they should call him. He gets a third name; thus it is known (from the *Vedas*)".[21] The *Hiraṇyakeśi-gṛhya* tells us that in the *upanayana* rite the teacher asks the student his name and the student pronounces his name with the word 'This' and with the words 'Hail, O Savitṛ, etc.' he mentions two names (I.5.4-6).[22] The commentator explains that these two are his *vyāvahārika* name and his *nakṣatra* name. The *Bhāradvāja-gṛhya,* I.26 (ed. by Salomons) speaks of giving a name only in *nāmakaraṇa* and closely follows the *Hiraṇyakeśi-gṛhya*. The *Pāraskaragṛhyasūtra* (I.17) speaks of giving a name only on the tenth day after birth, specifies the details as in *Gobhila-gṛhya* (II.8.14) and adds "with an uneven number of syllables ending in *ā*, with a *Taddhita* suffix, in the case of a girl. The name of a brāhmaṇa (should end in) *śarman,*[23] that of a kṣatriya in *varman*, that of a vaiśya in *gupta*." It will be noticed that here for the first time we come across the words *śarman, varman* and *gupta* added at the end of the names of individuals respectively belonging to the three *varṇas*. The *Mānavagṛhyasūtra*[24] (I.18.1-2) says "on the tenth night (after birth) he (the father) should give a name to the son, which should have a sonant at the beginning and a semi-vowel in the middle, a name of two syallbles or four: (the names) of girls should have three syllables and end in *dā*, in order that he may bow at the feet (of his teacher), (a name should be given) avoiding the father's (own) name; a name derived from a deity or *nakṣatra* tends to fame; but it is forbidden to give the name of a deity directly" (i.e., one may be called Rudradatta but not Rudra). The *Vārāha-gṛhya*[25] after stating the usual rules about the names of males on the 10th day after birth adds "the father's name should be avoided, or the son should have a name derived from a *nakṣatra* or a deity or (any other) desirable one but a brāhmaṇa should have two names; in this way the name of a girl should end in *ā* and should have an *a* intercepted, should have an odd number of syllables, and should not be the name of a river, a *nakṣatra*, the moon, the sun, the god Pūṣan, or it should not be a name ending in *dattā* or *rakṣitā* preceded by the name of a god". Manu also recommends that one should not marry a girl who bears a name which is the name of a *nakṣatra*, a tree, a river (III.9). The same *gṛhyasūtra* (5) refers to the *abhivādanīya* name in *upanayana*. The *Baudhāyana Gṛhyasūtra*[26] (II.1.23-31) refers only to the giving of a name on the 10th or 12th day after birth, gives almost the same details as to the letters of the name (but allows even six or eight syllables) as in *ĀpGṛS* and adds 'the name should show that the child is a descendant of a *ṛṣi* or connected with a deity or he should have one out of the names of the father's ancestors'. The *Baudhāyanīya Gṛhyaśeṣa-sūtra*[27] (1.11.4-18) gives more details about *nāmakaraṇa* on the 10th or 12th day after birth. It says "he bestows on the boy a name by means of a *nakṣatra* name; he has another and a second name which is used at the time of bowing down (*abhivādanīya*), which only his father and mother are acquainted with till (the boy's) *upanayana* . . . It is known that one who performs a *Soma* sacrifice should take a third name. To a girl (one should give) a name consisting of an odd number of syllables and ending in a long vowel as *Śrī*, Somyā. They also recite — The name of a brāhmaṇa should end in *śarman*, of a kṣatriya in *varman*, of a vaiśya in *gupta* and of śūdra in *bhṛtya* or *dāsa* or it may only end in *dāsa* . . . In the case of the *nakṣatra*s Rohiṇī, Mṛgaśīrṣa, Maghā, Citrā, Jyeṣṭhā, Śravaṇa Śatabhiṣaj, Revatī and Aśvayuk, the first vowel undergoes *vṛddhi*; and the name Rauhiṇa is given after the *nakṣatra* Rohiṇī; others also (are similarly formed). In the case of Tiṣya, Aśleṣā, Hasta, Viśākhā, Anurādhā, Asāḍā, Śraviṣṭhā the name is the same as the original (*nakṣatra*) as in Tiṣya (from Tiṣya); the others (also yield the same names). In Phālgunī the name of Phālguna" (results), etc. Saṅkha-Likhita as quoted in Aparārka prescribes *nāmakaraṇa* on the tenth day after birth and add '(the father) or some other elder in the family should bestow on males a name containing four or two syllables having a sonant at the beginning and a semi-vowel in the middle, in the case of girls (a name) ending in *ī*; if a name is bestowed in this way the family becomes pure.'[28] The *Mitākṣarā* on Yājñavalkaya, 1.12 quotes a passage of Śaṅkha that the father should give a name connected with the family deity. Baijavāpa[29] as quoted by Aparārka says 'the father gives a name containing one, two, three, four syllables or more without any restriction, which (name) has a *kṛt* (termination) and is not a *taddhita*; for a girl he gives (a name) ending in *ī*. The *Vaikhānasa-smārtasūtra*[30] (III.19) after prescribing a name of two or four syllables ending in a long vowel or a past participle ending in *ta* and having a sonant, etc. proceeds '(he should give) two names (of which) the *nakṣatra* name is the secret one; after a man consecrates the solemn Vedic fires he gets a public name (*prakāśa*) such as *āhitāgni* ending in the solemn rite he may have performed.' The same *sūtra* (1.7) shows that in Puṇyāhavācana when requesting the brāhmaṇas to pronounce *puṇyāha* the man's *nakṣatra* name, *gotra* name, his father's name, a matronymic name and his own name should be repeated. Some of the *gṛhyasūtras* speak of a name derived from a *nakṣatra*. In the whole of the Vedic literature hundreds of names occur, but there is hardly any name of a teacher or well-known person derived directly from a *nakṣatra*. In the *Śatapatha Brāhmaṇa* (VI.2.1.37) we are told of a person called Āṣāḍhi Sauśromateya (son of Aṣāḍha and Suśromatā) for whom the heads of unconsecrated animals were put and who on account of that mistake quickly perished. Here the name Āṣāḍhi is probably connected with the *nakṣatra* Aṣāḍhā. It appears therefore that in ancient times the *nakṣatra* name was a secret name and so we do not find it mentioned in most of the Vedic texts. Gradually however names derived from *nakṣatras* became very common and ceased to be used as secret names. We find that for several centuries preceding the Christian era, names derived from *nakṣatras* were very prominent. Pāṇini (who cannot be placed later than 320 BC and may be several centuries earlier still) gives some elaborate rules about names derived from *nakṣatras*. He says (IV.3.34) that names of males (and females also) are derived from Śraviṣṭhā, Phālgunī, Anurādhā, Svāti, Tiṣya, Punarvasu, Hasta, Aṣāḍhā, and Bahulā (i.e., Kṛttikā) without adding any termination in the sense of 'born on'. Examples would be Śraviṣṭhaḥ, Phālgunaḥ, etc. In another rule (IV.3.36) he states that in forming names from Abhijit, Aśvayuj and Śatabhiṣaj, the termination is optionally dropped, e.g., we shall have Śatabhiṣaj, Śātabhiṣajaḥ and Śatabhiṣaḥ. By VII.3.18 he says the name Proṣṭhapādaḥ is derived from Proṣṭhapada. He states (in IV.3.37) that terminations are frequently dropped when names are formed from *nakṣatras*; e.g. we have both Rauhiṇaḥ and Rohiṇaḥ from Rohiṇī. In the Junāgaḍh Inscription of Rudradāman (AD 150), we are told that the brother-in-law of Maurya Candragupta was a Vaiśya named Puṣyagupta (*EI*, Vol. VIII, p. 43). This is a name derived from the *nakṣatra* Puṣya and used in the fourth century BC. We know that the founder of the Śuṅga dynasty was Senāpati Puṣyamitra (*EI*, Vol. XX, p. 54). The *Mālvikāgnimitra* also mentions him and so does Patañjali on Pāṇini, III.2.123. His name also is derived from Puṣya. This is not the place to go into the interesting question of the formation of Buddhist names. But a few examples of Buddhist names derived from *nakṣatras* will be interesting. We have the well-known name of Moggaliputta Tissa (from Tiṣya) in which a *gotra* name and *nakṣatra* name are both combined. A *parivrājaka* Poṭṭhapāda (Proṣṭhapāda) occurs in *Dīgha*, I. p. 187 and III. p.1. In the Sāñcī. Inscriptions of the third century BC (*EI*, Vol. II, p. 95) we have such names as Āsāḍha (from Aṣāḍhā), Phāguna (from Phālgunī), Svātiguta (Svātigupta), Pusarakhita (Puṣyarakṣita). In the Karle Inscription there is Sātimita (Svātimitra) from Sopara (*EI*, Vol. VII, p. 54) and a nun Asāḍhamitā (p. 56). In the Sārnāth Inscription of Kaniṣka's time there is a Bhikṣu called Puṣyavṛddhi. In the Palitana Plate of Dhruvasena I dated (Valabhi) *Saṃvat* 210 (about AD 529) there is a brāhmaṇa named Viśākha. In the plates of Śivarāja dated (Gupta *Saṃvat*) 283 (i.e., AD 602-3) we find such names as Puṣyasvāmī, Rohiṇīsvāmī, Jyeṣṭhasvāmī and Revatisvāmī (*EI*, Vol. IX, p. 288). The Ājñapti of Cārudevī, queen of Pallava Vijayabuddha-Varman was Rohiṇīgupta (*EI*, Vol. VIII, p. 146). It is not necessary to adduce more examples.

Another rule stated about Abhivādanīya names was that they should be derived from deities. From the times of the *TaitS* (IV.4.10.1-3) different presiding deities had been assigned to the *nakṣatras* from Kṛttikā (such as Agni, Prajāpati, Soma, Rudrā etc. for Kṛttikā, Rohiṇī, Mṛgaśīrṣa, Ārdrā, etc.). When it was said that the name should be derived from a deity, what was understood according to the commentators was a name derived from the presiding deity of the *nakṣatra* on which a man was born (e.g. Āgneya for one who was born on Kṛttikā). In modern times we find people named after the names of deities (e.g. such as Viṣṇu, Śiva, Śaṅkara etc.). But ancient works do not show that that was the usage then. In the Vedic literature we hardly find any individual name which is the same as the names of the Vedic gods, Mitra, Indra, Pūśan, etc. We no doubt find from the *TaitUp*, III.1 that Bhṛgu learnt Bhārgavī Vāruṇī *vidyā* from his father who was named Varuṇa. But this is a solitary instance. So also we have such names as Indrota (protected by Indra) and Indradyumna (both cited above); but we have in the Vedic literature no human being who is named Indra. In the *PraśnaUp* (I.1) there is a Sauryāyaṇī Gārgya, whose first name is derived from Sūrya. *Gṛhyasūtras* like the Mānava (note 24) prohibited the giving of the names of deities of human beings directly. When the practice of giving the names of gods to human beings arose it is difficult to say. It is clear however that it could not have been much earlier than the first few centuries of the Christian era. We have historic examples from the fifth century onwards where persons bore the same names as gods; e.g. in the Eran stone pillar inscription of Buddhagupta of Gupta *Saṃvat* 165 (AD 484-85) there is a brāhmaṇa Indraviṣṇu, son of Varuṇa-Viṣṇu, son of Hari-Viṣṇu.

There is also another way of deriving names from *nakṣatras*. In some of the mediaeval *jyotiṣa* works, each of the 27 *nakṣatras* is divided into four *pādas* and to each *pāda* of a *nakṣatra* a specific letter is assigned (e.g. *cū, ce, co,* and *lā* for the four *pādas* of Aśvinī) from which a person born in a particular *pāda* of Aśvini was called either Cūdāmaṇi, Cedīśa, Coleśa, Lakṣmaṇa. Even so late a work as the *Dharmasindhu* (AD 1790) disapproves of such names, as not warranted by *śruti*. These names are called *nakṣatranāma*; they are secret and muttered into the ear of the *brahmacārī* at his *upanayana* even now.

Manu omits all these elaborate rules about giving a name in the case of males, makes no reference to the *nakṣatra* name of *abhivādanīya* name given to a boy, but gives two simple rules

(II.31-32) viz. that the name of a brāhmaṇa should be indicative of *maṅgala*, of a kṣatriya strength, of a vaiśya wealth and of śudra lowness (or contempt) and that to the name of a brāhmaṇa an *upapada* (addition) should be joined indicating *śarman* (happiness or blessing), of a king an *upapada* connected with protection, of a vaiśya indicating prosperity and of a śūdra indicating dependence or service. We find that the *Gṛhyasūtra*s (except *Pāraskaragṛhya*) are silent about these *upapada*s added after the names of individuals of the four *varṇa*s. Therefore it may be inferred that this practice had come into vogue only some time before the extant Manu and long after the older *Gṛhya-sutra*s. Even among the Buddhists we find names ending in Śarman: e.g. in the Amarāvatī Buddhist sculptures the word *mugudasamputasa* (*Mukundaśarma putrasya*) occurs (*ArchS* of *SI*, Vol. I, p. 103). The rule of Manu was not universally observed but there were frequent breaches. In the Udayagiri cave inscription of Candragupta II dated (Gupta Saṃvat) 82 (AD 401-2) there is a Mahārāja Viṣṇudāsa (*Gupta Inscriptions*, p. 21). In *EI*, Vol. X, p. 71 (of AD 436) we have a Viṣṇupālitabhaṭṭa (a Brāhmaṇa whose name ends in Pālita as that of a vaiśya should). We find that *vadhana* (*Vardhana*) is added to the names of Śaka kings (*Corpus Inscriptionum Indicarum*, Vol. II, p. 16). Brāhmaṇa names ending in *bhūti* (which should be the *upapada* of vaiśyas) and *dāsa* are found in *EI*, Vol. XIX, pp. 248-49. In the *Sabhāparva* (30.13) both Śarmakas and Varmakas are described as kṣatriya tribes. On the other hand in the Talguṇḍa Inscription of the Kadamba King Kākustha-varman (*EI*, vol. VIII, p. 24) we find that the original founder of the family was a brāhmaṇa Mayūraśarman, while his son and great-grandson who had become kings had *varman* affixed to their names (viz. Kaṅga-varman and Kākusthavarman).

A few words may be said about matronymics. In the first place they are not at all so many not so frequent as the other names. They were probably mentioned to show the high or pure descent of the persons so described on their mother's sides also. Vasiṣṭha (III.19) in enumerating those who are *paṅktipāvana*s mentions one whose ten ancestors in the father's and mother's families were *śrotriyas*. Similarly Yājñavalkya (I.54) lays down that the wife should be selected from a big family of *śrotriyas* who have been famous for ten generations. In the Nasik Insription No. 2 (*EI*, Vol. VIII, p. 60) Siri Puḷumāyi is described as Vāsiṭhīputa. Similarly the Ābhīra King Īśvarasena is described as Māḍharīputra (*EI*, Vol. VIII, p. 88). Here the mother's *gotra* names are probably specially emphasized to show that though the paternal side may not be of the bluest Āryan blood, the mothers were of the best Āryan families. In the Nāgārjuṇakoṇḍa Inscription (*EI*, Vol. XX, p. 6) Siri Virapurisa is said to be Mādharīputa and his father Siri Chāntamūla is said to be Vāsiṭhīputra. We find comparatively late writers describing the *gotra* of their mother's family; e.g. Bhavabhūti says that he was a Kāśyapa while his mother was a Jātūkarṇī. We learn from a *kārikā* in the *Mahābhāṣya* that the great grammarian Pāṇini was styled Dākṣīputra.[31]

In some of the later *smṛtis* named derived from the presiding deities of the twelve months of the year are prescribed. The *Laghu-Āśvalāyana Smṛti* (published by the Ānandāśrama Press, Poona) prescribes (VI.2-3) three names, one derived from the *pāda* of the *nakṣatra* on which one is born and so-called *janmanāma*, another called *saṃvyāvahārika* (i.e., in ordinary use) which may be the same as the child's paternal grandfather's and a third name derived from the presiding deities of the months beginning with Mārgaśirsa. The *Śaunaka Kārikās* (Ms. in the Bombay University Library) quotes Garga to the effect that a name derived from the month of birth should be given and says that Kṛṣṇa, Ananta, Acyuta, Cakrī, Vaikuṇṭha, Janārdana, Upendra, Yajñapuruṣa, Vāsudeva, Hari, Yogīśa, Puṇḍarīkākṣa are respectively the names of the twelve months (*Cāndra*) of the year (from Mārgaśīrṣa). The *Nirṇayasindhu* quotes this verse and says that according to the *Madanaratna* these names are meant for months beginning with Mārgaśīrṣa or Caitra. These names are being given to this day in various parts but not necessarily in accordance with the month of birth.

Resumé

The above discussion may be summarised thus:

(1) In the times of the *Ṛgveda* and *TaitS*, usually two names were given to a person, one of which was a secret name (*vide* note 7 above); but the *Ṛgveda* was not unacquainted with even three or four names for a person (*vide* notes 1 and 3).

(2) Throughout the Vedic literature, the names given to a person were his own secular name and one or more other names derived either from his father's or grandfather's name, or from his *gotra* or from a locality or from the name of his mother. The *Śatapatha* speaks of giving even a third name, but how it was to be formed is not stated. Most of the names of authors whose views are mentioned by such an ancient work as Yāska's *Nirukta* are either *gotra* names or patronymics e.g. Āgrāyaṇa, Aupamanyava, Audumbarāyaṇa, Kautsa, Gārgya, Maudgalya, Vārṣyātyaṇi, Sākṭāyana, Śākalya, Sthaulāṣṭhīvi, though a few like Carmaśiras and Śākapūṇi are probably individual names.

(3) It is not quite clear from the Vedic literature how the secret name was given. Hardly any secret name except that of Indra as Arjuna is known as given to any person in the Vedic literature. It is natural that the names being secret do not appear in the texts.

(4) All the *Gṛhyasūtras* (except *Baijavāpa*) insist on the name given to a boy being one containing an even number of syllables, usually two or four, though even six syllables or eight are allowed by a few *sūtrakāras*. This rule is deduced from the Vedic usage. Most of the names in the Vedic literature contain either two syllables (like Baka, Trita, Kutsa, Bhṛgu) or four (like Trasadasyu, Purukutsa, Medhyātithi, Brahmadatta, Satyakāma), though names of three syllables (like Cyavana, Kavaṣa, Bharata) or

five syllables (Nābhānediṣṭha, Hiraṇyastūpa) are not wanting.

(5) Most of the *sūtras* recommend that the names should begin with a sonant and contain in the middle a semi-vowel. That this is a very ancient rule follows from the fact that even Patañjali (about 140 BC) in his *Mahābhāṣya*[32] (ed. by Kielhorn Vol. I, p. 4) mentions the rule that 'the father should bestow on the son on a day after the 10th from birth a name having a sonant at the beginning, a semi-vowel in the middle, (a name) the first syllable of which is not long, or which shows the descent from one of the three male ancestors (of the father) and which is not borne by the adversary (of the father).

(6) Some *Sūtras* (*vide* notes 16 and 23) prescribe that the name should end in a *visarga* or a long vowel. This rule is probably deduced from such names as Sudās, Dīrghatamas, Pṛthuśravas (occurring even in the *Ṛgveda*), and such names as Vatsaprī Bhālandana (*TaitS*, V.2.1.6).

(7) Some *gṛhya-sūtras* like *Āpastamba* say that the name should have two parts the first being a noun and the second being a derivative from a verb (generally a past passive participle ending in *ta*). This rule is derived from such ancient names as Brahmadatta (which occurs in the *BṛUp*, I.3.24 and which figures very much in ancient Pāli Buddhist works), Devadatta and Yajñadatta (which figure very frequently in the *Mahābhāṣya*,[33] *Śabarabhāṣya* as the stock names of persons).

(8) Most are agreed that a secret name is to be given to the boy by the parents (notes 13, 15, 18, 19) according to some at birth (notes 18, 19), according to others at the time of *nāmakaraṇa* on the 10th or 12th day after birth (note 21).

(9) There is some divergence of opinion as to the secret name among the *sūtrakāras*. Āśvalāyana appears to prescribe that the name with a sonant at the beginning,

etc. is to be one known to all and the parents have to find out at the same time a secret name which the boy is to use at the time of *upanayana* for respectful salutation; while the *Śāṅkhāyanagṛhya* prescribes that the ordinary name (which is required to be only pleasing to brāhmaṇas) as to be given on the 10th day, while the secret name is to be given at the time of birth and is to have all the characteristic details of being *ghoṣavadādi*- etc. There is a further difference of views. *Hiraṇya-keśigṛhya, Baudhāyanagṛhyaśeṣasūtra* and *Vaikhāna-sasmārtasūtra* (prescribe that the *nakṣatra* name is to be the secret one (notes 21, 27, 30), while others like the *Khādira-gṛhya* speak of a secret name but do not connect it with *nakṣatras*. There is a further difficulty. Several *gṛhyasūtra* like *Gobhila, Khādira* require that there should be an *abhivādanīya* name (notes 17, 20). This is an ancient practice. But these say that the *abhivādanīya* was to be derived from a *nakṣatra* or a deity and *Gobhila* adds that according to some the *abhivādanīya* name should be derived from the *gotra*. This latter is supported by the usage of the *Upaniṣads*. When the *abhivādanīya* was a *gotra* name there could have been no secrecy about it.

(10) The name derived from a deity was originally derived from the deity presiding over the *nakṣatra* of birth. Later on the names of gods were directly used as the names of individuals, though this appears to have been originally forbidden.

(11) The *upapadas śarman, varman, gupta, dāsa* were added at a later date than most of the *gṛhyasūtras*.

(12) Some later *smṛtis* prescribe names derived from the names Kṛṣṇa, Annata, etc. given to the twelve months.

(13) The names of girls were to contain an odd number of syllables, generally three; and were to end in a long letter either *ā* according to some and *ī* according to others. Some said that it should end in *dā*.

References

[This paper is published in *IHQ*, Vol. XIV, pp. 224-44. 1938. This topic of *Nāmakaraṇa* is already discussed by Dr. P.V. Kane in his *History of Dharmaśāstra*, Vol. II/I, pp. 238-54. The present paper may be treated as an addition to the matter presented in the above volume particularly in the light of the practices preserved in the *Gṛhyasūtra* literature.]

S.G. Moghe

1. तुरीयं नाम यज्ञियं यदाकरस्तदुश्मसि। आदित्पतिर्न ओहसे। — ऋ०, VIII.80. 9.
2. अग्न्याधानात्परमाहिताग्न्यादि स्वकर्मान्तं प्रकाशं नाम भवेत्। — वैखानसस्मार्तसूत्र, III.19.
3. दधाति पुत्रः पित्रोरपीच्यं नाम तृतीयमधि रोचने दिवः। — ऋ०, IX.75.2.
4. *Vide* बौधायनगृह्यशेषसूत्र, I. 11.4-8. नामास्मै दधाति नक्षत्रनामधेयेन। द्वितीयमस्य नामधेयं गुह्यमस्यान्यदभिवादनीयमोपनयनकालान्मातापितरौ संविदितौ भवतः। . . . सोमयाजी तृतीयं नाम कुर्वीतेति विज्ञायते।।
5. स चिद्विवेद निहितं यदासामपीच्यं गुह्यं नाम गोनाम्। — ऋ०, IX.87.3.
6. अर्जुनो ह वै नामेन्द्रो यदस्य गुह्यं नामार्जुन्यो वै नामैतास्ता एतत्परोक्षमाचक्षते फल्गुन्य इति। — शतपथ, II.1.2.11.
7. तस्माद् द्विनामा ब्राह्मणोर्धुकः। — तै० सं०, VI. 3.1. This sentence is quoted in several *Gṛhyasūtras*.
8. मम नाम प्रथमं जातवेदः पिता माता च दधतुर्यदग्ने।
   तत्त्वं बिभृहि पुनरा मदैतोस्तवाहं नाम बिभराण्यग्ने।। — तै० सं०, I. 5.10.1.
9. E.g., the काठकसंहिता (VII.3) reads '. . . दधतुर्न्वग्रे।
   तत्त्वं गोपाया पुनर्ददै ते वयं विभराम तव नाम।।'
10. तस्मात्पुत्रस्य जातस्य नाम कुर्यात्पाप्मानमेवास्य तदपहन्त्यपि द्वितीयमपि तृतीयम्। शतपथ, VI. I.3.9.
11. तस्माद् ब्राह्मणोऽनृध्यमाने द्वितीयं नाम कुर्वीत राध्नोति हैव य एवं विद्वान् द्वितीयं नाम कुरुते। — शतपथ, III. 6.2.24.
12. प्रत्येकं गृह्णीयाद्यजमाननामधेयानि यानि स्युः। — द्राह्यायणश्रौत, I. 3.9. on which one interpretation in the *Dhanvibhāṣya* is that they are अभिवादनीय, व्यावहारिक and नक्षत्रनाम्।
13. कुमारं जातं पुरान्यैरालम्भात् सर्पिर्मधुनी हिरण्यनिकाषं हिरण्येन प्राशयेत्। . . . नाम चास्मै दद्युः। घोषवदाद्यन्तरन्तःस्थमभिनिष्ठानान्तं द्व्यक्षरं चतुरक्षरं वा। द्व्यक्षरं प्रतिष्ठाकामश्चतुरक्षरं ब्रह्मवर्चसकामः। युग्मानि त्वेव पुंसाम्। अभिवादनीयं च समीक्षेत तन्मातापितरौ विद्यातामोपनयनात्। — आश्व० गृ० सू०, I, 13.1 and I.13.4-

9. Sonants (*ghoṣa*) are the 3rd, 4th, 5th letters of the five classes from क वर्ग to प वर्ग, य, र, ल, व and ह पाणिनि (VIII.3.86) derives अभिनिष्ठान.

14. जातं वात्सप्रेणाभिमृश्य . . . जापः। नक्षत्रनीम च निर्दिशति। तद्रहस्यं भवति। . . . दशम्यामुत्थितायां स्नातायां पुत्रस्य नाम दधाति पिता मातेति। द्व्यक्षरं चतुरक्षरं वा नामपूर्वमाख्यातोत्तरं दीर्घाभिनिष्ठानान्तं घोषववदाद्यन्तरन्तःस्थम्। अपि वा यस्मिन्स्वित्युपसर्गः स्यात्तद्धि प्रतिष्ठितमिति ब्राह्मणम्। अयुजाक्षरं कुमार्याः। — आप० गृ०, VI. 15.1-3 and 8-11. Such names with two or four syllables would be गोप्रीः, हिरण्यदाः, द्रविणोदाः, सुदर्शनः।

15. पुमानयं जनिष्यतेऽसौ नामेति नामधेयं गृह्णाति। यत्तद् गुह्यमेव भवति। — गोभिलीय गृह्य, II. 7.15-16.

16. जननाद्दशरात्रे व्यष्टे शतरात्रे संवत्सरे वा नामधेयकरणम्। आहस्पत्यं मासं प्रविशासावित्यन्ते च मन्त्रस्य घोषवदा . . . निष्ठानान्तं कृतं नाम दध्यात्। एतदतद्धितम्। अयुग्दान्तं स्त्रीणाम्। — गोभिलीय, II.8.8 and 14-16.

17. को नामासीति नामधेयं पृच्छति तस्याचार्यः। अभिवादनीयं नाम कल्पयित्वा देवताश्रयं नक्षत्राश्रयं वा। गोत्राश्रयमप्येके। — गोभिलीयगृह्य, II.10.21-25.

18. अथ जातकर्म। . . . असाविति नामास्य दधाति घोषव . . . चतुरक्षरं वापि वा षडक्षरं कृतं कुर्यान्न तद्धितम्। तदस्य पिता माता च विद्याताम्। दशम्यां व्यावहारिकं ब्राह्मणजुष्ठम्। — शाङ्खायन (कौषीतकि) गृह्य, I.24.

19. असाविति नाम दध्यात्। तद्गुह्यम्। — खादिरगृह्य, II.2.31-32. The com. adds नामापरिज्ञाने अभिचाराद्यसिद्धिः फलम्।

20. को नामासीत्युक्तो देवताश्रयं नक्षत्राश्रयं वाभिवादनीयं नाम ब्रूयादसावस्मीति। — खादिरगृह्य, II.4.12; the com. रुद्रस्कन्द exemplifies the names derived from नक्षत्रs (such as कार्त्तिकेय, रौहिणेय, चैत्र) and the names derived from deities presiding over नक्षत्रs (such as आश्विन, याम्य, आग्नेय, मैत्र).

21. पुत्रस्य नाम दध्यात्। द्व्यक्षरं . . . प्रतिष्ठितमिति विज्ञायते। पिता मातेत्यग्रेभिव्याहरेयाताम्। विज्ञायते च मम नाम प्रथमं जातवेद इति। द्वे नामनी कुर्यात्। विज्ञायते च तस्माद् द्विनामा ब्राह्मणोर्धुक इति। नक्षत्रनाम द्वितीयं स्यादन्यतरद्गुह्यं स्यात्। अन्यतरेणैनमामन्त्रयीरन्। सोमयाजी तृतीयं नाम कुर्वीतेति विज्ञायते। — हिरण्यकेशिगृह्य, II.4.10-15.

22. तं पृच्छति को नामासीति। असौ इत्याचष्टे यथानाम भवति। स्वस्ति देव सवितरहमनेनामुनोदृचमशीय इति नामनी गृह्णाति। — हिरण्यकेशिगह्य, I.5.3-6.

23. दशम्यामुत्थाप्य . . . पिता नाम करोति द्व्यक्षरं चतुरक्षरं वा घोष . . . भिनिष्ठानं कृतं कुर्यान्न तद्धितम्। शर्म ब्राह्मणस्य वर्म क्षत्रियस्य गुप्तेति वैश्यस्य। — पारस्करगृह्य, I. 17.

24. दशम्यां रात्र्यां पुत्रस्य नाम दध्यात्। घोषव . . . स्थं द्व्यक्षरं चतुरक्षरं वा। त्र्यक्षरं दान्तं कुमारीणाम्। तेनाभिवादयितुं त्यक्त्वा पितुर्नामधेयम्। यशस्यं नामधेयं देवताश्रयं नक्षत्राश्रयं देवतायाश्च प्रत्यक्षं प्रतिषिद्धम्। — मानवगृह्य, I.18.1-2.

25. एवमेव दशम्यां कृत्वा पिता माता च पुत्रस्य नाम दध्याताम्। घोष . . . ष्टानान्तं कृतं

न तद्धितं द्व्यक्षरं चतुरक्षरं वा त्यक्तपितृनामधेयान्नक्षत्रदेवतेष्टनामानो वा। द्विनामा तु ब्राह्मणो नामैवं कन्याया आकारव्यवधानमाकारान्तमयुग्माक्षरं नदीनक्षत्रचन्द्रसूर्यपूषादेवदत्तरक्षितावर्जम्। — वाराहगृह्य, 2.

26. नामास्मै दधाति। . . . षडक्षरमष्टाक्षरं वा। . . . प्रतिष्ठितमिति विज्ञायते। ऋष्यनूकं देवतानूकं वा। यथैवैषां पूर्वपुरुषाणां नामानि स्युः। अयुगक्षरं कुमार्याः। अमुष्मै स्वस्तीति। — बौ० गृ०, II. 1.24-31.

27. *Vide* note 4 above for a portion. 'अयुगक्षरं कुमार्यै स्वस्तिश्रीसोम्येति दीर्घवर्णान्तम्। अथाप्युदाहरन्ति — शर्मान्तं ब्राह्मणस्य वर्मान्तं क्षत्रियस्य गुप्तान्तं वैश्यस्य भृत्यदासान्तं शूद्रस्य दासान्तमेव वा। अथ नक्षत्राणि रोहिणीमृगशीर्षमघाचित्राज्येष्ठाश्रवणशतभिषग्रेवत्याश्वयुक्षु प्रथमाक्षरवृद्धिः स्याद्रोहिण्यां रौहिणायेति। तथेतराणि। तिष्याश्लेषाहस्तविशाखानुराधाषाढाश्रविष्ठासु प्रकृतिवत्तिष्यायेति। तथेतराणि। फल्गुन्यां फाल्गुनायेति। — बौ० गृ० शेषसूत्र, I. 11.9-18.

28. 'अन्यो वा कुलवृद्धश्चतुरक्षरं द्व्यक्षरं घोष . . . न्तःस्थं पुंसामीकारान्तं स्त्रीणामेवं कृते नाम्नि शुचि तत्कुलं भवति। — अपरार्क, p. 27.

29. बैजवापः। पिता नाम करोत्येकाक्षरं द्व्यक्षरं त्र्यक्षरं चतुरक्षरमपरिमितं वा कृतं कुर्यान्न तद्धितम्। ईकारान्तं स्त्रियै। — अपरार्क, p. 27.

30. अथ नामकरणमाचत्वारिंशाद्दिवसात् . . .। दीर्घान्तमभिनिष्ठानान्तं घोषवदाद्यन्तरं द्विप्रतिष्ठितान्तस्थं मृष्टाक्षरपदस्वरं द्विवर्णं चतुर्वर्णं वा नाम शस्यते यथोक्तं मम नाम प्रथममिति गोत्रनामयुक्तं तदर्हं नाम कुर्यात्। द्वे नामनी तु नक्षत्रनाम रहस्यमग्न्याधानात् परमाहिताग्न्यादि स्वकर्मान्तं प्रकाशं नाम भवेत्। — वैखानसस्मार्तसूत्र, III.19. The printed text is rather corrupt.

31. सर्वे सर्वपदादेशा दाक्षीपुत्रस्य पाणिनेः। महाभाष्य on पाणिनि, I.1.20 (Vol. I, p. 75). Pāṇini is also called शालातुरीय। *Vide* भामह's काव्यालंकार, VI.62, 'शालातुरीयमतमेदनुक्रमेण' and the Nogawa plate of ध्रुवसेन II (Gupta 320, i.e., AD 649-50) where the name occurs राज्यसालातुरीयतन्त्रयोरुभयोरपि निष्णातः (*EI*, Vol. VIII at p. 192) पाणिनि (IV. 3.94) derives the word.

32. याज्ञिकाः पठन्ति। दशम्युत्तरकालं पुत्रस्य नाम विदध्याद्धोषवदाद्यन्तरन्तःस्थमवृद्धं त्रिपुरुषानूकमनरिप्रतिष्ठितं तद्धि प्रतिष्ठिततमं भवति द्व्यक्षरं चतुरक्षरं वा नाम कृतं कुर्यान्न तद्धितमिति। — महाभाष्य, Vol. I, p. 4. अनूक means 'descent, family' कैयट explains it as 'पिता तस्य ये त्रयः पुरुषाःताननु कायति अभिधत्ते'.

33. *Vide* माहाभाष्य, Vol. I, p. 38 लोके तावन्मातापितरौ पुत्रस्य जातस्य संवृतेऽवकाशे नाम कुर्वाते देवदत्तो यज्ञदत्त इति। तयोरुपचारादन्येपि जानन्तीयमस्य संज्ञेति। This shows that in Patañjali's time the ordinary name was given immediately on birth and that was the *vyāvahārika* name.

21

Prof. Kane's Method and Interpretations — A Review

Dr. S.G. Moghe

DR. P.V. Kane completed the last section of his *History of Dharmaśāstra* (Vol. V, Part II) in the year 1962. Thereafter he revised the first volume which was then published in two volumes by the Bhandarkar Oriental Research Institute in the years 1968 and 1975.

About the importance of the voluminous work of Dr. Kane, Jan Gonda of Utrecht remarks that it is a huge encyclopaedia which contains innumerable extracts from original sources, quotations from hundreds of texts, references to inscriptions and legislative enactments, thought-provoking theories, sharp observations and conscientious judgements. He observes that these erudite surveys of the *Dharmaśāstra* that embrace far more than the *śāstra* itself will no doubt prove to be an indispensable tool for many generations of scholars in the times to come.

In this article, I have attempted to show as to what extent the views and chronological dates proposed by Dr. Kane can be modified, corrected or added upon. In this context, I have also surveyed various articles, books and Ph.D. theses written on *Dharmaśāstra* literature since the completion of Dr. Kane's last volume on *History of Dharmaśāstra.* I have studied the aspects by best utilizing, to my knowledge, the works on the subject in the last thirty years or so that I could obtain and peruse.

I would like to mention that, for the work done on this subject in foreign countries, my principal source is the *Journal of the Bhandarkar Oriental Research Institute* and particularly, the reviews that have appeared therein. In this context. I have consulted an important work, *Bibliography on Dharma and Artha* published by Ludwik Sternbach many years ago though I have not referred to all the books and articles mentioned in that important work.

I would also remind my readers that in the year 1974, I wrote an article on the contribution of Dr. P.V. Kane in the domain of *Dharmaśāstra* (pp. 65-82) for the *Dr. P.V. Kane Commemoration Monograph* published by the University of Bombay. The same article has also appeared in my book, *Studies in the Dharmaśāstra* published in the year 1991. I propose to discuss in this paper some new aspects which are not featured in my article of 1974.

I. For the proper study of *Dharmaśāstra*, Dr. Kane has laid down the pattern of restoring lost texts of *Dharmaśāstra* which involves collecting the references to a lost work from the *Dharmaśāstra* works. He has restored the text[1] of *Śaṅkha-Likhita-Dharmasūtra* for the Bhandarkar Oriental Research Institute. He has also restored the text of the *Kātyāyana-Smṛti-Sāroddhāra,* which he himself published. These efforts have influenced the other writers on *Dharmaśāstra*. In this very context, it may be noted that I have also restored[2] the portion from the *Vyāghra-smṛti* covering 142 stanzas (pp. 108-26) after editing the text of *Vyāghra-smṛti* with the help of two manuscripts — one published by Mansukhalal Mor in the fourth volume of the *Smṛti-Sandarbha*. It is included as Appendix II in my edition of the *Vyāghra-smṛti* published by the Bhandarkar Oriental

Research Institute. I have restored the *Ṛṣyaśṛṅga-smṛti* in the *Mysore Orientalist*, Vol. XIV (pp. 65-77) and this has appeared in my *Studies in the Dharmaśāstra* (pp. 65-80). Here, I have collected about 73 stanzas as those of Ṛṣyaśṛṅga and have thrown light on his novel insight.[3] The text of Pulastya has been restored by Lallanjī Gopāl and Kṛṣṇa Kānti Gopāl and published in Varanasi in the year 1992, and it has been reviewed by Prof. M.L. Wadekar in the *Journal of the Oriental Institute*, Vol. XL, March-June 1991, pp. 337-40. It is also heard from reliable sources that the restoration of the *Devala-smṛti* is underway.[4] It may be relevant to note that the model laid down by Dr. Kane has been followed verbatim by later scholars.

II. In studies on *Dharmaśāstra*, editing of the manuscripts also forms the basis of further research. Dr. Kane himself has edited the text of the *Vyavahāra Mayūkha* published by the Bhandarkar Oriental Research Institute in the year 1925 and *Madana Ratnapradīpa* for the Anup Sanskrit Library, Bikaner, in 1948. In Appendix 'E' to his edition of the *Vyavahāra Mayūkha*, Dr. Kane has quoted the passages where Nīlakaṇṭha has expressly quoted *Madana-Ratna* and has either agreed with him or criticized him (pp. 513-15). This kind of editing of the *Dharmaśāstra* texts has much influenced the scholars, both oriental and occidental. Here a reference could be made to the article of Dr. J.D.M. Derrett who edited the rare manuscript on *Dharmaśāstra* particularly during the early regime of British India. The translation of this manuscript,[5] entitled *Śvaśrū-snuṣā-Dhana-Saṁvāda*, has been published by him in *Dr. Umesh Mishra Commemoration Volume* brought out by the Ganganath Jha Research Institute, Allahabad, in the year 1970. Miss. J.H. Dave, guided by Prof. H.D. Velankar, edited the text of *Śrāddha-Prakāśa* of Pṛthicandra in a Ph.D. thesis (unpublished) for the University of Bombay, in the year 1959. This thesis is deposited in the library of the University of Bombay.[6]

I have edited *The Budha-smṛti* with the help of six manuscripts (two from the Bhandarkar Oriental Research Institute, Poona, and one each from Benares, Adyar Library,

Madras, Oriental Institute, Baroda, and the India Office Catalogue as noted by Dr. Kane) for the *Journal of the Annals of the Bhandarkar Oriental Research Institute* (*JABORI*), Vol. LXIV, 1983, pp. 259-68. I have published the critical edition of the *Śrāddha-Sāgara of Kullūkabhaṭṭa* on the basis of a solitary manuscript from the Sanskrit College, Calcutta in 1994, with an introduction discussing several problems connected with the *Śrāddha-Sāgara*.

The *Divyatattva of Raghunandana* has been published by Richard W. Lariviere with the help of 50 manuscripts, and it has been reviewed by Dr. G.V. Devasthali in the *JABORI*, Vol. LXIV, 1983, pp. 272-74. His other important publication in this respect is the text of the *Nārada-smṛti* with English translation and notes. The manuscript entitled *Dāyabhāga-Vyavasthā-Saṁkṣepa* has been edited by Ludo Rocher for *Dr. R.N. Dandekar Felicitation Volume* (pp. 351-58). The important manuscript of the *Śrāddha-pradīpa* of Vipramiśra has been published by Dr. Braja Kishore Swain (in 1982) with his own commentary in Sanskrit entitled *Raśmi*. This book has been reviewed by me for the *JABORI*, Vol. LXIX, pp. 298-301 (1988) and Dr. P.D. Navathe (p. 304). Both qualitatively and quantitatively, remarkable progress is noticed in the last thirty years or so in respect of editing rare manuscripts of *Dharmaśāstra*.

III. In the domain of research, deciding the chronological dates of the authors and works on *Dharmaśāstra* is important. Some of the dates fixed by Dr. Kane can be challenged and new dates suggested where he has not mentioned any. A few of my attempts in this regard are noted below:

1. Dr. Kane has placed Kullūkabhaṭṭa, the commentator of the *Manusmṛti*, between AD 1150 and AD 1300. I have, however, placed him between AD 1520 and AD 1620. For further discussion on this aspect, please refer to my paper on the date of Kullūkabhaṭṭa published in *Studies in the Dharmaśāstra* (pp. 103-13).

2. As regards the date of Govindasvāmī, the commentator of the *Baudhāyana-Dharmasūtra*, the two scholars Dr. Burnell and Dr. Kane differ. Dr. Burnell treats him to be a modern commentator; while Dr. Kane takes him to be a very late writer. I have placed him in AD 1650-90 and treated him as a medieval writer. For further discussion on this point, attention is drawn to the *Studies in the Dharmaśāstra* (pp. 114-17).

3. As regards the *Budha-Smṛti*, Dr. Kane has not expressed a definite view and he has only fixed the general period of the *smṛti* literature. I have placed this work between tenth and eleventh centuries AD in a paper published in the *JABORI*, Vol. LXIV, 1983, pp. 259-68.

4. Dr. Kane has not specified the date of the *Vyāghra-smṛti* in his *History of Dharmaśāstra*. I have placed the work in the tenth century AD in my introduction[7] to the *Vyāghra-smṛti* published by the Bhandarkar Oriental Research Institute in 1985.

5. Dr. Kane is also silent regarding the date of *Ṛṣyaśṛṅga-smṛti*. I, however, place Ṛṣyaśṛṅga in the tenth or eleventh century AD in a paper,[8] 'Ṛṣyaśṛṅga Smṛti — restored' contributed to *Mysore Orientalist*.

6. As regards the date of Vaidyanātha Dīkṣita, Dr. Kane has placed him in the seventeenth century. However, I have placed him between AD 1700 and 1750 in a paper[9] 'Vaidyanātha Dīkṣita' contributed to the *Journal of the Asiatic Society*, Bombay, Volume 60-61 for 1985 and 1986, pp. 56-61.

IV. Interpretation of *Dharmaśāstra* texts also becomes an interesting topic in research. In interpreting the texts, the views of Dr. Kane can be contested in some cases:

1. Dr. Kane interprets the famous line from the *Manusmṛti* — *nakṣatraiḥ yaśca jīvati*, III.162, as a reference to the

professional astrologer who should not be invited for lunch at the *śrāddha*-ceremony. I, however, believe that it is a reference to the sham astrologer who does not possess the proper knowledge of astrology. The paper[10] dealing with this was contributed to the *Journal of the Bharatiya Vidya*, Bombay.

2. In the case of the famous Śunaḥśepa, Dr. Kane treats him as a *datrima* son, relying upon the authority of the *Vāsiṣṭha-dharmasūtra.* I have pointed out in a paper[11] contributed to the *Journal of the Ganganath Jha Kendriya Sanskrit Vidyapitha* that Śunaḥśepa belongs to the category of a *kṛtrima* son of Viśvāmitra, if at all the authority of the text of *Aitareya Brāhmaṇa* is respected. I have also shown that in the history of adoption, the case of Śunaḥśepa is a unique one.

3. Dr. Kane has not considered the interpretation of the *Dharmaśāstra* texts by non-*Dharmaśāstra* authors like Abhinavagupta. I have considered[12] the interpretation of the text of the *Gautama-dharmasūtra*, IX.35 by Abhinavagupta, particularly in comparison with the interpretations of the regular commentators, Haradatta and Maskari and demonstrated that the interpretation offered by Abhinavagupta is, no doubt, novel but it suffers from the fault of *Parisaṁkhyā* — well-known in the science of *Pūrvamīmāṁsā*. This paper was published by the research journal of Allahabad and it is included in my *Studies in the Dharmaśāstra*, (pp. 172-77).

4. I have, however, followed the viewpoint of Dr. Kane in interpreting[13] the *Kauṭilīya Arthaśāstra*, III.5.28, by suggesting that the word *strī* occurring in the *Kauṭilīya Arthaśāstra* has a reference to a kept woman or a concubine who is entitled to the property of a person and not to a wife. This paper is published in the *Journal of the Oriental Research Institute*, Baroda. For the interpretation of the interesting passages from the *Kauṭilīya Arthaśāstra*,

the attention of the readers is drawn to my book *Studies in the Dharmaśāstra* (pp. 220-70).

V. In the field of research, it is important to be in touch with developments on the nature and significance of concepts and technical terms. With specific reference to Dr. Kane's views on the texts of *Dharmaśāstra*, the following may be noted:

1. In explaining the significance of the expression *ananyapūrvikāṁ* in the *Yājñavalkya-smṛti*, I.51, the commentators of the *Yājñavalkya-smṛti* have simply given a faithful rendering of the expression. I have attempted to show the significance of this expression in the light of the *Mahābhārata* evidence with reference to Aṁbā and Śiśupāla, particularly by applying the rules of the *Dharmaśāstra* texts. This paper is published in my *Studies in the Dharmaśāstra* (pp. 159-64).
2. The concept of *Nyāsa* is fully explained by Dr. Kane in his *History of Dharmaśāstra*, Vol. III. I have tried to explain how this concept has undergone evolution in the classical Sanskrit literature by including the evidence from the *Rāmāyaṇa* and the *Mahābhārata* in 'Dharmaśāstra Concept of Nyāsa and Sanskrit Literature' contributed to the *Journal of the Oriental Institute*, Tirupati, Vol. XXX, 1987 (pp. 87-94). The paper has found a place in my book, *A Peep at Indology* (pp. 35-42).
3. In appreciating the sense of the word *bhrūṇa* in the *Dharmaśāstra*, Dr. Kane has failed to consider the evidence from the *Rāmāyaṇa* and the *Mahābhārata*. I, however, have attempted this in an article 'Dharmaśāstra Aspects of the Rāmāyaṇa' which is awaiting publication from a research journal but which has a place in my book *A Peep at Indology* (pp. 31-32).
4. In appreciating the concept of a witness, Dr. Kane has

highlighted some significant aspects. But I have considered this concept[14] in the light of the *Mahābhārata* and *Dharmaśāstra* literature in one of my books.

5. As regards the concept of *sāpiṇḍya*, i.e., consanguinity, there is a lot of discussion in Dr. Kane's *History of Dharmaśāstra*. The generally accepted view is that *sāpiṇḍya* is accepted up to fifth degree on mother's side and seventh degree on the side of one's father. But I have pointed out in the *Budha-smṛti* edited by me for the *Annals of the Bhandarkar Oriental Journal* of 1983 that *sāpiṇḍya* is accepted up to the tenth degree on the father's side.[15] This view is corroborated in the commentary *Keśava-Vaijayantī* by Nandapaṇḍita (17th century AD) on the *Viṣṇu-smṛti* which has been published by the Adyar Library, Madras.

6. Dr. J.D.M. Derrett contributed an article, 'An Aspect of the Arranged Marriage in Dharmaśāstra' to the Diamond Jubilee Volume of the Annals of the Bhandarkar Oriental Research Institute published in the year 1978 (pp. 107-20). This aspect has, however, not been discussed by Dr. Kane.

7. In Dr. Kane's work, one does not find the clarification of the term *svayaṁpāka* used in the context of the *śrāddha* ceremony. Here the attention may be drawn to the significant explanation[16] of Vyāghra who says that when the food for the *śrāddha*-ceremony is cooked either by the *yajamāna* himself, his wife or his son, then the cooked food is called *svayaṁpāka*. Regarding the *śrāddha*-ceremony, the question often arises as to whether some persons are seen as disqualified from preparing or cooking the *śrāddha*-food. Dr. Kane has not touched this point. It may be pointed out that, according to Vyāghra, the food for the *śrāddha*-ceremony is not to be prepared by a daughter, a widow, a childless woman, a pregnant woman and a woman with bad appearance. It seems

that Dr. Kane could not use this view of Vyāghra for the simple reason that at the time of his writing the volumes of *History of Dharmaśāstra*, the *Vyāghra-smṛti* had not been critically edited by any scholar.

8. The concept of a widow needs some explanation. Generally it is accepted that when a husband is dead, his wife is treated as a widow. But in the *Dharmaśāstra* literature, Dr. Kane has not taken any note[17] of the *Kapila-smṛti*. This *smṛtikāra* holds that a woman is treated as a widow when her husband and son are no longer alive. This means that when she has a son alive, she is not to be treated as a widow. This revolutionary view of *Kapila-smṛti* has escaped the notice of Dr. Kane for the reason that an edition of the *Kapla-smṛti* was published later in the volume of the *Smṛti-Sandarbha* (Vol. V, 1955) published by Mansukhalal Mor, Calcutta, 1955. (Gurumaṇḍala edition).

9. In Dr. Kane's work, one does not find adequate information on the question of persons to whom the daughters may not be given in marriage. Hemādri in *Darpaṇa* on *Raghuvaṁśa*, VI.23 quotes a stanza[18] from the text of *Vṛddha-Parāśara*. The stanza says that householders should not give daughters in marriage to those persons who are always away from home, who are not educated, whose minds are intent on emancipation, who are brave and who are paupers.

10. Dr. Kane has shown that in the matter of sacrifices, a woman is given a subordinate position and that she is not entitled to perform a sacrifice as such. For such a view, he has relied on the *Manusmṛti*, V.155, *Viṣṇu-dharmasūtra*, 25.15 and *Āpastamba-dharmasūtra*, II.6.15.17. I beg to differ[19] from Dr. Kane on the basis of weighty historical evidence obtained from Anantadeva's *Mīmāṁsā* interpretation, Śabara's important observations and the views of MM. Ganganath Jha on the

Mīmāṁsāsūtra, VI.1.13. I think that women are entitled to perform sacrifices.

11. As regards the three rates of donation, Dr. Kane has clarified his position relying on *Mitākṣarā* on the *Yājñavalkya-smṛti*, I.203. But I have combined[20] the sources of the *Rāmāyaṇa* and the *Mahābhārata* to suggest somewhat different rates of donation in my article 'Dāna Section of the Dharmaśāstra' (based on the *Mahābhārata*).

12. In *Ṛṣi-Kalpanyāsa*, Dr. Kane holds that it is not obligatory for women to apply *tilaka* mark on the forehead. It is difficult to agree with him on this point. One can quote here the stanza[21] No. 192 (of my critical edition) of the *Vyāghra-smṛti* which clearly means that a brāhmaṇa without a *tilaka* mark on his forehead and a pious lady without the *tilaka* mark of saffron on her forehead are condemned among the people and particularly in respect of *daiva* and *pitṛya* rites. This point has been raised by me in my introduction to the *Vyāghra-smṛti*.

13. There is a controversy between Dr. Kane and Dr. V.M. Apte on the point of *vrata*. This is already referred[22] to by Dr. Kane in his rejoinder in the first part of the fifth volume of the *History of Dharmaśāstra*. Dr. R.N. Dandekar says high-handedly that the interpretations suggested by both Dr. Kane and Dr. Apte are unacceptable[23] to him personally. As Dr. Dandekar has not clarified his standpoint with some Vedic evidence so far, his opinion need not be taken seriously.

VI. Dr. Kane has written special chapters in the fifth volume of the *History of Dharmaśāstra* on the relation of *Dharmaśāstra* to *Sāṁkhya*, *Yoga*, *Tarka*, *Purāṇas* and *Pūrvamīmāṁsā*. But on topics like *Dharmaśāstra* and *Gṛhyasūtras*,[24] *Dharmaśāstra* and *Kāmaśāstra*,[25] *Dharmaśāstra* and *Āyurveda*,[26] and *Dharmaśāstra* and Sanskrit lexicons,[27] Dr. Kane has not written chapters though he has utilised the matter in these works for *History of Dharmaśāstra*. Some of these topics have been discussed by me in journals and they have been brought together in the *Studies in the Dharmaśāstra*. So my work can be seen as filling some of the gaps in the work of Dr. Kane. Here, incidentally, it may be added that Dr. Derrett finds fault with Dr. Kane's work, for the latter not having consulted the sources of sociology and anthropology in his *History of Dharmaśāstra*. It may also be added that a gap[28] in the work of Dr. Kane has been filled by considering evidence from the classical Sanskrit literature and relating it to the *Dharmaśāstra*. This work has been done by Dr. A.N. Deo and he has been particularly guided by me. For the above topic, the period covered is from Bhāsa to Śrī Harṣa (the author of *Naiṣadhīyacaritam*).

It is universally acknowledged that Dr. Kane's is a voluminous work; nevertheless, some major omissions on his part need to be mentioned. It appears that the topics of the digest works of *Vaidyanātha Dīkṣita* and *Vaidika Sārvabhauma* have escaped the eagle eye of Dr. Kane. I have contributed an article[29] on *Vaidyanātha Dīkṣita* in an attempt to make up for the omission. The work of *Vaidika Sārvabhauma* deserves good treatment. Besides, it will be admitted by any serious reader of *Dharmaśāstra* that some of the *smṛti* works have received only a partial treatment at the hands of Dr. Kane.[30] These should be accorded a full treatment by research scholars in the future. Unless such *Smṛtis* are properly restored, nothing can be said about their contribution to the *Dharmaśāstra* thoughts. We may note that Mansukhalal Mor from Calcutta has published some *smṛtis* (in six volumes), but not a single chapter on these *smṛtis* is found in the *History of Dharmaśāstra*.[31]

The importance of the manuscripts in writing the history of any subject is supreme. It can be stated here without any fear of contradiction that though Dr. Kane has consulted some descriptive catalogues of the manuscripts for his monumental *History of Dharmaśāstra*, some important references have escaped his notice. For example. in his section on the *Budha-smṛti* or

Budha-dharmasūtra, Dr. Kane refers to the two manuscripts on the *Budha-smṛti* in the Bhandarkar Oriental Research Institute and in the list of the works on *Dharmaśāstra*, he makes a reference to the manuscript of the *Budha-smṛti* printed in *India Office Catalogue*, Vol. III, p. 386 (No. 1323). But there are some additional manuscripts which are not at all mentioned by Dr. Kane. These include the manuscript No. TR 690 at the Adyar Library and Research Centre, Madras and another in the Oriental Research Institute, Baroda. He could have obtained another manuscript printed in the *Smṛti-Sandarbha*, Vol. IV, pp. 2137-38 from the Royal Asiatic Society of Calcutta.

It should be remarked here that in the list of works on *Dharmaśāstra* prepared by that great scholar, there is no mention of any manuscript on the *Vyāghra-smṛti*. But there is a manuscript of the *Vyāghra-smṛti* in the Bhandarkar Oriental Research Institute, Pune, bearing No. 163 and of 1884-86. In addition to this, the manuscript of the *Vyāghra-smṛti* is also published in the *Smṛti-Sandarbha*, Vol. IV, pp. 2491-2528. This manuscript is also available from the Government Sanskrit College, Benares. I am happy to mention here that for critically editing the *Vyāghra-smṛti*, I made the best use of both these manuscripts.

The two illustrations cited above are sufficient to prove that where use of manuscripts of *Dharmaśāstra* for editing is concerned, the work done by Dr. Kane is insufficient. One, hence, feels that the *Catalogus Catalogorum* prepared by Dr. V. Raghavan and others from Madras, is of supreme importance. Every cautious worker on Indology is expected to make the best use of such catalogues for doing methodical work. It may be noted that Dr. Kane has not made a claim that he has consulted all the catalogues for the purpose of his volumes. I have only casually cited the above illustrations to caution the future readers of Indology and particularly the readers interested in *Dharmaśāstra*.

The importance of the manuscript is also supreme for

filling gaps in the previously printed texts. This point has already been clarified by me in a paper[32] 'Nīlakaṇṭha's Vyavahāra Mayūkha and Śvaśrū-snuṣā-Dhana-Saṁvāda'. It should be noted that some matters supplied by manuscript are missing in the critical edition of the *Vyavahāra Mayūkha* so ably brought out by Dr. P.V. Kane. In one instance, the portions supplied by the manuscript added in the matter of the *Vyavahāra Mayūkha* shows that Nīlakaṇṭha is rejecting the viewpoint of *Madana-ratna*. Thus the importance of the manuscript can be gauged well. This manuscript, however, is recorded by Dr. Kane in his *History of Dharmaśāstra*, Vol. I, Part II, p. 1131. In passing, it may be noted that recently interested scholars of *Dharmaśāstra* have been taking pains to publish some rare manuscripts in the journals. A few such cases are mentioned in this article.

VII. There are also some cases of improvement on the part of Dr. Kane.

1. As regards the expression *āmikṣā* Dr. Kane's explanation in his *Notes on the Harṣacaritam*, p. 94 is based on the Sanskrit dictionary. The same is the case with the explanation given by Raṅganātha on the *Harṣacaritam*. It is Dr. Ganganath Jha who has given the correct explanation in his *Mīmāṁsā-Maṇḍana*, p. 162. But if one consults Dr. Kane's *History of Dharmaśāstra*, Vol. II, Part II, p. 1092 and particularly the footnote No. 2448, one is convinced that Dr. Kane has given a more correct explanation. This is a case of improvement on the part of Dr. Kane.

2. Dr. Kane has correctly explained the word *upasaṅgrahaṇam* when it occurs in the *Harṣacaritam*. In his notes, p. 57, he translates it into 'who made a respectful salutation'. Even Raṅganātha, the commentator of the *Harṣacaritam*, explains it as 'salutation by embracing or touching the feet of another person'. These two explanations, though satisfactory

from the point of view of a general reader, will not satisfy the interested readers of *Dharmaśāstra*. For a proper explanation of this word, however, attention may be drawn to Dr. Kane's explanation in the *History of Dharmaśāstra*, Vol. II, Part I, pp. 334-35. This is, again, a case of improvement on the part of Dr. Kane. It appears that while writing the *History of Dharmaśāstra*, he attempted to do complete justice to such words as have occurred in his *Notes on the Harṣacaritam*.

In the collection of papers of Dr. Kane which are presented in this book, one will notice Dr. Kane's tendency to make improvements upon the matter presented previously. Here, in passing, it may be noted that Dr. Kane in the third volume of the *History of Dharmaśāstra* adds a respectable amount of matter especially on *kalivarjyam*. He added to the subject as and when he went on reading and finalising the matter and improved it further. Similarly Dr. Kane's statement in his *History of Dharmaśāstra*, Vol. I, Part I, p. 548 that Asahāya probably wrote a commentary on the *Manusmṛti* also may be treated as a case of addition to his views on Asahāya.

VIII. It is said that the study of the *Dharmaśāstra* cannot be complete without the study of *Pūrvamīmāṁsā*. Dr. Kane has written a chapter on "Mīmāṁsā and Dharmaśāstra" in the fifth volume of the *History of Dharmaśāstra*, pp. 1152 to 1351. Here he has explained the *Mīmāṁsā* doctrines and theories, and clarified the matter with the help of *Dharmaśāstra* and *Pūrvamīmāṁsā*. This has influenced a number of scholars including young and upcoming researchers.

In this context, I have evaluated the concept of Śaṅkarācārya[33] and Sāyaṇācārya[34] in *Purvamīmāṁsā* and have brought to light some aspects[35] of the *Paribhāṣās* of *Vyākaraṇa* and *Mīmāṁsā* rules of interpretation. I have made a proper comparison[36] between the two commentaries, *Sāravivecanī* and *Prabha* on the *Mīmāṁsā Nyāya Prakāśa* of Āpadeva and written papers on *Atideśa*,[37] *Punarvacana*,[38] *Vākyabheda*[39] and *Ūha*. I have also tried to show how the *Mīmāṁsā* principles of interpretation are utilised by the writers on classical Sanksrit works and the *Kāmandakīya Nītisāra*.[40] I have made an attempt to evaluate[41] the contribution of Dr. Kane in the domain of *Pūrvamīmāṁsā* in a special article for the Dr. P.V. Kane Commemoration Monograph published by the University of Bombay in 1974.

IX. Dr. Kane had also made some suggestions for the codification of the Hindu law. These were considered by the modern legislature and some points were found acceptable:

1. During the British regime, the Hindu law was based on the *Dharmaśāstra* texts of Manu, Yājñavalkya-Nīlakaṇṭha and others. Dr. Kane made the suggestion that the Hindu law should be codified in view of the changing circumstances — as a result of which the importance of the *Dharmaśāstra* texts decreased. This suggestion of Dr. Kane was favoured by the modern legislature.
2. For the Hindu Adoptions and Maintenance Act, Dr. Kane made a vital suggestion in respect of the age of the boy to be adopted. Dr. Kane stated that no boy is to be adopted after the age of 5 years. If at all he is to be adopted, he must be adopted before the *saṁskāra* known as *cūḍā-karma* is performed on him. But it is evident from the provision of Section 10(4) of the Hindu Adoptions and Maintenance Act that the boy or girl should not have completed the age of 15. Besides, Dr. Kane's suggestion that no one can be adopted after the *upanayana*-ceremony is performed on a boy is not favoured[42] by the modern legislature.
3. Dr. Kane's further suggestion that no one can be adopted after his marriage in the natural family is also set at naught by the provision of Section (10)(iii) of the Hindu Adoptions and Maintenance Act of 1956. The

modern legislature further held that if a custom in a particular community permits the adoption of the married person, then there is nothing wrong in it.

4. The modern legislature has not accepted the *Mīmāṁsā* principle of *adṛṣṭa* approved by the ancient *smṛtikāras*, commentators and digest authors. In the Madhavarao *vs.* Raghunatharao case particularly argued by Dr. Kane on the basis of the *Mīmāṁsā* principle of *adṛṣṭa* and *sagotra* marriages and relying on the *Mitākṣarā* arguments, his view was not accepted[43] by Justice P.B. Gajendragadkar.

5. Dr. Kane made a vital suggestion for the chapter of the *strīdhana* of the Hindu Law. He recommended that *strīdhana* should be the absolute property of the married lady, the woman's sons and daughters should succeed together, and the husband should succeed to the estate of a married lady when there are no heirs. This suggestion was made by him in his *History of Dharmaśāstra*, Vol. III, pp. 801-802. This view of the learned doctor has been accepted by the modern legislature.

X. I would wish to end this note by referring to some of the interesting papers on *Dharmaśāstra* and important books on the subject published in the last thirty years or so. A list of some important papers is as follows:

1. "The Doctrine of Prāyaścitta in Hindu Law and Jaina Doctrine of Karma" by Y. Krishan, in *ABORI*, Vol. LXIV, 1983, pp. 109-17.
2. "The Doctrine of Karma and Śrāddhas", in *ABORI*, Vol. LXVI, 1987, pp. 97-115.
3. "Caṇḍeśvara and his Rājanīti-Ratnākara" by Upendra Thakur, in *VIJ*, Vol. VII, parts 1 & 2, 1969, pp. 56-58.

4. "MM. Dr. P.V. Kane on Muhūrta-Śāstra and Astrology" by Dr. M.D. Paradkar, *Mysore Orientalist*, Vol. XIV, pp. 83-87.

5. "Position of Widows in Early Medieval India in the Light of the Kathāsaritsāgara" by Aparna Chattopadhyaya, in *JOI*, Baroda, Vol. XXIV, Nos. 3 & 4, 1975, pp. 393-402.

6. "Gotra and Exogamy" by K.C. Mishra, in *JOI*, Baroda, Vol. XXIV, Nos. 3 & 4, 1975, pp. 422 to 427.

7. "Saṁskāras — Their Purpose and Significance" by Dr. M.D. Paradkar, in *Mysore Orientalist*, Vol. IV, No. 1, 1971, pp. 8-14.

8. "Bṛhaspati on State Patronage to Free Booters" by Raghavendra Vajpeyi, in *Kane Centenary Volume* issued by Asiatic Society of Bombay, 1977-78, pp. 212-17.

9. "Adoption — Unmarried Woman" by H.S. Ursekar, in *Bhāratīya Vidyā*, Vol. XXXIX, No. 1, 1979, pp. 55-58.

10. "Law in Ancient India" by Prof. R.P. Kangle, in *Bharatiya Vidya*, Vol. L, 1990, Nos. 1-4, pp. 50-57.

11. "Prostitution in Ancient India" by Dr. Krishna Murari, in *JGJKSV*, Vol. XLI, 1985, pp. 57-65.

12. "Śunaḥśepa and Dattaka-Vidhāna" by S.G. Moghe, in *JGJKSV*, Vol. XXXV, 1979, pp. 85-96.

13. "Dāsa Varṇa in the Ṛgveda" by Ram Gopal, in *JGJKSV*, Vol. XXXIV, 1978, pp. 1-12.

14. "Glimpses of Ācāra and Vyavahāra in Early Indian Literary and Epigraphic records" by D.C. Sircar, pp. 3-14 of the *Studies in the Dharmaśāstra*.

15. "Father Bouchet's Letter on the Administration of Hindu Law" by Ludo Rocher, pp. 15-48 of the *Studies in the Dharmaśāstra*.

16. "A Sanskrit Jayapatra from 18th Century Mithila" by

Richard W. Lariviere, pp. 49-80 of the *Studies in the Dharmaśāstra.*

17. "Renouncer and Renunciation in the Dharmaśāstras" by Patrick, pp. 81-152 of the *Studies in the Dharmaśāstra.*
18. "Legal and Symbolic Significance of the Menstrual Pollution of Rivers" by Richard Salomon, pp. 153-78.
19. "What Dharmaśāstra has to say about Dowry" by J.D.M. Derrett, pp. 179-93 of the above volume. (This book is edited by Richard W. Lariviere).
20. "The Origin of the Gotra System in the Ṛg-Veda" by V.G. Rahurkar, in *ABORI*, Vol. LIII, 1972, pp. 93-99.
21. "Mahābhārata and Dharmaśāstras" by M. Bhavanachari, in *J.H. Dave Volume*, issued by Bharatiya Vidya, pp. 253-59.
22. "The Theory and Practice of Punishment as Recorded in Vardhamāna Upādhyāya's Daṇḍaviveka" by Bhabatosh Bhattacharya, in *Proceedings of the AIOC*, 26th Session, 1972, pp. 335-44.

XI. The names of important books on the subject in the last thirty years or so include the following:

1. *Dharmaśāstra and Juridical Literature*, by J.D.M. Derrett, pp. 1-75 published by Otto Harrassowitz, Wiesbaden.
2. '*The Socio-legal Position of Women in the Smṛtis of Manu and Yājñavalkya*' (A Ph.D. thesis deposited in the Poona University, 1971) and an article on the above topic in homage to Dr. Mainkar, pp. 1-17.
3. *Oaths and Ordeals in Dharmaśāstra* — Ph.D. thesis (published) of Dr. S.N. Pendse, deposited in the M.S. University of Baroda.

4. *Vipramiśra's Śrāddha-Pradīpa with Raśmi commentary* by Dr. B.K. Swain

5. *The Vyāghra-Smṛti*, edited by S.G. Moghe, published by Bhandarkar Oriental Institute, Pune, 1985.

6. *Studies in the Dharmaśāstra*, (A collection of 35 papers on *Dharmaśāstra* and *Kauṭilīya Arthaśāstra*) by S.G. Moghe, published by Ajanta Books International, Delhi, 1991.

7. *A Critical Edition of the Śrāddha-Sāgara of Kullūkabhaṭṭa* by S.G. Moghe, published by D.K. Printworld (P) Ltd., Delhi, 1994.

8. *Mensuration in Ancient India* by Dr. (Smt.) Sarala Srinivasan.

9. *Slavery in Ancient India* by Dr. Dev Raj Chanana, published by People's Publishing House, New Delhi, 1960.

10. *Studies in the Pūrva-Mīmāṁsā* (A collection of 22 papers) by S.G. Moghe, published by Ajanta Books International, Delhi, 1984.

11. *Studies in Applied Pūrva-Mīmāṁsā* (A collection of 22 papers) by S.G. Moghe, a forthcoming publication of Ajanta Books International, Delhi 1996.

12. *Dāya-Vibhāga* by I.S. Pawate, published by Karnatak University, Dharwar, 1979.

13. *The Indian Society in the Mahābhārata* by S.C. Banerji.

14. *The Sacrament of Marriage in Hindu Society* by U.M. Apte.

15. *Mīmāṁsā, the Vākyaśāstra in Ancient India* (A Ph.D. thesis partly published) by Dr. G.V. Devasthali.

16. *Smṛti — Material in the Mahābhārata* by Dr. S.C. Banerji, published at Calcutta.

17. *The Divya-Tattva*, edited by Dr. Lariviere.

References

1. *Journal of the Annals of the Bhandarkar Oriental Research Institute* (*JABORI*), Vols. VII and VIII.
2. *The Vyāghra-Smṛti* published by Bhandarkar Oriental Research Institute (BORI), Pune, 1985.
3. For the peculiar views of Ṛṣyaśṛṅga, ***see*** the *Mysore Orientalist*, Vol. XIV, pp. 66-67; ***Also see***, Dr. Moghe's *Studies in the Dharmaśāstra*, pp. 67-68.
4. Dr. M.L. Wadekar, *Devala-Smṛti — Reconstruction and Critical Story*'. Vol. I. (Introduction and reconstructed text) (pp. 99-657). Published by Koshal Book Depot, Delhi, 1996 and Vol. II Crtical Study and Appendices (in press).
5. P.V. Kane, *History of Dharmaśāstra*, Vol. I, Part II, p. 1131 refers to this manuscript of 'Śvaśrū-snuṣā-Dhana-Saṁvāda', as per Burnell's catalogue of Tanjore manuscripts, p. 143a.
6. It may be noted that Miss Parvati S. Moholkar has written a thesis entitled "A Critical Edition of the Vivādacandra of Misaru-Miśra" which is deposited in the library of the University of Bombay (1984).
7. S.G. Moghe, *The Vyāghra-Smṛti*, introduction, pp. 18-21.
8. "Ṛṣyaśṛṅga-Smṛti", restored, *Mysore Orientalist*, Vol. XIV, p. 67.
9. ***Also see*** this paper in S. G. Moghe's *Studies in the Dharmaśāstra*, pp. 165-71.
10. S.G. Moghe's paper, "A Fresh Interpretation of the Manu-Smṛti, III.162" is published in the *Bhāratīya Vidyā*, Vol. XXXIX, No. 1, pp. 59-63; ***Also see*** this paper published in *Studies in the Dharmaśāstra*, pp. 41-46.
11. S.G. Moghe's paper, "Śunaḥśepa and Dattaka-Vidhāna" is published in the *Journal of the Ganganath Jha Kendriya Sanskrit Vidyapitha*, Allahabad, Vol. XXXV, Parts 1-2, 1979, pp. 85-95.
12. ***Also see*** Moghe, *Studies in the Dharmaśāstra*, pp. 172-77. ***Also see*** *GJKSV*, Vol. 46, 1990, pp. 13-18.
13. S.G. Moghe's paper, "Kauṭilīya Arthaśāstra, III.5.28 — A reappraisal" in *Studies in the Dharmaśāstra*, pp. 240-44; ***Also see*** this paper published in the *Journal of the Oriental Institute*, Baroda, Vol. XXXVI, Nos. 1-4, 1986-87, pp. 97-101.
14. "Concept of Witness in the Mahābhārata and Dharmaśāstra Literature" published in the book *A Peep at Indology*, pp. 19-22. ***Also see*** *Oriental Journal*, Tirupati, Vols. 32-34, 1989-91, pp. 135-40.
15. Consult *JABORI*, Vol. LXIV of 1983, p. 263 for the views of Budha. ***Also see*** this published in the *Studies in the Dharmaśāstra*, p. 56.

16. ***See*** S.G. Moghe, *The Vyāghra-Smṛti*, introduction, pp. 27-28 for the concept of *svayaṁpāka* in the context of *śrāddha*.

17. For the concept of a widow, consult S.G. Moghe's *Studies in the Dharmaśāstra*, pp. 183-90 and particularly, p. 184 of the article "Smṛtis, Smṛtikāras and Digest Authors — Retrospect and Prospect".

18. दूरस्थानामविद्यानां मोक्षधर्मानुयायिनाम्।
श्रराणां निर्धनानां च न देयाः कन्यका बुधैः।।

Hemadri's *Darpaṇa*, p. 132.

19. S.G. Moghe's paper, "Are Women Entitled to Perform Sacrifices?"is published in *Studies in the Dharmaśāstra*, pp. 190-94.

20. ***See*** S.G. Moghe's paper on "Dāna Section of the Dharmaśāstra" (based on the *Mahābhārata*) published in *Studies in the Dharmaśāstra*, pp. 196-97 for the rates of donation; ***Also see*** "Prasanna-pārijāta" (Datta Mahārāja Kavīśvara felicitation volume in Marāṭhī), 1990, pp. 89-93. ***Also see*** *The Mysore Orientalist*, Vol. XVII, 1995, pp. 91-95.

21. *tilaken vinā vipro puṇyastrī kunkumaṁ vinā* I
dvau etau garhitau loke daive pitṛye ca karmaṇi II

st. 192 of the *Vyāghra-Smṛti* edited by S.G. Moghe, p. 69.

22. Dr. P.V. Kane, *History of Dharmaśāstra*, Vol. V, Part I, pp. 1-21 for the differing views between Dr. Kane and Prof. V.M. Apte on the point of *vrata*.

23. Dr. R.N. Dandekar's paper, "Professor P.V. Kane – A Tribute" published in *MM. Dr. P.V. Kane Commemoration Monograph* published by the University of Bombay, 1974.

24. "Relation of the Gṛhyaśūtras to the Dharmaśāstra Literature" by S.G. Moghe in *Tattvāloka*, Vol. V, No. 1, April 1982, pp. 15-28; ***Also see*** *Studies in the Dharmaśāstra*, pp. 1-12.

25. "Relation of Kāmaśāstra to the Dharmaśāstra" by Dr. S.G. Moghe in *Bhāratīya Vidyā*, Vols. XLV, XLVI, XLVII for 1985-86-87, pp. 126-36; ***Also see*** this paper in *Studies in the Dharmaśāstra*, pp. 13-26.

26. "Relation of Indian Medical Science (Āyurveda) to Dharmaśāstra" by Dr. S.G. Moghe in *Bhāratī-Śodha Sāra Saṁgraha*, Vol. II, 1973, pp. 51-57; ***Also see*** this paper published in the *Studies in the Dharmaśāstra*, pp. 27-35.

27. "Dharmaśāstra and Sanskrit Lexicons" by S.G. Moghe published in the book *Studies in the Dharmaśāstra*, pp. 36-40.

28. Dr. A.N. Deo "Dharmaśāstra Thoughts in Classical Sanskrit Literature" (from Bhāsa to Śrī Harṣa, the author of the Naiṣadhīyacaritam"), a Ph.D. thesis in the library of the Marathwada University. This thesis written in the Marathi language was deposited in the year 1993.

29. S.G. Moghe's paper "Vaidyanātha Dīkṣita" published in the *Journal of the Asiatic Society of Bombay*, Vols. 60-61, pp. 56-61; ***Also see*** this paper published in *Studies in the Dharmaśāstra*, pp. 165-71.

30. A few such *smṛtis* may be mentioned here — Hārīta, Saṁvarta, Laugākṣī, Viśvāmitra, Marīci, Prajāpati, Pracetas, Paiṭhīnasi, Dakṣa, Pitāmaha, Kārṣṇājini, etc.

31. *Kapila-Smṛti, Vādhūla-Smṛti, Lohita-Smṛti, Nārāyaṇa-Smṛti, Kāṇva-Smṛti, Dālbhya-Smṛti, Bhāradvāja-Smṛti*, etc. which are printed in the volumes of the *Smṛti-Sandarbha* by Mansukhalal Mor from Calcutta. It is observed here that though these *smṛtis* were published before the revision of the first volume of *History of Dharmaśāstra*, Dr. Kane's attention was not drawn to these *smṛtis*; otherwise he would have given a thorough treatment to these *smṛtis*, in keeping with his other chapters or sections on the *smṛtis*. Hence a work on these *smṛtis* is a desideratum.

32. S.G. Moghe's paper, "Nīlakaṇṭha's Vyavahāra-Mayūkha and Śvaśrū-snuṣā-Dhana-Saṁvāda", was published in the *Journal of the Asiatic Society of Bombay*, Vols. 52-53/1977/78, pp. 200-7. (This volume is treated as *MM. Dr. Kane Birth Centenary Volume*.)

33. S.G. Moghe, "Śaṅkarācārya and Pūrva-Mīmāṁsā", in *Mysore Orientalist*, Vol. IV, No. 2, 1971, p. 79-89. ***Also see*** his paper on "Śaṅkarācārya's Approach to Arthavāda", published in *Journal of the Oriental Institute*, Tirupati, Vol. XXVII, Parts 1 & 2, 1984, pp. 43-56.

34. S.G. Moghe, "Sāyaṇācārya's Equipment of Pūrva-Mīmāṁsā", in *Journal of the Oriental Institute*, Baroda, Vol. 24, Nos. 3 & 4, 1975, pp. 257-68.

35. S.G. Moghe, "Paribhāṣās of Vyākaraṇa and the Mīmāṁsā Rules of Interpretation — A Comparative Study", published in '*Ṛṣi-Kalpa-nyāsa-Rajeshvara Shastri Felicitation Volume*, 1970, pp. 90-100.

36. S.G. Moghe, "The Comparative Study of the Commentaries, Sāravivecinī and Prabhā on the Mīmāṁsā-nyāya-prakāśa of Āpadeva", in *Bhāratīya Vidyā*, Vol. XL, Nos. 2-3, 1980, pp. 95-100.

37. S.G. Moghe, "The Evolution of the Mīmāṁsā Technical Term, Atideśa", in *ABORI* (Diamond Jubilee Volume, 1977-78), pp. 777-84.

38. S.G. Moghe, "Motivations of Punarvacana", in *Journal of the Asiatic Society of Bombay*, Vols. 49, 50, 51/1974-75-76, pp. 128-35.

39. S.G. Moghe. "Some Evolutionary Aspects of Vākyabheda", in *JGJKSV*, Vol. 37, Parts 1-4, 1983 (*Prof. Baladeva Upadhyaya Felicitation Volume*), Allahabad, pp. 169-87.

40. S.G. Moghe, "Mīmāṁsā Principles as Envisaged by Śaṅkarācārya in Jayamaṅgalā on the Kāmandakīya Nītisāra", in *JGJKSV*, Allahabad, Vol. XLII, Parts 1-4, 1986, pp. 121-30.

41. S.G. Moghe, "MM. Dr. P.V. Kane's Contribution to the Domain of Pūrva-Mīmāṁsā", in *MM Dr. P.V. Kane Commemoration Monograph* (published by the University of Bombay, 1974), pp. 83-99.

42. S.G. Moghe's paper "The Hindu Adoptions Act — Ancient, Medieval and Modern — A Comparison", was published in the *Journal of the Oriental Institute*, Baroda, Vol. XL, Nos. 3-4, March-June, 1991, pp. 235-42; ***Also see*** this paper published in *Studies in the Dharmaśāstra*, pp. 134-41.

43. This has a reference to 48 Bom. L.R. 196.

Topical Index

Author/Title Index